# Basic Psychology for the Work Life

### A. Christine Parham, Ed. D.
San Jacinto College, Pasadena, Texas

Published by

P10   SOUTH-WESTERN PUBLISHING CO.

CINCINNATI   WEST CHICAGO, ILL.   DALLAS   PELHAM MANOR, N.Y.   PALO ALTO, CALIF.

# PREFACE

The primary goal of *Basic Psychology for the Work Life* is to provide knowledge of the basic psychological concepts, principles, and theories that may be applied during an individual's work life in order to promote a career and to achieve better mental health. My personal observation has been that a successful work experience depends to a great extent on the development of the ability to understand one's self and others and the ability to adjust or adapt to environmental conditions, as well as the development of the skills necessary for the work. If from the study of psychology a person develops a greater understanding of behavior and the ability to deal more effectively with life's problems and stresses, it is believed that person will be happier, more effective, and more likely to advance up the career ladder.

Having experience in a business career and in instruction of business and psychology courses, *Basic Psychology for the Work Life* is my attempt to integrate the principles of psychology with the techniques of teaching in such a way as to meet the practical needs of those individuals preparing for the work life. Preparation for a career often includes either an introductory course in psychological theory and/or a course in applied psychology; however, the psychology course may not make applications of the theories and research to work experiences. An applied or practical applications course may not expose the theories, research, and psychological concepts used to develop an explanation of behavior. The two approaches are combined in this book to teach the theoretical concepts of psychology and to make the application of them to work situations and work behaviors. Perhaps the most unique feature of this book is the attempt to combine an introductory psychology text approach with an introductory industrial/organizational psychology text approach.

Influences on an individual's behavior are so numerous, and the study of human behavior includes so many areas that only an introduction to the basics is attempted in this book. *Basic Psychology for the Work Life* introduces the standard theories and principles of behavior presented in introductory psychology courses with emphasis on those that will enhance understanding of behavior in a work environment and be highly relevant in work experiences.

A specific attempt is made to organize the material in *Basic Psychology for the Work Life* in such a way that the student is guided in study according to psychological principles of learning and remembering—specifically the *SQ3R* method (survey, question, read, recite, and review) introduced by Frank P. Robinson (1941). To aid in surveying, each chapter begins with an outline. Additional aids for surveying are provided in a supplementary book, *Study Guide to Accompany Basic Psychology for the Work Life*. These surveying aids include a list of learning objectives for each chapter, a list of new terms, and a more detailed outline of the chapter. The survey is intended to provide a framework for studying each chapter and give an overview of the content of each chapter.

To aid in questioning, the *Study Guide to Accompany Basic Psychology for the Work Life* includes a self-quiz for each chapter which may be used as a pretest before reading the chapter. Also, students may transform topic headings which are shown throughout the chapters into questions. Questions are intended to motivate reading and to increase concentration, comprehension, and interest during the reading process. To aid in reading, an effort is made to keep the language as nontechnical as possible and to present the material in such a manner and at a reading level that will facilitate learning. Suggestions for further reading are provided for each chapter since *Basic Psychology for the Work Life* is also intended to provide the background and to arouse interest for further reading and study.

Each chapter in the textbook has examples, applications, and implications for the theories and principles presented to enhance understanding. A constant attempt is made to relate psychological theory to practical applications in a work situation. Activities are provided in the content material to facilitate understanding and application and to add variety and interest. Additional activities are provided in the accompanying Study Guide and instructor's Manual. Boxed inserts appear in the text to add in-depth treatment of an issue, to stimulate interest, or to provoke thought. Visual materials in the form of drawings, charts, graphs, and photographs provide clarification of concepts and add variety to the presentation. Psychological terms are set in italics and are defined as they are introduced.

To elicit reciting, the accompanying Study Guide contains a programmed review and a self-quiz for each chapter. The programmed review as well as the summary at the end of each chapter in the textbook presents the main ideas of the chapter in a concise form for reviewing.

The following steps are suggested for using the *SQ3R* method with this text and the accompanying Study Guide to learn about psychological topics. Step 1—Survey each chapter before reading by looking over the learning objectives and the outline in the Study Guide and the outline and summary of the chapter in the text. Step 2—Note topic headings and formulate questions, read over the questions in the self-quiz section of the

Study Guide, and then read the chapter carefully, focusing on the answers to the questions. Pay attention to any activities or visual material when reading the chapter. Step 3—After reading the content for a topic heading, stop before proceeding to another topic and try to answer the questions formulated that are related to the topic heading and any questions in the self-quiz related to the topic heading. Then close the book and try to verbalize the content of the topic. If a satisfactory answer cannot be given to the questions or the content cannot be verbalized, reread the topic and try again. Once the content is understood, go to the next topic and repeat the process until the entire chapter is read. Step 4—Read the summary again at the end of the chapter. Step 5—Evaluate the acquisition of knowledge and understanding by trying to define in your own words each of the new terms listed in the Study Guide, by filling in the blanks in the programmed review in the Study Guide, and by taking the self-quiz in the Study Guide. Step 6—Correct any incorrect responses made in the evaluation process and reread the content in the text related to those responses.

*Basic Psychology for the Work Life* is organized in such a way that it may be adapted to courses of varying lengths. Depending on instructor and student interest, more time may be allotted to some chapters than others, or some chapters may be omitted. There is integration from chapter to chapter, and all 14 chapters should be used as written to achieve maximum coverage and integration. However, one chapter may be read independently of the other chapters, or parts of a chapter may be used without using the entire chapter since a glossary of psychological terms and concepts is available at the end of the text for any definitions which may be needed that were presented in an omitted chapter.

*Basic Psychology for the Work Life* is divided into fourteen chapters grouped into five parts. The first part contains three chapters and introduces the reader to psychology. Part One is concerned with the origins and development of psychology, psychology as a science and as a profession, and the contribution psychology can make in the world of work. Part Two contains two chapters and provides information about the nervous system—especially the brain, the endocrine system, heredity, and development. The biological processes and the role they play in behavior provide background and foundations for behavior. The focus is on the biological aspects of behavior. Part Three deals with cognitive processes and emphasizes the behaviors of learning, remembering, and thinking. Intelligence, perception, and creativity are other cognitive processes discussed. The three chapters which comprise Part Four are concerned with motivation and emotion. The theoretical concept of motivation is explained and then applied to work environments. Stress and coping with stress are dealt with in Part Four. Part Five, on individual and social processes, is comprised of three chapters. Personality, both normal and abnormal, and therapeutic change of personality; social influences on behavior, particularly attitude formation, attitude change, and behavior change; and human behavior in a social context with focus on group dynamics are discussed in Part Five.

If *Basic Psychology for the Work Life* serves the needs of those involved in training others for the work experience and is enjoyable and personally rewarding to those who are preparing for the work life, my goal will be realized.

A. Christine Parham

# CONTENTS

| Chapter | Page |
|---|---|

# Part 1
# Introduction to Psychology

# Chapter 1

# Development of Psychology

**I. SOME IDEAS ABOUT PSYCHOLOGY**
   A. A Definition
   B. The Word Psychology

**II. GOALS**
   A. Explanation
   B. Prediction
   C. Control

**III. BACKGROUND**
   A. Demonology
   B. Gods and Goddesses
   C. Philosophers
   D. Scientific Thought

**IV. EMERGENCE**
   A. Wundt in Germany
   B. James in America

**V. EARLY VIEWS**
   A. Structuralism
   B. Functionalism
   C. Behaviorism
   D. Gestalt Psychology
   E. Psychoanalysis

**VI. LATER VIEWS**
   A. Cognitive Psychology
   B. Humanistic Psychology
   C. Existential Psychology
   D. Physiological-Biological Approach
   E. Eclectic Approach

**SUMMARY**

**SUGGESTIONS FOR FURTHER READING**

Interest in the subject of psychology has increased in recent years, and no doubt almost everyone has heard the word "psychology." However, psychology may mean many different things to different people. Usually, students enroll in a first course in psychology with some idea about what psychology is and is not based on some experience, hearsay, or the media. (See Figure 1–1.) Before reading further, write down your idea of what psychology is so that you can compare it with your idea after completing this course. Often psychology is misunderstood. This beginning course attempts to clarify what psychology is.

Figure 1-1 Is this your idea of psychology?

## Some Ideas About Psychology

Some people hold the view that a study of psychology prepares one to be a fortune-teller with a college degree—to read a person's past, to analyze a person's present, and to predict a person's future. Others may think that psychology is the study of rats finding their way through mazes or the study of hypnosis. Still others may think that psychology is a game that people play to manipulate other people or is "spychology" (Morgan, 1970), i.e., spying on the inner lives of people. Some people may have the idea that psychology is a study of individuals who are different from the majority of people, such as the mentally retarded, the neurotic, the psychotic, the problem child, the genius, or the social deviate; these people may not realize that ordinary people may also be studied. One's idea of psychology may be similar to the blind men's perceptions of an elephant. The blind man who felt the elephant's leg thought the elephant to be like a tree, while the one who touched the elephant's tail thought the elephant to be like a rope. The one who came in contact with the elephant's trunk perceived the elephant to be like a snake. The fourth blind man, having encountered the elephant's side, said, "You're all wrong; the elephant is like a wall." After reading this book, one should have an overall, integrated view of psychology which will include the idea that psychology is also a study of an individual's work behavior and a study of organizational behavior.

### A Definition

*Psychology* is defined as the scientific study of behavior and mental processes and the application of knowledge gained through that study. The term *behavior* refers to any movement or activity of an organism in *response* to a specific *stimulus* or set of stimuli. A stimulus may be any physical event either internal, such as a pain or a thought, or external, such as something heard, seen, felt, or smelled. Since behaviors or responses consist of mental, physical, internal and external activities, one can see that psychology as a study of behavior is a rather broad field. Behavior is anything one does and includes one's behavior while on the job. Psychology then must include a study of job-related behaviors, using the scientific method, and the application of these findings to the world of work.

### The Word Psychology

The word psychology was coined near the end of the sixteenth century and first appeared in the dictionary near the end of the seventeenth century. The word actually comes from two Greek words—*psyche* meaning mind, life, spirit, or soul and *logos* meaning knowledge, study of, or wisdom.

In mythology, Psyche was a beautiful young woman who fell in love with Cupid, the god of love. Cupid's mother, Venus, the goddess of love, did not like Psyche because she was human; therefore, she separated the lovers and imposed hardships on Psyche. Psyche's love for Cupid was so strong that it impressed the other gods and goddesses; so they turned Psyche into a goddess, thus making her immortal, and the lovers were reunited for eternity. To the Greek, true love was the highest achievement of the human soul, and Psyche became the symbol of the human soul. Thus, the word psychology originally meant the study of the soul as contrasted with its present definition—the scientific study of behavior.

## Goals

Throughout history, people have tried to understand human behavior by using the best available knowledge to explain behavior. Prediction and control of behavior was then attempted based on the explanation of behavior. The boxed material on this page is an example of early attempts to explain and control behavior. These are also the goals of psychology today—to explain, to predict, and to control behavior.

### Explanation

Perhaps explanation is really what psychology is all about. Understanding and explaining behavior is the process of isolating the reasons for the behavior observed. This isolating process involves describing and

---

DEMONOLOGY

Evidence indicates that some half million years ago during the Stone Age, cave men performed an operation on human beings who exhibited behavior problems. With crude stone instruments, they would chip a circular hole through the skull of the individual to allow the evil spirits, believed to be causing the problem behavior, to escape. Exorcism, which included other treatment techniques such as noisemaking, drinking horrible-tasting concoctions, starving, flogging, and burning, was the primary treatment for changing behavior. Since the problem behavior was explained by the presence of evil spirits inside the person, it was predicted that these treatments would drive out the evil spirits. Administering these treatments was an attempt to control behavior.

measuring behaviors which requires the development of tests and techniques for measuring. The explanation process also includes the organization of known facts and the production of reasonable guesses in the formulation of theories. A *theory* is a set of assumptions used to explain a number of facts and to predict future events. Achieving adequate explanations for human behavior has innumerable implications. For example, a theory explaining job satisfaction or motivation has practical application in a variety of work-related situations.

### Prediction

Present or past measurements of behavior may be used by psychologists as a basis for predicting the future occurrence of behavior. College entrance exams may be used to predict success in a particular college. A score on a mechanical aptitude test may be used to predict how well a factory worker may do on a particular assembly line. A vocational interest test may be used to predict the likelihood of job satisfaction for an individual by comparing his or her personality traits and characteristics and likes and dislikes with those of other individuals who have been successful and satisfied in that occupation. (See Figure 1-2.) Predictions may be based on such phenomena as personality traits, abilities, past behaviors, or particular conditions. These predictions affect the lives of just about everyone.

Figure 1-2 Special tests are administered as an attempt to predict educational or vocational success.

## Control

Being able to predict behavior allows one to control behavior; one could intervene and thus influence behavior. If one has the knowledge to make accurate predictions regarding behavior, then one should apply that knowledge in a beneficial manner. Intervention could possibly prevent undesirable behaviors or produce desirable behaviors. Modifying or changing behavior is often the primary aim of the psychologist. An employer may be engaged in modifying the behavior of employees, a psychotherapist may be engaged in modifying a patient's behavior, or an individual may be engaged in modifying personal behavior. One goal of psychology is to improve the present or future circumstances of individuals and society. Of course, safeguards must ensure against the unethical use of such knowledge to modify and control behavior for one's own end such as in brainwashing.

# Background

Although psychology as a discipline is only about one hundred years old, and the application of psychology to work and organizational behavior is even more recent, the notion of psychology is perhaps as old as humanity.

## Demonology

The theory of *demonology* was one of the earliest explanations of behavior and existed even during the Stone Age. (See the boxed material on page 5.) Spirits were believed to possess a person's body and to direct behavior. Evil spirits or demons were considered to be the cause of mental disorders or unacceptable behaviors. A revival of this ancient superstition of demonology occurred, with some modification to conform to religion, during medieval times after the collapse of the Greek and Roman civilizations. Good and evil spirits were replaced by God and Satan (the devil). People possessed by the devil were of two types: (1) those who were allowed by God to be unwillingly seized as a punishment for their sins and (2) those who were voluntarily in alliance with the devil. This theoretical explanation of behavior continued to dominate popular thought into the nineteenth century.

## Gods and Goddesses

The ancient gods and goddesses of mythology were invented to be the supernatural beings responsible for every unexplainable human thought and action. There was a god or goddess of almost everything—war, love, fertility, worry, marriage, the dead, and even drunkenness. The heavens became filled with mythical gods that people used to explain human behavior. As human activities became more complex as civilizations advanced, it became too complicated to explain every behavior with a mythical god. Some people began to realize that behavior was not really being explained.

## Philosophers

Many of the early philosophers such as Hippocrates and Aristotle discussed psychological questions and elaborated on views of human behavior. Hippocrates (460-377 B.C.) denied the intervention of demons and deities and suggested that the human body consisted of a brain and four humors (blood, black bile, yellow bile, and phlegm) which were the cause of behavior. For example, those mad from an imbalance of phlegm would be quiet, depressed, and withdrawn; those mad from an imbalance of black or yellow bile would be excited, noisy, or mischievous; and those mad from an imbalance of blood would be in angry rages. Aristotle (384-322 B.C.) thought that one could learn by association. Aristotle also decided that something inside the person that cannot be seen does the thinking, produces the feelings, and controls behavior. He called it the soul.

## Scientific Thought

During the Middle Ages, philosophers developed opinions and beliefs about how the soul affected behavior which were not based on factual evidence. However, many philosophers were impressed with observation and maintained that humans might also be understood by this scientific method. This position led to casual observations and a lot of speculation without truly systematic observations. (See the boxed material on page 9).

During the Renaissance, the physical sciences departed from the medieval way of arriving at truth, and scientists began to develop theories about the world based on systematic observation. Some of the philosophies and scientific findings in the fields of biology, physiology, and physics during the Renaissance contributed to the emergence of psychology as a discipline, especially the following ones: René Descartes' *mechanism*, the view that the physical aspect of humans obeys mechanistic laws and is explainable by them; Charles Darwin's theory that evolution is a continuous process for man and other animal species; the discovery of the living cell and the finding that all organisms are composed of cells; the study of reflex actions; and Hermann von Helmholtz's measurement

---

### THE MEDIEVAL WAY OF ARRIVING AT TRUTH

During the sixteenth and seventeeth centuries, there were beginnings of more scientific thought. The following is an excerpt from the writings of Sir Francis Bacon (1561-1626) who was not very impressed with the medieval way of arriving at truth.

In the year of our Lord 1432, there arose a grievous quarrel among the brethren over the number of teeth in the mouth of a horse. For thirteen days the disputation raged without ceasing. All the ancient books and chronicles were fetched out, and wonderful and ponderous erudition, such as was never before heard of in this region, was made manifest. At the beginning of the fourteenth day, a youthful friar of goodly bearing asked his learned superiors for permission to add a word, and straightway, to the wonderment of the disputants, whose deep wisdom he sore vexed, he beseeched them to unbend in a manner coarse and unheard-of, and to look in the open mouth of a horse and find answer to their questionings. At this, their dignity being grievously hurt, they waxed exceedingly wroth; and, joining in a mighty uproar, they flew upon him and smote him hip and thigh, and cast him out forthwith. For, said they, surely Satan had tempted this bold neophyte to declare unholy and unheard-of ways of finding truth contrary to all the teachings of the fathers. After many days of grievous strife the dove of peace sat upon the assembly, and they as one man, declared the problem to be an everlasting mystery because of a grievous dearth of historical and theological evidence thereof, so ordered the same writ down.

---

of the nerve impulse demonstrating that nerve impulses are not mysterious movements at the speed of light but slower electrical events.

## Emergence

Psychology emerged as a science when precise observations of and experiments on human behavior began to replace philosophers' speculations and arguing. By the end of the nineteenth century psychology became a scientific discipline of its own and joined other sciences in establishing research laboratories. Prior to this time there had been no separate discipline called psychology and no one with the title of psychologist.

### Wundt in Germany

The "birth" of modern psychology is usually said to have occurred in 1879 when Wilhelm Wundt set up a laboratory in Leipzig, Germany, to study conscious experience in a search to find the elements of the human mind. Earlier Wundt had written a book called *Principles of Physiological Psychology* which presented the idea that the mind must be studied just as other natural laws, then under investigation, were studied. He believed that the elements of the mind could be found just as scientists had found elements of matter.

### James in America

William James, a young American physiology professor at Harvard, traveled to Europe where he turned to philosophy and became a student of Wilhelm Wundt. When James returned to Harvard, he combined physiology and philosophy into a course in psychology. Out of this course came his book in 1890 called *The Principles of Psychology*. In 1889, William James changed his title to psychologist and set up the first laboratory for psychological experimentation in the United States. He was primarily interested in how the mind functions and enables one to adapt to different situations rather than in determining the structural elements of the mind. This new science called psychology spread quickly throughout the world.

## Early Views

By the beginning of the twentieth century, Wundt's view of psychology had become known as *structuralism*, while James' view was referred to as *functionalism*. Wundt and James had produced the first two major psychological theories. By 1910, the viewpoints known as *behaviorism* and *Gestalt psychology* had also appeared. In addition, Freud's practice of *psychoanalysis* was becoming well known by this time.

### Structuralism

Wundt believed that developing a science of conscious experience was parallel to developing a science of physical reality. He wanted to explore the mind more directly than had the medieval philosophers. Wundt hoped to discover the structure of the mind by analyzing conscious sensory experience and reducing it to its basic elements. Because of this emphasis on structure, his position became known as structuralism.

The structuralists used *introspection* to investigate the contents of the mind; i.e., a person would be asked to describe his or her feelings or conscious awareness of the stimulus presented. The structuralists had difficulty arriving at a set of basic sensations because what was loud to one individual was not loud to another or what was pleasant to one was unpleasant to another, and what was loud or unpleasant one day might not be on another day.

## Functionalism

William James felt that the structuralists were on the wrong track. He became interested in the functioning of the mind. James believed that the mind consisted of the abilities to make decisions and to adapt to an environmental situation and was not just a collection of building blocks. This view extended the study of psychology to include such phenomena as learning, motivation, and emotion. Because James and his followers emphasized the functioning of the mind, they became known as the functionalists.

## Behaviorism

The functionalists and structuralists often disagreed because they relied on introspection, which is not a very objective or reliable method of securing information. John B. Watson was troubled by this lack of objectivity and reliability and by the method's limitations. Introspection was limited to normal human adults and excluded from study young children, animals, or insane individuals who could not report or describe their sensory experiences or answer questions about it. Since behaviors (responses) and environmental events (stimuli) are observable, definable and verifiable, Watson argued that the only thing that psychology could study was the relationship between stimuli and responses. Thus, Watson and his followers became known as the behaviorists. Today they are sometimes referred to as stimulus-response (S-R) psychologists.

The behaviorist's position of eliminating the structure and functioning of the mind entirely from the concern of psychology produced controversy with both the structuralists and the functionalists. The behaviorists did not ignore the mind or deny the mental processes; they explained human behavior in terms of stimuli and responses which gave psychologists something to study empirically and objectively. Thus, psychology became a full-fledged science. Behaviorism became the most popular viewpoint in America. First, psychology "lost its soul," now it was "losing its mind." Today, psychologists using the behavioral approach vary stimuli, observe the response, and develop laws and principles about how stimuli and responses are related. They reason that any internal change should produce some change in external behavior; therefore, the internal behaviors which cannot be observed directly do not have to be studied.

## Gestalt Psychology

The behaviorists were not the only ones who were not in agreement with the structuralist position. In Germany, Max Wertheimer and his followers argued that each experience is a complete and organized whole perceived according to a specific pattern and that the characteristics of all the various parts of that experience are determined by that pattern. Behavior should, therefore, be studied as an organized whole rather than as separate individual parts. These psychologists focused on how one interprets or perceives a three-dimensional object such as a table from the experience of the pattern of impulses arriving in the brain from the physical energy in the environment (sensation). The interpretation or perception of an experience rather than sensation came to be the primary interest of these psychologists. Wertheimer and his followers became known as the Gestalt psychologists, since gestalt is a German word meaning form, pattern, or whole. Their position is illustrated by pointing out that most people perceive the patterns in Figure 1-3 as a line, a triangle, and a square rather than merely dots. Viewing a film is another example of how perception of a whole can differ from perceptions of its parts. When viewing a film, most people perceive continuous movement even though a film is nothing more than a series of still pictures.

## Psychoanalysis

At the same time, another view of psychology, psychoanalysis, was developing in the field of medicine. Sigmund Freud, an Austrian physician, developed a theory of behavior based on clinical observation. His

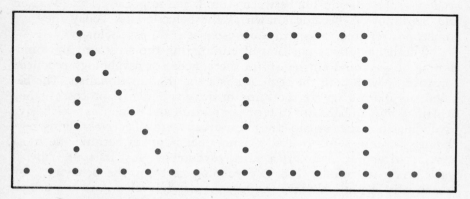

Figure 1-3 Gestalt psychologists believed that mental content and behavior are not merely the sum of the perceptions of their separate parts.

theory proposed that a vast amount of human behavior is the result of unconscious forces hidden within the person. This model of human behavior is sometimes referred to as the "iceberg" model (Figure 1-4) because only part of a person's mind is conscious or exposed to view. This model is still an accepted view today. The unexposed part of the iceberg represents unconscious thoughts, conflicts, and desires; the person has no awareness or knowledge of them. Freud proposed that they are repressed when they are kept in the unconscious or below the level of awareness. He believed that they are repressed because they are usually threatening in some way to the person or forbidden by society. He also believed that most adult problems could be traced back to childhood experiences. The process of discovering these repressed forces that are unconsciously causing a behavior is psychoanalysis. Freudian theory had a tremendous impact on psychology, although some parts of this theory are controversial and are not accepted by some psychologists. Freud laid the foundation for psychotherapy and contributed particularly to the study of personality.

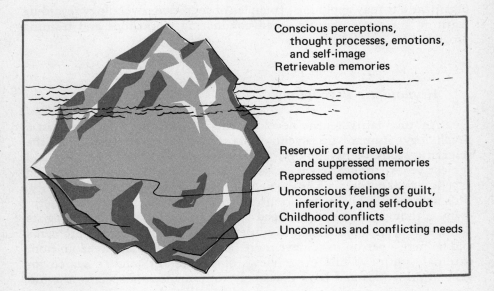

Conscious perceptions,
    thought processes, emotions,
    and self-image
Retrievable memories

Reservoir of retrievable
    and suppressed memories
Repressed emotions
Unconscious feelings of guilt,
    inferiority, and self-doubt
Childhood conflicts
Unconscious and conflicting needs

Figure 1-4 The unexposed part of the iceberg represents the unconscious part of the mind—childhood conflicts, conflicting needs, feelings of guilt or inferiority, and repressed emotions.

## Later Views

Although the behavioral and psychoanalytic views are still major approaches to psychology, they have undergone some modifications. Structuralism, functionalism, and Gestalt psychology no longer are considered major approaches although some of the principles have been incorporated into newer views.

### Cognitive Psychology

One of the newer approaches is the view that the human mind knows more than just the information it takes in directly from the environment. The mind processes or acts on information by producing new thoughts, making comparisons, and making decisions. Basically, *cognitive psychology* is a study of the way perception influences behavior and the way experience influences perception. Cognitive psychologists explain behavior through the thought processes, emphasizing the role of memory which is at the core of thought. Some business and industrial organizations may apply the principles of cognitive psychology regarding learning and remembering when conducting workshops and training programs for employees.

### Humanistic Psychology

Another fairly recent development in psychology is *humanistic psychology*. Humanistic psychologists tend to be less interested in the scientific study of psychology. They prefer to emphasize feelings and subjective experience, such as self-esteem and self-actualization, and psychological needs, such as the need for love, achievement, or creativity. This approach has been important in work on personality and psychotherapy, although it has not produced a great deal of research. Psychologists using this approach are basically interested in solving human problems and helping a person to achieve more personal growth and freedom from external control. While other views of psychology tend to search for general principles and laws that apply to humans as a species, the humanists emphasize the importance of free will and an individual assuming responsibility for his or her own behavior. Carl Rogers and Abraham Maslow were two of the several theorists who developed this viewpoint. Humanistic psychology is applied by business and industrial organizations when psychologists are employed to administer tests and use therapeutic techniques in order to help employees solve problems and achieve personal growth.

## Existential Psychology

*Existential psychology* is the product of a loosely organized group of European theorists and, like humanistic psychology, is more philosophical and less scientific. Existential psycholgists stress that human existence is in the here and now and is emerging or becoming. The past and future are relevant only to the extent that they affect immediate existing. The focus is on the person's immediate experience, the role of feelings, attitudes and values, and finding meaning in life. Victor Frankl, an early leader in existentialism, and his followers emphasized that the goal of therapy is not to eliminate anxiety, but to give it meaning to enable the person to deal with it more constructively. Existential views are sometimes applied in business and industrial organizations when psychologists are employed to conduct sensitivity sessions for employees to examine feelings, attitudes, values, and common experiences.

## Physiological-Biological Approach

The physiological-biological psychologists search for relationships between physiology and behavior. For example, the brain is studied to determine how memory is stored; heredity and development are studied as factors of behavior; and biochemical conditions are studied in terms of their effect on behavior. The findings from this approach have been important in many areas of psychology such as perception, learning, memory, motivation, emotion, and psychotherapy. When business and industrial organizations provide medical examinations and treatments for physical conditions that might affect behavior on the job or provide gymnasiums for physical fitness programs, views of physiological psychologists may be applied.

## Eclectic Approach

Each of the views previously described defines psychology somewhat differently. A psychologist who accepts one approach may see most issues and attack most problems differently from a psychologist who accepts another approach. However, psychologists seem to be becoming more and more *eclectic;* they select from each of the many theories and approaches available and use what seems to fit the situation. (See Figure 1-5).

What then is psychology today? It has been suggested that psychology is the systematic study of how animals, particularly humans, function—dealing especially with how they perceive, think, learn, behave, and cope with the environment. Psychology also tries to describe and explain every aspect of human activity—simple and complex, external and internal, observable and inferable (Freedman, 1978). Certain physical

Cognitive    Humanistic
Existential    Behavioristic
Psychoanalytic    Gestalt
Physiological-Biological

Figure 1-5 An eclectic psychotherapist draws from many sources.

mechanisms and reactions, however, are left mainly to the fields of
biology, physiology, and medicine and the complex workings of societies
are usually in the realm of sociology and anthropology. With only a few
exceptions, any question that can reasonably be asked about human
beings falls within the field of psychology. Psychology then is relevant to
the world of work by enabling people to understand their own behavior,
the behavior of co-workers, the behavior of anyone with whom contact is
made, and even in understanding organizational behavior.

## SUMMARY

1.    Although some people may have different ideas, psychology is
      usually defined today as the scientific study of behavior, including
      mental processes, and the application of knowledge gained through
      the study.

2.    The word psychology comes from two Greek words, psyche and

logos, meaning study of the soul.

3.  The goals of psychology are to explain, to predict, and to control behavior.

4.  Attempting to explain, to predict, and to control behavior has a long and varied background—demonology, gods and goddesses, philosophy, and Satanic possession; however, psychology as a science and separate discipline had its beginning in 1879 when Wilhelm Wundt set up a laboratory in Germany.

5.  William James set up a psychology laboratory at Harvard University in 1889, wrote a psychology textbook in 1890, and became the first American psychologist.

6.  Leaders and their early view of psychology are as follows: structuralism—Wilhelm Wundt; functionalism—William James; behaviorism—John B. Watson; Gestalt psychology—Max Wertheimer; and psychoanalysis—Sigmund Freud.

7.  Structuralism was concerned with sensory experience in an effort to find the structure (elements) of the mind; functionalism emphasized the functioning of the mind; behaviorism studied only the relationship of stimuli and responses; Gestalt psychology focused on perception; and psychoanalysis stressed the unconscious part of the mind.

8.  Some of the later views and approaches to psychology are cognitive psychology which emphasizes the role memory plays in the thought process; humanism which emphasizes personal growth; existential psychology which emphasizes giving anxiety and the immediate experience meaning; and physiological-biological psychology which emphasizes the role of the nervous system, endocrine glands, heredity, and development in behavior.

9.  A psychologist using an eclectic approach selects from many theories or views and combines and uses what seems to fit the situation.

## SUGGESTIONS FOR FURTHER READING

Atkinson, R. C. Reflections on psychology's past and concerns about its future. *American Psychologist*, 1977, 32, 205-210.

The *American Psychologist* is a journal published monthly which includes official papers of the American Psychological Association and articles of general interest to psychologists.

Chaplin, J. P., & Krawiec, T. S. *Systems and theories of psychology* (4th ed.). New York: Holt, Rinehart and Winston, 1979.

This book analyzes some of the basic issues in psychology and provides a history of the development of psychology.

Hebb, D. O. What psychology is about. *American Psychologist*, 1974, 29, 71-79.

A journal article that helps one understand better the goals of psychology.

Murphy, G., & Kovach, J. K. *Historical introduction to modern psychology*. New York: Harcourt Brace Jovanovich, 1972.

Many of the specialty areas within psychology are discussed along with the history of psychology.

Nordby, V. J., & Hall, C. S. *A guide to psychologists and their concepts*. San Francisco: W. H. Freeman, 1974.

Written for the beginning psychology student, this book contains brief biographies of prominent contemporary psychologists who helped shape psychological thought.

Robinson, D. N. *An intellectual history of psychology*. New York: Macmillan, 1976.

Special emphasis is placed on the philosophical foundations of psychology in this history of psychology.

Schultz, D. *A history of modern psychology* (2nd ed.). New York: Academic Press, 1975.

A history of psychology which emphasizes the views of psychology popular in the late nineteenth and early twentieth centuries.

Sexton, V. S., & Misiak, H. *Psychology around the world*. Monterey, Calif.: Brooks/Cole, 1976.

This book gives the history and present status of psychology in 40 different countries.

Watson, R. I. *The great psychologists* (4th ed.). Philadelphia: Lippincott, 1978.

Information about the lives of some of the great psychologists and their important contributions to the development of psychology are presented in this book.

Wertheimer, M. *A brief history of psychology* (rev. ed.). New York: Holt, Rinehart and Winston, 1979.

The material in this book deals with the history and basic issues of psychology.

# P sychology as a Science

Chapter 2

S ince science is the search for truth and attempts to find out whether various statements are true or false, psychology is indeed a science. Scientific investigation involves three steps. The first step is the formulation of the statement to be evaluated. The second step is the gathering of information relevant to the statement. Finally, the information is analyzed and an evaluation is made about the probable truth of the statement. These steps will be discussed in this chapter.

## Scientific Study

Since psychology emerged as a science and is defined as the scientific study of behavior, a student of psychology should be familiar with the characteristics of scientific study. One may think of a laboratory full of test tubes and beakers with someone wearing a white smock; however, this does not qualify one as a scientist. The manner in which investigations are planned and carried out, the procedures employed in collecting data, and the way findings are interpreted are the criteria for scientific study.

### Common Sense Assumptions

Saying that something makes sense, meaning that it is believable, does not necessarily mean that it is factual. *Common sense assumptions* are ideas one holds to be true without any proof that they are true—statements that are "taken for granted." People can easily agree on the plausibility of these assumptions. Sometimes common sense assumptions about behavior are not correct or are only partially correct. Consider the following common sense statements: (1) A lot of people dream very little, if any. (2) Schizophrenics have split personalities. (3) Rewarding an employee every time a task is completed compared with rewarding only half the time will produce longer performance of the task after the rewarding ceases. An individual may agree with some of these statements since they are all plausible descriptions of human behavior; however, none of the statements are true. Consider these common sense statements: (1) "Absence makes the heart grow fonder;" and "Out of sight, out of mind." (2) "Never too old to learn;" and "You can't teach an old dog new tricks." Much of what passes for common sense is inconsistent and vague. Science cannot tolerate such inconsistencies. All common sense assumptions are not false, but they can act as blinders which can prevent one from seeking information that would verify the truth. Whether an assumption is true or false is simply not known without a systematic scientific study.

## Empirical Approach

Scientific study implies the *empirical approach*, which is the pursuit of knowledge through observation and experimentation. The empirical method of science deals with information that is available to the senses and can be validated and confirmed by other individuals. In this approach, methods are used to improve and extend observation and to avoid the pitfalls of common sense assumptions. Psychologists have two things in common—an interest in behavior and an insistence on evidence.

**Hypotheses.** One of the first steps in scientific study is to formulate a *hypothesis*. A hypothesis is a belief, hunch, tentative statement, or explanation that has not been proven or disproven. In order for everyone to know exactly what is meant, scientists operationally define each term in the hypothesis. For example, in the hypothesis that success in a particular job is a result of years of experience, success on the job might be defined for an employee as earning a rating by the supervisor of three or higher on a one-to-five rating scale. For a salesperson, job success might be defined as a particular number or amount of sales made in a particular time period. Once the terms are operationally defined, the researcher can proceed with the observations necessary for collection of information. A hypothesis may be evaluated or tested by the collected evidence.

**Theories.** A theory is an integrated set of interrelated hypotheses that attempts to explain a phenomenon. Theories allow the results from many observations to be summarized in a way that accounts for existing information, predicts new observations, and guides further research.

## Scientific Methods

Psychologists employ many different methods in collecting evidence to test hypotheses and formulate theories. Some of the most commonly used methods will be described in the following sections.

## Naturalistic Method

Methods referred to as *naturalistic* or *field methods* involve careful observation and recording of behavior in a natural setting without any interference by the investigator, or at least as little as possible. An observation of the number of days absent from work per year for an employee or the number of complaints made to a supervisor per week would be examples of a naturalistic observation.

## Survey Method

In the *survey method*, questions are usually prepared to which answers are obtained through a direct interview, by mail, or by telephone. A survey is usually an investigation of the attitudes, feelings, traits, opinions, or behaviors of large groups of people. This method may be used to obtain information from a large number of people in a relatively short period of time. Public opinion surveys such as those conducted by Gallup are probably familiar, since the results are regularly reported on television, in newspapers, and in popular magazines. Market research predicts buying preferences on the basis of consumers' answers to questions obtained in surveys. Data concerning attitudes and perceptions of employees toward some aspect of the organization for which they work may be obtained by the survey method. Since computers are available to analyze the data from the large number of responses, the survey method is used extensively.

## Case Study Method

The *case study method* is an intensive investigation of a single case which results in a large amount of information. The information may include personality traits, social relationships, important life events, academic and vocational data, or other biographical information. Psychologists may use this information to understand an individual or an event, or the information may be used for more general purposes in exploring the nature and causes of behaviors. By examining a number of case histories, some significant general factors may possibly be noted.

## Correlational Method

The *correlational method* is an investigation of the relationships between measurable events. The researcher might determine whether a relationship exists between two sets of information (such as the number of business courses completed and supervisor rating of job performance) collected about an employee. For example, one might be interested in the relationship between an individual's score on a finger dexterity test and the number of pages typed per day.

Correlational studies identify relationships between measurable events without explaining why the relationship exists. For example, the number of cigarettes smoked per day might be inversely related to some measure of job performance; however, anxiety might be a third factor accounting for an increase in cigarette smoking and a decrease in productivity. Or a relationship might be found to exist between palm width and reading ability of elementary school children; however, this does not mean that palm width has a causal effect on reading. Another factor, growth, may be affecting both simultaneously. The correlational method has been especially useful in predicting behaviors. An example of a correlational study may be found in the box on this page.

## Experimental Method

The method of investigation that seeks to define cause and effect relationships is referred to as the *experimental method*. The experimental method is a powerful tool for the psychologist seeking to understand causes of behavior or to explain behaviors. A primary difference between this method and previously mentioned methods is that the researcher controls and manipulates variables. A *variable* is any characteristic, attribute, or event that can vary in amount when measured, or be present or absent. One variable is manipulated by the experimenter in order to observe how another variable is affected. The variable that is manipulated is referred to as the *independent variable*. The variable that is measured in order to observe the effect of the manipulation of the independent variable is referred to as the *dependent variable*. The logical reasoning for this approach is that if the only difference between two groups is the variation of the independent variable, then any difference in the

---

### A CORRELATIONAL STUDY

McClelland (1961) of Harvard University related the amount of achievement imagery in children's stories to national economic growth. He and his associates reasoned that the level of achievement concern in books for children would reflect the motivational level of these children when they became adults. McClelland further reasoned that if achievement motivation is responsible for economic growth, then the higher the amount of achievement imagery in children's books, the higher the economic-industrial index should be. A high relationship was found between achievement imagery in children's books and the economic-industrial index. If books transmit cultural values and influence development of motivation in children, then it should be possible to predict economic growth by examining children's books. Children's books from 20 different countries that were in print in 1925 were analyzed by McClelland. The achievement motivation index was found to be related to the economic-industrial index in 1950 when the children were adults.

measured behavior between the two groups is likely to have been caused by the independent variable. Usually, one thinks of an experiment in terms of manipulating only one variable and measuring only one behavioral response; however, with modern methods of analyzing data, the experimenter may manipulate a number of variables and measure the effect on more than one behavioral response.

## The Experimental Procedure

Since experimentation is the basic research tool used to test hypotheses explaining behavior, the understanding of this procedure is important in a study of psychology. The essence of the experimental procedure is controlling variables to obtain equivalency of groups and then manipulating a variable.

### Control Methods

**Randomization.** Random selection of the participants or *subjects* in the experiment is one way to control differences in variables and obtain equivalency of groups. By *randomization*, randomly selecting subjects, various traits and characteristics will be distributed equally or in an unbiased way. If a large sample of subjects is randomly selected from the total set of all the possible cases, and the subjects are then randomly assigned to the groups, only chance differences in measurable variables will exist between the groups to be contrasted or compared. The total set of all possible subjects is referred to as the *population.*

**Matching.** When randomization is not possible, equivalency may be obtained by matching the subjects in each group according to relevant variables. For example, if age is the relevant variable to control, placing a subject 20 years of age in one group would require placing a subject of 20 years of age in the comparison group. Placing a subject of 60 years of age in one group would require placing a subject of 60 years of age in the comparison group.

**Same Subjects.** Equivalency may be obtained by using the same subjects for each of the comparison conditions. A pretest or measure may be made on the behavior to be studied prior to the manipulation of the independent variable. Then a measure may be made after the test to determine if manipulating the variable produced a change in the behavior. A change in behavior for the different conditions may be attributed to the experimental treatment.

**Blind Technique.** A blind technique may be used to control possible behavior changes in subjects who may behave a particular way due to the knowledge of experimental treatment. In this technique, the subjects in the experiment would not know whether they were receiving the experimental treatment (Figure 2-1). For example, to study the effects of a particular motion picture instructing and motivating employees on job performance, each group would view a film—one group a neutral film and the other group the film on employee job performance. Since neither group would know which film is the one being studied, subject's reactions would not be influenced by what they *thought* the experimenters expected.

The blind technique may also be used to control bias in recording and measuring the behavioral response. If a researcher expects a subject to behave in a particular way due to the experimental treatment, evaluation and perception of the response may be altered and unconsciously

Figure 2-1 When the subjects participating in the experiment do not know whether they are in the experimental group or the control group, the experiment is referred to as a blind experiment.

biased. In using the blind technique, the researcher measuring and recording the behavioral response would not know whether the subject received the experimental treatment. A group which receives the experimental treatment is called an *experimental group*. A *control group* is a group in the experiment that does not receive the experimental treatment. Having a control group in the experiment helps insure that no special attention will be given to the subjects actually receiving the experimental treatment.

### A Sample Experiment

An example of the experimental procedure might be as follows. One may hypothesize that typists perform better on typing tasks when the noise levels are lower. Typing performance may be operationally defined as the average number of correct words typed per minute (dependent variable). Noise level might be operationally defined in decibels (independent variable). A sample of 100 typists might be randomly selected from the population of typists. From the sample of 100, 50 typists might be randomly selected to be in the experimental group which is to be exposed to high noise levels of 80 decibels. The remaining 50 typists would comprise the control group which is to be exposed to average office noise levels of 40 decibels. Each group would be assigned to type in two different rooms without knowing that the noise levels would be different. All other conditions that might affect the typing such as average typing speed, brand of machines, condition of machines, or illumination would be the same, whenever possible, for each group. The scorer of the typing tests would not know which typists had been in the experimental group. If a *significant difference* was found in the average performance of the two groups, then the difference might be reasonably attributed to the noise level. A significant difference means that the difference between the groups is so great that it is unlikely that it was due to chance factors. Obviously, the average words typed per minute by each group would not be identical to the nearest hundredth. A difference of 15 or 20 words per minute, however, probably would not be attributed to chance. If such a significant difference occurred, a more logical conclusion would be that the difference was due to the noise level difference rather than to chance. Mathematical formulas are used to determine the amount of difference that would be significant.

## Statistics

When drawing conclusions from the observations made in an experiment, the question becomes whether the differences in the measured variable between an experimental group and a control group are great enough to assume that the difference was caused by the manipulation of the independent variable.

## Definition

The discipline of *statistics* is a body of scientific methods consisting of mathematical ways of handling data and deciding whether a difference in behavior is attributable to independent variables rather than to chance factors. As well as being a method of dealing with data, statistics may be a collection of numerical facts which have been collected through observation or from other numerical data such as averages, tables, and graphs.

## Categories

Statistics as a method may be subdivided into two categories: (1) *descriptive statistics* which is concerned with describing the data and presenting it in a convenient, usable, and understandable form; and (2) *inferential statistics* which is concerned with drawing conclusions and making inferences about populations based on samples taken from a population. Statistics is a mathematical discipline which includes both the theory and the methods that can be used in analyzing data.

# Descriptive Statistical Procedures

*Data*, often called scores, usually consist of a large number of observations presented in numerical form that represents a characteristic or a phenomenon. Because of the large number of observations, some organization and summarization of the data is needed in order to describe the observations.

## Distributions

The first step in providing a description of a set of data might be to organize the data by preparing a *rank distribution* which involves arranging the items of data or scores in a hierarchical order from highest to lowest. An arrangement referred to as a *frequency distribution* consists of grouping all identical scores together, or grouping together all scores which fall into a particular category such as 70 through 74, and determining how many times (frequency) items of data fall into that category. This makes the data more meaningful and manageable. See Table 2-1 for an example.

## Graphs

The researcher might want to prepare a graph of the data to get an idea of the shape of the distribution to see if the scores are evenly distributed or concentrated heavily in certain parts of the distribution such as near the middle or near the upper or lower end. "Seeing" the distribution can enhance understanding.

A *histogram* is a type of bar graph in which the frequencies are represented in terms of the lengths of the bars. The area of a bar is directly proportional to the frequency it represents. The scores are plotted along the horizontal axis (x) and the frequencies along the vertical axis (y). See Figure 2-2.

A *frequency polygon* is a line graph in which the frequency associated with the score, or the scores in a group, is plotted as a point. A frequency polygon is shown in Figure 2-3.

## Measures of Central Tendency

A *measure of central tendency* is a representative point or score for a set of data and tends to be near the middle of the score range. The measure of central tendency may relate to the average value of the scores, the value of the score that is in the middle position when the scores are in rank order, or to the most commonly occurring score.

**Mean.** The familiar arithmetic average obtained by totaling all the items of data and dividing by the number of items of data is one measure of central tendency and is known as the *mean*. The mean may be obtained for any set of observations that can be added and divided. Some data such as *supervisor rating on a scale of 1 through 5* or *agree—disagree—undecided* as a response to a question cannot be described by a mean.

**Median.** The *median* is a measure of central tendency based on the rank distribution. The median is the point or score below which half (50 percent) of the items of data fall when they are arranged in rank order. For an odd number of items of data, the median will be the score that falls in

---

### TABLE 2-1   Organizing Data

Data collected: The following scores were made on a work sample test taken by 35 applicants. (A minimum amount of data is used for illustration. In practice, one would need to have many more scores in the sample.)

83, 86, 84, 83, 87, 83, 82, 78, 85, 90, 75, 81, 78, 85, 80, 79, 85, 88, 81, 76, 85, 80, 79, 80, 81, 81, 83, 84, 82, 83, 86, 84, 82, 87, 82

*(continued)*

## TABLE 2-1   Organizing Data   (continued)

| Rank Distribution | Ungrouped Frequency Distribution (Category size = 1) | | Grouped Frequency Distribution (Category size = 3) | |
|---|---|---|---|---|
| | **Score** | **Frequency** | **Score** | **Frequency** |
| 90 | 90 | 1 | 90–92 | 1 |
| 88 | | | | |
| 87 | 89 | 0 | 87–89 | 3 |
| 87 | | | | |
| 86 | 88 | 1 | 84-86 | 9 |
| 86 | | | | |
| 85 | 87 | 2 | 81-83 | 13 |
| 85 | | | | |
| 85 | 86 | 2 | 78-80 | 7 |
| 84 | | | | |
| 84 | 85 | 4 | 75-77 | 2 |
| 84 | | | | |
| 83 | 84 | 3 | | |
| 83 | | | | |
| 83 | 83 | 5 | | |
| 82 | | | | |
| 82 | 82 | 4 | | |
| 82 | | | | |
| 82 | 81 | 4 | | |
| 81 | | | | |
| 81 | 80 | 3 | | |
| 81 | | | | |
| 81 | 79 | 2 | | |
| 80 | | | | |
| 80 | 78 | 2 | | |
| 80 | | | | |
| 79 | 77 | 0 | | |
| 79 | | | | |
| 78 | 76 | 1 | | |
| 78 | | | | |
| 76 | 75 | 1 | | |
| 75 | | | | |

Mean = 2888 ÷ 35 = 82.5
Median = 83
Mode = 83
Range = 90 − 75 = 15

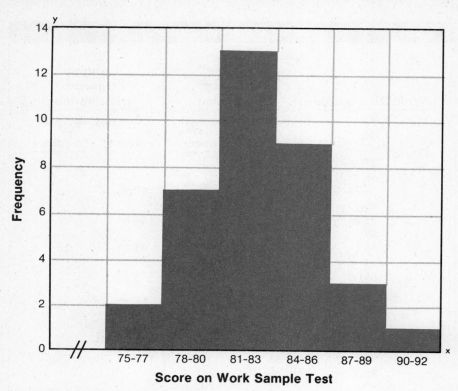

Figure 2-2 A histogram for the
grouped frequency distribution in
Table 2-1.

the middle and has an equal number of scores above it and below it. For
an even number of items of data, the median will be the average of the
two middle scores. The median may be calculated from a frequency
distribution by use of a mathematical formula.

**Mode.** The *mode*, another measure of central tendency, is the score
occurring most frequently and may be determined by inspecting the
frequency distribution. The mode is the only measure of central tendency
that can express data such as a response categorized as *strongly agree,
agree, undecided, disagree,* or *strongly disagree.* The mean, median, and
mode are given for the data in Table 2-1.

### Measures of Variability

**Definition.** A measure of variability describes the spread of the
observations or scores around the central tendency. A measure of variability is needed to indicate whether the items of data are widely scat-

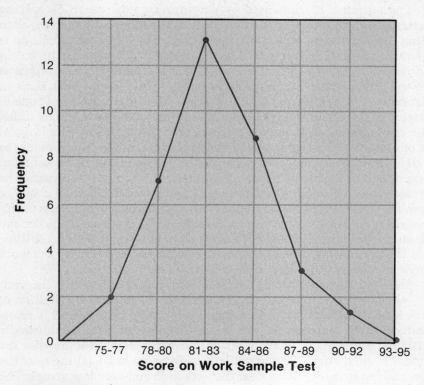

Figure 2-3 A frequency polygon for the grouped frequency distribution in Table 2-1.

tered or whether they cluster closely around the mean. If the variation is small, all individual scores will cluster around the mean; if the variation is large, some individual scores may be very different from the mean and there is less assurance that the mean is representative of a score in the distribution. For example, if the value of each of the items of data is 7, the mean will be 7 and the measure of variability will be 0. If the mean is 7 and the scores range from 6 to 8, the measure of variability will be smaller than if the mean is 7 and the scores range from 1 to 25.

**Methods of Calculation.** A number of different methods may be used for determining a measure of the degree of variability. The *range,* which is the difference between the highest and the lowest item of data, is the simplest measure of variability. Since only the two extreme items of data or scores are used to determine its value, the range tends to vary with the size of the sample, and it is not as stable as measures of variability which reflect the dispersion of the scores that are between the two extremes.

The *variance* is calculated by determining how much each score deviates from the mean of all the scores, squaring each deviation, then finding the average of the squared deviations. The *standard deviation* is the square root of the variance. The greater the variability of the scores from the mean is, the greater the sum of the squares of the deviations from the mean and the greater the average of the squared deviations or variance will be. The greater the variance is, the greater the standard deviation will be. The variance is a measure of variability in square units, while the standard deviation is a measure of variability in the original unit of measure. Expressing the variation in the same unit of measure as the data is advantageous because then the measure can be added to or subtracted from the mean. Thus, the position of a particular score may be expressed as a particular number of units (standard deviations) above or below the mean. The variance and standard deviation are very useful measures of variability, because each score in the distribution is considered rather than only two of the scores as in the range. Table 2-2 illustrates the calculation of the variance and standard deviation for the work sample scores given for data collected in Table 2-1.

**Standard Normal Curve.** The *standard normal curve* is a theoretical, bell-shaped, symmetrical curve which represents the distribution of scores for any population. If the sample selected to be observed is representative of the population, the set of scores (data) will be normally distributed and a graph of the distribution will resemble somewhat the standard normal curve. The graph will show more cases falling near the mean and fewer cases falling near the very high and very low scores. The graph of the distribution of scores for a sample is called a frequency polygon. (See Figure 2-3.)

The standard normal curve is divided into uniform, linear distances on each side of the mean (standard distances or deviations). These standard distances, however, do not represent equal percentages of the total area under the curve and, therefore, do not represent an equal percentage of the total number of cases falling within that linear distance. The average amount of the spread of the scores or data across each of the uniform, linear distances for a sample is whatever the standard deviation value is computed to be. Figure 2-4 shows a diagram of the standard normal curve. Based on the sample data given in Table 2-1 and a standard deviation of 3.28 as given in Table 2-2, the statement could be made that approximately 68 percent of all subjects taking the work sample test will score between 79.22 and 85.78, that is, between one standard deviation above and one standard deviation below the mean. The statement could also be made that approximately 95 percent of the population of applicants will score between two standard deviations above and below the mean, that is, between 75.94 and 89.06. An applicant who scored 92.34 scored three standard deviations above the mean. See the diagram shown in Figure 2-5.

## TABLE 2-2  Variance and Standard Deviation

| Score | Mean of Scores | Difference | Difference Squared |
|---|---|---|---|
| 90 | 82.5 | 7.5 | 56.25 |
| 88 | 82.5 | 5.5 | 30.25 |
| 87 | 82.5 | 4.5 | 20.25 |
| 87 | 82.5 | 4.5 | 20.25 |
| 86 | 82.5 | 3.5 | 12.25 |
| 86 | 82.5 | 3.5 | 12.25 |
| 85 | 82.5 | 2.5 | 6.25 |
| 85 | 82.5 | 2.5 | 6.25 |
| 85 | 82.5 | 2.5 | 6.25 |
| 85 | 82.5 | 2.5 | 6.25 |
| 84 | 82.5 | 1.5 | 2.25 |
| 84 | 82.5 | 1.5 | 2.25 |
| 84 | 82.5 | 1.5 | 2.25 |
| 83 | 82.5 | .5 | .25 |
| 83 | 82.5 | .5 | .25 |
| 83 | 82.5 | .5 | .25 |
| 83 | 82.5 | .5 | .25 |
| 83 | 82.5 | .5 | .25 |
| 82 | 82.5 | −.5 | .25 |
| 82 | 82.5 | −.5 | .25 |
| 82 | 82.5 | −.5 | .25 |
| 82 | 82.5 | −.5 | .25 |
| 81 | 82.5 | −1.5 | 2.25 |
| 81 | 82.5 | −1.5 | 2.25 |
| 81 | 82.5 | −1.5 | 2.25 |
| 81 | 82.5 | −1.5 | 2.25 |
| 80 | 82.5 | −2.5 | 6.25 |
| 80 | 82.5 | −2.5 | 6.25 |
| 80 | 82.5 | −2.5 | 6.25 |
| 79 | 82.5 | −3.5 | 12.25 |
| 79 | 82.5 | −3.5 | 12.25 |
| 78 | 82.5 | −4.5 | 20.25 |
| 78 | 82.5 | −4.5 | 20.25 |
| 76 | 82.5 | −6.5 | 42.25 |
| 75 | 82.5 | −7.5 | 56.25 |
|  |  | Total | 376.75 |

Variance = 376.75 ÷ 35 (number of scores) = 10.76

Standard Deviation = $\sqrt{10.76}$ = 3.28

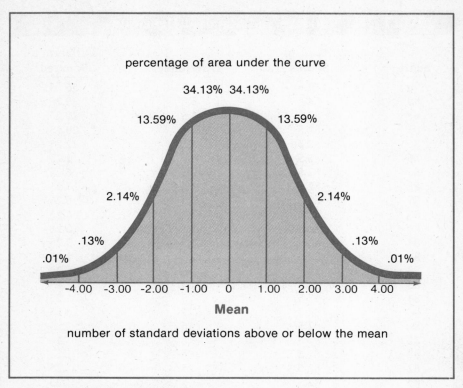

percentage of area under the curve

Figure 2-4 The standard normal curve.

## Correlations

Sometimes the data collected are paired measures, making it possible to determine the correlation—in other words, to describe the data in terms of the relationship between the two variables. For example, the data in Table 2-1 might also include the number of months of work experience the subject has on the job as well as the score on the work sample test. Some sample scores paired with number of months of work experience are listed in Figure 2-7 on page 37.

**Correlation Coefficients.** If higher work sample scores are associated with more experience and lower scores are associated with less experience, a positive relationship (correlation) is said to exist. If the lower work sample scores are associated with more experience and the higher work sample scores with less experience, a negative relationship (correlation) is said to exist. If either a positive or negative correlation is found to exist, the score that an applicant would make on the work sample test

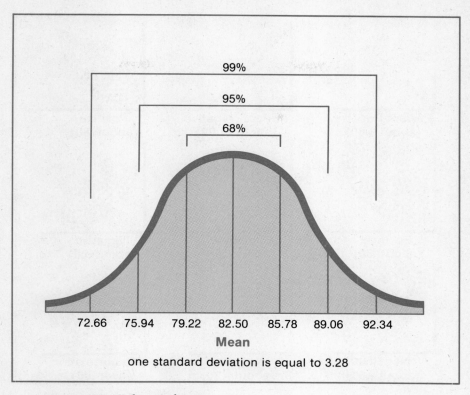

Figure 2-5 Work sample test
scores comparable to one, two, or
three standard deviations above or
below the mean.

could be predicted by knowing the number of months of experience. Formulas are available for computing a numerical representation of the relationship which is called a *correlation coefficient*. A correlation coefficient may range from 0 to + 1.00 or from 0 to − 1.00. The plus or minus sign indicates the direction of the relationship (positive or negative), and the numerical value indicates the degree of the relationship. The higher the degree of the relationship, the more accurately one variable in the pair can be predicted from the other known variable.

**Scattergrams.** A visual representation of the correlation can be prepared in the form of a *scattergram* which is a two-dimensional plot of points—each point representing the paired measurements on the two variables. Figure 2-6 shows scattergram patterns for several correlation coefficients. A lower-left-to-upper-right pattern represents a positive correlation. An upper-left-to-lower-right pattern represents a negative correlation, while an undifferentiated or circular pattern indicates no

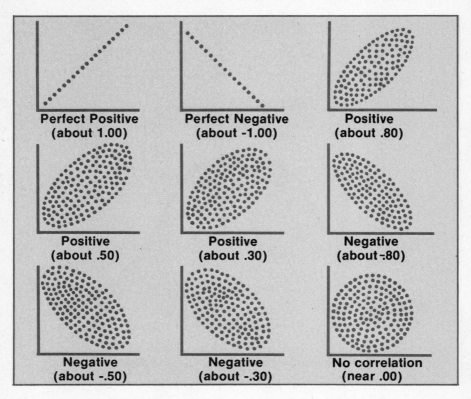

Figure 2-6 Scattergram patterns illustrating various correlations.

relationship. The closer the pattern approaches a straight line, the higher the degree of relationship. A scattergram for a set of paired measures is shown in Figure 2-7.

## Inferential Statistics

Two of the basic concerns of inferential statistics are (1) making assumptions about or estimating population characteristics and (2) testing hypotheses. Since it is usually impossible or impractical to measure an entire population, the data collected from a sample group are used to estimate the mean and the standard deviation of the population. Mathematical formulas are used to make the estimates. The method of selecting samples randomly from all possible members of the population is crucial. Also, there are mathematical ways of estimating how large a sample is needed for a given level of accuracy.

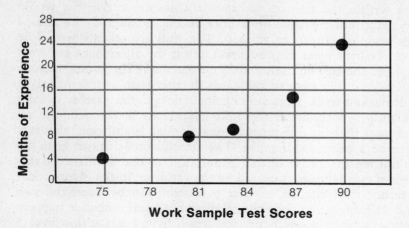

**Work Sample Test Scores**

The following data were collected on five applicants. (A minimum of data are used for illustration. In practice more data would be collected.)

| Applicant | Work Sample Test Scores | Months of Experience |
|---|---|---|
| B. Jones | 90 | 24 |
| T. Arnold | 83 | 9 |
| J. Mound | 75 | 4 |
| S. Dickens | 80 | 8 |
| J. Doe | 87 | 15 |

Figure 2-7 A scattergram for a set of paired measures.

The logic of hypothesis testing is based on the laws of probability and chance. Theoretically, if the means of all possible samples that could be drawn from a population could be plotted as a frequency polygon, one would have a standard normal curve which represents the total population of means. Since only one sample is drawn from which to obtain data to represent the population, one hypothesizes that the mean of the sample drawn is not significantly different from the mean of the population of means (the true population mean). If more than one sample is drawn from a population such as for a control group and an experimental group, one hypothesizes that the means of the two samples are not significantly different from each other, since they represent the same population. These kinds of hypotheses are referred to as null hypotheses. A *null hypothesis* states that no significant differences exist between the sample mean and the population mean, or between the means of two samples from the same population, or between a correlation coefficient and 0.

Usually, a researcher accepts that any differences between the mean of a sample and the population mean, or between the means of two samples, or between a correlation coefficient and 0 are caused by chance if they are within the area on the standard normal curve that would include 95 percent of the cases—not more than approximately 2 standard deviations from the mean or from 0. The null hypothesis would be accepted or retained when this occurs. Only if the differences are great enough to be in the area on the standard normal curve that would include the most extreme 5 percent of the cases (further than approximately 2 standard deviations from the mean or from 0) does the researcher usually reject the null hypothesis. If the null hypothesis is rejected, the researcher accepts that the difference is great enough (significant) that it is unlikely to be a chance difference. The conclusion is drawn that the sample is not representative of that population, or that a difference this great between two samples is caused by the variation in the independent variable rather than chance, or that a relationship between the two variables does exist rather than the relationship being a chance happening. Of course, when a researcher rejects a null hypothesis at this level (5 percent) there is a 5 percent chance that the conclusion is wrong and a 95 percent chance that the conclusion is correct. Sometimes a researcher will not reject a null hypothesis unless the difference is significant at the 1 percent level and there is only a 1 percent chance that the conclusion is wrong and a 99 percent chance that the conclusion is correct. Inferential statistical procedures involve determining probabilities of chance and deciding whether to reject or retain null hypotheses to support research hypotheses.

Psychology is a science because it employs scientific methods to investigate behavior, to interpret the information collected from the investigation, and to draw conclusions about behavior based on the information collected. Professional journals in the field of psychology publish the findings from these investigations. The following boxed material describes a publication that is helpful in locating research on a particular topic.

---

### PSYCHOLOGICAL ABSTRACTS

The _Psychological Abstracts_ is an index by subject of the published articles (usually research studies) in professional psychological journals and may be found in many libraries. The journal articles are abstracted (summarized) as well as referenced. Issues appear monthly with an index for that month, and an index is published for each of the six-month periods January through June and July through December. Using the index, research on topics in the field of psychology can be located.

## SUMMARY

1.  Scientific study implies the empirical approach, the pursuit of knowledge by observation and experiment, rather than the common sense approach which is often vague, inconsistent, false or only partially correct.

2.  Scientific study consists of formulating hypotheses, applying operational definitions, and making systematic observations to evaluate the hypotheses.

3.  Theories are integrated sets of interrelated hypotheses that attempt to explain phenomena.

4.  An empirical approach employs such scientific methods as naturalistic observations, surveys, case studies, correlational studies, and experimental studies.

5.  The correlational method investigates relationships among measurable events and is especially useful in predicting behaviors.

6.  The experimental method seeks to determine cause and effect relationships and employs procedures to manipulate independent variables, measure dependent variables, and control other variables to obtain equivalency of groups.

7.  Random selection and assignment of subjects ensures that various traits and characteristics will be distributed equally or in an unbiased way among the groups to be compared.

8.  Matching subjects on variables, using the same subjects, and using blind procedures are other methods of controlling an experiment.

9.  Statistics is a body of scientific methods consisting of mathematical ways of handling recorded observations (data) to evaluate a hypothesis. Statistics is also a collection of numerical facts expressed in summarizing statements.

10. Descriptive statistics is concerned with organizing, describing, and summarizing the data collected by observation.

11. Descriptive statistics involves the use of rank distributions; grouped or ungrouped frequency distributions; graphs such as histograms and frequency polygons; indexes of central tendency such as the mean, median or mode; indexes of variation such as the range, variance, or standard deviation; or indexes of correlation.

12. The mean is the arithmetic average of the observed measures or scores, while the median is the score below which 50 percent of the scores fall when they are arranged in rank order. The mode is the most frequently occurring score.

13. The variance, a measure of variability, is the arithmetic average of the squares of the amounts each score deviates from the mean of the scores. The standard deviation is the square root of the variance.

14. The standard normal curve is a theoretical, bell-shaped, symmetrical frequency polygon which represents the distribution in the population of the trait or characteristic that is measured.

15. Correlation coefficients and the visual representation of them (scattergrams) indicate the direction (positive or negative) and the degree (0 to 1.00) of relationship among the variables.

16. Inferential statistics is concerned with estimation of population characteristics and hypothesis testing.

17. A null hypothesis states that no differences exist between the sample mean and the population mean, between the means of the two samples from the same population, or between a correlation coefficient and 0 other than what might occur by chance.

18. A null hypothesis is usually accepted or retained if the difference is small enough that it is expected to occur by chance in 95 percent of the cases. A null hypothesis is rejected if the difference is great enough that it is expected to occur in 5 percent or fewer of the cases.

19. Psychology is a science in that it employs scientific methods to study behavior, to evaluate hypotheses about behavior, and to formulate theories explaining and predicting behavior.

## SUGGESTIONS FOR FURTHER READING

Anderson, B. F. *The psychology experiment* (2nd ed.). Monterey, Calif.: Brooks/Cole, 1971.

Experimental design is emphasized in this orientation to the scientific method.

Ary, D., & Jacobs, L. C. *Introduction to statistics: Purposes and procedures.* New York: Holt, Rinehart and Winston, 1976.

A book that provides an introduction to statistical procedures. The concepts are presented in a style of writing that beginning students in statistics will find readable. Extensive mathematical training is not presumed on the part of the reader.

Deese, J. *Psychology as science and art.* New York: Harcourt Brace Jovanovich, 1972.

This book examines methods of psychology as well as attitudes and values. The position is taken that the study of psychology ranges from scientific methods to humanistic approaches. The beginning psychology student will probably find the book rather difficult.

Fleishman, E. A. *Studies in personnel and industrial psychology* (2nd ed.). Homewood, Ill.: The Dorsey Press, 1967.

Scientific studies conducted in the area of industrial psychology are presented in this book. The studies are grouped by subject such as those pertaining to motivation and those pertaining to learning.

Heinze, D. *Fundamentals of managerial statistics.* Cincinnati: South-Western Publishing Company, 1980.

A book that explains introductory statistical procedures in a manner that beginning psychology students can comprehend.

Hinkle, D. E., Wiersma, W., & Jurs, S. G. *Applied statistics for the behavioral sciences.* Chicago: Rand McNally College Publishing Company, 1979.

A thorough but readable book that provides an opportunity for the reader to gain a conceptual understanding of the basic statistical procedures used in research and the computational skills needed to carry out statistical procedures in practical settings.

Huff, D. *How to lie with statistics.* New York: W. W. Norton, 1954.

A book that points out many important principles of psychological research in a unique manner by exposing how people misuse numbers and statistics both knowingly and unknowingly.

*Organizational Behavior and Human Performance, Journal of Applied Psychology, Journal of Applied Behavioral Science, Personnel Psychology*

Journals in the field of industrial/organizational psychology which are published periodically and contain research studies and reading material related to psychology and work.

Rosenthal, R., & Rosnow, R. L. *Primer of methods for the behavioral sciences.* New York: Wiley, 1975.

A brief introduction to research methods, covering observation, experimentation, causality, research biases, and ethics. This is a book that is easy to read.

# **P**sychology and Work  Chapter 3

**S**ince the study of psychology is so broad, intermingles with other disciplines, and includes both theory and application of theory, psychology as a profession offers a variety of work activities in several different areas. Whether one chooses to work in the field of psychology or to work in other occupations, a knowledge of the work of psychologists is needed in order to make occupational choices and to understand the function of psychologists in industrial and organizational settings. In this chapter the work activities of psychologists and areas of psychology are discussed with special emphasis on industrial/organizational psychology. The benefits an individual may derive from knowing and applying the principles of psychology are also a point of focus.

## Areas of Psychology

Because psychology is such a broad field, it is subdivided into a number of separate specializations; however, these areas overlap, and a psychologist may work in several different areas of specialization. Also, findings in one area concerning some behavior may directly relate to studies of behavior in another area. Furthermore, work activities may be common to more than one area of specialization. For example, a psychologist in each area of specialization may teach or conduct experimental research. Areas are sometimes classified as either pure psychology or applied psychology depending on whether the psychologists are primarily concerned with acquiring or developing further knowledge, or whether they are concerned with immediate practical application to current problems.

### Developmental Psychology

*Developmental psychology* is an area in which psychologists are concerned with the growth and development of a person from the beginning of life until death. Behavior and behavioral changes characteristic of each period of development are studied. The periods of development include the prenatal period, infancy, early childhood, later childhood, adolescence, adulthood, and old age. Developmental psychologists work in a wide variety of settings which may include serving as consultants to children's television programs, to special federal programs, or to schools. Developmental psychologists may also work with children who have learning problems or work in institutions where they may do psychotherapy with emotionally disturbed children.

## Educational Psychology

*Educational psychology* is the area of psychology concerned with increasing the efficiency of learning in school. Educational psychologists may work in teacher training institutions or school settings to develop further knowledge about the process of learning, but they primarily apply their psychological knowledge in school settings to improve learning. Psychologists in education may administer psychological tests, evaluate learning and emotional problems, advise parents and teachers on how to improve academic performance and social adjustment, organize training programs to help teachers, teach psychological principles, conduct research to answer questions of practical significance, or study teacher morale. Educational psychologists often serve as consultants to school systems.

## Social Psychology

The area of psychology which deals with the behavior of people in groups is called *social psychology*. Social psychologists are concerned with how other people influence an individual's behavior. The interactions or relationships among people in families, peer groups, professional groups, and cultural groups are of special interest. Social psychologists focus on such topics as attitude formation and change, group pressures, interpersonal relations, and socially deviant behaviors. Friendship formation, romantic attraction, bargaining, or the effect of violence in the mass media on aggressive behavior may also be topics of study.

## Experimental Psychology

Another area of psychology referred to as *experimental psychology* uses rigorous research methods to experimentally investigate basic psychological processes, usually in laboratory settings (Figure 3-1). Experimental psychology is a laboratory science in the strictest sense because it uses precise instruments for measurement and seeks to refine control and measurement. It is an area which applies the scientific method to the study of behavior. Experimental psychologists design research projects and have a specialized knowledge of the methods and logic of the scientific approach. Answers to questions that contribute to the practical areas of psychology are provided by experimental psychology. A relatively small number of psychologists label themselves experimental psychologists,

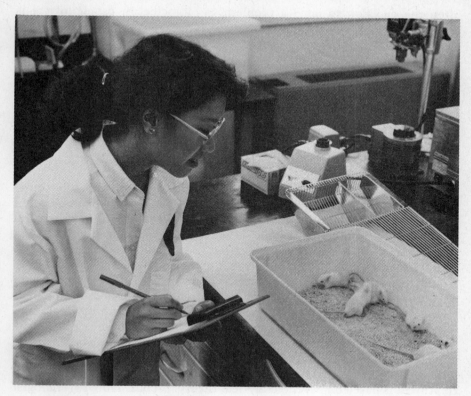

Figure 3-1 Experimental psychology uses rigorous research
methods, usually in the laboratory,
to study behavior.

but all areas of psychology include some experimental psychology since
some scientific research is necessary to all psychological investigations.
Experimental psychologists are usually based at a university where they
combine research with teaching.

### Physiological Psychology

*Physiological psychology* is an area in which behavior is studied as a
function of physical changes in the body, especially in the brain, the
nervous system, and the biochemistry of the body. Psychologists in this
area study the underlying physical mechanisms that control behavior. In
addition to searching for physical mechanisms, physiological psychologists also investigate the contribution of inherited characteristics. Physiological psychology is the area closest to the biological sciences, and

often the decision to label a problem as biological or psychological is arbitrary.

### Clinical Psychology

Probably the most familiar area of psychology is in applied psychology and is referred to as *clinical psychology*. Psychologists engaged in clinical work are concerned with helping individuals achieve psychological well-being and thus are involved in diagnosing and treating psychological disturbances. Clinical psychologists use a wide variety of diagnostic techniques and therapeutic treatments.

The difference between psychology and psychiatry is often confused. *Psychiatrists* are medical doctors who specialize in the treatment of psychological disorders. Psychiatrists have completed medical school and have followed this with three to five years of specialized schooling in psychological disorders. A clinical psychologist holds graduate degrees— usually a Ph.D. (Doctor of Philosophy) and an M.S. (Master of Science), having earned those degrees from a psychology department in a college or university other than a medical school. Clinical psychologists may have completed more courses in psychology, conducted more psychological research, or done more psychological testing than a psychiatrist; however, psychologists cannot prescribe any kind of medication, perform surgery, or refer patients for surgery or shock therapy. A *psychoanalyst* may be either a clinical psychologist or a psychiatrist whose approach to treatment is based on psychoanalytical theory. A *counseling psychologist* may or may not have a Ph.D. and works primarily with people who have less serious problems—perhaps problems associated with educational and vocational choices or individual and family adjustment problems. Those who work in the area of clinical psychology usually work in hospitals or have private practices.

### Industrial/Organizational Psychology

*Industrial/organizational psychology*, sometimes designated as business psychology, is an area of applied psychology that specializes in applying psychological principles in work-related situations and in conducting research to expand knowledge of psychological principles that are applicable. Psychologists with this specialized interest work in organizational settings (industrial or business) and are concerned with personnel selection, training programs, morale, supervision, productivity, job classification, and job satisfaction (Figure 3-2). Industrial/organizational psychologists often serve as part-time or full-time consultants for government agencies and private industry.

Figure 3-2 An industrial/organizational psychologist may discuss an employee's personal problems, management problems, or the effectiveness of a training program.

The industrial/organizational psychologist may be concerned with questions that involve the study of individual behavior; group behavior; department, division, or overall organizational behavior; and behaviors that are more global or environmental in nature. Questions that may be asked at the level of individual behavior focus on an employee's needs, abilities, values, and interests and how these variables relate to absence, turnover, grievances, theft, individual productivity, career progress, or job attitude. In studying group behavior, psychologists focus on communication, conflict within the group, cohesion of the group, decision-making, leadership, and group productivity. When the psychologist studies the behavior of a department, division, or the overall organization, the concern may be with such issues as size, structure, available technology, conflict between departments or divisions, and resources. Studying environmental behavior, which is the broadest and most global behavior, might include analyzing the effects of factors such as the employment level in a community, the stability or instability of a community's population, or the political attitudes (liberal versus conservative) within a community.

### Occupational Outlook

A survey of more than 35,000 members of the American Psychological Association indicated that more psychologists are engaged in the applied practice of psychology than in research (Boneau & Cuca, 1974). The survey also indicated that more psychologists are classified as clinical psychologists than any other area of specialization and that only about 7 percent of the psychologists with Ph.D. degrees and 10 percent of psychologists with M.S. degrees are classified as being in the field of industrial/organizational psychology. Industrial/organizational psychology, however, is presently one of the most rapidly expanding areas of specialization (Rathus, 1981) since organizations are finding that the application of psychological principles can be helpful in increasing production and resolving work-related problems. This expansion was foreseen when a survey of over 300 personnel administrators indicated that about 75 percent of the administrators believed a professionally trained psychologist could be useful in their companies and only about 11 percent of the companies reported the employment of an industrial/organizational psychologist (Thornton, 1969).

## Development of Industrial/Organizational Psychology

The percentage of psychologists working in the area of industrial/organizational psychology is still small compared to the percentage of psychologists working in other areas of psychology; nevertheless, the application of the principles of psychology to the work environment has experienced tremendous acceptance. The application of psychology in a business environment has expanded into many different areas since the first application at the turn of the century.

### The Beginning

Industrial/organizational psychology had its beginning in 1901 when W. D. Scott gave a short talk to a group of Chicago business executives about the potential uses of psychology in advertising (Ferguson, 1961). In 1903, Scott wrote a book concerned with the application of psychology to advertising called *The Theory of Advertising*. Scott was the first to apply psychology in business. Frederick W. Taylor pioneered efficiency engineering in 1911 and found that the amount of pig iron being loaded onto a freight car could be increased from 12½ tons to 47½ tons a day by giving the workers rest periods at various times during the day. With this, scientific management had its beginning. In 1913, the first industrial psychology textbook, authored by Hugo Münsterberg, was published.

### Time and Motion Study

An early aspect of industrial psychology was time and motion study developed by a husband and wife team—Frank B. Gilbreth, an industrial engineer, and Lillian Gilbreth, an engineer and psychologist. The Gilbreths did laboratory studies to determine the most efficient way to operate machines and observed workers to find more efficient ways for them to do their jobs. In one of their early studies on bricklaying, the Gilbreths devised a method to reduce the number of movements required thus enabling a worker to lay three times as many bricks in the same amount of time. Many people have read *Cheaper by the Dozen* (written by two of their twelve children) which is a humorous account of the application of time and motion study in the Gilbreth home environment.

### Later Developments

In the 1920s, industrial psychology began to be concerned with individual differences in aptitude and proficiency for work as well as the physical factors of the work place such as noise, lighting, and temperature and the effect of these variables on productivity. In the 1940s, interest in the effect of social factors such as worker morale and attitude on productivity was added to the study of industrial psychology. In the 1960s, an individual's interactions within different types of organizational settings became a concern. Also, an interest developed in communication networks as well as in physical and social factors. The 1970s saw an interaction develop between the employee and the psychologist, since the total physical and psychological well-being of the employee seemed to be related to productivity.

### Status Today

Industrial psychology has expanded its concerns to include many highly relevant social issues since its beginning about 80 years ago. Today an industrial/organizational psychologist may deal with questions related to equal employment opportunity, alcoholism and drug abuse, work motivation, and organizational effectiveness. Industrial psychology has become a blend of practice, theory, and research. There is more concern with organizational behavior and an interest in designing organizational and administrative systems best suited to human functioning. Organizational theory has become important and some psychologists have become known as organizational psychologists. The term industrial/organizational psychology is being used more often than industrial or business psychology. The strongest emphasis today is on organizational characteristics and the impact of social psychological forces on the interaction processes between organizations and persons. Today, the practice of industrial/organizational psychology is emerging not as a technique but as a field of knowledge developed out of research and theory. Research, practice, and theory in industrial/organizational psychology are interdependent, and they will become more so in the years ahead (Dunnette, 1976).

## Subdivisions of Industrial/Organizational Psychology

Since the area of industrial/organizational psychology has become so broad and has so many concerns, a number of specialized subdivisions have emerged. Some of these specialized subdivisions are identified in this section.

### Consumer Psychology

*Consumer psychology* is that branch of industrial/organizational psychology which studies the dynamics underlying decisions and behavior regarding the acquisition, use, and disposition of products, services, time, and ideas (Jacoby, 1969). The subject of motivation is of central concern to consumer psychologists. They draw most heavily from the social psychological literature on attitudes, communication, and persuasion, directing a great deal of attention to the study of persuasive communication. Consumer psychology employs motivation research to determine why a consumer chooses to buy a particular product or brand (see Figure 3-3). The study of consumer behavior includes both purchase and consumption behaviors, and many consumer psychologists are now more interested in the consumption rather than the purchase aspect.

Donald Laird was one of the first consumer psychologists. More than 40 years ago he did a study in which homemakers were asked to select one of four pairs of stockings that were identical in price, color, and weave. The pairs of stockings differed only in odor; however, only about 3 percent of the homemakers gave odor as the reason for their choice. Laird's research led to additional study of unconscious motives in motivation research. Most often the consumer's choice cannot be explained in terms of conscious reasoning (Laird, Laird, Fruehling, & Swift, 1975).

Figure 3-3 Consumer psychology employs motivation research to determine why a consumer chooses to buy a particular product or brand.

Industrial/organizational psychology is concerned with the behavior of people as workers and producers of goods inside organizations, while consumer psychology is concerned with the behavior of people as purchasers and users of goods outside organizations. Some psychologists have questioned whether consumer psychology is a subdivision of industrial/organizational psychology or a separate area of psychology (Jacoby, 1976). An example of the work of consumer psychologists appears in the box on page 52.

## Engineering Psychology

The subdivision of industrial/organizational psychology which specializes in the discovery and application of information about the relationship between human behavior and machines, tools, jobs, and work

CONSUMER PSYCHOLOGY

Some years ago a manufacturer of instant coffee sought the help of psychologists. The psychologists had hundreds of people characterize the type of person who would be most likely to buy the list of items shown them. Some were shown a list that specified coffee; others were shown an identical list except, instead of coffee, it specified the brand name of the instant coffee. The person who would be most likely to buy the list containing the instant coffee was more often characterized as being lazy, taking shortcuts in preparing meals, and not caring as much for family members. As a result of the study, an advertising campaign was developed based on the time saved by using instant coffee which would allow one to spend more time with one's family and thus show love and caring for family members. Sales of that brand of instant coffee went up significantly (Haire, 1950).

environments is called *engineering psychology*. Engineering psychology attempts to design equipment, tasks, work places, and work environments to best match worker abilities and limitations. Instead of regarding the job as a constant element and the worker as an element to be trained to suit the job, these psychologists take the opposite view. They regard the worker as a biological and psychological constant and see the task of the psychologist as that of changing the machines, the tools, or the environment to make the job better suited to the worker.

An example of the work of an engineering psychologist is demonstrated by the typewriter keyboard. About 40 years ago a typewriter keyboard called the Dvorak-Dealey "Simplified" Typewriter Keyboard was developed (Lekberg, 1972). (See Figure 3-4.) The most frequently used keys are in the home row, and the right hand does about 12 percent more work than the left hand. Developers of this keyboard produced evidence that by using this keyboard a typist's speed could be increased up to five times with no increase in errors. Actually, the standard typewriter keyboard was designed to place the most frequently used letters as far apart as possible to slow down typing speed because the keys of the earliest typewriters would jam up if the typist went too fast. The standard keyboard is still in common use today, however.

Engineering psychologists are often referred to as human factor psychologists because they are particularly concerned with human factors such as vision, hearing, and other sensory capacities in the design of safer and more efficient operation of machines by people. The term engineering psychologist needs to be broadened today to include those who have an interest in going beyond the design of machines and into the design of organizations and administrative systems best suited to human functioning. Although it may be important to be concerned with dials, gauges, knobs, and levers, some of the most challenging and important problems of engineering psychology today arise in the design of large systems and the integration of people into these systems. The design of systems requires the psychologist to consider the following: (1) the selection of workers and their training, (2) the design of the system's hardware and its environment, and (3) the design of operating manuals, instructions, and procedures. The engineering psychologist is often involved in the evaluation of systems that involve the behavior of both people and machines.

## Personnel Psychology

*Personnel psychology* is the study of individual differences in performance and of methods to assess such differences. Personnel psychology is also the application of psychology to management and employee training, supervision of personnel, communication, and employee counseling.

Personnel psychology involves *job analysis*, which describes the work to be done, the skills needed, and the training required. Assessing the relative value of a job to the organization or *job evaluation* is also a part of personnel psychology. The employee's actual performance may be measured against the *job description* which represents the standard performance for the job. Personnel psychologists attempt to ensure that employee appraisal is as reliable, relevant, and free of bias and distortion as research, development, and resources can make it. Applying motivational techniques including goal setting is another specific function of personnel psychology. Tests of interests, values, personality, aptitudes, and abilities are frequently used to provide information about job applicants and to predict job success. Personnel psychologists may be concerned with determining the reliability and validity of such tests as well as with determining the costs involved in gathering information, training employees and meeting selection ratios. Personnel psychologists may be directly associated with training programs such as on-the-job training, apprentice training, job rotation, and off-site programs such as lectures, films, and conferences.

## Environmental Psychology

*Environmental psychology* is a new specialized subdivision of industrial/organizational psychology which studies the relationship between psychological processes and physical environments, both natural

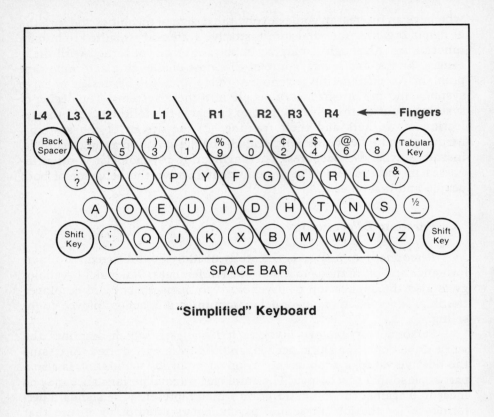

**"Simplified" Keyboard**

## DISTRIBUTION OF WORK LOAD
## AMONG FINGERS OF RIGHT AND LEFT HANDS
(As a % of Total Letter Occurrences)

| Fingers | Universal | Simplified | Difference |
|---------|-----------|------------|------------|
| Left first | 22.4% | 16.1% | − 6.3% |
| Left second | 19.4 | 12.7 | − 6.7 |
| Left third | 8.2 | 8.6 | + 0.4 |
| Left fourth | 7.8 | 7.6 | − 0.2 |
| | 57.8% | 45.0% | −12.8% |
| | | | |
| Right first | 19.4% | 15.8% | − 3.6% |
| Right second | 7.9 | 14.4 | + 6.5 |
| Right third | 12.5 | 14.6 | + 2.1 |
| Right fourth | 2.4 | 10.2 | + 7.8 |
| | 42.2% | 55.0% | −12.8% |

*(continued)*

## DISTRIBUTION OF WORK LOAD
## AMONG ROWS OF KEYBOARD
(As a % of Total Letter Occurrences)

| Rows | Universal | Simplified | Difference |
|------|-----------|------------|------------|
| Home | 30.4% | 69.5% | +39.1% |
| Third | 54.2 | 22.6 | −31.6 |
| Bottom | 15.4 | 07.9 | −07.5 |

Figure 3-4 The Dvorak-Dealey "Simplified" Typewriter Keyboard. The percentage of usage of the rows, fingers, and hands is compared with the conventional or Universal keyboard.

and human designed. Environmental psychology makes the assumption that it is extremely difficult to understand human behavior without understanding the environment in which it occurs. Environmental psychologists are concerned with the effects on human behavior of environmental conditions such as noise, air, and water pollution; physical space; and toxic agents (see Figure 3-5). Environmental psychologists are also interested in how behavior affects the environment. They often work with architects, sociologists, pollution experts, and others concerned with the physical environment. To illustrate a concern of environmental psychology, research on the effects of noise is cited in the box on page 57.

## Need for Psychology

Psychology has become a topic of general study because it is worthwhile, informative, and indirectly related to many occupations and interests. Every person can apply the principles of this science of behavior since every person exhibits behavior and interacts with other people who exhibit behavior.

### Individual Benefits

The study of psychology may prepare one for a career as a psychologist or indirectly prepare one for other careers. Although one may not plan to become a professional psychologist, gaining a knowledge of psychology and applying those principles in any work situation should help one deal more effectively with the people with whom one may work. Work situations almost always involve other people in some way and

Figure 3-5 Environmental psychologists are concerned with the effects on human behavior of environmental conditions such as noise, air, and water pollution; physical space; and toxic agents.

definitely involve one's own behavior, which creates a need to understand human behavior.

Every person is a psychologist of sorts, and everyone is a living example of psychology. George Miller (1969) believes that psychological principles should be made known to all people since there are not enough psychologists, even including nonprofessionals, to meet every individual need for psychological services. Miller believes people should be their own psychologists. Perhaps through the study of psychology people can become their own psychologists and enjoy better mental health.

Many employees underestimate the importance of human relations in the world of work. Often, an employee mistakenly believes that human relations is just getting people to like you, using common sense, or agreeing to everything that others may suggest. Human relations involves understanding your own behavior as well as the behavior of others. Most experts agree that employees who concentrate on good human relations get the best jobs. Since people will control your job future, the importance of building the best possible working relationships cannot be overemphasized.

Human relations is more important to the worker today than 40 or 50 years ago for several reasons: (1) businesses today are larger and more complex, which requires more group effort; (2) more people today are employed in service occupations where customer relations determine the future of the business; (3) more supervisors are being trained in human relations and are, therefore, more aware of the behavior of the workers they supervise; (4) employees in an organization today may be from a variety of cultures and personalities. A study of psychology can enable an employee to understand human relations and to have better working relationships which are assets necessary for career advancement.

---

### SOME RESEARCH ON THE EFFECTS OF NOISE

Glass and Singer (1972) measured people's ability to work problems while being exposed to brief episodes of very loud noise. The noise was quite disruptive at first, but after about four minutes, the experimental group was doing as well on the tasks as a comparison group of people who were not exposed to noise. This finding suggests that humans are capable of adapting to noise.

Research by Broadbent (1957) indicates that high noise levels interfere if the person is required to concentrate on more than one task, as when the subject was required to monitor three dials at a time, similar to the task of an airplane pilot or air traffic controller. Although noise did not interfere with the ability to track a moving line with a steering wheel, the noise did interfere with the subject's ability to repeat numbers while tracking (Finkelman and Glass, 1970).

In another study, Glass and Singer (1972) found predictable and unpredictable noise equally annoying when both loud and soft bursts of noise spaced one minute apart and at random intervals were presented to subjects who were proofreading. However, different results were found when the subjects were required to proofread written material with no noise. Unpredictable noise produced more errors in the later proofreading. Glass and Singer also found that if the person knows that he or she can control the noise, the annoying effects at the time seem to be eliminated, even if the person never exercises the option to turn the noise off.

---

Adapting to change is an important factor in the world of work. Estimates indicate that two-thirds of the jobs which will be available in the year 2000 do not exist today. With any change, whether desirable or undesirable, adjustments are required. How people react and adjust to change is closely related to how they see that change affecting their immediate needs, wants, and long-range goals. Change may be resented if it interferes with feelings of security, or change may be welcomed if it makes life more challenging. A knowledge of psychology will be helpful to anyone who must make adjustments to the inevitable changes that will occur during one's work experience.

Efficiency, or accomplishing a task in the shortest time and in the easiest and least expensive way, is really what connects psychology to the work environment. Behavior has a direct bearing on efficiency, and almost everything one person does will have an effect on someone else's efficiency. Understanding and applying the principles of psychology should improve an individual's efficiency and the efficiency of co-workers. Improved efficiency will most likely be noticed by supervisors.

The *holistic approach* to psychology deals with the whole individual as an organized system interacting within the context of the whole environment. This approach has become a popular way of viewing people at work. A person's home life, social life, religious life, work life, etc., are not viewed as a collection of parts but rather as a whole, each one influencing the other. Work is at the center of life; and success in life, a sense of achievement, security, and prestige all may be tied to one's work. Human behavior is too complex to be completely understood, but the holistic approach to the study of human behavior is probably the best approach available. Applying the principles of psychology will help one become a better adjusted person overall, not only in work but in life as a whole.

## Organizational Benefits

From an organizational point of view, human relations is motivating employees to develop teamwork which will fulfill the employee's needs and also achieve the objectives of the organization (Figure 3-6). Knowledge and application of psychological principles are important to human relations as viewed by organizations.

The concept of *organizational behavior* is concerned with understanding and describing behavior in an organizational environment. Organizational behavior attempts to explain the whole complex human factor in organizations by identifying causes and effects of that behavior, incorporating findings of the behavioral sciences, relying heavily on empirical research, and emphasizing that organizations are composed of people not just positions. Certain principles of psychology that are important to organizations have evolved as a concept called organizational behavior.

Many factors gave rise to the development of the concept of organizational behavior. These factors include the following:

1. Today workers are better educated and this has prepared them to demand better leadership.
2. With greater specialization today, more conflicts tend to arise between specialized groups such as those producing goods and those inspecting them. Also, an employee may work on such a small part of the whole that a feeling of accomplishment is lost.
3. Increasing labor costs create a greater need to make full use of labor.
4. Under subsistence living conditions, most of one's time is occupied trying to meet physiological needs, but with today's higher standard of living, more of an employee's time may be occupied in trying to meet psychological needs.
5. Increased size of organizations creates new problems. In many cases, some employees may never have met any of the officers or members of higher management.

In a survey of over 300 diversified companies, approximately three-fourths of the respondents reported that psychological principles brought new and valuable insights to management (Rush & Wikstrom, 1969). The

Figure 3-6 Human relations is motivating employees to develop teamwork which will fulfill the employee's needs and also achieve the objectives of the organization.

survey also indicated that an interest in psychology was increasing at all levels of management.

The need for knowledge and application of psychological principles in organizations was emphasized by Williams (1978) when he stated quite emphatically that

> Only progressive and efficient organizations can survive and only sophisticated and knowledgeable managers can succeed. Managers must have more than technical knowledge and an intuitive grasp of what is required to organize and lead effectively. They must become aware of the subtleties of formal organizations, informal group processes, authority, power, and communication within an organizational setting. . . . Managers must gain a deep understanding of human behavior as it is expressed in an organizational setting. In the final analysis, organizations are made up of individuals who are increasingly demanding to be viewed as individuals, rather than as economic units in a heartless, impersonal bureaucracy. (p. 5)

Most psychologists believe that organizational behavior is a legitimate study. The concept of organizational behavior is not complete; new opportunities are being provided for research each day.

## SUMMARY

1. Psychology is such a broad field that it is subdivided into specialized areas.

2. Developmental psychology is concerned with growth and development from the beginning of life through old age and death.

3. Educational psychology specializes in developing knowledge about learning and the application of that knowledge in schools.

4. Social psychology is the study of how other people influence an individual's behavior and deals with the behavior of people in groups.

5. The strict application of the scientific method to investigate behavior is experimental psychology.

6. Physiological psychology is concerned with the contribution of physical mechanisms to behavior, with biochemistry, and with inherited characteristics that control behavior.

7. Clinical psychology uses diagnostic and therapeutic techniques to help individuals achieve psychological well-being.

8. A psychiatrist is a medical doctor who specializes in the treatment of psychological disorders while a psychologist usually has a doctor of philosophy degree, or at least a master's degree in psychology.

9. Industrial/organizational psychology specializes in applying psychological principles in work-related situations and in conducting research to expand knowledge of psychological principles that are applicable.

10. Since its beginning in 1901 in the field of advertising, industrial/organizational psychology has expanded to include time and motion study, the effects of individual differences, physical factors, social factors, communication networks, and environmental factors. It is now a blend of theory, research, and practice with emphasis on organizational behavior.

11. Consumer psychology is that branch of industrial/organizational psychology which studies the dynamics underlying decisions and behavior regarding the acquisition, use, and disposition of products, services, time, and ideas.

12. The discovery and application of information about the relationship between human behavior and machines, tools, jobs, and work environments is called engineering psychology.

13. Personnel psychology applies psychological principles to problems of management and employee training, personnel supervision, communication, and employee counseling. Personnel psychology also includes the study and assessment of individual differences in performance.

14. The effects on human behavior of such environmental conditions as noise, physical space, air and water pollution, and toxic agents is the concern of environmental psychology.

15. Even if psychology is not to be a person's career, one should gain a knowledge of psychology while preparing for employment. A knowledge of psychology allows a person to be more effective on any job, to have better human relations, to achieve better mental health, to improve efficiency, and to adjust to inevitable change.

16. Organizational behavior has evolved as a concept of behavior in an organizational environment and is needed for progressive and efficient organizations in today's world. Factors that gave rise to the development of organizational behavior were better educated employees, greater specialization, increased labor costs, increased size of organizations, and higher standards of living.

## SUGGESTIONS FOR FURTHER READING

Altman, I. *The environment and social behavior.* Monterey, Calif.: Brooks/Cole, 1975.

An introduction to environmental psychology that discusses the human need for privacy, reactions to intrusion by other people, and the effects of overcrowding on behavior. The design of human environments is also discussed.

American Psychological Association. *Careers in psychology.* (3rd ed.). Washington, D.C.: American Psychological Association, 1978.

A publication provided by the American Psychological Association which discusses traditional and innovative careers in psychology.

American Psychological Association. Psychology's manpower: The education and utilization of psychologists. *American Psychologist,* 1972, *27* (5).

This issue of the official journal of the American Psychological Association is devoted to the careers of psychologists. It examines salaries, specialized types of employment, job markets, the status of women, and future prospects.

Bass, B. M., & Barrett, G. V. *Man, work, and organizations* (2nd ed.). Boston: Allyn and Bacon, 1981.

This book conveys to the reader the idea that the role of industrial/organizational psychology today is more than the application of principles from learning, perception, and motivation in general psychology, but also includes theory and concepts derived directly from research on people and organizations at work.

Siegel, L., & Lane, I. M. *Psychology in industrial organizations.* Homewood, Ill.: Irwin, 1974.

The function of psychology in industrial/organizational settings is discussed in this book.

Super, D. E., & Super, C. M. *Opportunities in psychological careers today* (3rd ed.). Louisville, Ky.: Vocational Guidance Manuals, 1976.

A book that provides guidance for people interested in careers in psychology.

Woods, P. J. (Ed.). *Career opportunities for psychologists: Expanding and emerging areas.* Washington, D.C.: American Psychological Association, 1976.

This book describes new career possibilities in psychology that have received an unusual amount of attention and may offer special job opportunities for the future. Each chapter is written by a different author and deals with general problems of securing employment in psychology.

# Part 2
# Biological Processes

# Nervous and Endocrine Systems

Chapter 4

# A

**ny behavior,** from opening a desk drawer to solving a management problem, depends on the integration of the nervous system, the sense organs, and the endocrine system. Much of human behavior and mental functioning cannot be explained or fully understood without knowledge of these biological processes. Even one's perception of an event depends on how the sense organs and brain function. Although much is not known about these physiological mechanisms, there are findings that explain certain human behaviors. A brief overview of these biological processes which are fundamental to behavior is presented in this chapter.

## Neurons

The human body is composed of billions of cells. Each cell is a separate entity enclosed by a membrane and contains the main cell body and nucleus where most of the complex chemical reaction occurs that keeps the cell alive and functioning. Although all the cells of the body have the same general organization and the same biochemical mechanism, they vary in size, shape, appearance, and unique features according to the specialized job they perform. For example, blood cells are different from bone cells or skin cells. The specialized cells of the nervous system are called *neurons*. The human brain is thought to consist of about $10^{11}$ (100 billion) neurons (Stevens, 1979). To learn as much as possible about how these cells function is especially important because they are at the foundation of human behavior and mental functioning.

### Structure

Neurons have short, delicate branch-like extensions called *dendrites* protruding from the main cell body. The name dendrite is derived from the Greek word "dendron" which means tree. Dendrites receive messages or impulses from neighboring cells and conduct that information to the main cell body.

The *axon* of a neuron is a long, slender tubelike fiber ranging in length from one or two inches to three feet. The axon extends away from the main cell body and carries messages out from the cell, either passing them on to another neuron in the nervous system or to cells in a muscle or gland. Some axons may have axonal branches. As shown in Figure 4-1, some axons are covered with fatty nodules called a *myelin sheath* which serves to insulate the fiber of the axon and speed up the transmission of a message. The message is transmitted faster since the myelin sheath is not continuous and the message jumps along between nodes. (See Figure 4-1.) A *nerve* is a bundle of axons from many neurons much like a telephone cable that consists of many wires. At the end of an axon are small fibers called *terminal branches*. A knob at the end of each terminal branch releases chemical substances when the outgoing message reaches the end of the branch. Studies indicate that these chemical substances carry the message to the next neuron.

## Types by Function

Neurons have different characteristics depending on their specialized function. An *afferent neuron,* sometimes referred to as a sensory neuron, receives input directly from cells in the sense organs. The cells in the sense organs are activated by some stimulus in the environment (inside and outside the body) and send messages to the afferent neurons in

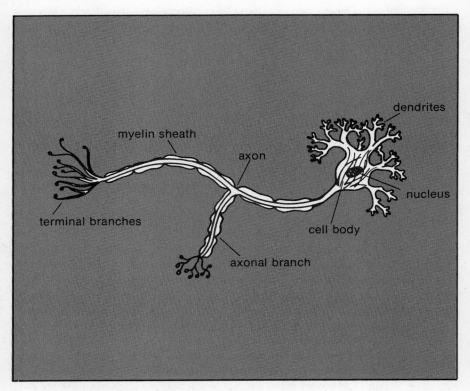

Figure 4-1 Structure of a neuron.

the nervous system. An *efferent neuron*, sometimes referred to as a motor neuron, carries messages out from the brain and spinal cord to cells in muscles that control outward external movement as well as to the smooth muscles that control glands and internal organs. *Interneurons*, sometimes referred to as association neurons, carry messages to and receive messages from other neurons in the brain and spinal cord. These neurons generally have shorter axons which are not covered by a myelin sheath. All living systems, including the cells of the body, carry out three functions—inputs, internal activities, and outputs. Figure 4-2 illustrates these three functions in the nervous system.

## The Neural Impulse

Since the neurons are not physically joined together, the message or neural impulse must cross a small space, called a *synapse*, that separates the terminal branch of one neuron from the dendrites of the next neuron.

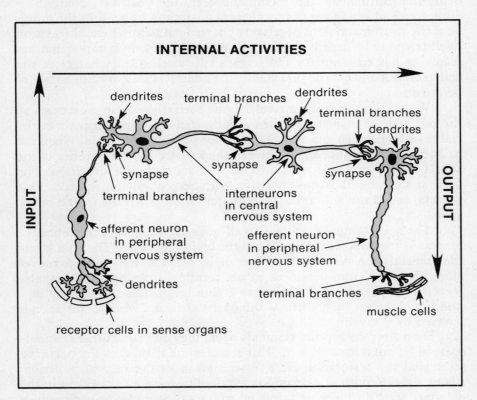

Figure 4-2 Structures and
functions of the nervous system.

A typical neuron may have anywhere from 1,000 to 10,000 synapses and may receive information from something like 1,000 other neurons (Stevens, 1979). The transmission of the neural impulse, therefore, consists of the synaptic transmission which is the movement of the impulse across the synapse, and the axonal transmission which is the movement of the impulse along the axon of a neuron.

### Axonal Transmission

The movement of the impulse along the axon of the neuron is electrical in nature. The cell membrane separates two fields of electrically charged *ions*, particles formed when a neutral atom or group of atoms loses or gains one or more *electrons*. Electrons are negative charges of electricity that are parts of all atoms. The area outside the cell membrane is composed primarily of positively charged sodium ions. The area within the cell membrane is composed primarily of negatively charged potassium ions. When a neuron is in the resting state with no message being transmitted, the cell membrane keeps out positively charged sodium ions and lets in negatively charged potassium ions. Since the interior of the neuron is rich in negatively charged potassium ions, the neuron itself is said to be negatively charged. When the neuron is at rest, neither receiving nor transmitting messages, and the electrical charges of the cell's interior and exterior are stable, the neuron is said to be in a state of *polarization*.

When the axon is stimulated, having been triggered in most cases by the cell body in response to the synaptic transmission, channels in the cell membrane open and allow sodium ions to enter the axon. When the balance of electrical charges between the interior and the exterior of the cell is altered, the cell is said to be in a state of *depolarization*. The interior of the cell is now positive with respect to the outside. This process, called the neural impulse, repeats itself down the length of the axon.

The neural impulse follows an all-or-none principle in that once the process is triggered, it is repeated to the end of the axon. The strength of the transmission does not decrease or increase as the impulse moves along the axon from dendrites to the terminal branches. The impulse travels at a speed from about two to 200 miles per hour, depending on a number of factors such as the width of the axon and whether the axon is covered by a myelin sheath.

Soon after the sodium channels open, they close and other channels open to let potassium ions in. This restores the neuron to the polarized state, and the restoration time is referred to as the *refractory period*. About a thousandth of a second is required to restore the neuron to the polarized state during which time no amount of stimulation can produce an impulse. During the next few thousandths of a second the neuron is capable of depolarization only if a much stronger than minimal stimulation occurs. Thus, a stronger stimulation may produce more impulses in a given amount of time.

## Synaptic Transmission

The transmission of the message across the synapse is chemical in nature. Thus, the entire process of transmitting the neural impulse is electrochemical. Some knowledge of the chemical nature of the nervous system also helps to understand behavior.

What takes place in the knobs at the end of the terminal branches is not fully understood; however, recent discoveries indicate that each knob contains the chemical acetylcholine which is released into the synapse after which the knob is quickly refilled for future release. The released acetylocholine seems to be destroyed by other chemicals present in the environment of the synapse. Some chemicals such as those in pesticides and nerve gas which enter the bloodstream and then the environment of the synapse are thought to prevent this destruction of acetylcholine and interfere with the transmission of the neural impulse (Kimble, 1977).

Other chemical transmitter substances released from the knobs of the terminal branches are norepinephrine and probably epinephrine, serotonin, and dopamine (Axelrod, 1974). The norepinephrine and dopamine are taken back into the knobs. Amphetamines prevent this reabsorption and can cause neurons to send an impulse over and over again. Some drugs, such as tranquilizers, probably produce mood-altering effects by changing the chemical activity at the synapse. The arrival of the nerve impulse at the knobs of the terminal branches also opens calcium channels and allows calcium to flow into the knobs, but the precise function of this process is still not known (Stevens, 1979).

Some of the chemicals released from the knobs of the terminal branches of a neuron have an inhibitory effect; they counteract the excitatory chemicals that would cause depolarization of the surrounding neurons. Thus, there is a constant chemical interplay at the synapse which determines whether a neuron will receive and carry the message.

A person is aware of the external and internal environment only from the messages received in the brain, and behavior is exhibited only as a result of messages carried by the neurons in the nervous system to the muscles and glands. Some psychologists believe that most human behavior will become explainable at the physiological level when more is known about the synaptic transmission of the neural impulse. Problems related to memory and mental illness may also become understandable when more is known about the synaptic transmission of the neural impulse.

## Divisions of the Nervous System

Although all its parts are interrelated, the nervous system can be divided structurally into two main divisions: the *peripheral nervous system* and the *central nervous system* (Figure 4-3). An understanding of the structure of the nervous system is an important part of understanding human behavior.

### The Peripheral Nervous System

The system which consists of all the nerves carrying messages to and from the brain and spinal cord and which go out to all parts of the body is referred to as the peripheral nervous system. The peripheral nervous system is composed of two parts: the somatic nervous system and the autonomic nervous system. The *somatic nervous system* consists of the spinal nerves and the cranial nerves such as the auditory nerve

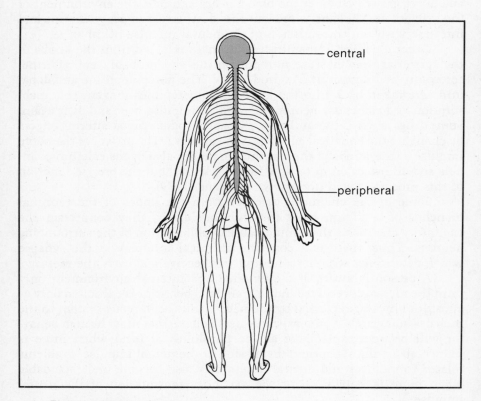

Figure 4-3 Main divisions of
the nervous system.

and the optic nerve. These nerves carry messages from the sense organs about the external and internal environment to the central nervous system and carry messages from the central nervous system back to muscles of the body where action is initiated.

The *autonomic nervous system* serves the internal body organs, such as the heart, stomach, and glands (Figure 4-4). The internal organs send messages to and receive messages from the central nervous system. This autonomic system consists of two subsystems: (1) the *parasympathetic system* which is activated in the normal maintenance of life support functions; and (2) the *sympathetic system* which is activated in emergency situations, in emotional experiences, and in preparation of the body to react to stress, whether physical or psychological. The two systems work together but achieve different results. The sympathetic system arouses the body to handle stress placed upon it; the parasympathetic system sends relaxation messages instructing the body to resume normal functioning. The sympathetic system acts more as a unit affecting the whole body while the parasympathetic system tends to

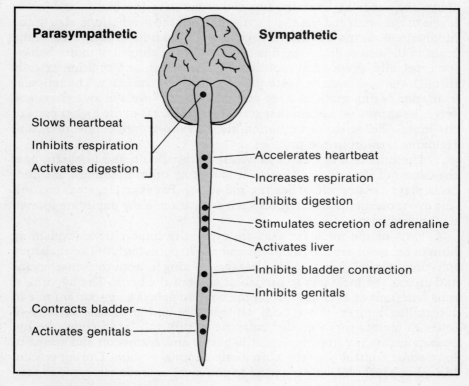

Figure 4-4 The autonomic nervous system.

affect only one organ at a time. However, sometimes one system tends to dominate in a person.

## The Central Nervous System

The central nervous system consists of the brain and the spinal cord. The spinal cord has two primary functions, one of which is the regulation of reflex behaviors. In a reflex response, a message for a specific body movement may be processed in the spinal cord before the message reaches the brain. The second function of the spinal cord is to carry messages from nerves in the peripheral nervous system to the brain and from the brain back to the nerves in the peripheral nervous system.

The brain is composed of three basic divisions—the hindbrain, the midbrain, and the forebrain. The lower part of the brain which merges with the spinal cord is known as the hindbrain (see Figure 4-5). This division of the brain includes the *medulla*, the part adjoining the spinal cord. The medulla controls reflex behaviors such as breathing and heart rate and helps maintain our upright posture. The *pons*, positioned just above the medulla, contains fibers that connect the higher and lower levels of the brain and the two hemispheres of the *cerebellum*, also in the hindbrain. Body movement messages are relayed from higher levels of the brain to the cerebellum which is involved in the control of motor behavior, especially balance and coordination. The *reticular formation* extends through the hindbrain and into the center core of the brain. The reticular formation is important in sleep and attention or levels of awareness and serves as an arousal system that activates large areas of the higher parts of the brain. The reticular formation also has downward connections and regulates tension in the muscles.

The midbrain is located between the hindbrain and forebrain near the center of the brain. Although it has many other functions, the midbrain plays a major role in hearing and seeing. For example, areas controlling eye movements and reflexes such as dilation of the pupils are located in the midbrain.

Parts of the forebrain that are especially important in explaining human behavior are the *thalamus* and the *hypothalamus*. The thalamus functions as a relay station for messages coming in from the sense organs and directs the messages to particular areas of the brain. The hypothalamus functions as a thermostat for the body and plays an important role in controlling hunger, thirst, body temperature and endocrine activity in order to maintain the needed balance for survival. In addition, the hypothalamus is involved in sexual behavior and aggression and seems to have some control over the autonomic nervous system. During physiological or psychological stress the hypothalamus sends messages to activate the autonomic nervous system.

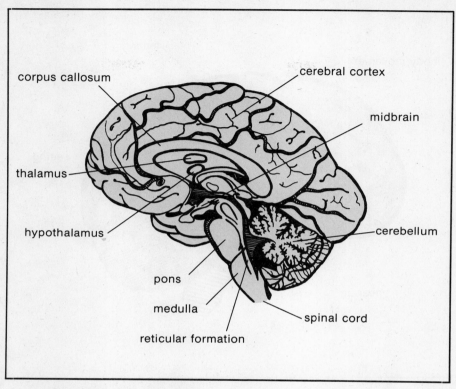

corpus callosum

cerebral cortex

midbrain

thalamus

hypothalamus

cerebellum

pons

medulla

spinal cord

reticular formation

Figure 4-5 The right hemisphere of the brain (medial view).

The *cerebral cortex* is a mass of cell bodies and unmyelinated axons that covers the two hemispheres of the brain that form an "umbrella" over the structures in the center of the brain. The hemispheres are connected by the *corpus callosum*. The cerebral cortex is crumpled into folds to fit inside the skull. If it were spread out smoothly, it would cover many square feet of surface area. Each area of the cerebral cortex has a specific responsibility. Specific areas of the cerebral cortex are responsible for the projection of messages that arrive from specific sense organs, and specific areas of the cerebral cortex activate specific muscle responses. The left hemisphere of the cerebral cortex governs the functions of the right side of the body, and the right hemisphere governs the functions of the left side of the body. Other specific areas of the cerebral cortex are concerned with the control of certain aspects of more complex behaviors such as thinking and speaking. Figure 4-6 is a diagram showing some of the specific areas of the cerebral cortex. The two hemispheres are not equal partners; one hemisphere will dominate over the other. Being right- or left-handed is one indication of this domination. The left hemi-

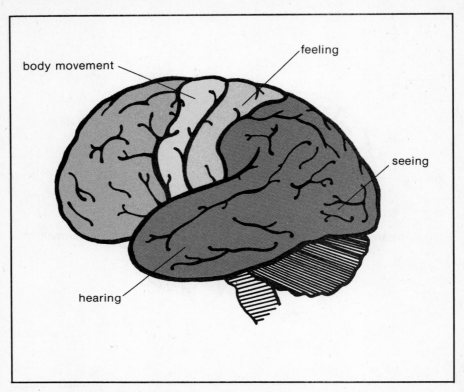

Figure 4-6 Some of the specific areas of the cerebral cortex.

sphere is the center for language control and analytical thought; the right
hemisphere governs artistic abilities and is generally believed to be responsible for creative thinking.

The *limbic system* is an interconnection of several structures in the
center core of the brain, including parts of the thalamus and hypothalamus. The limbic system seems to be related to motivation and emotion
and includes the pleasure centers of the brain.

An understanding of the functioning of the nervous system is an
important part of understanding human behavior. The brain is the master
organ of the body because it directs behavior, feelings, and thoughts and
is, in one sense, the person. A number of behavioral problems are beginning to be understood as more is understood about the functioning of the
brain. For example, damage to a specific area of the brain may result in
very specific behavioral problems such as visual or hearing difficulties,
problems with speech or reading, numbness or immobility of particular
body parts, memory problems, or thinking problems. Recent research
indicates that abnormally high concentrations of a particular chemical

transmitter substance in the area of the brain controlling emotion is associated with a mental illness called schizophrenia (Iversen, 1979). A drug commonly used in the treatment of schizophrenia blocks the action of the chemical transmitter substance. Also, evidence is now available that the abnormal fatigue, slowness of movement, decreased appetite, and disheartened mood associated with depression may result from lack of a chemical transmitter substance in the brain (Coppen, 1972). Electrical stimulation of certain areas of the brain has been shown to produce feelings of intense pleasure. Delgado (1969) reported the case of a woman patient who became more communicative and flirtatious when electrical stimulation was repeatedly applied to an area of the brain where electrodes had been implanted in an attempt to control a disorder. Evidence also indicates that pain is suppressed by chemicals produced by the brain. Hypnosis and acupuncture as methods of reducing pain are believed to be effective because they in some manner stimulate the release of the chemicals in the brain that suppress pain (Cotman & McGaugh, 1980). The ability of different individuals to handle varying levels of pain may be explained by the amount of these pain-suppressing chemicals that each individual's brain produces.

## Sensation

Sensation was one of the earliest topics of interest to psychologists. Since information about the outside world comes through one's senses and all of the senses do not function in the same way, basic research on sensation is concerned with what a sense organs responds to and how the sense organ registers information and transmits it to the nervous system. This understanding then leads to applied research relating capabilities to task requirements.

### *Transduction*

Since psychology is a study of behavior, a student of psychology should have a general overall picture of how behavior occurs. As was previously mentioned in the discussion of the nervous system, all living systems carry out three functions—inputs, internal activities, and outputs. The human organism is no exception. The sense organs of the body serve the function of input. (See Figure 4-2.) Sense organs translate energy in the environment such as warmth, cold, pressure, light rays, sound waves, chemical energy, and gravitational pull into a common kind of energy the nervous system can understand. This translation of energy is called *transduction*. The energy received from the environment is translated at the sense organ level and relayed to the peripheral nervous system, both the somatic and autonomic parts. The somatic and autonomic parts of the peripheral nervous system relay the messages to the central nervous system where the information is processed, decisions are made, and orders are given. Messages in the form of neural impulses are sent to the muscles of the body that control both the external and internal behavior. Thus, the muscles of the body serve the function of output. The level of a person's awareness of the environment is directly related to how well his or her sense organs and nervous system function. Similarly, a person's behavior is limited to the messages issued by the central nervous system and to the extent to which the person's muscles are capable of executing those messages.

The minimum level of energy that is required for transduction to occur is called the *threshold*. Different species have different thresholds for transduction to occur in a particular sense organ. For example, a dog can hear sounds a human cannot. There are also variations in thresholds within a species. For example, one person's threshold for hearing might be 18 decibels and another's might be 20 decibels. One person may not hear, see, smell, or feel something in the environment that another person does. Some things exist in the environment of which most people are unaware unless the energy is magnified to the threshold level for transduction to occur. For example, germs cannot be seen except under a microscope, and radio signals cannot be heard without amplification.

The principle of *adaptation* explains why some people have a different awareness of the environment and why a person's awareness may not be the same at different times. When the cells in sense organs are exposed to a constant level of stimulation, adaptation occurs; that is, the cells become less sensitive and thus raise the threshold for transduction to occur. For example, one may adapt to a particular odor, such as that of cigarette smoke or of some industrial chemical, and not smell it. Or one may adapt to certain noises, such as a loud office environment, the sound of a pounding hammer, or the sound of trucks passing, and not be as sensitive to them.

### The Senses

**Vision.** In the eye, the cells responsible for transduction are located at the back of the eyeball on the *retina*. Light rays enter first through the transparent *cornea* of the eye and then pass through the *pupil*, a small hole in the front of the *lens* of the eye. The pupil enlarges and contracts to control the amount of light entering the eye. Muscles are connected to the lens and tighten to increase the curvature of the lens thus focusing the image as it is projected onto the retina. The major parts of the human eye are shown in Figure 4-7.

The back layer of the retina is composed of two general types of cells

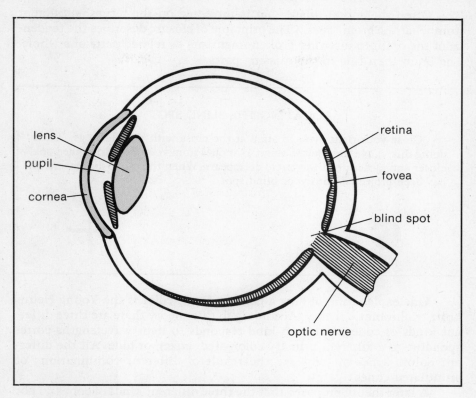

Figure 4-7 A cross section of
the human eye.

called *rods* and *cones*. The cells called rods are sensitive to brightness or
differences in light intensity and are involved in night vision. If only rods
composed the retina, people would see only in black and white, not in
color. The cells called cones respond to differences in wavelength and
light intensity. In bright light, these cells are extremely sensitive to
wavelengths. Cones are involved in color vision.

Only cones are found in the *fovea*, an area on the retina. The fovea is
the most sensitive part of the retina and, therefore, vision is sharpest
when the image is projected on this area. The place where the *optic nerve*,
which carries the neural impulse to the brain, leaves the retina has
neither rods nor cones; light rays falling here will not stimulate a neural
impulse. This area of the retina is referred to as the *blind spot*. Usually a
person does not notice the blind spot because there are two retinal images
(one from each eye). The part of the image that is not received by one eye
will be received by the other eye. The boxed material on page 78 shows
how to locate the blind spot.

Often the actual image that is projected on the retina is different from what the brain "sees." The principle of closure describes the tendency of the brain to interpret broken fragments as related parts of a whole. The brain then fills in the missing parts.

---

### LOCATING THE BLIND SPOT

Close your right eye and stare at the cross with your left eye. While doing this, move the book to about 12 inches from your face. Bring the book closer and closer until the circle disappears. When the circle disappears, it has been projected onto your blind spot.

---

One explanation of how a person sees in color is the Young-Helmholtz trichromatic theory. According to this theory there are three different kinds of cones, and each kind responds to light wavelengths corresponding to a different primary color—red, green, or blue. All the different colors a person sees are the result of different combinations of stimulated cones.

A later theory proposed that the three different kinds of cones do not respond to just three separate primary colors, but rather respond according to an opponent process. This opponent process theory proposes that each type of cone is capable of responding to either color of a pair of primary colors that oppose each other. But the cone cannot respond to both the colors at the same time, since stimulation by one color is associated with inhibition by its opposite. One kind of cone responds to blue-yellow, another kind to red-green, and a third kind to black-white. Another explanation of the opponent process in color vision proposes that the level of electrical activity, or the rate of neural impulses in a cell, may be increased or decreased by a color. For example, a blue-yellow cone might send a yellow message with increased activity and would, when the level of electrical activity reversed (decreased activity), send a blue message. Or a red-green cone might send a red message with increased activity, but when reversed (decreased activity), would send a green message (Hurvich & Jameson, 1974).

Individuals who are missing either the red-green or the blue-yellow cones or both do not perceive color normally and are said to be colorblind. Those individuals who have one type of cone missing are called *dichromats*, and those who have two types of cones missing are called *monochromats.* Individuals who have all three kinds of cones have normal vision and are called *trichromats.* A monochromat sees only blacks and whites or grays. His or her visual experience is much like a television picture with the color turned off. A dichromat with red-green color-blindness is only partially color-blind and cannot differentiate between red and green. His or her visual experience is much like a television picture with the blue and yellow turned on and the red and green turned off. A dichromat with blue-yellow color-blindness has a visual experience similar to a television picture with the red and green turned on and the blue and yellow turned off.

**Hearing.** The stimulus in the environment which causes transduction to occur in the ear is a sound wave, or vibration, in the air. (See Figure 4-8.) One cycle is the distance from the beginning of one wave to the beginning of the next wave. Sound waves are perceived in terms of loudness, pitch, and timbre. The *frequency* of the waves (how many cycles or waves arrive per second) determines the *pitch* of the sound—how high or low it is. The *amplitude* (height of the cycle or wave) determines the loudness. The *timbre* (quality or texture of the sound) is

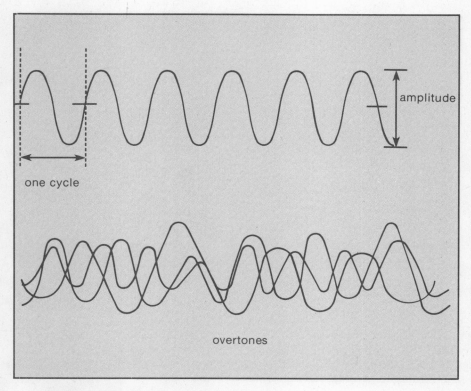

Figure 4-8 The sound wave.

determined by a complex pattern of overtones which are produced by accompanying sound waves that are different multiples of the basic frequency.

Sound waves are collected by the outer ear and channeled through the ear canal where they hit the eardrum and cause it to vibrate. The eardrum vibration puts three tiny bones commonly called the hammer, anvil, and stirrup into sequential motion. The eardrum vibration moves the hammer which is attached to the anvil, and the anvil is attached to the stirrup. The stirrup is connected to a membrane so that when the stirrup moves, the membrane also moves or vibrates. This membrane covers part of the snail-shaped cochlea in the inner ear. Fluid inside the cochlea is moved with the vibration of the membrane. This movement of the fluid stimulates tiny hair cells located on a membrane inside the cochlea where transduction occurs. Afferent neurons in the auditory nerve are depolarized, and the patterns of neural impulses relayed to the brain by axonal and synaptic transmission are interpreted or perceived as loudness, pitch, and timbre. (See Figure 4-9 for a diagram of the structure of the ear.)

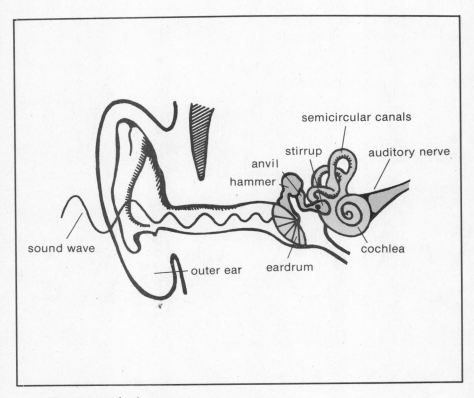

Figure 4-9 The human ear.

**Other Senses.** The sensations of pressure, warmth, cold, and pain are produced by the stimulation of different kinds of cells in the skin. Light pressure applied to the skin moves hairs on the skin some of which are too fine to be seen without a microscope. The movement of the hairs stimulates the cells of the nerve endings that are wrapped around the base of the hair to start the neural impulse. Heavy pressure disturbs capsules beneath the surface of the skin which contain nerve endings. The disturbance of these capsules stimulates cells and fires a neural impulse which travels through the nervous system. The impulses originating from the movement of hair on the skin or the disturbance of the capsules beneath the skin are perceived as touch or pressure.

Two kinds of cells in the skin respond to temperature. One kind of cell responds to temperatures above body temperature. Impulses originating from the stimulation of these cells are perceived as warmth. The other kind of cell responds to temperatures below body temperature. Impulses originating from the stimulation of these cells are perceived as cold. One may be able to locate cells which transmit impulses perceived as cold by touching various places around the bend of the elbow or on the forearm with the lead of a pencil. Lead is cooler than body temperature.

The sense of pain functions differently from the other senses. Any of the cells in any sense organ, if overstimulated, may produce impulses which are perceived as pain. Different types of cells that respond to different types of pain have not been found. But two kinds of nerve fibers have been found that seem to carry different pain messages—fast, sharp, and more localized pain or pain that is slow, aching, widespread, and of a longer duration (Liebeskind & Paul, 1977). A network of free nerve endings in the layers of the skin is thought to send pain messages to the brain. More variation among individuals seems to exist for pain than for any of the other senses. One theory proposes that there are neurological pathways with areas that either refer pain to other pathways or stop pain by a flood of impulses from another pathway. These areas function as a gate to let through or block out impulses perceived as pain (Melzack & Wall, 1965). This gate control theory explains the experience of arm pain during a heart attack and how acupuncture works. Recent research provides evidence that the body manufactures chemical substances in some areas of the brain and spinal cord which suppress pain impulses (Snyder, 1977).

The inner ear is responsible for more than the sense of hearing. Additional hairlike cells are located in the semicircular canals of the inner ear. (See Figure 4-9.) The movement of fluid in the semicircular canals stimulates the hairlike cells which send neural impulses to the brain. Impulses originating from these cells provide an awareness of body position or balance and make it possible to maintain an upright posture. This is the sense of *equilibrium*.

The muscles and tendons of the body have some cells which respond when a muscle is expanded or contracted. These cells also respond to different angles of position. This enables one to be aware of the movement and position of different body parts and is referred to as the *kinesthetic sense.*

Chemical substances stimulate cells in some sense organs. The cells which start neural impulses that are perceived as taste are located inside the taste buds on the tongue. One type of cell responds to bitter substances, another to sweet substances, another to salty substances, and another to sour substances. Taste is not the same as flavor which is perceived from a combination of impulses from the skin senses, taste, and smell. When chemical substances come in contact with the tiny hairlike cells in the taste bud, transduction occurs and starts a neural impulse through the nervous system. The hairlike cells in taste buds are replaced with new ones about every seven days. Children have many more of these cells than adults; the number decreases with age. This may account for differences in sensitivity to taste for some foods by children, adults, and elderly people or by any individual at different times.

The cells where transduction occurs for smell are located high in the nasal cavity in an area about half the size of a postage stamp. It is not known exactly how the sense of smell functions, but it is thought by some to be related to the distinctive size, shape, or electrical charge of the molecules of various chemicals in the air. The molecules fit into one or more of some basic types of socket-like holes in the nasal cavity just as a key fits into a lock (Amoore, Johnston, & Rubin, 1964) and, therefore, are differentiated and perceived as different odors.

## The Endocrine System

Some glands of the body are called duct glands because they empty secretions into a duct. The salivary glands empty secretions into the mouth, tear glands secrete into the eye cavity, and digestive juices are secreted into the stomach. The *endocrine glands,* however, are ductless and secrete substances called *hormones* directly into the bloodstream; consequently, these hormones have a widespread and immediate effect on behavior. Hormones are secreted to help maintain a physiological balance in the body. The released hormones are carried by the bloodstream to the tissues they affect; some hormones affect many organs, some affect only one organ, and some affect other endocrine glands. An endocrine gland may secrete many hormones, or it may secrete only a few or only one hormone. Figure 4-10 shows the location of some important endocrine glands.

The *pituitary gland* in the brain produces more hormones and has a wider range of effects on the body than any of the other endocrine glands. One group of hormones produced by the pituitary controls the timing and amount of growth of the body. Another group of hormones produced by the pituitary controls other endocrine glands. Therefore, the pituitary gland is often referred to as the master gland of the body. The relationship between the pituitary gland and the hypothalamus provides a good example of the interdependence of body systems. Certain hormones produced by the pituitary gland (part of the endocrine system) stimulate the hypothalamus (part of the nervous system) in the brain which results in changes in behavior. Changes in behavior indirectly cause the pituitary to release more hormones.

The *thyroid gland* secretes a hormone that regulates the rate at which energy is produced and used by the body. A person with an overactive thyroid may be excitable, tense, nervous, and underweight. A person with an underactive thyroid may be overweight, inactive, slower, and prone to sleep more.

The *parathyroids*, embedded in the thyroid, release a hormone which controls the calcium and phosphate levels in the blood. Calcium and phosphate affect the excitability of the nervous system. Muscle

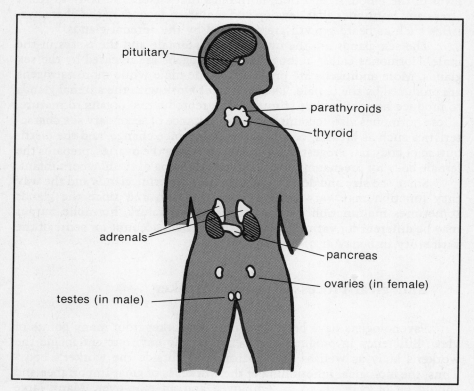

Figure 4-10 Endocrine glands.

spasms or twitches may result from insufficient secretions of this hormone. Secretion of too much of this same hormone may produce drowsiness.

The *pancreas* secretes two hormones that work against each other to control the level of sugar in the blood. Improper functioning of the pancreas may produce conditions commonly referred to as sugar diabetes or low blood sugar with such behavioral effects as moodiness, chronic fatigue, irritability, or decreased mental activity.

The *adrenal glands* release adrenaline (epinephrine) and noradrenaline (norepinephrine) into the bloodstream, resulting in a number of important changes in the body all of which prepare it for action. For example, heart rate and blood pressure are raised; stored sugar is released for quick energy; the muscles tense and receive more blood; the blood is prepared to clot more quickly; the blood vessels in the peripheral parts of the body constrict; all the body tissues become generally more tense; digestion stops; and the pupils of the eyes become larger. Other hormones are produced by the adrenal glands that regulate the sodium-potassium level in the blood. In addition, hormones that enable the body to resist stress and hormones that develop and maintain secondary sex characteristics such as beard growth are produced by the adrenal glands.

The sex glands are the *ovaries* in the female and the *testes* in the male. Hormones called androgens and estrogens are released by the sex glands. More androgens are produced by the male while more estrogens are produced by the female. The sex glands work with the adrenal glands to produce hormones that stimulate the reproductive organs to mature. These hormones also account for the appearance of secondary sex characteristics such as breasts, beards, pubic hair, voice change, and the distribution of body fat. Progesterone, also secreted by the ovaries, prepares the female body for pregnancy, childbirth, and nursing of the newborn infant.

Since the size and development of the endocrine glands and the way they function may vary from person to person and since the glands sometimes malfunction because of disease or injury, hormone output may be different for various individuals and may account for some of the variability in behavior of people.

## Biological Processes and the Worker

Psychologists have been studying the worker from many points of view. Efficiency in production depends on the environment inside the worker's body as well as the environment outside the worker's body. Thus, the biological functioning of the worker is of great importance and should be of concern to an employee and an employer. Many large companies provide the services of a medical doctor to deal with employees' physiological problems while at work (Figure 4-11). A company physician may also give physical examinations before an employee begins a new job or before a person is selected for employment with the company.

The physiological functioning of an employee while on the job may affect performance and may be the result of a number of factors. An employee's diet, for example, contributes to his or her body chemistry which in turn affects the functioning of the nervous system. Many companies have cafeterias that employ a dietitian who selects certain foods in order to provide a balanced diet or special diets for employees. Some conditions such as low blood sugar may be controlled by special diets. Low calorie foods may be supplied to aid in weight control. Also, rest breaks may be provided for food intake so that the body may restore chemical imbalances.

Measurements of such bodily functions as heart rate, blood pressure, oxygen consumption, and body temperature have been used to assess the physiological cost of work on a person's body. The physiological cost to the typical worker on the job averages about two calories per

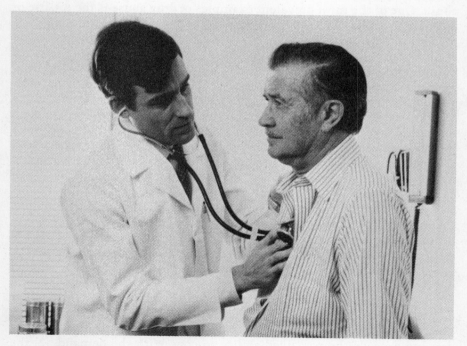

Figure 4-11 The worker's physical functioning is important to the employer. Many companies provide medical examinations for employees.

minute, which is less than the average physiological cost of off-the-job activities (Bass & Barrett, 1972). Under conditions of severe food rationing, the calorie intake of a worker is a predictor of production levels. Lower production levels may be the result of the physiological cost and inadequate calorie consumption. Physiological costs have shown extreme variations among individuals performing the same tasks. Physiological costs seem to be higher when a task is first begun, higher for those who are less skilled in performing the task, and higher for tasks requiring mental operations such as reading, writing, and arithmetic.

The power of drugs to change the body chemistry and thus influence behavior is well known. The introduction of chemicals which hinder or help the functioning of the nervous system is one of the most direct and immediate ways of influencing behavior. A *stimulant* is any drug that increases activity in the nervous system while a *depressant* is any drug that reduces nervous system activity. *Hallucinogens* produce changes in a person's ability to receive and interpret sensory information. Drug abuse by employees sometimes accounts for insufficient work or poor quality work. Absenteeism, however, is a primary consequence of drug abuse. One of the most prevalent examples of drug abuse is the misuse of alcohol. The main effect of alcohol is on the brain. Alcohol may seem to be a stimulant but is actually a depressant. The cerebral cortex of the brain becomes depressed first as the percentage of alcohol in the blood rises. Thinking, feeling, and problem solving are affected. As the midbrain becomes depressed, speech and vision may be affected. A person's sense of balance is lost as lower centers of the brain are affected. Death can result if the percentage of alcohol in the blood becomes high enough to depress activities in the medulla of the brain which controls such things as respiration. One of the problem areas in industrial/organizational psychology is the detection, management, control, and correction of ineffective performance due to drug abuse. A number of companies have established formal alcohol control programs.

Since either physiological or psychological stress causes the sympathetic part of the nervous system to effect the changes in body chemistry necessary for a person to cope with an emergency situation, stress is related to behavior. Stress is a part of the interaction between a person and the environment. The environment presents a person with a demand or constraint—an opportunity for behavior. Psychological stress may be a result of a person's belief that the demand or constraint exceeds his or her capabilities and resources. The degree of psychological stress experienced seems to be related to three factors; these are (1) the degree to which the demand exceeds the perceived ability to cope with the demand, (2) the consequences of a favorable versus an unfavorable outcome of a particular situation, and (3) the uncertainty of the outcome. Some activation of the sympathetic nervous system enhances performance, but beyond a particular level, which is individual for each person and each task, the level of performance decreases. Thus, body chemistry changes resulting from stress may account for ineffective job performance and accidents on the job. (See Chapter 12 for a more detailed discussion of stress.)

Industrial/organizational psychologists study job performance in relation to stress, particularly physical stress such as noise, loss of sleep, and extreme temperatures. Jobs requiring only limited skill are less likely to produce psychological stress. Psychologists may provide training for employees to learn to control the autonomic nervous system so that they are able to activate the parasympathetic system which elicits the relaxation response rather than activate the sympathetic system. A person may learn how to improve rather than decrease the level or quality of performance. Also, stress effects may be moderated by time which allows a person to make a physiological adaptation and a psychological adjustment.

Humans, as well as animals, experience cycles in a number of biological processes. Body temperature and sleep are related to such cyclic biological processes. As a result of the rhythm of biological changes, body temperature increases from about eight o'clock in the morning to about eight o'clock in the evening then drops to its lowest point about four o'clock in the morning. Sleep is part of a 24-hour biological cycle also and does not seem to depend on the sun for timing. Job performance seems to be related to these biological rhythms. People who engage in shift work or fly from one time zone to another may have their biological rhythms disturbed and their job performance affected. Biological rhythms may vary for different individuals, even though they are on a 24-hour cycle. Some individuals are more active at night and less active during the first part of the day. As a result, a person is sometimes labeled as a "day person" or a "night person."

These biological processes have an impact on behavior and need to be understood to explain some job-related behaviors. Although much new knowledge of the basic functioning of the nervous system has been gained during the last two decades, much of what is important about the brain and its interrelated systems still remains to be learned. Many questions about human behavior cannot be explained until more of the incredible complexities of the brain are understood. Research on the human brain is a new frontier in the study of human behavior.

## SUMMARY

1. The nervous system is composed of billions of specialized cells called neurons.

2. In addition to the nucleus, the main cell body, and the membrane that encloses it, each neuron contains dendrites, a main axon which may have branches, and terminal branches with knobs at the end. Some neurons are covered with a myelin sheath.

3. Afferent neurons are close to cells in sense organs and receive input from the environment directly from those cells. Efferent neurons are located next to cells in muscles and send messages to the muscles that elicit behavior. Interneurons carry messages to and receive messages from other neurons in the brain and spinal cord.

4. The neural impulse is the transmission of the message along the axon of a neuron and across the synapse or space between neurons.

5. The axonal transmission is electrical in nature and results in the depolarization of the neuron.

6. The synaptic transmission is chemical in nature and is accomplished by the chemicals released into the synapse by the terminal branches. Some released chemicals have an excitatory effect while others have an inhibitory effect.

7. The two main divisions of the nervous system are the peripheral system which is made up of the somatic and the autonomic nervous systems and the central system which is made up of the spinal cord and the brain.

8. The two subsystems of the autonomic nervous system are the parasympathetic system and the sympathetic system which work together but achieve different results. The sympathetic system prepares the body to react to stress while the parasympathetic system tells the body to return to normal functioning.

9. Some of the brain structures in the hindbrain are the medulla which controls reflex behaviors such as breathing and heart rate, the pons, the cerebellum which is involved in control of motor behavior, and the reticular formation which serves as an arousal system.

10. The thalamus which functions as a relay station, the hypothalamus which functions as a thermostat, and the cerebral cortex which covers the two hemispheres of the brain are structures in the forebrain.

11. The cerebral cortex has specific areas for specific responsibilities. One area is responsible for the projection of messages that arrive from specific cells in the sense organs. Another area of the cerebral cortex activates specific muscles.

12. The limbic system is an interconnection of several structures in the core of the brain and seems to be related to motivation and emotion.

13. Cells in the sense organs translate energy in the environment, through a process called transduction, into a form of energy that can be relayed through the nervous system as a neural impulse.

14. The threshold, a minimum level of energy required for transduction, varies according to species and from individual to individual for a particular sense organ.

15. Cells called rods located on the retina of the eye are stimulated by brightness or differences in light intensity. Cells called cones, also located on the retina, are stimulated by the wavelengths of light rays. Cones are involved in color vision, and rods are involved in night vision.

16. The trichromatic theory proposes that different combinations of the three kinds of cones that are stimulated accounts for how different colors are perceived. The opponent process theory proposes that one kind of cone is capable of responding to either color of a pair of primary colors that oppose each other.

17. Sound waves produce vibrations of the eardrum which initiate a series of motions that eventually stimulate cells in the cochlea of the inner ear to send neural impulses to the brain. These impulses are perceived as hearing.

18. Various cells in the skin are stimulated by pressure, warmth, and cold. Also, a network of nerve endings in the skin sends impulses which are perceived as pain. The gate control theory and the production of chemical pain killers in some areas of the brain help explain a person's perception of pain.

19. Cells in the inner ear send messages concerning the body's equilibrium or sense of balance. Cells in muscles and tendons enable one to be aware of the movement and position of body parts; this awareness is referred to as the kinesthetic sense.

20. Cells in taste buds on the tongue are stimulated by sweet, sour, salty, or bitter substances.

21. The pituitary, thyroid, parathyroid, pancreas, adrenal, and sex glands (ovaries and testes) are endocrine glands which secrete hormones into the bloodstream, have a very direct and immediate effect on behavior, and help to maintain the chemical balance necessary for the proper functioning of the nervous system. Hormone output accounts for some of the variability in behavior of people.

22. Efficiency in job performance is related to the physiological functioning of an employee; therefore, the services of a medical doctor, the maintenance of a proper diet, an awareness of drug abuse, the control of stress, and an understanding of biological rhythms may improve the level and quality of employee performance on the job. Employers concerned with efficiency in production should be concerned with the biological well-being of their employees.

# SUGGESTIONS FOR FURTHER READING

Benson, H., & Klipper, M. *The relaxation response.* New York: Avon Publishers, 1976.

An easy-to-read book that describes a simple method of relaxation and serves as a guide for controlling anxiety.

Goleman, D. Special abilities of the sexes: Do they begin in the brain? *Psychology Today*, November 1978, *12*(6), 48-59; 120.

Psychological research is discussed that suggests that some differences exist between the sexes, chiefly in spatial and verbal talents. Differences in neurological functioning determined by the way male and female brains are organized is suggested.

Hassett, J. *A primer of psychophysiology.* San Francisco: Freeman, 1978.

A good introduction to physiological psychology.

Iversen, S. D., & Iversen, L. L. *Behavioral pharmacology.* New York: Oxford University Press, 1975.

Research on the ways drugs affect the brain and behavior is summarized in this book.

Netter, F. H. *The CIBA collection of medical illustrations, Vol. 1, Nervous System* (11th ed.). Summit, N. J.: CIBA Pharmaceutical Company, 1978.

Contains a collection of color drawings of the structure of the nervous system.

Orstein, R. E. *The psychology of consciousness.* New York: Viking Press, 1972.

A theory of how the right and left hemispheres of the brain serve different functions to divide up the work and how they represent two different kinds of consciousness.

*Scientific American*, September 1979, *241*(3).

The entire issue is devoted to the brain and nervous system.

Snyder, S. H. *Madness and the brain.* New York: McGraw-Hill, 1974.

A popular book on the pharmacology of behavior disorders that is quite informative.

Telyer, T. J. *A primer of psychobiology.* San Francisco: W. H. Freeman, 1975.

A nontechnical introduction to biological psychology that provides a brief but entertaining discussion of the structure and function of the brain and nervous system.

# Chapter 5

# Heredity and Development

The biological factors influencing behavior are numerous. Some of these were discussed in the preceding chapter; but in addition, hereditary endowment and personal development are significant factors in shaping a person's behavior. These factors must be considered when attempting to understand the behavior of people in the work environment because both heredity and environment have been found to be important in explaining a person's actions and interactions with others.

## Heredity

Characteristics which are inherited are those determined by materials present at the moment the person was conceived and existed as one cell. The sequence of structural and behavioral changes which occur in the person over time as a product of both heredity and the environment is referred to as development. In the past, some psychologists have tended to ignore or minimize the role of heredity in studying human behavior, but currently a great deal of interest is being given to hereditary factors. Understanding the normal processes of development helps people put their own lives into perspective and understand others who are older or younger.

### Interaction

Although some hereditary differences appear from the time of birth, the development of many behavioral characteristics depends on the interaction between heredity and environment. Heredity seems to provide a framework for behavioral development by providing personal potentials and limitations that are altered by environmental factors such as education, nutrition, disease, or culture. An individual's own behavior may be a factor in development. For example, Jerome Kagan (1969) found that newborn babies differ in activity, irritability, distractability, and other aspects of temperament. Because some babies have a greater tendency to smile, pay attention, cry or vocalize, they become an active participant in their own development. A pleasant baby who smiles may encourage touching, feeding, and affection from others whereas an unpleasant baby may anger or frustrate others whose reactions in turn cause more unpleasantness.

Physical characteristics such as height, bone structure, hair color, or eye color depend more on heredity than environment. Psychologists are particularly interested in the degree to which psychological characteristics such as ability, temperament, and emotional stability are inherited. The controversy over heredity versus environment as determinants of human behavior has been particularly intense over the years and has now evolved into a concept that considers their interaction.

## Biological History

A human being can be viewed as having an evolutionary heredity extending back to the first traces of life, thus having a kinship with all other organisms. Human beings are not considered to be direct descendents of apes as they exist today. But humans do share with apes some common ancestors, now extinct, that go back millions of years. According to evolutionary theory, all forms of life have common roots. Charles Darwin (1859) proposed that a species changes over generations keeping those characteristics that enhance survival and rendering extinct those that do not.

A human being can be viewed as having a species heredity; i.e., an individual is the potential possessor of all the limitations and capacities with which humans are endowed. For example, humans cannot fly through the air or breathe under water without equipment, but humans do have a nervous system that enables them to invent ways of adapting to the environment.

Sociobiologists claim that much human behavior is rooted in preservation of the *genes* which are the carriers of heredity. Most people do not like to think that their genes control their behavior, but that is what sociobiologists claim. *Sociobiology* is defined as the systematic study of the biological basis of all social behavior (Wilson, 1975). Sociobiologists today point out that it is the survival of the genes, not the survival of the individual, that matters. For example, acts of self-sacrifice for others are explained in terms of their benefits to the survival of one's own gene pool. Some psychologists do not accept this theory and feel that more research is needed.

## Individual Heredity

Most important to the psychologist is a person's own individual heredity. People inherit from their parents specific structures, capacities, and limitations which account for their physical characteristics and have a profound effect on their behavior throughout life.

Human reproduction involves the uniting of a *sperm* from the father with an *ovum* (egg) from the mother. Since the sperm and the ovum each possess 23 *chromosomes,* their union forms a cell of 46 chromosomes. The chromosomes are the carriers of heredity. A chromosome is a complex structure composed of thousands of genes threaded together like a string of beads. Each gene, the basic unit of heredity, is composed of a biochemical substance called *DNA (deoxyribonucleic acid)* which carries chemically coded instructions that determine physical appearance, body functioning, and growth. Chemically, DNA is composed of four chemical bases which may be arranged in an almost infinite number of ways. The particular arrangement which exists in a given chain of DNA molecules is thought to constitute the genetic code responsible for the creation of a particular hereditary characteristic. It is the particular variations in the arrangement of these four chemical bases which account for the differences in all living organisms.

Theoretically, the 23 chromosomes coming from the father could occur in one of $2^{23}$ or 8,388,608 different combinations and the same could be true of the 23 chromosomes coming from the mother. In addition, during the process of germ cell division when sperm and ova are produced, genes may cross over from one chromosome to another. Thus, there is little chance that there will ever be two humans exactly alike genetically, except for identical twins. In the case of identical twins, a single fertilized egg divides once and then each of the two cells, with identical chromosomes, develops as a separate individual. Nonidentical twins develop from two separate fertilized eggs.

The chromosomes form 23 pairs, one from the father and the corresponding one from the mother composing a pair. Each gene pair influences a particular characteristic. Some genes are *dominant,* meaning they predominate the other gene; and some are *recessive,* meaning they defer to the dominant gene. If a person has two dominant genes or one dominant and one recessive, the characteristic controlled by those genes will reflect the dominant gene. Only if two recessive genes are paired will the recessive gene determine the characteristic. Examples of dominant characteristics are dark hair, dark eyes, or curly hair while examples of recessive characteristics are blonde or red hair, straight hair, or blue eyes. Sometimes the two genes can be co-dominant, as when the offspring of a black parent and a white parent has light brown skin.

Also, characteristics may be influenced by a variety of genes operating in a complex interaction. Important human characteristics such as intelligence, personality, temperament, physical structure, and probably also susceptibility to some forms of mental illness are predominantly *polygenic;* they are the result of the interactive effects of many genes. These traits are likely to show continuous variations from one extreme to the other rather than falling in distinct categories as do single-gene determined traits. A number of studies (Buss & Plomin, 1975; Vandenberg, 1967) suggest there is a hereditary basis for at least three aspects of temperament—activity, emotionality, and sociability. Some people have higher levels of activity and are more energetic and vigorous as they go about life. People differ in how aroused they become by events and how much emotion they feel. Some people desire the company of others and seem to enjoy interacting with people more.

The twenty-third pair of chromosomes carries the genes which determine the individual's sex. The sex chromosomes are labeled X and Y. Males have an X chromosome and a Y chromosome while females have two X chromosomes. All eggs then contain X chromosomes, but sperm may contain either X or Y chromosomes. If a sperm containing a Y fertilizes an egg, the newly formed cell will have an X and a Y chromosome and, thus, a male will develop. If a sperm containing an X fertilizes an egg, the newly formed cell will have two X chromosomes and, thus, a female will develop. Figure 5-1 illustrates the mechanics of heredity that determine the sex of an individual.

The pair of chromosomes containing the genes that determine sex contains other genes that determine other characteristics which are referred to as *sex-linked characteristics*. For example, the genes necessary

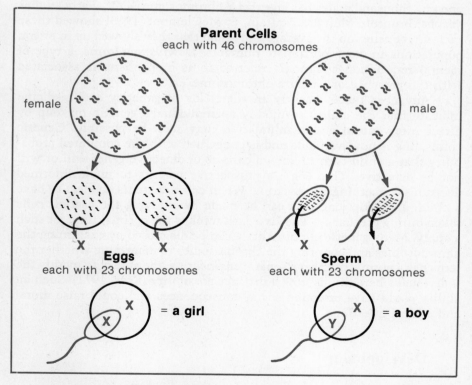

**Parent Cells**
each with 46 chromosomes

female

male

X          X
**Eggs**
each with 23 chromosomes

X          Y
**Sperm**
each with 23 chromosomes

X
X   = a girl

X
Y   = a boy

Figure 5-1 Hereditary mechanisms determine an individual's sexual identity.

for the formation of the cone cells of the eye which make color vision possible are carried by the sex chromosomes. The gene related to hemophilia, a disease that prevents the blood from clotting, is also on this pair. A female may have a defective recessive gene on one X chromosome, but will most likely have a normal dominant gene on the other X chromosome of the pair. The normal gene will be dominant and the defect will not show up. However, if a male has a defective recessive gene on the X chromosome, the other chromosome of his pair, the Y chromosome, is shorter and does not have as many genes on it. It may not provide a normal dominant gene and, thus, the defect will show up. This explains why a number of characteristics such as color blindness and hemophilia are found predominately in males.

Some genetically based disorders are caused by an abnormal number of chromosomes. Some individuals have only a single X chromosome instead of a pair of sex chromosomes and thus have only 45 instead of 46 chromosomes. Their external genitals are female, but their female organs are poorly developed, and they may not be able to have children. About one in a thousand males has an extra Y chromosome (XYY). Early studies (Jacobs, Brunton, Melville, Brittain, & McClemont, 1965) showed these males to be taller on the average and found that they showed up in prison populations in disproportionate numbers. *Down's syndrome*, a type of mental retardation commonly referred to as mongolism, is associated with the presence of an extra chromosome.

Advances made recently in the fields of genetics and medicine indicate that the ability to modify an individual's genetic makeup by direct intervention and manipulation may soon be possible. Genetic counseling is now available and is concerned with the computed probability that a child born to known carriers of defective genes will or will not be defective. This enables prospective parents to make informed decisions concerning childbearing. When carrier parents do elect to have a child, a genetic diagnosis can be made by studying the cast-off cells taken during pregnancy. The sixteenth week is the optimal time for such a study. Many genetic abnormalities can be diagnosed by examining the chromosomes and counting the chromosomes to determine whether the fetus has a normal number. *Genetic engineering*, the ability to modify the individual's heredity, is now a distinct possibility (Kass, 1971). Such an ability could have profound social consequences and could raise moral and ethical questions.

## Development

Developmental psychology traces the changes in behavior and mental processes which occur through the life span. Some changes which occur are a result of experience and some are a result of biological processes, but most are a combined outcome of both these factors. A discussion of development then involves biological maturation and the environment in which the hereditary traits are expressed.

## Maturation

*Maturation* refers to the control that the genes exert over the unfolding of biological events from conception to death. Maturation produces changes in the nervous system and other bodily structures which in turn make possible the appearance of certain behaviors. For example, the development of physical abilities is related to the maturation of the skeletal, muscular, and nervous systems. The maturation of the cortex of the brain is related to the acquisition of language and the growth of intelligence as well as the acquisition of motor skills and other behaviors.

One general trend of maturation is seen in the head-downward progression in physical growth and purposeful movements. The head develops sooner in proportion to the lower part of the body, and head movements come under control before movements of the legs and feet. (See Figure 5-2.) Another general trend is the center-outward progression. The center portions of the body develop and come under control before the peripheral parts; for example, the heart develops physically before the arms; and children can control the trunks of their bodies enough to turn over before they can control their fingers enough to write. Another general trend is the progression from massive, global, and undifferentiated responses to specific and integrated responses. For example, an infant's response to anger may involve the entire body, but an older child's response to anger may only involve striking or shouting.

Sometimes environmental conditions will have a greater effect on a behavior at a particular time or affect the behavior of an individual if and only if they occur at certain times in the development process. These periods, referred to as *critical periods*, exist when a set of environmental conditions has an optimal effect. For example, a skill may be learned at a later time, but with more difficulty than if mastered during a critical period. Critical periods usually correspond to times of rapid development. A readiness for learning is determined by maturation. Physical structures must be mature before practice will establish a skill.

## Environment

Every influence on one's behavior other than the influences of heredity and maturation is included in environmental influence. The environmental influences affecting an individual may be differentiated as *prenatal* (from conception to birth), *perinatal* (during the birth process), and *postnatal* (from birth until death).

Figure 5-2 The development of physical abilities is related to the maturation of the skeletal, muscular, and nervous systems.

During the prenatal period there is an exchange of nutrients and other materials between the developing organism and the mother. Materials in the mother's bloodstream are passed to the unborn child even though the mother's blood does not flow directly through the unborn child's circulatory system. Some viruses, some drugs such as alcohol, nutritional deficiencies, irradiation, and hormonal secretions associated with emotional arousal have been found to have an adverse effect on the development of the unborn child.

One of the major factors in the perinatal period is the supply of oxygen to the cells of the brain. Drugs administered during labor and complications such as kinks in the umbilical cord increase the chances of oxygen shortage. If the cells of the brain are deprived of oxygen for more than a few minutes, they are irreversibly damaged. Also, damage to brain cells may be caused by too much pressure on the skull during the birth process.

After birth, there are many environmental factors influencing behavior. Of course, the physical environment has an impact; but the social
environment, especially signficant people, also has a great impact on
behavior. The type of home environment with respect to such things as
the emotional and verbal responsiveness of the caretaker, the use of
punishment, the number of restrictions, opportunities for variety in day-
to-day stimulation, provision of appropriate play items, and involvement
with the child seems to be especially significant in development (Elardo,
Bradley, & Caldwell, 1975; 1977).

Early sensory stimulation from the environment is essential for
later sensory functioning. When a child is deprived of normal sensory
experiences such as those in some impoverished environments, sensory
retardation may result (Helms & Turner, 1976).

### Cognitive Development

Jean Piaget, one of the most influential psychologists of this century, believes that the development of knowledge, understanding, and the
thought processes or cognitive development has its roots in the biological
makeup of the individual; however, he also believes that the rate of
development may be influenced by the environment. Piaget has taken an
interactionist point of view and asserts that cognitive development progresses through a sequence of stages. Biology guides the sequence, but
special training and experience can speed progression through the stages,
if a certain level of maturation has been reached. The forces of heredity
and maturation interact with an individual's experiences in the environment; this results in a series of qualitative changes in the way an individual understands and adapts to the environment. Adaptation depends on
the processes of *assimilation* and *accommodation.* Equilibrium or understanding is acquired by applying existing rules or structures to new
situations (assimiliation) and by changing the rules or structures to acquire new information that does not fit existing structures (accommodation). Dissatisfaction or, in Piaget's term, *disequilibration,* is the result of
conflict and unresolved problems. Disequilibration occurs as a result of
one's experiences; then, through the processes of assimilation and accommodation, there is a qualitative change in the way one understands
and adapts, which brings about a state of equilibrium.

The *sensorimotor stage* which consists of approximately the first
two years of life is the stage that occurs prior to the development of
language. One intellectual achievement during this period is the ability
to exhibit goal-directed, intentional behavior. Another achievement during this period is the ability to coordinate and integrate information
coming in from the different senses. A third important achievement
during this stage is the understanding that objects are permanent and

exist even when not seen. In other words, during this period a child becomes capable of mentally representing objects and events.

During the _preoperational stage,_ the period from approximately two to seven years of age, the child becomes increasingly able to represent objects and events symbolically. This is exhibited in the child's use of language and mental imagery as when the child uses a stick to represent a gun or a doll to represent a baby. The preoperational child is egocentric; the child cannot recognize any role or viewpoint other than his or her own. Also, the preoperational child tends to focus attention on a single aspect of a visual stimulus, ignoring other relevant attributes. A third important characteristic of a child in this stage is the inability to reverse the thought processes. For example, a child in this stage thinks that a ball of clay when flattened contains more mass because the flattened clay takes up more surface area than the original ball of clay. The child does not realize that if the flattened clay were rolled up you would have the same ball you began with. (See Figure 5-3.) The child in this stage also has difficulty differentiating between objects and living creatures and injects

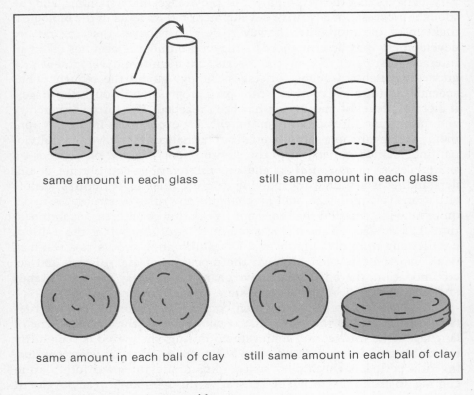

same amount in each glass          still same amount in each glass

same amount in each ball of clay   still same amount in each ball of clay

Figure 5-3 Conservation of liquid and mass.

human qualities and feelings into inanimate things. For example, the preoperational child may believe that a chair will hurt if it is kicked or that boats sleep at night.

The child develops the capacity to reason and solve problems in a logical manner during the *concrete operational stage*, the period from about seven to eleven years of age. Classification systems develop during this period so that a hierarchical relation of classes and subclasses is established. For example, if six yellow apples (three large and three small) and four red apples (one large and three small) were placed in view, the child could correctly respond to the question, "Are there more yellow apples or more large apples?" The ability to reverse thought processes characterizes this stage. Piaget's writing discusses *conservation* of numbers, length, liquid, mass, weight, area, and volume. Conservation of mass is illustrated when the child understands that changing the shape of the ball of clay does not change the amount of clay. Conservation of liquid is illustrated when the child understands that the amount of liquid remains the same whether it is poured into a tall, thin glass or a wide, low glass. During this period, a child is capable of understanding how a solid can be transformed into a liquid and changed back again to the original state.

The *formal operational stage* follows the concrete operational stage and is characterized by the ability to consider all possible combinations of events in problems presented and to exclude those that are irrelevant. The capacity to consider hypothetical situations is also characteristic of this stage. Imaginal representation in the younger child was limited to the child's experience; now hypothetical events or combinations can be imagined that the child has never actually experienced. The child can now think about how things could be rather than how they are. This ability is necessary for formulating hypotheses for scientific inquiry. The formal operational stage is also characterized by the ability to deal with abstract philosophical principles such as the meaning of life.

## Vocational Development

Theories of sequential stages in the process of choosing a career emphasize the developmental viewpoint. Ginzberg (1952, 1970, pp. 58-67) proposed that the first period, the Fantasy Period, lasts up to about age 11 and is characterized by the belief that a person can be anything he or she wants to be. The Tentative Choice Period lasts from about 11 to 17 years of age and may be subdivided into the following stages: (1) the Interest Stage when career possibilities are based on interest; (2) the Capacities Stage when personal skills and abilities are considered; (3) the Values Stage when personal values become important in the choice process; and (4) the Transition Stage when making plans to attend college or to apply for a job predominate. The third period, the Realistic Choice

Period, from about 17 years of age and older, may be subdivided into the following three stages: (1) the Exploration Stage when one last look is made at the range of alternatives; (2) the Crystallization Stage when a career choice is determined; and (3) the Specification Stage when a specific job or position is taken.

Super (1957) also views the process of making a career choice as developmental in nature. He proposes five sequential stages. During Stage I, the Growth Stage, careers are thought about in terms of fantasy, interests, and capacities. This stage lasts up to about 14 years of age. During Stage II, the Exploration Stage, careers are explored through self-awareness and role experimentation provided by school and part-time work (see Figure 5-4). This stage lasts from about 15 to 24 years of age. A commitment to work and to a permanent job develops within a particular career during Stage III, the Establishment Stage, which lasts from about 25 to 44 years of age. Stage IV, the Maintenance Stage, is from about 45 to

Figure 5-4 During adolescence, careers are explored through part-time work.

64 years of age. It covers the time when a person does whatever is needed to continue or maintain a career. During Stage V, the Decline Stage, from about 65 years of age and older, the pace and demands of the job may change and retirement will require new patterns of adjustment.

Job development may be horizontal or vertical. In horizontal progression there is little qualitative change. The work activities may change, the pay may increase with seniority, and extrinsic factors such as working hours, noise levels, or supervisors and co-workers may change, but there is no movement to a higher level of skill or to a position of more power. In vertical progression people move to higher levels of skill or to positions of more power as they proceed from relatively low entry positions to successively higher positions. Promotion may depend on the development of new skills or more mature judgment. Sometimes people may shift career directions and orient themselves toward new goals. However, vocational interests tend to be rather stable throughout the adult period (Troll, 1975).

## The Life Stages

Although each individual is unique, there are certain broad similarities in the universal life stages of infancy and childhood, adolescence, adulthood, and old age. Each stage represents a step in physical maturation and psychological development. According to Erikson (1963), a person is confronted in each stage with different tasks to be mastered. These tasks must be mastered successfully to insure healthy development and a satisfying life.

### Infancy and Childhood

Infancy and childhood may not be of immediate interest to some students, but one of the best ways to understand the adult is to understand the child. The value of childhood experiences in shaping character and personality is being recognized more and more.

The most rapid changes of the entire life span occur in the 38 to 40 weeks between conception and birth. The average newborn weighs about 7 to 7½ pounds and is about 20 inches long. The human newborn has well-developed sensory mechanisms and is capable of exhibiting many reflex responses.

Overall physical rates of growth continue to be very rapid during the first three years of life. By five years of age children have doubled their original birth length and increased to about five times their birth weight. Physical rates of growth are much slower during the middle years of childhood (ages five or six to approximately age ten or eleven), but rapid advancement is made in motor-skill abilities that require both large-muscle and fine-muscle movements and coordination. Bodily changes and efficiency in motor skills have an important influence on the developing self-concept.

According to Erikson (1963), the basic attitude of trust or mistrust is formed during the first year of life when the child is completely dependent on others for safety and comfort. Improper or unpredictable care as a child by those who are unloving and rejecting may account for an adult's insecurity, suspiciousness, or inability to relate to others. A sense of autonomy or independence is developed between the ages of one and three. Whether the child is encouraged to climb, touch, explore, and do things rather than being criticized, teased, or ridiculed when he or she falls, spills something, or fails, or is consistently overprotected is significant. Between the ages of three and five, a child develops the ability to take initiative in planning, undertaking, and carrying out a task through play activities. Initiative may be encouraged by allowing a child the freedom to choose activities, use imagination, and ask questions. Between the ages of six and twelve, children learn skills valued by society. They are more likely to develop a sense of industry rather than inferiority if they receive encouragement for productive activities.

Since work is one of the best ways to achieve a sense of mastery, children can discover their powers and limitations through work experiences. One study found that the most common age for beginning to work was ten, although boys from lower income backgrounds began by age nine (Engel, 1967). The children performed mostly physical work such as mowing lawns, delivering papers, running errands, or shining shoes (see Figure 5-5). The conclusion was drawn from the study that early work experiences helped by providing a model for behaving as an adult and for rehearsing work abilities before they were actually needed for self-support.

### Adolescence

Adolescence begins with the physiological achievement of sexual maturity which occurs, on the average, around age 13 and ends with adulthood, i.e., when people become economically independent and establish a residence apart from their parents. It is difficult to attach a specific age to the end of adolescence because people assume adult roles at various ages. They usually assume them, however, between the ages of 18 and 25.

Early adolescence is marked by a rapid physical growth spurt. An adolescent may grow four to six inches taller in a single year, and the body proportions change from child to adult dimensions. Sexual maturity follows the growth spurt. Young adolescents are usually critical of their parents and society. They can imagine ideal possibilities because they are

Figure 5-5 Children can discover their powers and limitations
through work experiences.

now capable of abstract logic. Their parents' actual beliefs and behaviors
may differ from their imagined ideal. Adolescents can argue endlessly
about minute details of parental errors, prejudices, and perceived foolish-
ness. This typical activity seems to serve the purpose of loosening bonds
between the parent and child thus helping the child become more independent. It also helps bring into focus adolescents' ideas about the kind of
person they do and do not want to become and provides an opportunity
for them to try out new ideas in a safe environment.

Young adolescents are usually very critical of themselves and are
easily shamed and embarrassed. Since their thoughts are often focused on
themselves, they believe others' thoughts are similarly focused on them;
young adolescents, then, are egocentric. If they dislike their looks or
behaviors, they are sure everyone else is similarly critical; and if they are
pleased with their behavior or appearance, they are sure everyone else
admires them as well. As adolescents mature and reach adulthood, they
become less egocentric and realize that others do not necessarily share

their thoughts and feelings. This realization is necessary if they are to form mutual relationships and to perceive another person's needs.

Much of the unsettled behavior that occurs during adolescence is an attempt to arrive at a consistent and satisfying identity. Adolescents try out different ways of behaving. They may shift from job to job, relationship to relationship, and life style to life style. Identity formation is not a process of which adolescents are totally conscious. By isolating select features from various models and combining them into a unique identity, adolescents develop a sense of self that is different from anyone else yet shares many characteristics with others. According to Erikson, the task to be mastered during adolescence is developing a sense of identity.

## Adulthood

Adulthood essentially coincides with a person's entrance into the world of work. It begins with the termination of a person's continuous schooling and ends with a person's retirement from his or her last job. Work consumes more of an adult's waking hours than any other activity. Occupational status largely determines social status which, in turn, relates to a person's values, customs, and expectations. Jobs determine many things such as where people live; how often they move; who cares for their children; the number of hours they spend working, eating or sleeping; their evening and weekend activities; their participation in organizations; and the amount of money they have to spend. Vocational choice and vocational development exert a great influence on an adult's life.

Adults are usually in the process of establishing themselves financially, rearing children, taking their place in the community, and making progress in their jobs. Older adults are usually more established than young adults and are reaping the consequences of their earlier years.

The maturing of personality is an important development in adulthood. One group of researchers (Levinson, 1978) believes that at about age 45 there is often a crisis during which a person experiences a period of doubt and confusion, and then restabilizes. If a crisis is not experienced or if the crisis is not resolved, a new maturity and satisfaction with life may not be achieved during later adulthood as it is by those who experience a crisis and restabilize.

Some research considers the major achievement of early adulthood to be the development of a meaningful love relationship or deep friendship with others (Erikson, 1963). (See Figure 5-6.) Failure to establish intimacy, i.e., the ability to care about others and to share experiences with them, results in isolation. In later adulthood, according to Erikson, fulfillment is achieved through productive or creative work, by guiding one's children, or by helping others—all of which broadens one's energies to include society in general.

Figure 5-6    Some research considers the development of a meaningful love relationship or deep friendship to be the major achievement of early adulthood.

## Old Age

Although some people are old at 65, some much sooner, and some much later, the common retirement age is considered to be 65 and is seen as a dividing line between adulthood and old age. Physical changes which accompany old age are dry and wrinkled skin, impaired strength and agility, brittle bones which break easily and mend slowly, white hair which becomes thinner, facial changes from loss of teeth and receding gums, and a bowing spine. Less time is spent in deep sleep and more naps may be taken during the day. A general slowing down of behavior usually becomes one of the noticeable effects of old age. Also, the sensory processes become less acute.

Older adults have a varied course of development. Some remain actively engaged in work, family, and society while others retire to a quiet, uninvolved life, and others are plunged into poverty and isolation by forced retirement and social neglect. The developmental tasks of the aged are to adjust to change and to develop a sense of integrity. Two principle theories have been proposed to explain successful adjustment to the changes of the aging. The *disengagement theory* assumes that as people grow older they voluntarily withdraw from their social surroundings, and society is satisfied to let them do so because withdrawal is seen as a natural part of aging that has psychological benefits. The aged welcome disengagement since it relieves them of roles and responsibilities they have become less able to fulfill. Society benefits from disengagement since younger people with new energy and skills fill positions vacated by the aging people.

In constrast to the disengagement theory, the *activity theory* assumes that activity is the essence of life. As people grow older they need to seek other activities to replace work so they can maintain a high level of activity and not lose the satisfactions that work brings. (See Figure 5-7.) Proponents of this theory believe that aging people should maintain the activities of their earlier years and their work responsibilities for as long as possible. Whether older people meet the challenges of life by withdrawing from some activities or by taking up new ones seems to be an individual matter according to some researchers (Elias, Elias, & Elias, 1977); however, the majority of studies conducted on aging support the activity theory (Barrow & Smith, 1979).

According to Erikson, whether a person successfully achieves the tasks of each of the developmental periods determines whether that person develops a sense of integrity or despair in old age. Old age is a time of reflection. If a person can look back with a sense of satisfication and acceptance and develop a sense of integrity, aging and death may be faced with dignity; otherwise, the aged person may fall into despair, and aging and death may be faced with fear and depression.

Based on extensive study of terminally ill patients, Kübler-Ross (1969) theorizes that dying progresses through five stages: (1) denial, when the person denies that death is impending; (2) anger, as frustration builds; (3) bargaining, when the person pleads with God, doctors, and others for postponement of death; (4) depression, when death is imminent; and (5) acceptance, when the person is almost void of feelings and seemingly ready for life on earth to end.

*Ageism* refers to discrimination or prejudice on the basis of age. The older person is often stereotyped, especially by the media, as being senile, meddling, lonely, dependent, unattractive, and incompetent. Youth may be stereotyped as being fresh, attractive, energetic, active, and appealing. Ageism applies to people of all ages and can affect young as well as old people. For example, a person applying for a job may be considered too old

Figure 5-7    Proponents of the
activity theory believe that as
people grow older they should
remain active in order to retain the
satisfaction that work gives.

or too young to adequately perform the job even though he or she may not
be told that age is a factor. Many older people refuse to accept stereotyped
images of themselves. One of the best ways older people can combat
ageism is to counter stereotypes with facts.

## SUMMARY

1.  Inherited characteristics are those determined by the genetic ma-
    terials present at the moment the person was conceived. Develop-
    ment refers to the sequence of structural and behavioral changes
    which occur in a person as he or she matures as a product of both
    heredity and environment.

2. Some behavioral characteristics may be a result of heredity and some may be a result of the environment; however, most depend on the interaction between heredity and the environment, with heredity providing potentials and limitations which may be altered by the environment.

3. According to evolutionary theory, some of an individual's heredity has common roots with all forms of life; some roots are common with the species and some roots are individual.

4. Sociobiology proposes that a biological basis exists for all social behavior; that basis is the biological instinct to preserve genes which are carriers of heredity.

5. A human being develops from one cell with 46 chromosomes made up of 23 chromosomes from a sperm provided by the father and 23 chromosomes from an egg provided by the mother.

6. A chromosome is made up of many genes composed of chains of DNA molecules. DNA consists of four chemical bases in various arrangements which constitute a genetic code for the creation of a particular characteristic.

7. The two genes for a specific characteristic (one from the father and one from the mother) may both be dominant or recessive, or one may be dominant and one recessive with dominant genes predominating over recessive genes. Therefore, some characteristics are determined by a single gene and some by both genes; some characteristics are polygenic—they are determined by a variety of genes operating in a complex interaction.

8. An individual's sex is determined by the twenty-third pair of chromosomes. The individual receives an X chromosome from the mother and either an X or a Y chromosome from the father, so that an XX combination forms a female and an XY combination forms a male.

9. Some characteristics are sex-linked and some are determined by an abnormal number of chromosomes, 45 or 47 instead of the usual 46.

10. Genetic counseling is now available so that the probability that a child born to carriers of a defective gene will inherit the gene can be evaluated, and genetic and chromosomal abnormalities can be diagnosed in the early prenatal stage of development.

11. Maturation, the control that genes exert over the unfolding of biological events from conception to death, follows some general trends as seen in the head-downward, center-outward, and massive-to-specific progressions.

12. A critical period refers to a time in the developmental period when an environmental condition will have an effect on the behavior of an individual.

13. Prenatal and birth conditions such as the materials present in the mother's bloodstream, the supply of oxygen to the brain, and damage to brain cells as well as the postnatal environmental conditions have an effect on the developmental processes.

14. Piaget theorizes that cognitive development progresses through a sequence of stages guided by the interaction between a person's biological makeup, or heredity, and a person's environmental experiences.

15. The four stages of cognitive development as proposed by Piaget are the sensorimotor stage, the preoperational stage, the concrete operational stage, and the formal operational stage.

16. Ginzberg proposed three sequential periods of vocational development: the Fantasy Period, the Tentative Choice Period, and the Realistic Choice Period. Super proposed five sequential stages: growth, exploration, establishment, maintenance, and decline.

17. The life stages may be delineated as infancy and childhood, adolescence, adulthood, and old age with each stage representing a step in physical maturation and psychological development.

18. Adulthood essentially coincides with a person's entrance into the world of work. Thus work has a profound influence on this stage often determining such things as social status, values, customs, expectations, and life styles. The maturing of personality is an important development in adulthood.

19. The important developmental tasks of old age are to adjust to change and to develop a sense of integrity.

20. Two different theories, disengagement and activity, have been proposed to explain successful adjustment to old age. The development of a sense of integrity depends on the successful achievement of the tasks of each of the preceding developmental periods.

## SUGGESTIONS FOR FURTHER READING

Caplan, F. *The first twelve months of life.* Princeton, N. J.: Edcom Systems, 1973.

Behaviors typical of each month of development are described in tables and in illustrations. This book also discusses current research on infancy.

DeVore, I. The new science of genetic self-interest. *Psychology Today*, 1977, *10*, 42-51.

This article explains and comments on the new sociobiology theory.

Kübler-Ross, E. *On death and dying*. New York: Macmillan, 1969.

Kübler-Ross proposes five steps by which one comes to terms with death. The author is the scientist best known for helping to call attention to the needs of the terminally ill.

McClearn, G. E., & DeFries, J. C. *Introduction to behavioral genetics*. San Francisco: W. H. Freeman, 1973.

This book is an understandable introduction to the study of how genes influence behavior and personality.

Nilsson, L. A. *A child is born: The drama of life before birth*. New York: Delacorte, 1968.

Many photographs of prenatal development are included in this book prepared especially for parents-to-be.

Phillips, J. L., Jr. *The origins of intellect: Piaget's theory* (2nd ed.). San Francisco: W. H. Freeman, 1975.

An introduction to Piaget's theory of intellectual development that is easy to read.

Sheehy, G. *Passages: Predictable crises of adult life*. New York: Dutton, 1976.

Psychological crises people encounter during their middle years are described in this best-selling book about adult development.

Shertzer, B. *Career planning: Freedom to choose*. Boston: Houghton Mifflin, 1977.

Recommendations and general guidelines for making a career choice are given in this comprehensive, easy-to-follow guide to career choices and vocational selection.

Why you do what you do. Sociobiology: A new theory of behavior. Time, August 1, 1977, pp. 54-63.

A theory of human behavior that is clearly related to behavior genetics is presented in this article.

# Part 3
## Cognitive Processes

# L Chapter 6
## earning

# A

**person** can learn, can see others in the process of learning, and can observe that one responds in a different way as a result of learning; but learning cannot be observed directly. Sometimes reading, studying, or teaching is considered to be parallel to learning; however, these activities are only a part of learning. Learning is an abstraction that is inferred by a relatively permanent change in one's behavior that occurs as a result of experiences with people, places, events, or objects. Reflex behaviors such as blinking when air is blown into the eye are not learned. Likewise, behaviors that result from maturation or from physiological changes arising from illness, fatigue, intoxication, or drugs are not learned. Learning is the process whereby behaviors change to insure survival under changing conditions and to meet the demands of the current environment. Learning is central in developing, modifying, and maintaining knowledge, skills, and attitudes necessary for success in the business world. Several forms of learning that have been identified and explained are discussed in this chapter.

## Classical Conditioning

*Classical conditioning* is a form of learning which is often referred to as signal learning. Associations are formed when a new event is paired with an event that brings forth a particular behavior. The new event comes to signal the previous event and brings forth the same behavior.

### *Discovery*

Ivan Pavlov (1927), a Russian physiologist, used dogs to study the digestive processes. Since the presence of food in the mouth brings forth the reflex response of salivation, Pavlov inserted tubes into the salivary glands to measure the amount of saliva produced when he fed the dogs. He became perplexed when, after being in the laboratory for a while, the dogs would salivate before they were given food. Pavlov then turned his attention to this phenomenon and demonstrated classical conditioning in the laboratory.

Pavlov demonstrated classical conditioning by immediately following the ringing of a bell with the presentation of food to the dogs. Initially, the dogs did not salivate when the bell rang. After repeating this several times, Pavlov rang the bell without presenting food. He discovered that the bell alone now produced salivation in the dogs. A form of learning referred to as classical conditioning had occurred (see Figure 6-1). The dogs responded differently to an environmental event (bell) as a result of an environmental experience (pairing of bell with food). Originally the bell was neutral; it did not bring forth a specific response in the dog. After the bell became associated with food, it came to signal the presentation of food and to produce the same response as the appearance of food—salivation. Classical conditioning had occurred by associating a *neutral stimulus* with an *unconditioned stimulus*. A neutral stimulus is a person, place, event, or object that does not bring forth a specific response. An unconditioned stimulus brings forth a reflex response referred to as an unlearned or *unconditioned response.*

Pavlov extended his experiment by turning on a light before ringing the bell. At first, turning on the light did not elicit salivation. However, after turning on the light and immediately following it with the ringing of the bell a few times, the dog would then salivate when the light was turned on without the light being followed by the ringing of the bell.

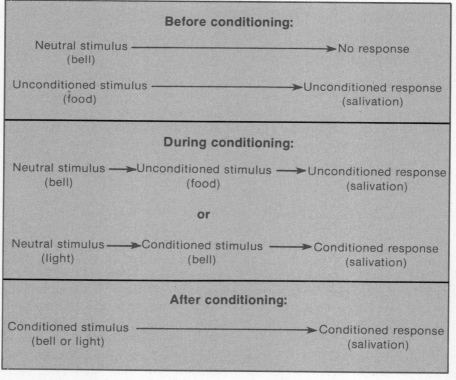

Figure 6-1    Classical conditioning.

Classical conditioning had also occurred by associating a neutral stimulus (light on) with a *conditioned stimulus* (bell), a learned stimulus. A response brought forth by a conditioned stimulus is referred to as a learned or *conditioned response.*

Classical conditioning may be defined then as the shifting of an old response to a new stimulus. In other words, when some event elicits a particular response, whether learned or reflexive, and another event becomes associated with the first event, the second event becomes a signal for the first event and elicits the same response. For example, classical conditioning has occurred when a company security guard has learned to respond to the presence of the company electrician at the gate by unlocking the gate for entrance to the premises. If the electrician arrives at the gate in a particular car on several successive occasions, just the appearance of the car may cause the security guard to respond by unlocking the gate.

The boxed material which follows describes how one may demonstrate classical conditioning by shifting the response of hand raising from one stimulus to a new stimulus.

---

A DEMONSTRATION OF CLASSICAL CONDITIONING

Instruct a group of people to raise their right hands whenever you raise yours. These instructions establish a reasonably reliable conditioned stimulus-conditioned response relationship. Try it a few times to make sure everyone is responding. Then begin to precede the raising of your hand with the word "now" as if to indicate when you are going to raise your hand. Do this for about 15 or 20 trials. Then just say "now" without raising your hand. Several people should be conditioned to raise their hands at the word "now." The word "now" was originally a neutral stimulus for hand raising; it has become a conditioned stimulus for hand raising (VanRijn, 1973).

---

Psychologists do not all agree on the importance of classical conditioning in explaining complex human behavior; however, for those subscribing to the behavioral approach, classical conditioning is the fundamental unit of change in behavior. Regardless of its importance in explaining complex human behavior, one will be exposed to classical conditioning frequently in the work environment.

## Conditioning of Emotional Reactions

John B. Watson, the American psychologist who developed behaviorist theory, was attracted to Pavlov's explanation of how old responses are shifted to new stimuli. He extended the principle to include emotional reactions such as fear, anger, likes, dislikes, and attitudes. Watson recognized three innate reactions—fear, anger, and love—as being similar to Pavlov's reflexes and proposed that all emotional reactions to stimuli are learned in association with these three. For example, a loud unexpected noise elicits fear responses reflexively. Any neutral stimulus immediately preceding the noise may be associated with the noise and will then bring forth fear responses.

The classic demonstration of conditioning of an emotional reaction (Watson & Rayner, 1920) was with an 11-month-old boy named Albert who showed no fear of white rats and enjoyed watching them. After the appearance of a white rat was immediately followed by a loud, frightening noise a few times, Albert showed signs of fear when a white rat appeared alone without the noise (see Figure 6-2).

An electrician may show no signs of fear when handed a particular tool to use. However, if there are loud, explosive sounds somewhere in the building each time that tool is handed to the electrician, fear reactions may then occur when that tool is presented even though no loud, explosive sound occurs. As another example, the director of a project may not experience feelings of anger when a particular worker appears. However, if the director happens to become angry about some incident every time the worker appears, the director may then experience feelings of anger when the worker appears even though there is no incident to elicit anger.

Figure 6-2    Albert developed
a fear of white rats after a white rat
was associated with a loud,
frightening noise.

## Basic Principles

**Extinction.** When an old response is shifted to a new stimulus, the new stimulus may not elicit the old response indefinitely. If the new stimulus is presented repeatedly without being paired with the old stimulus, the new stimulus may cease to elicit the old response. This phenomenon is referred to as *extinction*.

Pavlov demonstrated extinction in the laboratory by conditioning a dog to salivate to the sound of a bell. He then repeatedly sounded the bell without pairing it with the appearance of food. The amount of salivation relative to the sound of the bell decreased until finally no salivation occurred when the bell was sounded. The association of the bell with the absence of food had become stronger again than the association of the bell with the presentation of food.

The electrician previously mentioned may cease to experience fear when handed a particular tool if no further loud, explosive sounds are paired with the presentation of that tool. The security guard may cease to unlock the gate when a particular car is seen if the electrician does not appear at the gate in that car. The project director may cease to experience feelings of anger when the worker appears if incidents eliciting anger no longer occur when the worker appears.

**Spontaneous Recovery.** Sometimes after extinction has seemingly occurred and a period of time passes during which neither the old stimulus nor the new stimulus nor the pairing of them occurs, the new stimulus may be presented and again will elicit the response. This is referred to as *spontaneous recovery*.

Pavlov demonstrated spontaneous recovery in the laboratory by conditioning a dog to salivate to the sound of a bell, then sounding the bell without pairing it with food until extinction occurred. He then put the dog out of the laboratory and into the yard for a period of time. When he brought the dog back into the laboratory and sounded the bell, the dog salivated again even though it had previously ceased salivating in response to the sound of the bell. The association of the sound of the bell with no food had weakened during the time the dog was out of the laboratory, and the association of the bell with the appearance of food was stronger again.

Spontaneous recovery would be demonstrated by a person who is afraid of driving an automobile to work after being involved in a wreck but continues to drive without experiencing another wreck until extinction of fear occurs. If the person stops driving for an extended period of time and experiences fear again when driving is resumed, spontaneous recovery has occurred.

**Stimulus Generalization.** Pavlov also found that although conditioning a dog took place by pairing a bell of a particular tone and loudness with the presentation of food, the sound of a bell of any tone or loudness elicited the response of salivation. When a new stimulus comes to be associated with a stimulus that already elicits a particular response, any stimulus similar to that new stimulus may also elicit the response, even if direct conditioning has not occurred. This is the principle of *stimulus generalization*, an important aspect of learning since most often a person outside the laboratory does not have exactly the same stimulus presented each time (see Figure 6-3). People would not be able to read if the principle of generalization did not apply; no two people have handwriting that is identical and print is seldom exactly the same shape, size, or color as the print presented during the original act of learning.

If an employee walks into the company storeroom which has no windows and is frightened by something, conditioning may occur. The storeroom may elicit fear responses when it is entered again. Stimulus generalization may occur also and fear responses may be elicited by entering any room which has no windows.

**Stimulus Discrimination.** Another important aspect of conditioning is learning to react to a specific stimulus and not to respond in the same way to all similar stimuli. Learning to recognize the differences between similar stimuli is referred to as *stimulus discrimination*. Stimulus discrimination is as important to learning how to read as stimulus generalization. If one could not learn to discriminate between similar stimuli, reading would not be possible since the letters "b" and "d" would elicit the same response. Pavlov demonstrated in the laboratory that dogs conditioned to salivate to the sound of any bell could be conditioned to salivate to a specific bell such as a bell of 35 decibels and not to salivate to a similar bell such as a bell of 25 decibels. He accomplished this by pairing the bell of 35 decibels with food and not pairing the bell of 25 decibels with food. After a few trials the decibel level paired with food produced salivation and the decibel level not paired with food did not produce salivation. The process of stimulus discrimination involves learning to respond to a particular stimulus and to inhibit that response in the presence of other stimuli.

An automobile mechanic may learn to respond differently to very similar engine sounds. A manager may learn to discriminate between the handwriting of the president of the company and the handwriting of a fellow employee and to respond differently to each person's handwriting.

## Operant Conditioning

The laws of association explained by Pavlov were extended by B. F. Skinner. Skinner was primarily concerned with the association of a response with the consequence (stimulus) which followed the response. Pavlov was concerned with the association of stimuli preceding and

Figure 6-3    Stimulus
generalization occurs when an
employee likes a co-worker because
of a particular feature similar to
another person with whom the
employee has had a pleasant
experience in the past.

eliciting a response. Skinner proposed and demonstrated experimentally, primarily with rats and pigeons, that a randomly or spontaneously emitted behavior becomes associated with the consequence or effect the behavior has on the environment and may increase or decrease in frequency (Skinner, 1953). A device referred to as a Skinner box (see Figure 6-4) was used to demonstrate this proposition. A Skinner box provides an opportunity for a particular response to occur, such as pressing a bar, and a consequence for that response, such as a pellet of food. The spontaneous behaviors that an organism is capable of emitting such as pressing, pecking, turning, making a sound, or moving particular body parts are referred to as operants; they operate on the environment. The term *operant conditioning* is applied to this type of learning.

### The Theory

According to Skinner's theory, operants (responses) may operate on the environment to produce either a reinforcing or a punishing consequence, or there may be no operation on the environment and no consequence. A reinforcing consequence increases the frequency of the operant, and a punishing consequence decreases the frequency of the operant. For example, turning a door knob is an operant that may be followed by the consequence of the door opening. Therefore, this operant will be associated with the opening of the door and will probably increase in frequency when one wants a door open. If an employee criticizes his or her supervisor and is demoted as a consequence, the operant of criticizing will probably decrease in frequency.

Whether a consequence is reinforcing or punishing depends on the effect of the consequence not the consequence itself (see Figure 6-5). The

Figure 6-4    A Skinner box is equipped with a bar or button that, when pressed or pecked (a response), supplies the subject with a pellet of food (a consequence).

consequence might be pleasing, rewarding, or satisfying for one person but would not be for another person. Likewise, the consequence of a response might be unpleasant, aversive, or painful for one person but not for another person. Whether a consequence is reinforcing or punishing is determined by the effect it has on the response emitted. If the consequence increases a response, it is reinforcing; if the consequence decreases a response, it is punishing. For example, at one company arriving late to work results in being sent to a job site on the east side of the city. One employee might like the consequence because it enables the employee to work with a friend; the frequency of this employee's tardiness would increase. Another employee might not like the consequence because the job site is not air-conditioned; this employee's tardiness would decrease in order to avoid the consequence.

Figure 6-5   Presenting a report may be a pleasant consequence of working on a project for one person. To another person, however, such a presentation would be a painful and punishing experience.

Reinforcing consequences may be of two general types. *Positive reinforcement* is a consequence that increases a response since it pleases, rewards, or satisfies the person. If a person desires a cup of coffee and placing a coin in a machine results in receiving a cup of coffee, positive reinforcement is illustrated. Something pleasing is delivered. *Negative reinforcement* is a consequence that increases a response if that response either removes an aversive stimulus, provides escape from it, or prevents an aversive stimulus from occurring. Negative reinforcement would be illustrated if an employee is dawdling (aversive stimulus to the supervisor), the supervisor yells in an angry voice (response), and the employee stops dawdling (reinforcement for the supervisor). The supervisor's yelling in an angry voice when an employee is dawdling will probably increase. Something aversive is removed.

The term *punishment* refers to an aversive consequence that follows the occurrence of a response and decreases the occurrence of that response. The consequence may be physiologically or psychologically unpleasant to the person. Physical punishment in a job situation would be illustrated if a worker pushed the red button rather than the green button on a machine, releasing a piece which mashed a finger. Harsh criticism from the manager would be an example of psychological punishment. *Time-out* or *response-cost* refers to a consequence that delays (time-out) or removes (response-cost) a pleasant stimulus situation. If an employee is caught sleeping on the job and is docked two days' pay, response-cost as a type of punishing consequence would be illustrated. In general, learning through association with aversive consequences involves either the withdrawal of pleasant stimuli (time-out or response-cost) or the administration of unpleasant stimuli (punishment). See Figure 6-6.

The basic principles of extinction, spontaneous recovery, stimulus generalization, and stimulus discrimination also apply in operant conditioning just as in classical conditioning. If a response ceases to operate on the environment and, therefore, is no longer paired with a reinforcing consequence, extinction will occur and the response will cease to be emitted. For example, an employee in the office may tell jokes which are followed by laughter and attention from others in the office (reinforcement). If everyone suddenly ignores the jokes, reinforcement is no longer paired with the response and the joke telling by the employee will cease—extinction occurs. If the employee is out of the office for an extended period of time but tells a joke again upon returning, spontaneous recovery in operant conditioning has occurred.

Stimulus generalization would be demonstrated if one learns to emit a particular response in a particular situation and then emits the same response in similar situations. When one learns to discriminate between similar situations for emitting the response, stimulus discrimination is demonstrated. For example, cursing may occur in frustrating

Figure 6-6    Types of punishing consequences. (1) Time-out: "You exceeded the speed limit; therefore, you must delay driving your car for one week." (2) Response-cost: "You exceeded the speed limit; therefore, your car will be taken away permanently." (3) Punishment (physiological): "You exceeded the speed limit; therefore, you will do hard labor for one week." (4) Punishment (psychological): "You exceeded the speed limit, you unreliable, incompetent, uncaring person."

situations with peers on the job but may not occur in a similar situation with a supervisor present who has shown disapproval of cursing.

**Response generalization.** The emission of similar but physically different responses in a particular situation refers to *response generalization.* One may always speak a greeting to the manager on arrival to work, but it may be a little different each time—louder, softer, with different words such as "hello" or "good morning," or with a little or big smile.

**Response discrimination.** When two or more similar but physically different responses are emitted in a particular situation and one response is reinforced but the other responses are not, *response discrimination* occurs. Such selective reinforcement is referred to as *differential reinforcement*. When greeting the manager upon arrival at work, saying hello loudly may be reinforced with a return hello and smile while saying hello softly may not be reinforced. The employee learns to say hello loudly. Response discrimination may occur when learning a new behavior such as learning to operate a word processor. When the correct response is made, the word processor operates properly; thus, the correct response is reinforced. When any other similar response is made, the word processor does not operate properly. The use of the correct response will increase, while the use of all other responses will decrease or cease even though they may be very similar to the correct response.

*Shaping* is an important tool in teaching or training. Most of one's behaviors would never occur spontaneously. To create a new behavior, differential reinforcement may be used to gradually shape the behavior by reinforcing closer and closer approximations of the desired or target behavior. "Operant conditioning shapes behavior as a sculptor shapes a lump of clay" (Skinner, 1953, p. 91). The responses necessary for piloting an airplane do not occur spontaneously. Instead, the responses are shaped by reinforcing closer and closer approximations. One small part of the task may be accomplished, then another, until the piloting is attempted under simulated conditions, then attempted with an instructor, and then attempted alone.

### Reinforcement

**Effectiveness.** According to Miller (1975) there are four main factors that determine the effectiveness of reinforcement. These factors are:

1. Contingency—for maximum effectiveness, the reinforcement must be delivered only if the organism makes the response;
2. Immediacy—the more immediately the reinforcement follows the response, the greater the effect;
3. Size—the greater the quantity of reinforcement, the greater the effect;
4. Deprivation—the more deprived one is of the reinforcement, the greater the effect.

*Correlated reinforcement* in which the quantity of reinforcement varies in proportion to the quantity or intensity of the response is also very effective in conditioning. Correlated reinforcement is effective because it provides the learner with more information concerning the value of the behavior modification. This then enables the learner to discriminate responses and thus have more control over the behavior (Travers, 1972). Money paid in proportion to the number of pages typed and a grade on a test assigned in proportion to the number of correct responses given are examples of correlated reinforcement.

**Types.** Although each consequence must be tested to determine if it is a reinforcer for a specific individual, there are types of consequences that are generally considered to be reinforcers. *Primary reinforcers* are those which satisfy a biological need such as food. They may lose their effectiveness due to overuse but, subsequently, may regain their effectiveness after a period of deprivation. *Conditioned* or *secondary reinforcers* are those which satisfy a learned need. These conditioned reinforcers may lose their effectiveness due to either overuse or extinction. A conditioned reinforcer gains its effectiveness from association with other reinforcers such as a smile from a person followed by friendly conversation with that person, which is reinforcing. If this happens frequently enough, the smile may become a reinforcer by being associated with friendly conversation. *Generalized conditioned reinforcers* are associated with many different reinforcers and, therefore, extinction or ineffectiveness from overuse does not usually occur. Some generalized conditioned reinforcers are money, approval, attention, affection, diplomas, and grades.

Sometimes responses may be reinforcers. Premack (1965) demonstrated that a behavior which occurs often can be used as a reinforcer of a behavior which occurs less frequently. The *Premack principle* is sometimes referred to as "Grandma's Law"—"eat your spinach, then you may eat your ice cream." A response such as talking with co-workers occurs more frequently for an employee than a response such as writing a report. If the employee is allowed to talk with co-workers only following the completion of a report, report writing would probably increase.

*Intrinsic reinforcers* are those internal feelings of satisfaction that people get from a particular behavior (see Figure 6-7). An employee's work may produce a feeling of competence, achievement, or self-actualization which satisfies a need and increases the work response. Intrinsic reinforcers have limitations in work situations because managers cannot directly control them. Managers can only hope that the employee will receive a feeling of satisfaction from the work which will increase productivity. Tangible things that can be used as reinforcers are referred to as *extrinsic reinforcers*. A manager can give extrinsic reinforcers such as money, fringe benefits, promotions, approval, or privileges.

**Schedules.** Reinforcement can be applied according to many different schedules, and the relationship of these schedules to a response has been investigated (Ferster & Skinner, 1957). Research has been concerned with two general types of reinforcement schedules: *continuous reinforcement* in which a reinforcer follows the response every time it occurs and

Figure 6-7   Sometimes people
engage in certain activities only
because those activities are
stimulating or satisfying within
themselves.

*intermittent reinforcement* in which a reinforcer follows the response only some of the time. Learning is more rapid with continuous than with intermittent reinforcement. Continuous reinforcement produces a steady rate of performance as long as the reinforcement continues; however, the reinforcer may cease to be effective rather rapidly from overuse. A continuous schedule leads to more rapid extinction of the response or to weakening of the behavior when the reinforcement is suddenly withheld. A reinforcer is less likely to become ineffective with intermittent reinforcement. Also, intermittent reinforcement is capable of producing a high frequency of the response that is resistant to extinction.

Intermittent schedules may be of many different types. Two general types are (1) *interval schedules* based on a period of time and (2) *ratio schedules* based on a number of responses. On an interval schedule a person who repairs television sets might receive reinforcement in the form of praise from the supervisor only after a three-hour time lapse since the last reinforcement. On a ratio schedule the person might receive praise following each fifth television set repaired.

Schedules may be further classified as to whether they are fixed or variable. The preceding examples of praise given the person repairing television sets represent a *fixed interval* and a *fixed ratio schedule.* If the praise is given at variable or random time intervals such as after one hour, again after four hours, after eight hours, and after one half hour, then a *variable interval schedule* is in effect. If the praise is given when four television sets are repaired, when one is repaired, and when ten are repaired, a *variable ratio schedule* is in effect. If an employee receives a paycheck at the end of each month, a fixed interval schedule of reinforcement is in effect. If an employee is paid $30 on the completion of each twenty pages typed, a fixed ratio schedule is in operation. A commission salesperson probably receives reinforcement on a variable ratio basis—a sale may be made to the fifth person attempted, or to the next one, or the tenth one, or the twentieth one. The slot machines in gambling houses are set up on a variable ratio schedule of reinforcement. A variable interval schedule occurs commonly in the irregular dispensing of promotions to higher-level positions within many companies.

Different types of intermittent schedules have different effects on the response. Ratio schedules tend to produce a higher rate of response than interval schedules because in a ratio schedule one gets the reinforcer faster by making more responses. Ratio schedules also tend to produce steady responding. In this psychology course, if you are to receive reinforcement in the form of test results every four weeks on a fixed interval schedule, the response of studying will probably slow down immediately following the test and increase immediately preceding the next test. Fixed schedules tend to produce an uneven response pattern with a pause immediately following reinforcement. (See Figure 6-8.)

A fascinating relationship between a response and reinforcement called *superstitious behavior* may occur when there is no schedule of reinforcement. B. F. Skinner (1948) demonstrated that if food is delivered regularly to pigeons regardless of what they do, the pigeons will develop particular behaviors. One pigeon might flap its wings frequently. Another might turn its head to one side frequently or peck the wall frequently even though these behaviors would have no effect on obtaining food. This

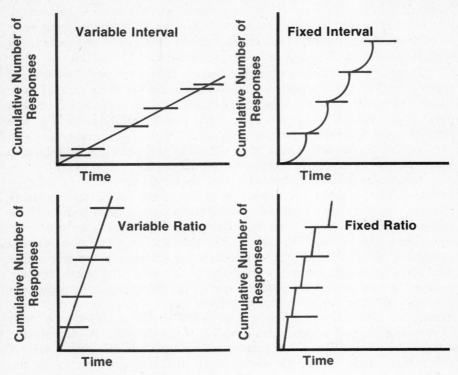

Figure 6-8    Different
schedules of reinforcement affect
the rate of responding differently.
The steeper the line the faster the
responding is. The dashes across the
line represent when reinforcement
is given.

phenomenon was explained as follows. A random response occurred
accidentally just before a food award was delivered. This association caused
the response to be repeated again and again. The response frequently
coincided with the delivery of food and came to be reinforced on a
variable ratio schedule. In a like manner, a person may just happen to
wear a particular color on the day he or she has to perform a specific task
and may do well on the task. The person may then wear that particular
color when the task is to be performed again and may do well again.
Enough intermittent reinforcement may be received to maintain the
superstition that wearing this color influences the performance of the
task. A salesperson may carry a rabbit's foot on a key chain when attempting to make a sale. Enough coincidences of making a sale when
carrying the rabbit's foot may maintain the superstition that the rabbit's
foot has an effect on whether or not a sale is made.

## Punishment

The use of punishers is not as predictable or desirable as the use of reinforcers in modifying behavior. Even though punishment may suppress a response, various undesirable side effects may occur. There are several reasons for not using punishment. First of all, the suppressive effects may generalize to related behaviors. A person who is punished for inappropriate aggression may become generally unassertive, even in situations in which assertive behaviors would be appropriate. Secondly, the use of punishment creates an aversive situation and the punished person may learn a response to avoid the aversive situation (negative reinforcement) rather than to learn a response to bring positive reinforcement. One may learn to avoid criticism by not attempting the task. Sometimes another inappropriate behavior may be increased, if it removes or avoids the punishment for some other response (negative reinforcement). For example, lying may avoid the punishment for stealing, or physically attacking the punisher may remove the punishment being administered; as a result, lying and attacking would be likely to increase. Next, punishment produces frustration and emotional responses which may disrupt the normal functioning of a person and produce unpredictable behaviors. Also, humanitarian, ethical, moral, and legal grounds must be considered in using punishment. Lastly, in using punishment to modify behavior, even though the inappropriate behavior may be suppressed, if no attempt is made to replace it with an acceptable behavior, little "growth" will take place. In general, if punishers are used to suppress a behavior, reinforcers should be used in conjunction with them to shape an acceptable alternative behavior. In too many work situations, feedback is usually aversive—"here's what you are doing wrong" rather than "here's what you are doing right" or a combination of the two.

The boxed material on page 132 describes how one may demonstrate operant conditioning by using positive reinforcement. Operant conditioning is a basic form of learning that accounts for much of human behavior. The principles of operant conditioning should be applicable in many instances in understanding, predicting, and obtaining desired responses in the world of work.

## Biofeedback

Recently it has been demonstrated that biological functions such as heart rate, blood pressure, brain wave pattern, or temperature and such human physiological problems as pain, headaches, drug abuse, and paralyzed muscles may be controlled by the application of feedback information or reinforcement (Miller & DiCara, 1967; Schwartz, 1975; Shapiro & Zifferblatt, 1976). Such feedback, known as *biofeedback*, is in the form of a bell, light, or image on a screen that is controlled by the biological

---

A DEMONSTRATION OF OPERANT CONDITIONING

Select an operant such as eye contact with a teacher during a lecture. Measure the operant level for a period of time, such as ten minutes, by making a tally mark on your note paper each time the lecturer has eye contact with you. Be sure not to give any reinforcement during this time. Reinforcement would include looking directly at the lecturer to indicate interest or attentiveness, nodding your head to indicate understanding, or smiling to indicate you heard or comprehended what was said. Then, for an equal amount of time, measure the eye contacts in the same manner; however, this time give reinforcement immediately when eye contact occurs. Compare the number of eye contacts made without reinforcement and those made with reinforcement. Did the response of eye contact increase when reinforced?

---

function being studied. Although biofeedback holds promise, much remains to be explained before this application of operant conditioning becomes a cure for one's physical problems or stress which may be important factors in one's work life. Although much human learning and behavior can be explained with the principles of classical and operant conditioning, there is much behavior that cannot be explained completely with these principles.

## Other Forms of Learning

Learning occurs in ways other than by classical and operant conditioning. Learning may occur by observing the behavior of others or by insight. These ways of learning save time and effort. Behaviors that are observed to be reinforced when others perform them can be imitated, and behaviors that are observed to have negative consequences for others can be avoided.

### Observational Learning

**Basic Principles.** Albert Bandura (1965) focused on *modeling* whereby a person learns to do something by watching someone else do it (Figure 6-9). This larger, more general approach to learning expands on operant conditioning and is often referred to as *social learning theory* (Bandura, 1977). Social learning theory explains how people have the ability to acquire large integrated patterns of behavior without having to form them gradually through shaping by tedious trial and error reinforcement.

Figure 6-9    Some behaviors
are learned by observing a model
and imitating the observed
behavior.

Modeling can be more than just learning a specific behavior; it can be
learning to govern one's behavior by the same rules models have been
observed to follow—called *rule modeling*. The model may be another
person making a response, a picture of a person making a response, or a
cartoon character making a response. The model may be imagined with
the image being supplied by reading, by hearing verbal descriptions, or by
creative imagination.

The prerequisites for observational learning are: (1) a model; (2) attention to, recognition and differentiation of what is distinctive in the model's response; and (3) coding of what is distinctive in the model's response into images or words in the person's memory.

**Determinants of Effectiveness.** The effectiveness of modeling in learning depends on whether the imitation of the model is reinforced, since the principles of operant conditioning apply to learning from a model. Therefore, the consequence following imitation is central to whether the imitation will increase or decrease. If followed by punishment, the imitation will decrease; if the imitation is not reinforced, extinction will take place; if the imitation is reinforced, the imitation will increase. Also, schedules of reinforcement affect the imitation of a model by determining the amount of time necessary for acquisition of the behavior, maintenance of the behavior, and extinction of the behavior. The likelihood that the behavior of a model will be imitated depends on the following factors: the greater the similarity between the learner and the model; the greater the need for the reinforcement anticipated; the more the model's behavior is seen as being reinforced; the more prestigious or the greater the expertise of the model; and the greater the number of models observed.

**Imitation and Identification.** Many personality traits are a product of observational learning. The attitudes and dispositions of parents, fellow workers, peers, supervisors, or teachers may be imitated after observing what happens to them as a result of their outbursts of emotion, expressions of affection, openness, or secrecy with others. For example, when words and actions of parents are contradictory, most children imitate the actions of their parents rather than behave as they are told. The same could possibly be said concerning adults and models. Often one is not consciously aware of modeling. When unconscious modeling occurs, it is referred to as *identification* rather than imitation. A worker's values, attitudes, or ways of coping with stress may be examples of identification whereby the thoughts, feelings, and behavioral tendencies of important people in the worker's life have been internalized unconsciously and modeled.

### Insight Learning

**Characteristics.** Some human learning is difficult to account for without introducing the cognitive processes or thought processes. Contemporary cognitive psychologists believe that the development of learning capacities consists of stages and that each stage requires previous learning. Learning abilities seem to build on a hierarchy of past learning and *learning sets*. Learning sets are formed when one encounters problems or tasks based on the same principle. A correct solution or learning of a task provides reinforcement for the manner in which the problem was solved or the task was learned. When new problems or tasks with a common principle underlying their solutions or learning arise, the person already has a "set" or a "learned way" to solve the problem or learn the task. A sudden awareness of how a problem can be solved without any trial and error preceding it describes insight learning.

**Illustration.** To illustrate insight learning, arrive at the solution to the following problem using cognitive processes. The solution may be found at the end of this chapter on page 147. Connect all the dots with four straight lines without lifting your pen or pencil from the paper or going through any dot more than once.

**Insight.** If you solved the problem, it probably suddenly struck you that you could go beyond the boundaries of the square. If so, that realization was an insight. Without it, you might never have solved the problem. Insight occurs when the solution to a problem suddenly becomes completely clear. Insights that are less dramatic seem to occur frequently in ordinary thought processes that affect or give direction to one's behavior. At this stage of learning, the complexity of the processes has reached a point where learning can be discussed more easily under headings of reasoning and thinking. Insight does seem to be another kind of learning which occurs without obvious reinforcement and can occur in a single trial or without any trials at all.

## Application of Learning Principles

The principles of learning are now being applied in management situations. The systematic use of learning principles to shape behavior in order to accomplish desired goals is becoming more common. Training programs are also becoming more effective through the application of principles of learning.

## Behavior Modification

*Behavior modification* is the application of learning theory or the use of learning technologies. Although behavior modification was originally associated with B. F. Skinner and operant conditioning, it does not involve any one set of learning principles. Today behavior modification may involve the use of a variety of learning principles—classical conditioning and observational learning as well as operant conditioning—with emphasis on goal setting to achieve target behaviors and on the measure of behavior change.

Behavior modification was first used in industry in the 1930s when B. F. Skinner and his co-workers trained pigeons to guide missiles (Skinner, 1960). The pigeons were conditioned to peck a target on a screen which had a feedback system that directed the missile; however, Skinner was unable to convince the military that he could actually control the behavior of pigeons and no pigeon ever really guided a missile. Today this technology of behavior is used in industry, psychological therapy, schools, prisons, mental institutions, and homes. Getting things done anywhere often requires the modification of much behavior.

Edward J. Feeney was a pioneer in the application of behavior modification principles to the business environment (Hilts, 1974). At age 22, he took a job with Emery Air Freight Corp. After taking a course in behavior modification, Feeney began to apply behavior modification principles at Emery Air Freight Corp. Probably his dock-loading project is best known. A performance audit showed that packages headed for the same destination were not being sent with maximum efficiency. Forty-five percent of the time, these packages were sent separately to the same destination rather than more efficiently sent together in one large container. The employees and supervisors on the dock, however, thought their performance was good. Training was not the answer, Feeney decided, because the employees knew how and when to use the containers. It was a matter of behavior modification. Feeney devised a plan whereby reinforcement was given in the form of checklists which allowed the employees to keep track of their own performance and thus receive immediate feedback. Reinforcement was also given in the form of graphs of group performance placed on bulletin boards and through praise and recognition by supervisors for performance improvement. Container use jumped from 45 to 95 percent in offices all over the country and has been maintained for several years by continued use of feedback and reinforcement. Savings from this program alone for one year were $650,000.

More recently, managers in other organizations have applied behavior modification to change work-related behavior. In 1976 Michigan Bell Operator Services, Connecticut General Life Insurance Company, B. F. Goodrich Co., and ACDC Electronics Division of Emerson Electric initiated programs of positive reinforcement in an effort to discourage such behaviors as absenteeism, tardiness, and excessive turnaround time on repairs and to stimulate behaviors that increase productivity and efficiency. Reinforcers such as praise, recognition, self-feedback, system feedback, earned time off, and freedom to choose work activity were used. Michigan Bell Operator Services improved attendance by 50 percent. B. F. Goodrich Co. increased production over 300 percent. ACDC Electronics Division of Emerson Electric increased attendance from 93.5 percent to 98.2 percent, reduced turnaround time on repairs from 30 to 10 days, increased profits by 25 percent, and experienced a return of 1900 percent on the investment associated with the project (Hampton, Summer, & Webber, 1978).

**Steps in a Behavior Modification Program.** Generally, programs of behavior modification using positive reinforcement follow a series of steps as follows:

1. *Identify a specific target behavior.* Work with a single behavior and define the behavior in such a way that everyone involved is referring to the same behavior.
2. *Devise a way to measure the behavior and identify how much of the target behavior currently exists.*
3. *Determine and state the desired target behavior in terms of goals or objectives.* This is often done in organizations with employee participation. Think of the desired target behavior as composed of several interrelated units. For example, the goal of increasing production to 100 units might be broken down into subunits of increasing from the current response of 75 units per week to 80 units the first week, to 85 units the second week, to 90 units the third week, to 95 units the fourth week, and to 100 units the fifth week. This would be an application of the learning principle called shaping.
4. *Design and apply positive reinforcement.* (See Figure 6-10). Be sure to reinforce the behavior immediately after it occurs, not to demand too much effort for too little reward, to reinforce each successive approximation to the target behavior when first beginning, and to shift to an intermittent schedule once the target behavior is acquired in order to maintain it.
5. *Monitor and record on a continuous basis the behavior that is to be modified.* Measurement of the behavior after beginning a program of reinforcement is essential if the effectiveness of the program is to be evaluated.
6. *Change the program—target behaviors, reinforcers, schedules, etc.—as necessary based on whether or not the plan is working.*

These general steps apply to any behavior modification program whether it is intended to modify individual behavior or group behavior.

Figure 6-10   Positive
reinforcement in the form of
feedback, praise, or recognition has
been found to be effective in
changing work-related behaviors in
industrial/organizational settings.

**Self-control.** The techniques previously presented represent one individual managing the contingencies to alter the behavior of someone else; however, the techniques can be applied to control one's own behavior and the behaviors one deliberately undertakes to achieve self-selected outcomes (Kazdin, 1975). Individuals sometimes perform better when they plan and choose the behaviors to perform and the reinforcement to receive rather than having these behaviors and reinforcements imposed on them. In the final analysis, external control is really just a means to achieve self-control. Some behaviors can be modified only by self-control since they are not always accessible to others. These behaviors might include such private events as thoughts, fantasies, or images.

There are several techniques of self-control. *Physical restraint* is the technique whereby the individual places physical restrictions in order to achieve a particular end, such as not having any cigarettes in the house to avoid smoking. *Stimulus control* is a technique in which the environment is designed so that certain cues increase the likelihood that specific behaviors are performed; selecting a place to relax where there are few cues associated with work or selecting a place to study, such as a particular room or a particular desk, that is used only for studying. The technique of *self-monitoring and recording* works on the premise that becoming aware of the behavior sometimes controls that behavior. Most people are not aware of the extent to which they engage in some behaviors. *Self-instruction*, a technique that encourages individuals to make specific comments or suggestions and direct language towards themselves, has often been used to develop self-control. In the *alternate response technique*, one engages in responses which interfere with or replace the response to be controlled or eliminated. For example, learning to relax controls tension, since relaxation and tension are incompatible; chewing gum controls eating or smoking or increasing smiling decreases frowning since they cannot occur simultaneously. Another technique used in self-control is *observation of others* who have achieved the goal and to model what they do. Remember that once a goal is set, shaping may be used to start moving toward it. Sometimes one may need to engage another person to administer the reinforcers if cheating cannot be resisted (see Figure 6-11). Those who succeed in self-control seem to try longer and tend to use more techniques than those who fail; therefore, one should try several techniques (Watson, 1978).

### Training Programs

Training programs consist of organized experiences used to develop or modify knowledge, skills, and attitudes of people in the organization; therefore, learning principles may be applied to the variety of training programs that are conducted in industrial/organizational settings. Training programs may be casual and general or highly organized and specific. Training programs in business and industry may consist of orientation programs, on-site training such as on-the-job training, apprentice training, or job rotation. Off-site training in business and industry may take the form of lectures; assigned readings, films and slides; television programs; programmed instruction; computer-assisted instruction; conferences; group discussion, which may include case studies and role playing; training simulations including business games and computer-based simulations; and laboratory or sensitivity training. (See Figure 6-12.)

Training programs should have goals. The main question in a training program is whether the employee's goals are the same as the planner's goals. For example, if the planner has the goal of producing the maximum units of a given quality in a given time and the trainee has the goal of producing just enough units to keep from losing the job, the training

Figure 6-11    The main
problem with one administering his
or her own reinforcement is
cheating.

program may not be as effective as it could be if the planner and trainee
were working toward the same goal. An employee's personal goals will
affect learning in an orientation training situation. If one's personal goals
are long-range, the individual will be likely to learn all that is possible. If
one's personal goals are short-term or immediate, the individual will be
likely to learn only enough to do the job just well enough to stay on the
payroll.

A training program should recognize which reinforcers are operative
and most effective in a particular situation. The satisfaction of a basic
physical need is seldom an important reinforcer. Social reinforcers such
as the approval or recognition from others for a job well-done seem to be
more important. Also, a personal feeling of accomplishment, self-satis-
faction, information about progress and achievement, or monetary reward may be effective. Too often money is used as a reinforcer when
other, less tangible reinforcers are more important.

Figure 6-12    Training
programs can take a wide variety of
forms. A lecture is pictured here.

The principle that the employee learns best through participation is important in training programs. Participation allows for immediate feedback and immediate reinforcement of the response. Some techniques used to obtain active participation in supervisory or managerial programs are role playing, games, or discussion meetings. An audience participation technique first developed by Donald Phillips (1948) has received a high degree of acceptance in business and industry. This technique permits small group discussions within the framework of a larger group situation. The technique is often referred to as "Phillips 66" since the group is divided into committees of six, each of which holds a six-minute discussion on some specific question or situation previously put to them. The technique has also been adapted to role playing and combinations of role playing and discussion to permit small group participation within the framework of the larger group.

Active participation may also be obtained in training programs through management games which provide simulated situations. One or more teams, each representing a business firm, makes a series of decisions governing their firm's operations during the period of play. A model of how the industry or business operates is used to calculate the outcomes of the teams' decisions. If the model is simple, calculations can be made by hand; otherwise, they are made by computer. The teams get partial or complete information about the results of their decisions as they are made. Sometimes, supervisory training may employ action mazes for the trainee to work through, choosing a response which will be followed by a supposed consequence.

Active participation is achieved in some training programs by employing a technique called *programmed instruction*. B. F. Skinner was instrumental in developing this educational practice which presents the learner with a small segment of information, and then calls for a response to make sure the material is learned before a new segment is presented. As soon as the response to the question, which may be multiple choice, fill-in-the-blank, true-false, or something similar, is made, the learner checks the correctness of the answer immediately with the correct answer which is usually printed in a second column or on the next page. In addition to being in textbook form, such programmed instruction may be designed for machines and computers that automatically provide feedback before presenting the next segment of information. Programmed instruction is based on the principle of shaping since learning of each segment of information in the sequence moves the learner closer and closer to the final objective of the course of study.

Achievement in training programs should always be measured. This measurement may take different forms. But often, since the objective of training programs is increased productivity, important measurements are statistics concerning output such as the number of items produced per hour or day, the percentage of workers meeting an established standard, or the amount of time required to complete a job. More indirect measures may relate to the number of rejects or the decrease in costs and breakage. Even more indirect measures may be changes in absenteeism or employee turnover. If the goal is gaining information, as in some orientation training programs, measures used may be similar to those used in school classrooms. The most difficult training programs to evaluate are those in the area of human relations skills such as supervisory and managerial training programs.

## SUMMARY

1. Learning cannot be observed directly but is inferred by a change in behavior as a result of an experience. Behaviors resulting from reflexes, maturation, or physiological changes arising from illness, fatigue, intoxication, or drugs are not learned.

2. Classical conditioning, discovered by Pavlov in laboratory experiments with dogs, concerns the association of stimuli; that is, a new stimulus comes to elicit a response by being associated with an old stimulus that elicited the same response.

3. Emotional responses such as feelings of fear, anger, and love, and likes, dislikes, and attitudes may be learned according to principles of classical conditioning.

4. Extinction, spontaneous recovery, stimulus generalization, and stimulus discrimination are basic principles of classical conditioning.

5. Operant conditioning, demonstrated by B. F. Skinner, concerns the association of a response with the consequence that follows it.

6. Consequence stimuli may reinforce and increase responses, or may punish and decrease responses.

7. Response generalization and response discrimination as well as extinction, spontaneous recovery, stimulus generalization, and stimulus discrimination are basic principles of operant conditioning.

8. Most behaviors do not appear suddenly full-blown, but are shaped in small steps by differential reinforcement of closer and closer approximations to the target behavior.

9. The effectiveness of reinforcement is related to contingency, immediacy, size, and deprivation. Correlated reinforcement is especially effective because the size of the reinforcement varies in proportion to, or is correlated with, the size of the response.

10. Reinforcers may be classified as primary, those that satisfy a biological need, or as conditioned, those that satisfy a learned need. Reinforcers may also be classified as intrinsic, those that elicit internal feelings of satisfaction, or extrinsic, those tangible things such as money, benefits, or promotions.

11. Reinforcement may have different effects depending on whether it is continuous, occurring each time the response is made, or is intermittent, occurring only part of the time according to a variety of schedules classified as fixed ratio, fixed interval, variable ratio, or variable interval.

12. While learning occurs more quickly with a continuous reinforcement schedule, a continuous schedule also results in more rapid extinction when reinforcement is withheld.

13. Ratio schedules tend to produce a steadier and higher rate of response while fixed schedules tend to produce an uneven response pattern with pauses immediately following reinforcement.

14. A random response occurring accidently just before a reinforcing event may result in a superstition—a belief that the reinforcement is contingent on the response.

15. Reinforcement, rather than punishment, should be used for behavior control whenever possible because results are more predictable, side effects are less likely, and reinforcement is more humane.

16. Using biofeedback as reinforcement has been demonstrated to be a promising form of operant conditioning.

17. Learning may occur from observation of a model. Whether a model is imitated depends on the perceived consequences, the need for the reinforcement anticipated, the prestige or status of the model, and the number of models observed.

18. Insight learning is complex and occurs in the thought processes.

19. Behavior modification is the application of learning principles to shape individual, group, or one's own behavior.

20. Behavior modification involves identifying the behavior to be modified, devising a way to measure it, setting goals, applying reinforcement, monitoring and recording progress, and changing the program as needed.

21. Learning principles may be applied to training programs in industrial/organizational settings in order to modify the knowledge, skills, or attitudes of employees.

22. Goal setting, reinforcement, and active participation should be employed in training programs, and achievement of goals should be evaluated.

## SUGGESTIONS FOR FURTHER READING

At Emery Air Freight: Positive reinforcement boosts performance. *Organizational Dynamics*, Winter 1973, pp. 41-50.

> A report of a successful use of positive reinforcement in a business and industrial setting. The program described is one of the most widely publicized programs of behavior modification in the area of industrial and organizational psychology.

Calvin, A. Social reinforcement. *Journal of Social Psychology*, 1962, 56, 15-19.

> The experiment discussed in this article demonstrates the control of the color of clothes worn by peers through the use of social reinforcement.

Claiborne, R. Behavior modification and its positive aspects. *The New York Times*, April 28, 1974.

The many positive aspects of behavior modification and how it operates naturally in many areas of daily life are presented in this article.

Dill, W. R. Management games for training decision makers. In E. A. Fleishman, *Studies in personnel and industrial psychology.* Homewood, Ill.: The Dorsey Press, 1961.

A chapter in this book describes management games that are sometimes used in management training programs.

Hilts, P. J. *Behavior modification.* New York: Harper's Magazine Press, 1974.

An interesting and easy-to-read book about behavior modifiers—what they do, how they do it, and what it means.

Jablonsky, S. F., & DeVries, D. L. Operant conditioning principles extrapolated to the theory of management. *Organizational Behavior and Human Performance,* 1972, 7, 340-358.

This journal article illustrates schedules of reinforcement with familiar practices in management.

Kazdin, A. E. *Behavior modification in applied settings.* Homewood, Ill.: The Dorsey Press, 1975.

This book provides an introduction to behavior modification techniques in applied settings. The major focus is on the application of operant principles, the implementation of behavior modification techniques, and the measurement and evaluation of program effectiveness. It contains one chapter on self-control.

Lang, P. J. Autonomic control, or learning to play the internal organs. *Psychology Today,* October 1970, pp. 37-41, 86.

Discusses the use of operant conditioning techniques to control behaviors of the autonomic nervous system like heart rate, blood pressure, etc. and discusses some intriguing possibilities for the future.

Latham, G. P., & Yukl, G. A. A review of research on the application of goal setting in organizations. *Academy of Management Journal,* 1975, *18*, 824-845.

A journal article concerned with the use of goal setting in organizations to achieve desired outcomes. It provides a review of the related research to 1975.

Luthans, F., & Kreitner, R. *Organizational behavior modification.* Glenview, Ill.: Scott, Foresman, 1975.

A book which applies principles of behavior modification to organizations.

Mahoney, M. J., & Thoresen, C. E. *Self-control: Power to the person.* Monterey, Calif.: Brooks/Cole, 1974.

Demonstrates how behavior modification techniques can be used for self-control.

Miller, L. K. *Principles of everyday behavior analysis.* Monterey, Calif.: Brooks/Cole, 1975.

An excellent book designed to teach the principles of behavior modification to the beginning student. It is simply written, easy to understand, and uses many everyday examples of behavioral principles. A concept-programmed instruction approach is used to teach the application of conditioning principles.

Nord, W. Beyond the teaching machine: The neglected area of operant conditioning in the theory and practice of management. *Organizational Behavior and Human Performance*, November 1969, 4, 375-401.

A journal article which discusses managers' failure to use operant conditioning and benefits that may be derived from application of operant conditioning in management theory and practice.

Reynolds, G. S. *A primer of operant conditioning.* Glenview, Ill.: Scott, Foresman, 1968.

A detailed but easily understood treatment of basic principles of operant conditioning.

Stern, R. M., & Ray, W. J. *Biofeedback: How to control your body, improve your health, and increase your effectiveness.* Homewood, Ill.: Dow Jones-Irwin, 1977.

An interesting book on use of biofeedback to control internal behaviors or the involuntary bodily responses.

Ullmann, L. P., & Krasner, L. (Eds.). *Case studies in behavior modification.* New York: Holt, Rinehart and Winston, 1965.

An application of behavior modification principles to personal problems.

Where Skinner's theories work. *Business Week*, December 2, 1972, pp. 64-65.

This short article points out some applications of Skinner's operant conditioning theory in the business world.

Whyte, W. F. Skinnerian theory in organizations. *Psychology Today,* 1972, 5 (11), 67-69.

An article that discusses Skinner's operant conditioning theory in relation to organizational behavior.

Solution to the problem illustrating insight learning on page 135.

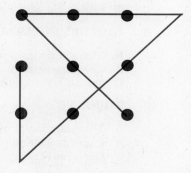

# Chapter 7

# Remembering and Thinking

# The processes

**T**he processes of remembering and thinking are essential for functioning on a job, for positively impressing others, or for communicating with others in the world of work. Without memory processes one would have to begin life anew each moment since past experience would not be available to one's consciousness. Remembering is holding on to or retaining any experiences with people, places, events, objects, or information. Memory is the persistence of learning over time. The process of memory is complex and consists of several processes and stages as will be pointed out in this chapter. Thinking involves manipulating one's world symbolically through images, words or signs, and through concepts and the generation of ideas. The primary focus on thinking in this chapter will be as it relates to problem solving and decision making. The building blocks of thought—imagery, language, and concept formation—will also be topics of discussion.

## Memory

Hermann Ebbinghaus (1885), who was the first person to study memory using systematic experiments, discovered much about memory and contributed to the later study of memory by the experimental techniques he devised. More recent research on human memory has revealed the complexities of the memory process and provided explanations of the memory system. Currently, memory is being viewed in an information-processing framework—the cognitive approach. The biological approach to the study of memory has also contributed to the understanding of the biological basis of memory.

### Early Studies by Ebbinghaus

The study of memory began when Ebbinghaus conducted a long series of experiments on himself. Ebbinghaus learned lists of nonsense syllables to avoid any effects on memory related to meaning and to avoid any of the recall being related to something previously learned. *A nonsense syllable* is a vowel between two consonants that does not form a meaningful word such as BAX, JUP, HEB, or LOM.

Ebbinghaus tried measuring memory by the *free recall* method—the percentage of nonsense syllables from the list remembered in any order;

by the *serial recall* method—the percentage of nonsense syllables remembered in the order learned; by the *recognition* method—the percentage of nonsense syllables recognized in a longer list of nonsense syllables that contained those from the learned list; and by the *relearning method*. In the relearning method, Ebbinghaus read a list of nonsense syllables until he could recall it perfectly, keeping a record of the amount of time or number of trials it took him to do that. Then after a period of time, hours or days, he relearned the list by reading it until he could recall it perfectly. Again Ebbinghaus kept a record of the amount of time or number of trials it took to achieve a perfect recall. He computed the difference between the original amount of time or number of trials it took to achieve perfect recall and the relearning amount of time or number of trials to achieve perfect recall. The percentage of savings in terms of time or number of trials required to relearn represented the percentage of retention or the percentage remembered.

Ebbinghaus made many contributions to the study of memory, one of which was the theory that the length of time between initial learning and recall affects the amount of information remembered (see Figure 7-1). He also found that in recalling a list, those items at the beginning and at the end of the list are recalled more readily than those items in the middle. In addition, Ebbinghaus found that the percentage of recall varies according to the method used for measurement.

## The Process View of Memory

The behaviorist approach to the study of memory emphasizes resistance to extinction or the persistence of a learned association. The behaviorists study only the relationships between stimuli and responses. The process view of memory is a cognitive approach to understanding memory. The cognitive processes (mental activities) that occur between a stimulus and a response are subdivided into three processes referred to as *encoding, storage,* and *retrieval.* Encoding is the process of entering information into a system for immediate or later use. Storage is the process of holding information in a system or the process of permanently storing information in a system. And retrieval is the act of getting at the stored information. All three processes must be intact in order for one to remember; if any one of the three processes breaks down, the result is failure to remember. Remembering is perceived as an act of construction, the means by which one actively builds a mental representation of the world. The steps in construction are as follows: An event changes from a physical event to a sensory event, then changes from a sensory event to a recognizable event, then changes to a condition for applying a rule.

The process view might be illustrated by the following example. One is introduced to a new employee at a business meeting. At the encoding stage, the sound waves (physical event) are changed at the

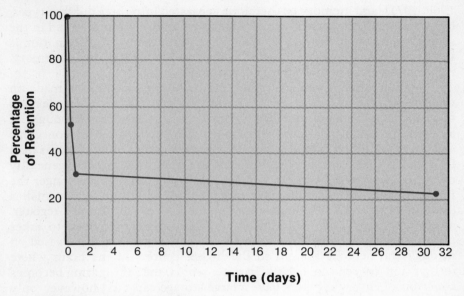

Figure 7-1    Retention as a function of time (data from Ebbinghaus, 1885). After 20 minutes, 53 percent was remembered; 34 percent after one day; and 21 percent after 31 days.

receptor cell level (transduction which was discussed in Chapter 4) to send a message to the brain where the code is placed in memory as something recognizable (perception). Possibly, visual codes and codes linked to the other senses such as touch or smell are also stored. The code is held in storage and may be retrieved a week later when the new employee is met while walking down the hall and is spoken to by name. Research suggests that retrieval involves a search process for the code which is stored in terms of features of the physical event (Sternberg, 1966, 1969). The new employee's name may be stored by the sequence of each syllable sound and the number of syllables (the features of the physical event which are the conditions for applying a rule) so that another word that rhymes with it or the sound of the first letter may serve as a *retrieval cue* (anything that helps retrieve a memory).

## The Structural View of Memory

In the structural view of memory, another cognitive approach to understanding memory, information is portrayed as being stored in the memory system in three types of storage systems (Atkinson & Shiffrin,

1968, 1971); and memory is, therefore, separated into three distinct types, or levels. At the first level, *sensory memory*, information is stored in the sensory register; at the second level, *short-term memory*, information is in the present consciousness; and at the third level, *long-term memory*, information is held in a permanent storage system.

Memory at the sensory level consists of the impressions made on the senses from energy in the environment. Information at this level is not conscious. Sensory memory is, therefore, not commonly thought of as memory since the impressions have not yet resulted in conscious awareness. A sound is held as an auditory impression or an object is held in a visual form. Sensory impressions are held only briefly—generally only a fraction of a second to perhaps a few seconds; but the longer the impression is held, the weaker it gets until it completely vanishes (Klatzky, 1975). While the information is held in the sensory register, attention may occur. In attention, the information attended to takes priority over other information in the sensory register and is passed on through the nervous system to the higher centers of the brain where recognition (perception) occurs. In other words, the information becomes conscious. Sensory registers have a large storage capacity; however, only a few inputs (sensory impressions) get attention, are recognized, and held in the short-term memory system. There are too many simultaneous sensory impressions to all be passed on through the nervous system and perceived.

Information held in the short-term system is in the present consciousness and awareness; however, it is held there only very briefly—10 to 30 seconds—unless it is repeated over and over. For example, the number 3 is not held in short-term memory as a visual sensory impression, but rather as an identified number, and it is kept in the present consciousness by repeating so that it does not slip away. The capacity of short-term memory storage is very small—only about seven meaningful units on the average—and corresponds to one's attention span. One's attention span is the amount of information that can be held in consciousness or present awareness at that moment. Short-term memory is an active, working system and is believed to be important in conscious thought. One's short-term memory seems to place a limit on the number of ideas that can be held in consciousness for thinking at one time (Baddeley & Hitch, 1974).

Long-term memory, which is a permanent storage system, has a large capacity and holds all of one's knowledge. Transfer to long-term storage is accomplished by acting on information while it is held in the short-term memory by repeating (Figure 7-2), grouping, organizing, coding, or using strategies such as rhyming, linking, or associating. Another strategy is to create a story around items of information or to imagine each item in a sequence in one of a previously learned sequence of locations.

Figure 7-2    Repeating the name of a new co-worker several times while it is in short-term memory will help transfer it to long-term memory.

More information is available in long-term memory storage than can be retrieved. Most forgetting is the result of the loss of access to the information rather than the actual loss of the information. An item in memory may be "filed" or organized under several different categories. The more categories an item is "filed" under, the more likely it can be "found" or retrieved. Coding and use of strategies provide cues for retrieval. What actively takes place while the information is in the present consciousness (short-term memory) is crucial to whether the information will be remembered later.

Because of the difficulties in trying to make all the complex operations and many codes fit the structural view of memory, an alternative explanation has been offered (Craik & Lockhart, 1972). Rather than viewing information as being stored or held for a period of time in a distinct structural storage system (sensory memory, short-term memory, or long-term memory), the information is viewed as passing through levels of a certain process. The processing may vary in depth from "shallow" (the processing of physical aspects) to "deep" (the processing of emotional aspects). The deeper the processing of the descriptive characteristics related to the information, the better the retention. Thus, short-term memory is just a lower level of processing and long-term memory is a deeper level of processing. This view is consistent with the biological concept of a memory trace referred to in the next paragraph.

## The Biology of Memory

Researchers have also studied memory from a biological approach. Some psychologists believe that as information is passed through the nervous system, a trace or mark is left, probably electrical in nature, which perishes quickly unless repeated or strengthened in some way until a chemical or structural change takes place. Once the chemical or structural change occurs the memory trace may be long lasting or relatively permanent. Thus, the more frequently the information is repeated and the deeper the processing, the more distinguishable and lasting the memory trace will be. Charles Morris (1979) compared the memory trace to a path taken through a forest. The path may be very faint and indistinguishable after only one or two walks over it (little repetition or shallow processing) and the path may be difficult to find again. However, after many walks (frequent repetition or deep processing) over the path, it may be easy to find again.

The representation of memory in the brain is often called an *engram*, a general term for a persistent structural change caused by stimulation of living neural tissue. One's brain is assumed to be packed with billions of engrams which are stored in different parts of the brain. The different senses involved in any one memory are thought to account for the storage in the different parts of the brain. Recent experiments with rats indicate that one form of memory, the location of objects, is localized in the hippocampus region of the brain (Olton, 1977).

Electrical activity in a nerve cell results in the production of several chemicals, including one commonly referred to as *RNA (ribonucleic acid)* which controls the production of protein molecules. Some theorists believe memory storage involves the creation of new chemical molecules in the brain. Studies have shown that learning produces a change in the RNA of specific cells (Hyden, 1969). Studies on planaria (flatworms) and rats have also shown that when RNA is transferred from an animal that has learned to respond in a particular way to a second animal, the second animal will learn to respond in that way more rapidly than the animals in a control group injected with RNA from an animal that has not learned to respond in that particular way (McConnell, 1974).

Some theorists propose that a change occurs at connections between brain cells (Hebb, 1949). Sensory information coming into the brain travels from one cell to the next until it makes a full round or circuit. When cued into, the circuit will be repeated (memory). When a structural change occurs, the circuit is relatively permanent and is called a *reverberating circuit*. One's brain may have billions of possible memory routes or circuits.

### Explanations of Forgetting

Various explanations have been given to explain forgetting of a specific, isolated fact. One explanation is the *trace decay theory* which proposes that with the passing of time the strength of the memory is weakened and, therefore, the memory itself is harder to remember. One may forget a business appointment that is made a month in advance if it is not strengthened by reminders (cued into and repeated).

The *interference theory* holds that the information gets mixed with other information and becomes harder to remember. Something previously learned may interfere with remembering something learned more recently (*proactive inhibition*), or something learned later may interfere with remembering something learned previously (*retroactive inhibition*). One may forget a business appointment because a number of events occurred immediately prior to or immediately after the appointment was made. Organizing and coding for storage of the appointment in long-term memory may have been lessened due to the processing of either previous or following events. Figure 7-3 outlines the experimental procedure for illustrating proactive and retroactive inhibition.

*Repression*, the psychoanalytic explanation for forgetting, is the unconscious blocking out of memories which may be unpleasant, emotionally disturbing, or in conflict with one's belief system. A business appointment may be forgotten because the person unconsciously did not want to keep the appointment. Psychological *amnesia* is the most extreme form of repression. A person's life may have been so frightening or miserable that all memory of personal events is blocked out. People suffering from psychological amnesia may not be able to recall who they are, where they work, anything about their family, or where they live; but they may be able to function on a job or be capable of functioning normally at the present and in the future.

The *reconstruction theory* proposes that sometimes events are not blocked out—only distorted. One may reconstruct an event as it is unconsciously desired to be, or the event may be reconstructed as it seems it should have been. Additional distortion may take place at the time of storage when the general idea is abstracted or summarized for storage. One does not store information passively by exact reproduction like a

|   | 1 | 2 | 3 |
|---|---|---|---|
| Experimental Group | Learn List A of nonsense syllables | Learn List B of nonsense syllables | Recall List B |
| Control Group | No learning activity | Learn List B of nonsense syllables | Recall List B |

**Proactive Inhibition**

|   | 1 | 2 | 3 |
|---|---|---|---|
| Experimental Group | Learn List A of nonsense syllables | Learn List B of nonsense syllables | Recall List A |
| Control Group | Learn List A of nonsense syllables | No learning activity | Recall List A |

**Retroactive Inhibition**

Figure 7-3    Experimental procedure for illustrating interference effects on recall. The experimental group usually does not recall as many nonsense syllables as the control group due to interference.

copy machine; rather one actively interprets information as it is received and stores the information as it is interpreted. As a result, memory may be incorrect because it was misinterpreted when stored. The boxed material on page 157 is an illustration of distorted reconstruction which explains some forgetting.

Sometimes an inability to retrieve an event or experience may simply be because a cue is not available to trigger the memory. One may forget a person's name and later remember it by going through the letters of the alphabet—the letter of the alphabet with which the name begins may serve as a cue for retrieval.

---

DISTORTED RECONSTRUCTION

Read the following list of words: bed, rest, awake, tired, dream, wake, night, eat, comfort, sound, slumber, snore. Close the book and reconstruct the list by writing down as many of the words you read as you possibly can without looking back at the list. Research indicates that the word "sleep" is included on the reconstructed list in more than half the cases. It seems sleep should have been there even though it was not (Deese, 1958). Including the word "sleep" when recalling the list is an example of distorted reconstruction which explains the forgetting of the exact words on the list.

---

Sometimes forgetting may have a physiological basis such as brain damage or some malfunctioning of the brain. Malfunctioning of the brain might be an explanation for a breakdown in the process of encoding, storage, or retrieval. A breakdown of any one of these could account for a failure to remember an event that had been experienced.

## Factors Influencing Memory

Memory is a function of many factors. Characteristics of the individual such as intellectual ability, motivation, anxiety, cognitive style, and use of imagery affect memory. Memory is also related to the characteristics of the material such as the degree of abstractness, the structure, and the association value. The procedure used in learning such as whether practice is massed or distributed, whether practice is by parts or by the whole, and whether practice is continued after learning occurs has been found to influence memory.

### Characteristics of the Individual

Factors within the individual who is doing the remembering affect what one remembers. Intellectual or mental ability and motivation (discussed in later chapters) have long been recognized as basic fundamental aspects of remembering what has been learned. Workers vary in their abilities to remember learned facts or behaviors that are related to the performance of a particular work task. Workers also have varying degrees of incentive (motivation) to remember. In addition, the ability to focus on certain aspects of the environment while ignoring other aspects of the environment varies among workers and is related to retention of an event. This ability was referred to earlier in this chapter as one's attention span, or the number of aspects of the environment that can be held in the short-term memory storage system. As noted, an average of seven items is typical, but for some workers nine or ten items or for others only four or five items may be held in short-term memory.

Anxiety is another factor that has been demonstrated to be important in remembering (Tobias, 1979). Some individuals have less anxiety than others, and some learn to reduce anxiety more than others by such methods as organizing effective programs of study and preparation. Sometimes the thought of learning something new and retaining it is so anxiety inducing that the person avoids the situation by not attempting it. If already in the situation, the person may escape by daydreaming, watching television, or engaging in social activities with friends. A little anxiety may enhance remembering by providing the motivation to prepare for later retrieval. However, extremely high levels of anxiety seem to interfere with remembering. The level of anxiety for maximum efficiency in remembering varies according to the nature of the task. Higher levels of anxiety interfere more with remembering a highly cognitive (thinking) or more complex task. The implication is that, for maximum performance, anxiety should be kept at an optimal level for each individual for each work task.

In recent years psychologists have become interested in *cognitive styles* which describe differences in the way individuals characteristically perceive events and draw inferences from them. One cognitive style that has been differentiated is the dimension of field independence-dependence. Field-independent individuals make perceptual judgments analytically and tend to disregard environmental information that may distort their judgment; whereas field-dependent individuals tend to make global judgments and are more influenced by the field or immediate environment of the stimulus being judged. In other words, distorted reconstruction may account for what is remembered more in some individuals than in others depending on whether the individual is more field-independent or more field-dependent. In a job situation, one manager may tend to perceive employee productivity more objectively than another manager and may disregard such environmental information as family problems, lack of educational opportunities, or financial needs which might distort the perception. Some unemployed persons may tend to be field-independent and perceive the unemployment rate more accurately than others who are field-dependent and whose perception is more influenced by their immediate environmental situation.

Memory of past events may be influenced by whether an individual tends to be a leveler or sharpener in cognitive style. Levelers tend to see new stimuli as very similar to those previously presented. Sharpeners tend to notice differences quickly and accurately between new stimuli and stimuli previously presented. Experimental studies have found sharpeners superior to levelers in recalling stories heard years earlier. Levelers are more likely to simplify the grammatical structure of verbal materials they have been asked to recall (Holzman & Gardner, 1960; Livant, 1962).

Another individual factor which influences memory is the degree to which one makes use of mental imagery. Before language was acquired, the environment was categorized in terms of mental images. Then with the use of language, imagery became less important; however, individuals vary in their use of imagery when encoding, storing, and retrieving. Stronger use of imagery is associated with better memory (Paivio, 1974). For example, when introduced to a new person, one might form an image of the name of the person. The name Rose Doe might be imaged as a rose bush growing out of a batch of dough on top of the person's head. The more bizarre or unusual the image, the more effectively it influences memory. One might remember a list of words by forming an image that chains the words together. Frog, magazine, elbow, missile, and photograph might be imaged as a frog with a magazine under its elbow standing by a missile having a photograph taken. Visualizing such an image should improve one's memory of the list.

### Characteristics of the Material

The degree of abstraction of the material to be remembered influences memory of it. Information that contains concrete concepts such as apple, chair, desk, or truck relies more on imagery than abstract concepts such as beauty, anxiety, or attitude. Concrete information is remembered better than abstract information. The difference is thought to be due to the stronger use of imagery (Paivio, 1974). A word with a high *imagery rating* is easier to remember. The imagery rating refers to the degree to which the word can bring to mind a concrete picture.

The meaningfulness of the information presented also has a profound effect on remembering it. When information is presented in terms of its relationship to other information already stored in one's memory, it is more meaningful. Knowing the "whole picture" and understanding how each element fits into it aids in forming a memory of it. An activity to illustrate this is contained in the boxed material on page 160.

The structure of the material—how easily it can be grouped or organized in some way—affects recall of the material. The amount of material to be remembered is also significant. To remember a list of ten bits of information requires about twice as much learning time as is required to remember a list of seven bits of information. Material that can be broken down and organized into smaller units can be remembered better.

---

### MEANINGFULNESS AFFECTS MEMORY

Look at the following sentence: "Idi du seth ema ter ialy est erd ay." Close the book and write the sentence. The sentence is gibberish, without meaning, and difficulty was probably experienced in recalling it. Now look at the following sentence: "I did use the material yesterday." Close the book and write the sentence. This sentence is the same as the first sentence except that the letters are grouped in such a way as to produce meaningful combinations. Much less difficulty was probably experienced in recalling the latter sentence.

---

The *association value* of the words in the content of the material affects remembrance of the material. The degree to which a word can bring to mind other words is referred to as the association value of the word. For some words the average person can think of 10 or 12 words in a minute that may be associated with them, while for other words only 6 or 8, 3 or 4, 1 or 2, or 0 words per minute may be associated with them by the average person. Words with a high association value are easier to remember than words with a low association value.

The content of material varies in the frequency with which the words are seen in print or used in speech. High-frequency words are remembered more easily than low-frequency words. Repetition is another factor in memory storage.

### Learning Procedures

Repetition is a factor in placing material in long-term memory storage, thus the procedures involved in repetition are also important. Practicing or repeating for short periods of time with rest periods intervening is called *distributed practice.* Doing all the practice or repetition from start to finish in one long, unbroken time interval is called *massed practice.* Usually distributed practice has been found to lead to superior retention for equal amounts of practice time for both verbal and sensorimotor learning (Ausubel & Youssef, 1965; Hintzman, 1974). The practice period should not be so brief that time is not allowed for repetition of a complete set of material; neither should the time between practice periods be so great that much of the learning from previous practices is forgotten (DiVesta & Thompson, 1970).

Whether one should learn material in small parts or tackle the whole thing at once is rather complex and has been studied extensively. Early research results tended to favor the whole method since the part method had the problem of putting the pieces together in a meaningful way. However, by using the part method, reinforcement for accomplishment of each part may be very effective. Some guidelines for deciding on learning by the whole or the part method for better retention in proportion to the amount of time spent in learning follow:

1. The more intelligent person can probably use the whole method more effectively.
2. The whole method is more effective if distributed practice, rather than massed practice, is used.
3. The effectiveness of the whole method increases with practice.
4. The whole method tends to be more effective for learning meaningful and highly organized material (McGeoch & Irion, 1952). However, the part method seems to become more preferable as the complexity of the material increases.

*Overlearning,* which refers to the continuation of practice or repetition beyond the point when the material has been learned, facilitates remembering (see Figure 7-4). Of course there is a limit to how much continued repetition will increase remembering. In order to remember a greater percentage of information, repetition of the material should be continued even after it has been learned.

*"Even though I know the details of the construction plans, I think I will go over this a few more times just to be sure I can remember them next week."*

Figure 7-4    Overlearning or continuing to repeat information after it can be repeated perfectly will increase retention of the material.

# Thinking

Thinking is the process by which one manipulates and combines the representations or symbols held in the mind for things or events that are physically absent. These representations or symbols may be in different forms, but the most important units of thought are motor representations, images, words, and concepts. Thinking is sometimes considered to be communication with one's self.

## *The Basic Units of Thought*

Thinking may involve motor representations, the reactivating of muscular patterns stored in the mind. For example, people who "talk" with their hands or move their lips while reading are using movement to help their thinking.

Imagery is believed to be a more efficient type of representation that is built up in the course of cognitive growth. Images held in the mind are not just visual. One may have an image of a sound, smell, taste, or touch. Stored images are used to evoke a previous experience. Research indicates that people mentally rotate images of geometric figures to determine whether they are alike or different (Shepard & Metzler, 1971). Such research suggests that an internal image corresponds directly to the physical stimulus. An image, however, may be stored in incomplete or distorted form, or it may be stored very vividly or only faintly. Only when one can construct language symbols, can representations go beyond imagery.

Language symbols or words represent transformations of thought according to a rule, abstraction, and inference. Although thinking can occur without language, most thought depends on language symbols because language allows the world to be encoded into symbols that are easily manipulated (see Figure 7-5). Since words do not resemble what they represent, they can be arranged in an infinite variety of ways to produce ideas.

Concepts, categories for representing or classifying environmental stimuli according to common characteristics, allow one to identify a new subject and guide one's action in a new situation. Concepts make it possible to generalize, discriminate, and abstract when thinking. Concepts vary in their level of abstraction. The concept of an apple is not as abstract as fruit or a hug as abstract as love. Concepts may be incomplete and not clearly defined. Words may be attached to concepts to become a symbol for the concept. The formation of concepts has a great impact on one's ability to solve problems.

Figure 7-5  Thinking relies heavily on language symbols.

### Problem Solving

Problem solving involves thinking and remembering. It is the application of past experience and presently available information. An individual in the world of work does a vast amount of problem solving each day. It may be as simple as figuring out how to open the office door or as complex as figuring out how to double the volume of business in the next year. A person has a problem to solve any time it is recognized that a gap exists between the way things are (the situation) and the way things ought to be (the goal).

**Steps in Problem Solving.** The first step in solving a problem is identifying or recognizing the problem. After the problem is identified, the second step is to define the problem. Facts about the problem have to be gathered to develop a reasonable definition. Concepts are used in defining the problem. For example, if the problem is how to open the door, one must have a concept of "open" and "door" and some facts about doors.

The third step in solving a problem is the "search" or the generating of a number of possible solutions, ideas, plans, or recommendations. With many alternative recommendations, one has more choices and a greater possibility of finding the most realistic and reasonable solution. This third step may involve either or both *convergent thinking* and *divergent thinking*. In convergent thinking one retrieves correct answers or previous solutions already stored in long-term memory. Thinking converges on the correct answer. Divergent thinking is the opposite in that new, unusual, or unheard-of solutions are sought. One uses imagination. Based on one's knowledge and experience, new answers are created. This may involve thinking at the subconscious level, similar to an incubation period, which may end with a seemingly sudden insight sometimes referred to as a "bright idea" (Figure 7-6).

The fourth step in problem solving may be referred to as anticipation or evaluation. This step involves thinking that mentally carries out the alternative recommendations before actually carrying out any. By doing this thinking, one may anticipate that some of the recommendations will create more problems than they resolve. The recommendation that is evaluated as the best alternative to accomplish the desired goal will be chosen. The fifth step involves the implementation or application of the chosen recommendation. This step should be followed by a sixth step—the reexamination of the problem at a later date to ensure that the applied actions are accomplishing the goals. The final or seventh step is to restudy the problem if the goals are not being accomplished and to make modifications.

**Factors Affecting Problem Solving.** A number of factors influence problem solving. One's short-term memory or attention span places limits on the number of combinations of problem-solving operations one can keep in one's consciousness simultaneously. All the facts, words, concepts, and procedures related to a problem cannot possibly be kept in mind simultaneously. Also, the amount of information stored in one's long-term memory and whether it is retrievable when needed to solve a problem are factors influencing problem solving.

The sets that a person has are also a factor. The concept of *set* refers to a habit of responding in a certain way because of experience. A set may serve as a cue for finding a solution to a problem or may be a hindrance in that it blinds one to seeing a more efficient solution (see Figure 7-7). A creative problem solver is more likely to use imagination while a conformist is more likely to rely on a set.

Functional fixedness is another way in which experience may affect problem solving. If an object has previously had a particular function, one may have difficulty thinking of another function for the object. For example, if one has had extensive experience using a hammer to drive nails, recognizing that a hammer may be used as a paperweight may be difficult.

Figure 7-6    Divergent thinking may lead to a seemingly sudden insight for solving a problem.

## *Decision Making*

A decision is a choice between two or more alternatives. The process of decision making involves thinking. One is constantly faced with making decisions in problem solving in one's work life as well as one's personal life (see Figure 7-8). Usually a number of possible solutions can

*"This is the way I've solved problems like this one for the last 20 years, and I'm not going to try anything new."*

Figure 7-7    A set or habit of responding in a certain way to similar problems may aid or hinder problem solving.

be generated. In most instances of decision making, a problem is given for which a decision must be made concerning which possible solution to implement.

The effectiveness of a decision may depend on a number of factors. One factor, for example, may be whether the decision maker had access to relevant, up-to-date information. Another factor may be the personality of the decision maker. A person with a well-balanced personality who is not overly rigid, overly cautious, or overly risk-taking would be more likely to make more effective decisions.

One's emotions and feelings influence the decision-making process. A decision to continue to manufacture an unprofitable product may be based on sentimentality rather than rationality. One's feelings may influence the decision without the decision maker's awareness of the influence. Sometimes how one believes others will react to the decision affects the choice. Rationality is an ideal that one should strive for in making effective decisions.

The time allotment for making the decision may be a factor also. Usually people think more clearly when they are not rushed. In performing a job, one does not always have a great amount of time to spend

*"My decision is to follow through with Plan B rather than Plan A."*

Figure 7-8    Making decisions
is a part of many jobs.

in analyzing the alternatives for each decision that must be made. However, one should attempt to gather as much useful information as possible during the time available before making a decision. More time may be allowed for significant decisions—those decisions that affect more people or have a greater effect on the profits of the business. The more significant the decision, the more serious the consideration given to each alternative should be. One method of evaluating the alternatives would be to list each alternative on a separate sheet of paper and then list side by side the disadvantages and advantages for each alternative. The advantages may be listed on the left and the disadvantages on the right. One can then see which alternative has more advantages than disadvantages. Sometimes a disadvantage might be serious enough to outweigh several advantages or vice versa.

Some decisions lead to highly favorable outcomes, while some lead to highly undesirable outcomes either economically or personally. One must consider personal satisfaction as well as economics when evaluating the outcomes of a decision. Most of the time people tend to make decisions that lead only to a minimum standard of satisfaction. Most decisions are made just to take care of the concern in an acceptable manner, rather than to lead to a big breakthrough (DuBrin, 1980).

Some forms of thought such as daydreaming and dreaming at night, often called associative thinking, are not directed toward a goal and are not subject to problem-solving operations which include decision making.

## SUMMARY

1. The first memory studies, conducted by Ebbinghaus in 1885, consisted of measuring retention levels of nonsense syllables by recall, recognition, and relearning. Time elapsed, position in the list, and method of measuring retention were found to influence the percentage of retention.

2. Cognitive psychologists view memory as an activity consisting of encoding, storage, and retrieval processes.

3. The structural view of memory storage proposes three types or levels of storage systems—sensory registers, short-term memory, and long-term memory; whereas the process view of memory storage defines storage as a continuous memory trace with varying degrees of distinguishability based on depth of processing.

4. Memory at the sensory level is unconscious and consists of impressions made on the senses which are held onto for only an extremely brief time. The capacity of memory storage, however, is large.

5. Short-term memory consists of what is held in consciousness; this system has small storage capacity. Only about seven items on the average can be stored in consciousness simultaneously and only very briefly without repetition.

6. Long-term memory has a vast capacity since it is a relatively permanent storage system of all one's knowledge.

7. The amount of information that can be retrieved from long-term memory and brought into short-term memory is less than the amount that is stored in long-term memory. Retrieval of such information depends on cues to find it and on the method of organization used when the information was stored.

8. Biological theories of memory propose that permanent structural changes in the connections between brain cells forming reverberating circuits and in the RNA of specific cells are responsible for memory. The physical representation of a memory is referred to as an engram.

9. Explanations for forgetting include decay of the memory trace, interference (proactive and retroactive inhibition), repression, reconstruction, unavailable cues, and malfunctioning of the brain.

10. Factors within the individual such as intelligence, motivation, attention span, anxiety, cognitive style, and use of imagery influence memory.

11. Characteristics of the material to be remembered such as the degree of abstraction, meaningfulness, grouping ability, and the association value and frequency rating of the words also influence memory.

12. Procedures used during the learning process such as massed versus distributed practice, part versus whole practice, and overlearning influence memory.

13. Thinking is the process by which one manipulates and combines mental representations or symbols for things or events that are physically absent.

14. The representations or symbols—basic units of thought—may be in the form of motor representations, images, words, and concepts.

15. A person has a problem to solve any time it is recognized that a gap exists between the way things are (the situation) and the way things ought to be (the goal).

16. Solving a problem may be as simple as opening a closed door or as complex as doubling the volume of business.

17. The steps in solving a problem are to identify the problem, define the problem, search for possible solutions, evaluate the alternatives, choose a solution and apply the chosen action. Later, the problem should be reexamined and modifications made if the goals are not being accomplished.

18. Memory, retrievable information and attention span; sets or habits of responding in a certain way; and functional fixedness, a set for a particular function of an object affect one's problem-solving ability.

19. One is constantly faced with making a choice between two or more alternatives—a process that is referred to as decision making.

20. The effectiveness of decision making may be influenced by the availability of up-to-date and relevant information, by whether one has a well-balanced personality, by emotions and feelings, and by whether there is time pressure.

21. Most of the time people make decisions that lead only to a minimum standard of satisfaction rather than to a big breakthrough.

## SUGGESTIONS FOR FURTHER READING

Adams, J. L. *Conceptual blockbusting.* San Francisco: Freeman, 1975.

This book contains suggestions that may be useful in helping individuals improve their problem-solving abilities.

Anderson, J. R. *Language, memory, and thought.* Hillsdale, N. J.: Erlbaum, 1976.

An integrated account of language and memory is included in this book.

Harrison, E. F. *The managerial decision-making process.* Boston: Houghton Mifflin, 1974.

This book is a recent and general treatment of decision making.

Higbee, K. L. *Your memory: How it works and how to improve it.* Englewood Cliffs, N. J.: Prentice-Hall, 1977.

A practical book that describes various mnemonic strategies and explains how they work.

Johnson, D. M. *A systematic introduction to the psychology of thinking.* New York: Harper & Row, 1972.

This book provides a survey of the literature on concept formation, problem solving, and judgment, along with some speculations about development.

Klatzky, R. L. *Human memory: Structures and processes.* San Francisco: Freeman, 1975.

Memory is discussed in this book as a system continuously active in receiving, modifying, storing, and retrieving information. Background information is not necessary for comprehension.

Lorayne, H., & Lucas, J. *The memory book.* New York: Stein and Day, 1974.

A practical book to help one read faster and remember what is read. Memory techniques are suggested for remembering things in everyday life such as shopping lists, speeches, or long numbers.

Lorayne, H. *Good memory—successful student.* New York: Stein and Day, 1976.

This book is a guide to remembering what is learned. A memory system is presented to aid in remembering the material of any course, with special instructions for particular subject areas.

MacCrimmon, K. R., & Taylor, R. N. Decision making and problem solving. In Marvin D. Dunnette (Ed.), *Handbook of industrial and organizational psychology.* Chicago: Rand McNally College Publishing Company, 1976.

Decision making and problem solving are examined in the form of strategies rather than in the traditional format. Strategies available to the decision maker in dealing with environments characterized by uncertainty, complexity, and conflict are identified. Types of decision problems and characteristics of decision makers which influence the use of the strategies are also discussed.

Mayer, R. E. *Thinking and problem solving: An introduction to human cognition and learning.* Glenview, Ill.: Scott, Foresman, 1977.

Many examples of reasoning and various forms of human problem solving are included in this book which also contains material on computer simulation of cognitive processes.

McConnell, J. V. *Understanding human behavior.* New York: Holt, Rinehart and Winston, 1974.

This is an excellent presentation of the latest research concerned with the physiology of memory. It is written at a reading level for the beginning psychology student.

Newell, A., & Simon, H. A. *Human problem solving.* Englewood Cliffs, N.J.: Prentice-Hall, 1972.

This book discusses computer simulation models of thinking.

Williams, J. C. *Human behavior in organizations.* Cincinnati: South-Western Publishing Company, 1978.

Chapter 14, "Managerial Decision Making: Nature and Process," is an excellent presentation of decision making that enhances an understanding of the process.

# I Chapter 8
# Intelligence

**M**ental or intellectual abilities or aptitudes, the differences in these among people, and the implications of these differences for achievements or outcomes in life are examined in this chapter. Some activities call for nonintellectual abilities such as hammering a nail into a board which calls for eye-hand coordination. Other jobs such as speech making or decision making require intellectual abilities. (See Figure 8-1.) In many higher level jobs both nonintellectual and intellectual abilities may be helpful. For example, the speaker may also be able to type the speeches, or a company president who makes policy decisions may also be able to elevate the swivel chair or paint a wall in the office. The primary focus in this chapter is on mental or intellectual abilities referred to as intelligence. First, an attempt will be made to define intelligence. Then, the relationship of intelligence to perception and creativity will be clarified. The theories and determinants of intelligence will be examined, and a review of the ways psychologists measure intelligence through testing will be presented. Finally, the relationship of intelligence to occupational success and personnel selection will be discussed.

## The Concept of Intelligence

Intellectual abilities, as well as other human abilities, are important for performing work activities; however, intelligence is not easy to define. Psychologists disagree on what intelligence means, and they disagree in their views of how one acquires intelligence. Since intelligence is a construct—it is not a pure characteristic and includes a variety of specialized abilities—it can be defined in many different ways.

### Intelligence vs. Achievement

**Achievement.** Psychologists generally distinguish between achievement and intelligence. *Achievement* is what a person has learned, the knowledge and skills that have been acquired through experience. Achievement presupposes an acquaintance with a specific body of material. For example, achievement in the area of calculus requires some mathematical knowledge, and achievement in the area of air conditioning repair and installation requires knowledge of those systems and equipment. Intelligence may include the ability to learn but does not require knowledge as learned in a particular course of study.

Figure 8-1　Many activities, such as riding a bicycle, require nonintellectual skills, while other activities, such as forming a strategy for a chess game, require intellectual abilities.

**Aptitude and Ability.** The terms aptitude and ability are often used interchangeably since the ideas are related; however, the ideas are not identical. *Aptitude* is thought of as an innate or natural capacity for performing or learning to perform some task such as repairing machinery (mechanical aptitude) or carrying out some mathematical function as in accounting (numerical aptitude). An *ability* is a current capability to learn that is based on both aptitude and experience. For example, a woman might have an aptitude for rifle shooting because of excellent vision and a steady hand. The ability, however, to shoot a rifle may only be present if enough experience with rifles has occurred so that she knows how to hold the rifle, how to load the rifle, and that pulling the trigger causes the rifle to fire. The ability to learn something includes not only the aptitude but prior knowledge or experience.

## Definitions of Intelligence

**Ability to Adapt.** Jean Piaget (1952), the Swiss child psychologist who spent many years researching intellectual development, defined intelligence as the ability to adapt to the environment and to new situations—to think and act in adaptive ways. Piaget theorized that intellectual development occurs through a sequence of stages. The capability to think in a particular way develops as one interacts with the environment. The order of the stages remains constant; however, the rate of progression through the stages varies for different individuals.

**Ability to Solve Problems.** A common definition of intelligence is the "degree of availability of one's experiences for the solution of immediate problems and the anticipation of new ones" (Hepner, 1973, p. 336). Thus, the term intelligence is often used to refer to problem-solving abilities. In general, people with higher intellectual abilities are more likely to identify problems and make good decisions than those of lesser intelligence.

**Ability to Learn.** Some psychologists think of intelligence as the aptitude for general learning. People who can understand instructions and basic principles and can reason and make better judgments are considered to be more intelligent. People who are more intelligent generally are found to be better in academic studies.

**Ability to Understand and Cope.** David Wechsler (1975) defined intelligence as the "capacity of an individual to understand the world around him and his resourcefulness to cope with its challenges" (p. 139). To Wechsler, intelligence involves the ability to exhibit effective behavior as well as to build an inner representation of the world—thinking and performing.

**Ability to Respond.** Behaviorally-oriented psychologists think of intelligence in terms of the types of responses available to an individual. As was explained in Chapter 1, the behaviorists eliminated the structure and functioning of the mind from the concern of psychology because the mind could not be observed directly. However, behavior or responses could be observed directly and could provide an objective, empirical, and scientific approach to the study of intelligence. Since behaviorists do not make assumptions about mental processes or mental abilities, they define intelligence as the responses or behaviors the person is capable of making.

**Ability to Perceive.** Combs and Snygg (1959) feel that intelligence is really the effectiveness of *perception* or perceptual skills—the process of assembling sensations into a meaningful and usable mental representation of the world. Perception determines the way the world looks, feels, smells, tastes, or sounds. Perception provides one's immediate experience of the world. Since behavior and thinking depend on one's perceptions of the world, intelligence is related to how adequate and varied a person's perceptions are. Intelligence then is really an individual's ability to adequately perceive the environment.

## Perception

The view that intelligence is related to perception calls for an understanding of perception and an understanding that intelligence may be changed through changing perceptions—that intelligence is not a fixed ability.

### The Concept of Perception

Perception is an active process, not just a passive reception of information directly from the outside world. In a broad sense, perception is the construction of meaning (Pylyshyn, 1973). An individual constructs a three-dimensional world filled with objects and events referred to as reality. Reality is constructed from the physical energy in the environment that is transformed at the sensory level and transferred to the brain where memory of previous constructions of reality, motivations, and expectations influence the construction. Perception is like guessing or hypothesizing about what is out there in the world. Perception is a process of building on sensation; one organizes and interprets the raw information or evidence that is received through the senses. Figure 8-2 demonstrates how two different realities may be perceived from the same physical information. This phenomenon was discovered in 1832 by the Swiss mineralogist L. A. Necker. The perception of a cube from the flat lines printed on a flat piece of paper is an illustration of how perceptions are constructed.

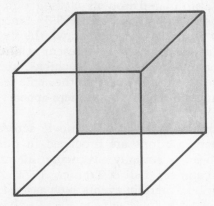

Figure 8-2 The Necker
cube. The shaded surface can appear
as either the top surface or the back
surface of a transparent cube.

In the process of perception, incomplete or ambiguous sensory information may be filled in and smoothed over; sensory information may be changed by the addition of information from memory; parts of sensory information may be amplified or may recede into the background; or sensory information may be noted and attended to or ignored. Meaning may be assigned to the sensory information and judgments and interpretations made.

## The Role of Experience and Heredity

Although both past experience and heredity play a significant role in perception, the extent of the effect of heredity and environmental experience is not agreed upon by all psychologists. The Nativist philosophers of the seventeenth and eighteenth centuries believed that one's perceptual ability is innate, that is inborn or inherited. However, the Empiricists insisted that one's perceptions come about through experience. Today, psychologists believe that perception is an integration of heredity and experience.

**Research Supporting Innate Perception.** Since the organization of some neural impulses seems to be predetermined by heredity, some perceptual constructions such as perception of space, events, and form are apparently innate. They appear to be built into the nervous system. A newborn when ten minutes old consistently turned its eyes in the direction of a clicking sound (Wertheimer, 1961) which illustrates that the ability to organize sensory information in such a way as to locate a sound in space is present at birth. Most crawling infants refuse to crawl across a glass surface where a simulated drop-off or *visual cliff* appears even when the mother beckons to them. (See Figure 8-3.) Since babies cannot be tested on the visual cliff until they can crawl, the findings are inconclusive as to whether depth perception is present at birth. However, when animals that are mobile at birth such as chicks, kids, and lambs were tested as soon as they were able to stand, the same results were found as those found with human babies. Thus, there appears to be some innate perception of space.

When a shadow is projected on a movie screen and then rapidly magnified, avoidance reactions are produced in humans and animals although no real object is actually advancing. Infants as young as two weeks of age stiffen and cry (Ball & Tronick, 1971). Apparently there is some innate perception of certain events such as the impending collision of an object in space with one's self.

Figure 8-3    An infant on the visual cliff refuses to crawl across the apparent drop-off which suggests that infants have depth perception.

When a three-day-old infant is presented with a triangle or some other simple form, photographs of the infant's corneas show that the eyes tend to orient toward the vertices and edges—the features of the pattern that define it (Salapatek, 1975). Also, infants as young as four days have a tendency to look at forms that resemble a human face in preference to others, which is thought to be based on a preference for curved rather than straight contours (Fantz, 1961). Thus, visual form perception also seems to be present to some extent at birth. Perceptual constructions that are already present at birth and are not a result of experience probably have survival value. They are important in the development of responses for self protection, in the development of intelligence, and in the development of attachment to other humans—all of which are essential for survival.

**Research Supporting Learned Perception.** Others have demonstrated that one's experience in the environment affects the development of perception. One psychologist (I. Kohler, 1962) had people wear goggles that inverted the visual world. Although very clumsy at the beginning, by the end of a month, they could generally perform visual motor tasks such as bicycling or fencing as well as before. When the goggles were removed, they were clumsy again and had to relearn motor behaviors. While wearing prisms that displaced the visual world to one side, human subjects who walked a route for several hours, compared to those who were pushed over the same route in wheelchairs, showed marked improvement on simple visual motor tasks involving locations of visual targets (Held & Freedman, 1963). Thus, motor activity and movement appear to be crucial in perceptual learning.

Studies of adults whose vision was restored by surgery after being blind from birth indicated that the patients could not identify simple, familiar objects by sight until they had several weeks of training. They could, however, distinguish figure from background (Senden, 1960). This suggests that one's perceptions develop gradually beginning with an innate perceptual construction. The perceptual construction becomes more accurate and more detailed with learning.

Segall, Campbell, and Herskovits (1966) found that people from different cultures have different perceptions. African tribespeople were not fooled by the Müller-Lyer illusion (see Figure 8-5) as were people from western cultures. The reason is believed to be because Westerners live in a world filled with angular shapes which provides many experiences in perceiving angular shapes; therefore, Westerners have a set or expectation which influences their perceptions that the African tribespeople do not have.

Studies of perception consistently show that environmental experience is essential to perceptual development. Heredity seems to provide the prewired organization of the sensory receptors, the brain, and the muscles. However, one must have sensory input or experience and must respond physically to it; activity and movement are essential. Perception is sensory-motor integration; it is the development of appropriate responses to incoming sensory messages.

### The Perceptual Systems

**Patterning.** Perception is organized along principles called the laws or rules of perceptual organization by the Gestalt psychologists. These principles seem to be the bases for *patterning* which permits rapid interpretations of sensory input so that one can act quickly on minimum information. Patterning puts together large amounts of information quickly and integrates the elements into meaningful wholes. The processes involved are referred to as *perceptual organization.* The principle of *figure-ground relationship* states that geometrical patterns are always organized as a figure against a background and appear to have a contour and boundary. Other basic grouping principles are as follows. Parts seem separate or grouped together depending on how close together they are, or their *proximity*, and how much alike they are, or their *similarity*. The principle of *continuity* states that continuous contours are grouped together and abruptly changing ones are disregarded. Missing pieces of a figure are automatically filled in according to the principle of closure. *Common fate* explains the tendency to perceive objects as a single whole if they move together. Figure 8-4 illustrates some of these principles.

**Stabilizing.** Stabilizing processes seem to make possible dependable interpretations of sensory input under different environmental conditions and are referred to as *constancy principles.* Stabilizing provides a standard, dependable way of interpreting events. Perception of size, shape, color, and brightness are all affected by constancy principles. The constancy principles which are interpretative rules for judging occurrences involve a decision to stabilize the world of moving, changing objects rather than to follow the movements. The interpretation of motion, contour, and texture are used to judge size, shape, distance, depth, and location. Although the actual size and shape of the image of an object on the retina of the eye changes with its distance from the eye and its movement to another position, the object is perceived as remaining the same size and shape. The actual change in size of the retinal image is perceived as distance.

**Illusions.** The patterning and stabilizing principles interact to interpret the world, and they operate so reliably that they sometimes misinterpret or produce an illusion. Figures 8-5 and 8-6 are examples of constancy illusions. Constancy illusions are products of experience. Interpretations or judgments of the actual sensory input are at fault, not the senses, when the perception is distorted and fails to correspond to reality.

Patterning principles produce the illusion of movement that everyone experiences when watching a motion picture. This illusion depends

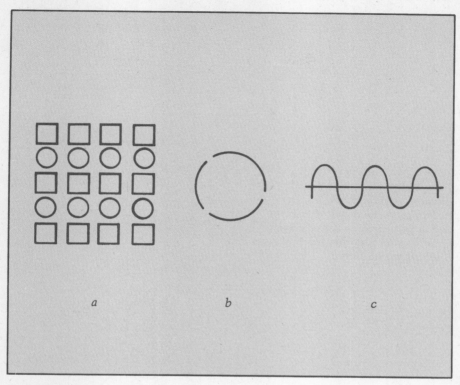

Figure 8-4    Grouping principles. The principle of similarity is illustrated by the fact that a person may perceive example *a* as horizontal rows of circles and horizontal rows of squares. Or a person may perceive example *a* as vertical columns of alternating squares and circles according to the principle of proximity. Example *b* is perceived by most people as a circle rather than three separate arcs, thus illustrating the principle of closure. People that see a wavy line and a straight line in example *c* are observing that figure according to the principle of continuity.

on the principle of closure—the blank spaces between the still pictures are filled in—and the principle of proximity—the still pictures are flashed rapidly enough that vision persists and is not switched off.

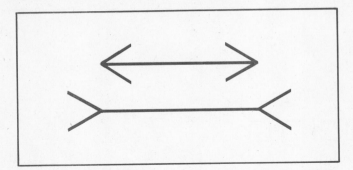

Figure 8-5    The Müller-Lyer
illusion. Although the length of the
two lines is the same, the lower
one is perceived as being longer.
This illusion was devised by Franz
Müller-Lyer in 1889.

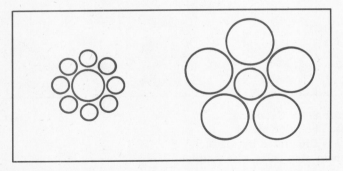

Figure 8-6    The Ebbinghaus
illusion. The inner circles are the
same size although the one on the
left is perceived as being larger.

**Perceptual Sets.** Perceptual expectancies called *perceptual sets* are created from combinations of one's prior experiences, what attracts one's attention, suggestions, and motivations. People see what they expect to see. These expectancies prepare a person to perceive or misperceive in a particular way. For instance, when proofreading, an error may not be seen due to a perceptual set.

**Malfunctions.** Sometimes one's perception is so inappropriate that it is said to be malfunctioning. Perceptual malfunctioning may be related to neurological damage or genetically determined brain dysfunctions, prolonged sensory deprivation, or chemical changes in the body affecting the nervous system. Drug intake or extreme nutritional deficiency may produce such chemical changes.

**Perceptual Learning.** *Perceptual learning* is a type of cognitive learning that has been defined by Eleanor Gibson (1969) as "an increase in the ability to extract information from the environment as a result of experience or practice with the stimulation coming from it" (p. 3). Focusing attention is important in perceptual learning. Skill in many occupations is based on the ability to perceive slight discriminations in sensory information. People who are trained can perceive distinctions that untrained people cannot. For example, a trained person may be able to distinguish the calls of birds, or sounds of motors, or textures of rocks. Perceptual learning usually comes from experience rather than from books.

**Feature Analysis.** One theoretical explanation of perception called *feature analysis* explains perception as an active, hypothesis-testing process. This theory emphasizes the role of context and experience and the interaction with the fixed, inherent structure of the nervous system. In perception, the person seems to abstract features of the signal or neural impulse and compare them with patterns stored in long-term memory. The information or abstracted features seems to pass through a series of stages wherein particular features are compared at each stage. At the first stage, the features of the incoming neural impulses are recorded. The next stage focuses on specific features of the signal or pattern of neural impulses such as lines, curves, or angles. The third stage focuses on the pattern of the features rather than the individual features. The next stage compares the pattern with the patterns stored in long-term memory and recognition of the stimulus occurs. In the last stage, special features of the pattern are compared with special features of stored patterns which are similar. This is a high-level task which enables a person to discriminate between patterns that are very similar.

## Person Perception

Psychologists have begun investigating a person's perception of other people which is referred to as *person perception*. Differences in relationships that exist among people at work are often related to perception. Making inferences rather than depending on facts sometimes causes people to make erroneous judgments which result in distorted perceptions of others.

**Halo Effect and Logical Error.** The *halo effect* is one example of distorted perception of others. In the halo effect, a favorable impression of an individual created by one characteristic spreads to other characteristics so that virtually everything the individual does is judged in a favorable light. When the halo effect occurs, the error is in assuming the presence of many positive traits from the existence of one favorable trait.

*Logical error* is the tendency to see different traits as belonging together when they logically do not. A person may be assumed to have a certain trait or traits because of a particular characteristic the person does have, or because of the person's relationship with another person, or because of the person's physical attractiveness. A person may be perceived as honest because he or she is physically attractive or dishonest because he or she is not physically attractive. A person may be assumed to be honest because he or she is a friend of an acquaintance who is an honest person. Or a person may be assumed to be a liar because he or she steals.

**The Influence of Set.** The influence of set, or expectation, based on prior information, may shape not only first impressions, but future interactions with a person. Just as a stereotype of a group of people may be formulated, a stereotype may be developed that can be applied to a single person. Stereotypes act as cognitive shortcuts which may produce selective bias in information processing and storing. They cause one to see only the evidence which fits the stereotype and to ignore evidence which is contrary to the stereotype. The *Pygmalion effect* is the tendency of an individual to act, perhaps unconsciously, in such a manner as to ensure the expected perception. For example, if a supervisor expects employees to be unproductive, they will be unproductive; and if the supervisor expects the employees to be highly productive, they will be—at least as perceived by the supervisor.

People also have a tendency to be evaluative and to categorize the traits used to describe others as generally good or bad. According to the principle of perceptual constancy, people are prone to perceive the behavior of others as more consistent than is actually true.

## Creativity

The view that intelligence is related to problem solving calls for an understanding of creativity, which is an important aspect of problem solving.

### The Concept of Creativity

**Definition.** Creativity may be thought of as the ability to produce original and worthwhile solutions to problems. The problems may be large, medium, or small. Creativity may arise in solving problems in one's daily life both on and off the job, as well as in trying to solve artistic or scientific problems. Creativity is the ability to respond uniquely and appropriately. Everyone is creative, but people vary in the extent to which they are creative.

**Divergent vs. Convergent Thinking.** Although some people have viewed intelligence and creativity as synonymous because both involve cognition or thought, others believe they are not synonymous. Some research indicates that creativity requires divergent thinking rather than convergent thinking (Guilford & Hoepfner, 1971). In convergent thinking, thought is limited to present facts and applies to questions that have one correct answer. In divergent thinking, many possible combinations of existing elements may be generated to construct new answers. Convergent thinking is the following of accepted patterns of thought, while divergent thinking is unique and diverges from customary thought patterns.

**Creativity in Problem Solving.** Problem solving usually includes both divergent and convergent thinking. First, the individual's thoughts diverge to recall possible solutions or generate new possible solutions (divergent thinking). Then, one's knowledge of facts and rules of logic are used to converge on the most appropriate solution (convergent thinking). People often alternate between divergent and convergent thinking in solving difficult problems. When a solution is discarded, it may become necessary to think of a new solution. Divergent thinking is associated with creativity and originality.

**Intelligence and Creativity.** Most measures of intelligence emphasize only convergent thinking; therefore, separate measures of creativity have been devised. Typically, intelligence test questions require the individual to engage in convergent thinking in order to focus on the correct answer—a unique answer may be scored as an incorrect response. Tests of creativity are designed to determine how flexible, fluent, and original one's thinking can be. Some psychologists believe that both convergent and divergent thinking are factors of intelligence (Guilford & Hoepfner, 1971).

Research has shown that as a whole, people with higher intelligence measures tend to have higher measures of creativity, and people with lower measures of intelligence tend to have lower measures of creativity. However, this trend is not true at the upper end of the distribution. Persons who have high measures of intelligence do not necessarily have high measures of creativity (Crockenberg, 1972). Often people who have only moderate measures of intelligence are highly creative.

**Stages in the Creative Process.** A sequence of stages appears as a common pattern in the process of generating a unique and appropriate solution to a problem. The first stage is preparation, during which time a person acquires all possible information that might relate to a problem. The second stage, called the *incubation stage,* consists of the time during which the information that has been acquired is absorbed and assimilated. This stage appears to be inactive and unproductive; no conscious attention is given to the problem. But undoubtedly there is a lot of unconscious mental activity. Suddenly and unexpectedly one may have insight into the problem resulting in the conception of an idea that seems to be a solution. This is referred to as the *illumination stage*. A final and very important stage is verification of the idea by mentally or experimentally trying it out. Sometimes people get so excited during the illumination stage that they act immediately without going through the final stage.

### Expression of Creativity

**Conditions That Enhance Creativity.** Whether the ability to be creative and engage in divergent thinking is innate or learned has been a question considered by psychologists. Eran Zaidel (1976) believes that up until approximately the time a child begins school or kindergarten, the two hemispheres of the brain are about equal in their abilities. Then with the development of language ability in the left hemisphere, the right hemisphere seems to take on creative and nonlogical abilities. During creative or divergent thinking, a person's thoughts seem to leave the world of logic and reason (Martindale, 1978).

Research has shown that environmental conditions may have an effect on creativity. Carl Rogers (1961) described three inner conditions (conditions within the person) and three outer conditions (conditions in the person's environment) that tend to foster creativity. Holland (1981) summarized these conditions described by Rogers as follows:

> The inner conditions fostering creativity are openness to experience, internal standards, and the ability to "toy" with ideas. A person who is open to experience is sensitive to things as they really are and does not jump to conclusions until all evidence is in. A person with internal standards strives to satisfy personal goals and expectations rather than someone else's. A person with internal standards decides what is good or bad on the basis of an internal standard of evaluation rather than on the basis of external standards established by others. A person with the ability to "toy" with ideas enjoys exploring new combinations of concepts and can see problems in fresh ways.

> The outer conditions fostering creativity are unconditional acceptance, absence of external evaluation, and empathetic understanding. Unconditional acceptance fosters creativity; people who are valued by those around them and accepted without reservations are more likely to be creative. The absence of external evaluation fosters creativity by permitting people to develop their own internal standards. Empathetic understanding fosters creativity; when people are truly understood by those around them, they are encouraged

to be fully themselves. These conditions together provide the optimum climate for creativity (p. 373).

**Creativity in Organizations.** In organizations and industry, overcontrol tends to reduce the expression of creativity on the job. Often managers set up rigid systems, job procedures and other means of control to the extent that employees are not encouraged to be creative. Conditions that promote conformity usually interfere with the expression of creativity. A person may be creative, however, without being a deliberate nonconformist. The boxed material which follows indicates some characteristics of creative organizations.

Psychologically unhealthy employees are not as creative. If a person is preoccupied with fear of punishment or anxieties, fear of rejection (overly concerned with the impression that is being made on others), or has feelings of insecurity (overly concerned with other's opinions of one's self), creativity will be inhibited.

---

CHARACTERISTICS OF CREATIVE ORGANIZATIONS

1. A trustful management that does not overcontrol people.
2. Open channels of communication among members of the organization; a minimum of secrecy.
3. Considerable contact and communication between outsiders and the organization.
4. Large variety of personality types.
5. Willing to accept change, but not enamored with change for its own sake.
6. Enjoyment in experimenting with new ideas.
7. Little fear of the consequences of making a mistake.
8. Selects people and promotes them primarily on the basis of merit.
9. Uses techniques for encouraging ideas, such as suggestion systems and brainstorming.
10. Sufficient financial, managerial, human, and time resources to accomplish its goals (DuBrin, 1980, p. 131).

---

# Views of Intelligence

Different theorists have different ideas of what intelligence is. Theorists also disagree about the impact of environmental experience and heredity as determinants of one's intelligence. Some of the views of intelligence will be discussed in the following sections on theories of intelligence and on research that has led to conclusions concerning the determinants of intelligence.

## Theories

The question has been debated for years as to whether intelligence is unified into a single general trait, or whether intelligence is composed of a group or cluster of abilities, or whether one's intelligence consists of many separate and independent abilities.

**Spearman's g Factor Theory.** In 1904, Charles Spearman reasoned that because of high positive correlations between scores on such items as mathematical ability, mechanical ability, etc., there must be a general level of intelligence responsible for the relationship. He called this general factor g. He further reasoned that this general intelligence is manifested in specific tasks which require specific abilities. He called the specific factors s. Most measures of intelligence that produce a single score are built around this theory of a general intelligence.

**Thurstone's Primary Mental Abilities.** In 1938, L. L. Thurstone identified seven primary mental abilities. This theory held that intelligence consists of seven abilities: numerical ability, word fluency, verbal meaning, memory, reasoning, spatial relations, and perceptual speed. The measure of intelligence based on this view is composed of tests measuring each of these abilities. One's intelligence score is then derived from a composite or average of these tests.

**Guilford's Structure of Intellect.** In 1961, J. P. Guilford developed a model for the structure of human intellect that is three-dimensional and provides for 120 independent factors in intelligence. Guilford (1967) claims there is no evidence for a general factor of intelligence. Guilford's model (see Figure 8-7) proposes that one dimension consists of five kinds of operations (convergent thinking, divergent thinking, memory, evaluation, and cognition); another dimension consists of four kinds of content such as semantic (verbal) or symbolic (nonverbal) used in intellectual operations; and a third dimension consists of products or outcomes of the operations such as relations, units, or classes. Each of the 120 factors represents a unique intellectual ability. Guilford has devised tests to measure many of the 120 factors for an individual.

**Cattell's Fluid and Crystallized Intelligence.** Raymond B. Cattell (1971) proposed that there are two major theoretical components of intelligence. *Crystallized intelligence* reflects what one has learned through experience. It reflects much more of one's cultural exposure and formal education and is composed primarily of knowledge and skills. It is the summation of all the particular perceptual skills acquired in specific fields. *Fluid intelligence* is a general perceptual capacity that is more dependent on the physiological functioning of one's brain. It is determined more by an individual's genetic endowment. These two components of intelligence are usually correlated because a person's crystallized intelligence depends on fluid intelligence, along with experience, years of formal education, and motivation. Fluid intelligence is believed to be

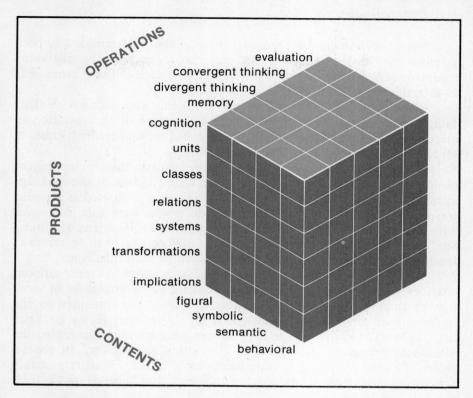

Figure 8-7    Model of
Guilford's structure of intellect.
Each cell of the cube is
representative of an independent
intellectual ability.

fully developed by about ten years of age and to begin to decline after age
20; crystallized intelligence is believed to be able to increase for many
years even after the end of formal schooling.

**Sternberg's Information-Processing Theory.** Recently, research has
shifted from abilities to information processing. Of primary concern is
what happens to the information from the time the problem is perceived
until a response is made. Robert Sternberg (1979) found that people with
higher intelligence take longer on encoding, the first step of information
processing, than do people with lower intelligence. By more careful encoding, they can then do the later steps more quickly and efficiently.
According to Sternberg's view, the general factor of intelligence proposed
by Spearman may refer to people's abilities to realize ahead of time the
type of problem to be faced and recognize that careful encoding is necessary.

## Determinants

Most psychologists believe that intelligence is determined by both heredity and environmental experience; however, there is still some confusion and controversy over the impact that each of these factors has in determining one's degree of intelligence.

Based on research with genetically identical twins, along with other data, it has been estimated that 40 to 60 percent of the variation in measures of intelligence of people is accounted for by heredity (Rubin & McNeil, 1981).

The importance of environmental experience on the development of intelligence was demonstrated by research with children in an orphanage in Iowa (Skeels, 1966). Ten orphans who had been evaluated as retarded were placed in a building with retarded adults who were able to interact with the children and provide sensory stimulation, love, and attention. Significant increases in intelligence were noted compared to decreases in intelligence in the control group who stayed in the orphanage.

Children who were adopted and raised by families in a more affluent environment were found to have considerably higher measures of intelligence than would have been expected if they had remained in the impoverished environment into which they were born (Scarr & Weinberg, 1976). The earlier in life the children were adopted, the higher the intelligence measure tended to be. This study and research in general emphasizes the influence of experiences early in life. Heredity probably sets limits, but whether one reaches that potential depends on environmental experience.

## Measurement of Intelligence

The history of intelligence testing dates back to the 1800s. Many different tests to measure intelligence have been devised; however, the two best-known, individually administered tests are the Stanford-Binet and the Wechsler Adult Intelligence Scale which are described in this section. Often tests are used in business and industry to evaluate aptitude and ability attributes of personnel. A few of these are also reviewed. Tests used to measure intellectual abilities are evaluated according to how reliable and how valid the tests are, and how well one person's test results can be compared to another person's test results.

### History

In 1869, Sir Francis Galton had some ideas about classifying and measuring human qualities and abilities. Galton reasoned that intelligence was related to speed of perceptual-motor skills, since information is acquired through the senses. He administered a battery of tests measuring such things as head size, reaction time, visual acuity, and memory for visual forms; however, his tests never proved to be very useful.

Although the term "mental tests" was introduced by James McKeen Cantell in 1890, the testing of intelligence did not begin until 1904 when Alfred Binet was commissioned by school authorities in Paris, France, to devise a way to differentiate between those students who did poorly in school because they were of low intelligence and those who did poorly because of lack of motivation or poor instruction. The first test, designed to measure a person's ability to deal with abstract relations, was published and began to be used in Paris schools which initiated a worldwide response. The measure yielded a score in the form of a mental age. For example, a child might be ten years old chronologically, but function mentally as the average six-year-old child does or as the average twelve-year-old child does.

In 1916, Lewis Terman of Stanford University translated, revised, and extended Binet's test producing what is now called the Stanford-Binet test which was further revised in 1937, 1960, and 1972. The test yields an *intelligence quotient* (IQ) which is a ratio of mental age to chronological age multiplied by 100 to remove the decimal fraction. For example, an eight-year-old child with a mental age of eight would have an IQ of 100 (8/8 × 100). An eight-year-old child with a mental age of nine would have an IQ of 112 (9/8 × 100), or an eight-year-old child with a mental age of six would have an IQ of 75 (6/8 × 100).

David Wechsler decided in the 1930s to develop a test that would include more performance skills such as picture completion and object assembly and not rely so heavily on verbal skills. He developed the Wechsler Intelligence Scale for Children (WISC) and the Wechsler Adult Intelligence Scale (WAIS). This test provides an overall IQ which is derived by combining the scores from all the subtests such as vocabulary, picture completion, object assembly, etc. Both the Stanford-Binet and the Wechsler tests are administered individually to one person at a time. Other tests have now been developed to assess large groups simultaneously and to assess a variety of specific aptitudes and abilities.

## Some Tests Used in Business and Industry

Tests often are administered to people applying for jobs to measure their achievement, aptitude, or ability in some area related to performance of the job for which they are applying. A few of the aptitude and ability tests (see Figure 8-8) commonly used in business and industry are reviewed in this section.

Figure 8-8    Personnel
administrators often give
achievement, aptitude, or ability
tests to job applicants.

The Otis Self-Administering Tests of Mental Ability (World Book Company) consisting of 75 items and the shorter version consisting of 50 items called the Wonderlic Personnel Test are two popular short intelligence tests used in industry. The items involve vocabulary, sentence meaning, proverbs, analogies, number trends, etc.

The Thurstone Test of Mental Alertness (Science Research Associates) is a 20-minute assessment of intelligence based on quantitative and linguistic items. Trainability for industrial jobs may be assessed using the Adaptability Test (Science Research Associates) for literates or the Purdue Non-Language Test, consisting of 48 geometric forms, for nonliterates.

A longer, more reliable measure of intelligence is provided by the Civilian Edition of the Army Classification Test. This test contains 150 items and requires 40 minutes to take. Average IQ scores are available for 125 civilian occupations.

Dunnette (1976) lists the three multiple aptitude test batteries described below among the better known and more widely used ones for predicting work performance in organizational settings.

The General Aptitude Test Battery (GATB) was developed by the United States Employment and Training Service for use in state employment offices. The factors currently measured by the GATB include numerical aptitude, verbal aptitude, spatial aptitude, form perception, clerical perception, motor coordination, finger dexterity, and manual dexterity.

The Differential Aptitude Tests (DAT) are used mostly for educational and vocational counseling of students in grades eight through twelve, but the DAT has come to be widely used in industry also. This battery of tests yields scores in verbal reasoning, numerical ability, abstract reasoning, clerical speed and accuracy, mechanical reasoning, space relations, spelling, and grammar.

The Employee Aptitude Survey (EAS) is a series of tests designed to measure problem-solving ability in a business environment. The EAS was developed primarily for use in industrial and organizational settings. The factors included might be regarded as basic components of intelligence: the ability to use words in thinking and communicating; the ability to handle numbers and work with numerical material; the ability to make rapid, accurate scanning movements with the eyes; the ability to perceive small detail rapidly and accurately within a mass of material; the ability to visualize objects in three-dimensional space; the ability to discover relationships and derive principles; the ability to produce words rapidly; and the ability to apply principles in order to arrive at a unique solution.

## Evaluation of Ability Tests

Some things should be considered in evaluating an intelligence test for use such as reliability, validity, and standardization. Of course other factors should be considered such as cost, time involved in administration, and the use to be made of the results of the test.

**Reliability.** The *reliability* of a test is related to the consistency or stability of the measures. Intelligence is considered to be a rather stable trait; therefore, the intelligence test should yield consistent IQ scores for an individual. The reliability of a test is usually reported as a correlation coefficient which expresses the relationship between test-retest scores, alternate forms scores, or split half scores—a score on half the items may be correlated with a score from the remaining half. The higher the correlation coefficient, the more reliable the test score. For example, short tests like the Wonderlic, which takes only 12 minutes to administer, yields a test-retest reliability of around .80 or above. But longer tests, like the Stanford-Binet, WAIS, or Army Classification Test, yield reliabilities as high as .97.

**Validity.** The *validity* of a test is the extent to which it measures what it is designed to measure. For example, a valid intelligence test would measure intelligence, not weight or reaction time. The validity of an intelligence test may be determined by whether it is based on a sound theory, or by how well it correlates with some other intelligence test that already is known to have a high degree of validity. Another way to assess the validity of an intelligence test is to determine how well it predicts whether a person does what intelligent people are described as being able to do that less intelligent people cannot do well.

**Standardization.** A *standardized test* is one that has been given to a large and representative sample of people and for whom the distribution of their scores has been determined. The scores made by the people in this group are called *norms*. These scores provide the comparison for determining if an individual's score is average, above average, or below average or for determining the percentile rank of the score. If a test is not standardized, an individual's score cannot be interpreted. If the standardization group is too small or not representative of the population, the interpretation may not be very valid.

**Shortcomings.** When using tests to measure intelligence, one should keep in mind that only a sample of behavior believed to reflect intelligence is considered. Behavior in the test situation may be influenced by many factors other than factors of intelligence such as motivation and emotions of the person taking the test, the behavior and characteristics of the person administering the test, environmental conditions such as noise level or temperature of the room, and cultural background. Especially, one should consider that so-called intelligence tests do not reflect all aspects of intelligence such as creativity and that IQ is a mathematical computation of a ratio of mental age to chronological age which is determined by a test compared to a norm group. Another limitation of intelligence tests is that most of them measure a certain type of perception "based on the assumption that academic, upper-middle-class intellectual perceptions are important. But are they?" (Combs & Snygg, 1959, p. 220). Thus, some psychologists avoid the controversy in defining intelligence by defining it operationally as being what is measured on intelligence tests.

## Intelligence and Occupational Success

Intelligence is a major characteristic which varies among people and affects job performance. Therefore, psychological tests measuring intellectual abilities have been used extensively by personnel administrators in the selection of people for employment. An employee's IQ may be reflected in the length of time it takes him or her to learn a job, in the amount of work produced, and in his or her abilities to perform complicated tasks. The degree of intelligence of employees may make a difference in whether a firm has a profit or a loss.

## IQ and Job Satisfaction

Some people are very satisfied with their work and find their jobs so rewarding they look forward to going to work, seldom missing a day. Other people are not satisfied with their work and find their jobs unpleasant, boring, and frustrating, missing a day as often as they can. One factor in job satisfaction seems to be the degree of intelligence of the person performing the job and the complexity of the job task. If a worker has too little intelligence or more than is required to perform the job, he or she may become dissatisfied. A high degree of intelligence may be an advantage in a complex job; but if a job is extremely simple, like stapling pages together all day, a low degree of intelligence might be an advantage. A person of low intelligence may be more satisfied and better able to perform some job functions than a person of high intelligence.

The upper limit of intelligence for a given occupation seems difficult to specify; however, a minimum or critical score is more easily established. The required intellectual ability of many occupations is not sharply defined by test scores. Sometimes there is a critical score below which workers are considered unsuitable for the job or a critical score above which workers tend to change jobs as soon as a promotion is available.

According to Guilford's view that a person has many different intelligences, job satisfaction may depend on whether a career choice matches one's abilities. If a person is constantly struggling to adjust to a job that is extremely difficult and if the person is constantly worried about failure, chances are the person is not very happy in the job. Working on a job that is easier, one that the person has the ability to perform without a difficult struggle, contributes to job satisfaction. Formal schooling provides an opportunity for one to become aware of individual strengths and weaknesses and make career choices that may enhance job satisfaction. For example, if mathematics is very difficult for a person, the idea of being an engineer, accountant, or mathematician might be abandoned. Or if one has great difficulty in English courses a career as an author might be dismissed.

## IQ as a Predictor of Success

Over the years intelligence tests have tended to predict successful training in a variety of skilled types of work such as electrical workers, structural workers, process workers, machine operators, machinery workers, computing clerks, general clerks, and recording clerks. Intelligence tests have not been very valid predictors of success, however, for such manipulative and observational occupations as machine tenders, bench assembly workers, inspectors, packers, wrappers, and manual workers. Dexterity tests and perceptual tests have been better predictors of success in these areas (Ghiselli, 1966).

## IQ and Occupational Status

People in occupations carrying high prestige such as lawyer, physician, or scientist tend to have higher levels of intelligence while people in occupations of lower prestige tend to have lower levels of intelligence. A correlation of .50 has been estimated to exist between adult IQ scores and occupational status; however, within an occupational group, IQ does not seem to relate to success (Jencks, Smith, Acland, Bane, Cohen, Gintis, Heyns, & Michelson, 1972). Thus, income which is most often used as a criterion of success is not very predictable from IQ scores.

Although there is no difference in the mean IQ scores of males and females, the proportion of women holding jobs in occupations of higher status is smaller than for men. For example, surveys in the 1970s indicated that 97.8 percent of all practicing dentists are men (Coombs, 1975) and 99 percent of the dental assistants are women (American Dental Assistants Association, 1978). It has been noted (Fernald & Fernald, 1978) that these distributions are apparently not based on differences in ability since women with intelligence comparable to male dentists generally have more nimble fingers, and show greater interest in cosmetics than male dentists. Thus, females would be expected to perform better than men in the dentist's role. Similar findings exist for various groups in diverse occupations. IQ scores seem to be better predictors of academic achievement than of occupational success. Of course, IQ tests were originally developed to predict academic, not occupational, success.

## Selecting Successful Employees

The basic task facing psychologists in the area of personnel selection is that of devising effective procedures for choosing applicants most likely to succeed in a given job. The following procedure does work;

however, it is costly in terms of time, depends on large samples, and assumes that over the years both the jobs and the people who fill them will remain very much the same.

The first step of the procedure is the *job analysis* in which the specific behaviors required for the performance of the job are determined. Following the job analysis, the traits and characteristics of persons believed most likely to succeed are described. The next task is to select employees and measure the variables (traits) believed to affect success. After a sufficient period of time, the performance of each selected employee is evaluated. The performance measures are then correlated with the measures believed to affect performance. In this way, the strength of the relationship may be determined. The stronger the correlation, the more accurately success on the job can be predicted from the measured trait. Even if the relationship is strong, the initial findings should be *cross-validated* which means the procedure should be repeated with another sample of applicants to see if the same results occur again. This is more likely to insure that the results have not been a chance or random occurrence. The final step then is to formulate specific recommendations regarding the selection of future personnel for the particular job.

Intelligence tests are likely to correlate with job success and prove to be valid predictors of success in a given job that calls for verbal, numerical, and/or spatial aptitude. When more skill has to be learned to perform the job, intelligence tests are likely to be more predictive of job success. Intelligence is very complex. IQ scores may be put into better perspective if one also recognizes the complexity of creativity. Although IQ scores have uses, one must keep in mind that they do not explain all that is good and valuable about a person.

## SUMMARY

1. Achievement is what a person has learned, while ability is a current capability to learn. Aptitude is thought of as an inborn capacity to learn.

2. Intelligence has been defined as the ability to adapt, to solve problems, to learn, to understand and cope, to make appropriate responses, and to perceive.

3. Perception is the construction of meaning from information received through the senses and involves the filling in of incomplete information and the changing, amplifying, attending to, or ignoring of parts of sensory information.

4. Research has shown that both heredity and past experience play a

significant role in perception. Heredity seems to provide the prewired organization of the sensory receptors, the brain, and the muscles; but the environment must provide sensory input (activity) and response to it (movement).

5. The organizing processes of perception involve grouping or patterning which puts together large amounts of information quickly following principles related to proximity, similarity, continuity, closure, and common fate.

6. Stabilizing processes provide a standard and dependable way of interpreting events by providing rules for perceiving objects as constant and any change in size, contour, or texture from sensory information as distance, depth, shape, size, or location.

7. The organizing processes operate so reliably that illusions or misinterpretations may be produced. Various other things may affect the physiological functioning of the nervous system to cause perceptual malfunctioning.

8. Environmental experience prepares one to perceive or misperceive by creating expectancies or sets. Environmental experience results in perceptual learning.

9. Principles of perception also apply in one's perceptions of other people. Making inferences rather than relying on facts sometimes leads to distorted perceptions related to the halo effect, logical error, stereotyping (set), the Pygmalion effect, evaluation, and consistency.

10. Creativity is the ability to produce original and appropriate responses and seems to require divergent thinking. Most measures of intelligence call for convergent thinking even though some theorists believe that both divergent and convergent thinking are factors of intelligence.

11. The creative process progresses through a sequence of stages: preparation, incubation, illumination, and verification.

12. The right hemisphere of the brain has been associated with creative thinking; however, research has shown that the environmental conditions of openness to experience, internal standards, ability to try out ideas, unconditional acceptance, absence of external evaluation, and empathetic understanding enhance the expression of creativity.

13. Overcontrol of employees and poor psychological health inhibits creativity. Organizations considered to be creative seem to have certain characteristics.

14. In 1904, Spearman proposed that intelligence consists of a single, general ability. In 1938, Thurstone proposed that intelligence consists of a group of seven primary abilities. Later, Guilford proposed that there is no general intelligence, rather 120 independent factors resulting from three dimensions of intelligence—operations, contents, and products.

15. More recent theorists have proposed that there are two components of intelligence—crystallized (learned) and fluid (genetically determined)—and that information processing, particularly encoding, is related to intelligence.

16. Research indicates that both environmental experience and heredity account for one's intelligence. Heredity sets limits and experience determines whether those limits are reached.

17. Alfred Binet developed the first measure of intelligence and the concept of mental age which initiated the development of many different measures of intelligence and specific aptitudes, abilities, and achievements.

18. Intelligence quotient (IQ) is a ratio of the mental age to the chronological age, multiplied by 100.

19. Some tests often used in business and industry to assess aptitude and ability are the Otis Self-Administering Tests of Mental Ability, the Wonderlic Personnel Test, the Thurstone Test of Mental Alertness, the General Aptitude Test Battery, the Differential Aptitude Tests, and the Employee Aptitude Survey.

20. Test reliability (how consistently the test measures), validity (whether the test measures what it was designed to measure), and standardization (adequate norms for interpreting a score) should be considered when attempting to measure intelligence.

21. Measures of intelligence do have some shortcomings in that they reflect only a sample of behavior, do not reflect all aspects of intelligence, and assume certain types of perception as intelligent.

22. Job satisfaction may be associated with too little or too much intelligence for what is required for a given job and whether one's specific abilities match the abilities required for a job.

23. IQ tends to predict success in a variety of skilled types of work that require learning and call for verbal, numerical, or spatial aptitude; but IQ has not been a very valid predictor of success in manipulative and observational types of occupations.

24. Occupations of higher status are associated with people who have

higher IQ scores; however, the ratio of some groups in these occupations is not in proportion to their intellectual ability.

25. A procedure for choosing employees most likely to succeed in a given job involves doing a job analysis, describing characteristics hypothesized for success, measuring these characteristics, evaluating performance on the job, correlating the characteristics and performance measures, cross-validating, and using the highly correlated characteristics as characteristics for selection of future employees.

## SUGGESTIONS FOR FURTHER READING

Anastasi, A. *Psychological testing* (4th ed.). New York: Macmillan, 1976.

A very thorough text covering the general aspects of testing. This book discusses tests of intelligence, achievement, aptitude, and personality and the limits and extent of proper testing.

Barron, F. *Creative persons and creative process*. New York: Holt, Rinehart and Winston, 1969.

In this book the creative process is analyzed and people in various occupations considered to be creative are studied.

Block, N. J., & Dworkin, G. (Eds.). *The IQ controversy*. New York: Pantheon, 1976.

Articles debating issues such as heredity vs. environment, validity of IQ tests, and class and race differences in IQ are presented.

Brody, E. B., & Brody, N. (Eds.). *Intelligence: Nature, determinants, and consequences*. New York: Academic Press, 1976.

All the major theories of intelligence are examined in this book as well as research on some new issues such as the effect of family size.

Buros, O. K. (Ed.). *The mental measurements yearbook*. Highland Park, N.J.: The Gryphon Press, 1938-1977.

A yearbook containing descriptive lists of published tests in various areas including costs and publishers and critical reviews. Eight editions have been published since 1938.

Butcher, H. J. *Human intelligence: Its nature and assessment*. New York: Harper & Row, 1973.

Attention is particularly directed to problems encountered in the area of intelligence testing.

Campbell, D. *Take the road to creativity and get off your dead end.* Niles, Ill.: Argus Communication, 1977.

This book is a good source for characteristics of organizations that encourage creativity.

Carterette, E. C., & Friedman, M. P. *Handbook of perception* (Vol. 4). New York: Academic Press, 1976.

The concept and principles of perception are discussed on a rather advanced level in this book.

Cronbach, L. J. *Essentials of psychological testing* (3rd ed.). New York: Harper & Row, 1970.

This book presents a comprehensive coverage of the subject of psychological tests. Construction, reliability, validity, and types of tests are reviewed. Many tests have sample items presented.

Hastorf, A. H., Schneider, D. J., & Polefka, J. *Person perception.* Reading, Mass.: Addison-Wesley, 1970.

A book about perception of people that should interest psychology students.

Hochberg, J. E. *Perception* (2nd ed.). Englewood Cliffs, N.J.: Prentice-Hall, 1978.

This book is an expanded and rigorous treatment of many topics being studied today by psychologists interested in perception.

Loehlin, J. C., Lindzey, G., & Spuhler, J. N. *Race differences in intelligence.* San Francisco: Freeman, 1975.

A very thorough review of the research regarding racial differences in IQ is included in this study. This book gives an objective, balanced view of the issue.

Raudsepp, E., & Hough, G. P., Jr. *Creative growth games.* New York: Harcourt Brace Jovanovich, 1977.

This book contains activities that require creative thinking and the riddance of mental set.

Taylor, I. A., & Getzels, J. W. (Eds.). *Perspectives in creativity.* Chicago: Aldine, 1975.

Various articles on creativity make up this book. The articles clarify the concept of creativity, its expression, and its improvement. It also covers the basic research on creativity.

Vernon, P. E. *Intelligence: Heredity and environment.* San Francisco: Freeman, 1979.

The author presents both sides of the issue of heredity and environment as determinants of intelligence as fairly as possible.

Whimbey, A., & Whimbey, L. S. *Intelligence can be taught.* New York: Dutton, 1975.

In this book suggestions for increasing intelligence test scores are given and the argument is made that many of the abstract skills that intelligence tests measure can be improved with training.

# Part 4
## Motivation and Emotion

# The Concept of Motivation

# Why do people behave as they do? Human behavior

**W**hy do people behave as they do? Human behavior poses a basic question for psychology, and the answer to why people behave as they do on the job has important applications in the world of work. (See Figure 9-1.) Why is one worker consistently absent, another rarely absent? Why does one have a high production rate, another a low production rate? Why is one dishonest, another honest? Why does one eat lunch, another skip lunch? Why does one join a union, another doesn't? Why does one pursue further education, another doesn't? Why does one resign to take a different job, another doesn't? Why does the same person behave differently at different times when in the same situation? The concept of motivation provides an explanation for this variability of behavior. This chapter is devoted to clarifying this concept of motivation which is basic to any study of human behavior.

Figure 9-1　Why does an individual work? Why does an individual engage in a particular type of work?

## Introduction to Motivation

Motivation is sometimes difficult to define since it must be inferred and cannot be observed directly; however, some defining characteristics that psychologists usually agree on are given as a definition. Motivation is considered to be an internal source of behaviors that are not elicited by an external stimulus as in reflex behaviors.

### Definition

Motivation is a concept concerned with the source, cause, or explanation of a behavior. The word motive comes from the Latin "movere" which means "to move" or "to activate." Literally, a motive is whatever moves one to action. Psychologists generally agree on the definition that motivation is that which activates or causes behavior to occur and gives direction to behavior—motivation leads to behavior which equals performance. Any manager therefore who is interested in performance is concerned with motivation. Motivation seems to be a *hypothetical construct* (invisible and impossible to measure directly) rather than a fact; therefore, psychologists sometimes have different views about what activates and gives direction to behavior. What one proposes as a definition of motivation seems to depend more on what theory of motivation one is committed to.

### Sources of Behavior

Reflex behaviors do not require very elaborate explanations, since all one has to do is identify the condition or stimulus which moved the person to the action or behavior. For example, a puff of air directed to the eye causes the eye to blink, food placed in the mouth causes one to salivate, or a very hot object causes one to withdraw his or her hand if that hand touches it.

Most behaviors are not reflexive, however, and an identifiable external stimulus cannot be specified as eliciting these behaviors. The behaviors are explained indirectly as being the result of learning from prior experience, thinking, or the physiological structure of the individual. If an internal source of these behaviors could be located, a direct explanation could be made as in the explanation of reflex behaviors. Several theories of motivation have been proposed to hypothetically identify different internal sources as causes of behaviors which are not reflexive.

# Philosophical Origins of Motivation

From the earliest of times, humans have attempted to explain their behavior by assigning it a source or cause. The source or cause of human behavior was a topic of great concern to early philosophers, and their speculations attributed the cause of behavior to different sources. Their speculations on the cause of human behavior are significant because they laid the foundation for basic assumptions about human behavior. These basic assumptions paved the way for the scientific study of behavior and influenced modern approaches to explaining behavior. Many of the questions of psychology today originated in philosophy.

## Free Will vs. Determinism

Two basic philosophical assumptions exist about behavior. *Free will* is the assumption that humans freely choose their own behavior—that humans have control of their own destiny. The assumption of *determinism* proposes that every event, act, or decision is the consequence of prior physical, psychological, or environmental events that are independent of the human will. The issue still is not settled. The humanistic approach to psychology assumes that individuals are free. Behaviorism and the more rigorous scientific approach to psychology assume that an individual's behavior is caused or determined. The dilemma is that humans want to believe that they have free will, but they desire predictability in dealing with others. The goal of psychology as a science is to be able to predict behaviors. When behavior is not predictable, the scientist assumes that it is only because of a lack of knowledge; a law governing the behavior does not cease to exist merely because it is not known. Some early philosophical ideas that gave rise to the assumptions of free will and determinism and made a distinct imprint on the concept of motivation are rationalism, mechanism, dualism, and empiricism.

**Rationalism.** The philosophical idea of traditional *rationalism* attributes one's behavior to thinking—conscious intentions and reasonings. Free will is assumed in rationalism, in that one consciously chooses a behavior, but rationalism does not explain why one reasons a particular way and chooses a particular behavior. Sigmund Freud, using the psychoanalytic viewpoint, emphasized the unconscious influences on people's thinking and behavior and, therefore, downgraded human rationality. Behaviorists hold that one may think rationally, if trained and rewarded for doing so; but they do not believe there is an innate rational force in humans. The humanistic psychologist, Carl Rogers, has drawn the conclusion from his extensive study of humans in psychotherapy that the innermost core of human nature is basically positive in that the nature is to become socialized, to move forward, to be rational, and to be realistic.

**Mechanism.** René Descartes is considered to have been the father of the mechanistic philosophy. Mechanism attributes all natural events, including human behavior, to physical causes. The assumption is made that all behavior can be explained, at least in principle, if enough can be learned about the physical systems. This philosophy holds that the physical aspect of humans obeys laws of mechanics and, if the laws are known, the behavior can be predicted. Behavior is viewed as being determined by forces beyond human control rather than as being chosen freely based on a conscious decision. The ancient philosophical idea of *hedonism* is an example of mechanistic philosophy since it attributed human behavior to physical causes. Hedonism states that behavior is determined by the desire to avoid pain and the desire to seek pleasure.

**Dualism.** The philosophy of *dualism* holds that human behavior is controlled by complex interactions of both the mind and the body, either of which may initiate behavior. Dualists assume that God creates humans in such a way that the mind guides behavior to satisfy bodily needs. According to dualism, the source of behavior is God; behavior is instinctive in nature.

**Empiricism.** The empiricists maintain that behavior is determined, not chosen, but they make no commitment about the cause or source of behavior. According to the philosophy called *empiricism*, relationships exist between stimuli and responses; therefore, stimuli, either external or internal, determine behavior. The British philosopher, John Locke, originated this view when he proposed that the mind at birth is a blank tablet, and environmental experiences determine behavior.

## Instinct

Hereditary, mechanistic, God-given behaviors were viewed by the dualists as instincts and as the source of behavior. In the late 1800s, Darwin's theory of evolution led to the view that defined instincts as the force that compels behavior—an inherited predisposition to respond to some stimulus in the environment with a particular kind of behavior. For example, people are compelled to gather in groups because of the "herd instinct" or to fight because of the "aggressive instinct." This view that patterns of human behavior are attributable to inborn conditions of the individual came under attack because many instincts believed to be shared by all humans did not appear in all cultures.

In 1932, E. C. Tolman put the idea of instincts into behavioral language when he defined instinct as wants or desires which are aroused by certain physiological conditions caused by some biological distress. A behavior must have a fixed outcome, but the behavior itself may vary. For example, the behavior must provide food intake for the person, but the pattern of the actual behavior of eating may vary. Thus, instinct came to be viewed as changeable rather than as mechanical in nature. As a result, behavior has come to be viewed as being caused by a striving toward a biological goal. If the striving is hindered by an obstacle, the striving merely intensifies until the goal is finally achieved. Today, the term "drive" has replaced this view of instinct.

Currently, instinct is merely a descriptive term designating unlearned, goal-directed behavior patterns which are universally unique to a particular species and are elicited by a particular environmental stimulus the first time the stimulus is presented. An example is nest building in birds. Birds have no previous knowledge of building nests and are not conditioned to build nests but do so instinctively. Instincts, as defined today, are found primarily in animals other than humans. Human behavior is either reflexive or learned.

## Views of Motivation

Researchers continue to try to discover the source of motivation, and a number of different views of motivation exist today. Drives, incentives, needs, arousal, reinforcement, expectancy, and homeostasis are viewed by various researchers as sources of motivation.

### Drive Theory

*Drive*, the term referring to the force that compels behavior that arises from physiological conditions which signify some biological distress, has continued to receive widespread acceptance as a source of motivation. One reason for this is the general belief that physiological research will disclose the source of motivation. Currently, however, the conclusion seems to be that drive cannot direct behavior; it can only energize behavior. According to the drive theory of motivation, a person's drive level provides the energy necessary for exhibiting a behavior. The drive level increases with increased deprivation of a biological need, but the drive level is reduced when the biological need is satisfied. For example, the longer one is deprived of food, the higher the drive level for exhibiting food-seeking behaviors. But the consumption of food reduces the need for food and the drive level for food-seeking behavior is lowered.

### Incentive Theory

The motivational components of behavior are explained today in terms of *incentive* as well as drive. The most fundamental distinction between incentive and drive is that drive is produced by internal events—biological states—while incentive is produced by external events—environmental cues. In effect, the innate part of motivation is attributed to drive, while the learned part is attributed to incentive. Incentive is of psychological origin and depends on previous experience and present environmental conditions. This external-internal model of motivation has implications for the practical control of behavior. The idea of two basic concepts of motivation—motivation as a pushing force (drives that are energizing behavior) and motivation as a pulling force (incentives that give direction to behavior)—dominates most psychologists' thinking about motivation. Motivation seems to be the combined action of drives and incentives—push and pull. Hunger is a drive producing a desire for food (a pushing force). A table laden with food is an incentive to eat (a pulling force).

### Needs Theory

*Needs* is only a broader term for drive and refers to psychological (social or learned) needs as well as physiological needs of the body. The need to achieve and the need to be loved and accepted by other people do not seem to have a physiological basis. Instead, they seem to be learned needs. Both physiological and psychological needs serve as sources of motivation. Association or learning seems to be the source of energy for some behavior; thus, acquired or learned needs are also important in the concept of motivation. In fact, evidence seems to indicate that much of the time, motivation itself is learned. Most psychologists agree that there are two kinds of needs—unlearned needs or drives which have a physiological basis and learned or psychological needs which are acquired through environmental experience.

### Arousal Theory

Recent evidence indicates that to think of one as being more easily aroused or more sensitive to or more reactive to a stimulus is probably more accurate than to think of one as being more energized. The view that behavior is the function of being aroused by a stimulus rather than a direct effect of deprivation is called *arousal theory*. The state of arousal or activation of the organism may vary on a continuum from deep sleep to alertness to intense excitement.

Theoretically, a person needs an intermediate level of stimulation and activation to function best. When conditions deviate too far from this optimum level of arousal, the person acts to restore the equilibrium. In an environment that is not stimulating enough, one begins to investigate, to explore, or to manipulate the surroundings in order to increase the stimulation. If the environment is too stimulating, one may withdraw or begin to focus on only a part of the environment in order to reduce the stimulation. There is an optimum level of arousal in terms of both internal and external conditions. For example, hunger or thirst might be an internal stimulus or condition causing one to be more sensitive to, reactive to, or aroused by cues such as the sight of food, the smell of food, or the presence of a kitchen or restaurant. Many contemporary psychologists reject the drive theory in favor of the arousal theory (Duffy, 1962).

The relationship between arousal or motivation and performance varies for different tasks. (See Figure 9-2.) A very simple or boring task may be performed better at a higher level of arousal to avoid losing concentration or falling asleep. A complicated, difficult task involving logical reasoning may be performed better at a lower level of arousal. As arousal or motivation increases, performance increases until the optimum point is reached; then as arousal or motivation increases, performance decreases.

The optimum level of arousal varies among different people for different tasks. Some people perform better at higher levels of arousal while others perform better at lower levels of arousal. Individual differences in need for stimulation can be measured by psychological tests such as the Sensation-Seeking Scale (Zuckerman, Kolin, Price, & Zoob, 1964). Each item in the Sensation-Seeking Scale presents a situation with two choices. An individual taking the test selects the choice that is believed to best reflect the way he or she would feel or act. The ones selected are scored such that the higher the total score, the higher the need for arousal.

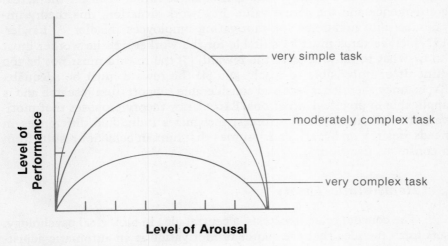

Figure 9-2    Level of performance is a function of arousal or motivation. The optimum level of arousal or motivation for the best performance varies with the complexity of the task.

### Reinforcement Theory

The reinforcement theory of motivation is based on the assumption that what is ordinarily called motivated behavior is simply learned behavior. This theory proposes one single source of behavior—reinforcement. Reinforcement theory is a modern version of the ancient philosophical idea of hedonism. The concept of reinforcement as an explanation of behavior is presented in Chapter 6. Learned associations between a behavior and the environmental consequence of that behavior account for an increase or a decrease in that behavior.

### Expectancy Theory

The cognitive psychologists propose that the motivation behind a person's behavior is his or her deliberate, conscious choice to behave in a particular way in order to achieve an expected outcome. A person thinks that a particular behavior will bring about a particular outcome or consequence. The motivation behind any behavior then is a function of the expectancy of a particular outcome or consequence and the value that the person places on the expected outcome. People perform behaviors that are likely to result in worthwhile rewards. Behavior occurs because it is believed to be a means to a goal. Motivation is based on what the person thinks the consequence of the behavior will be and what the person thinks will be the value of the consequence rather than on the actual consequence and the actual value. In a work situation, this theory implies certain guidelines for motivating employees (Nadler & Lawler, 1977): (1) rewards must be suitable for the worker; (2) the worker must know what to do to receive the reward; (3) the reward must not be too difficult or impossible to reach; and (4) the reward must be adequate. Expectancy theory has received considerable support from research and is applicable in practical situations. Expectancy theory proposes that motivation is an interaction of forces; recognizes individual differences in needs, desires, and goals; and assumes that human behavior results from a conscious decision.

### Homeostatic Theory

The concept of *homeostasis*, a central idea in biological psychology, sets forth the idea that the source of motivation is an automatic adjustment of behavior to maintain equilibrium. Many physiological states such as blood pressure, body temperature, glucose levels, and other chemical and metabolic processes must remain within a certain range of values for life to continue. Bodily mechanisms exist which restore an optimum level of physiological performance when deviations from that level are experienced. For example, high temperatures may trigger perspiration which cools the body and cold may cause one to shiver which generates body warmth. These mechanisms are involuntary. But the mechanisms for restoring equilibrium, such as building a fire or putting on a coat to protect one's self from cold, or turning on an air conditioner to cool one's self, are voluntary. These responses are the interaction of the physiological state, learning and habit, and stimulus conditions. In the concept of homeostasis, need refers to any physiological imbalance or deviation from the optimum level. When involuntary mechanisms do not maintain equilibrium, drive is activated in order to motivate the person to do something to restore equilibrium. Although the concept of homeostasis may account for many behaviors exhibited by a worker, it has been challenged as the explanation for all voluntary behaviors because some human behaviors create rather than correct a physiological imbalance such as in drug addiction, in food preferences, or in the amount or type of activities undertaken.

## Needs

The concept of need proposed in homeostatic theory as a source of behavior necessary for physiological equilibrium was extended to include the need to maintain a psychological equilibrium such as the need for power or the need for social acceptance. Since this broader concept of needs is accepted by psychologists as the explanation for many behaviors, especially those of workers, this view of motivation will be described in more detail.

### Classification

Human needs are classified by whether the basis for the need is biological (innate) or psychological (learned, social, acquired, or environmental). Needs which have a biological basis are called *primary needs*. Primary needs may be subdivided into those necessary for survival of the individual, those necessary for survival of the species, and those necessary for the survival of learning or the development of intelligence and attainment of knowledge. Individual survival needs include the need for food, fluids, air, tolerable temperature, sleep and dreaming, and the need to be free from pain. Survival needs of the species include the sex drive to insure reproduction and the maternal drive to insure adequate care of the young. Needs that promote survival of learning are referred to as *stimulus motives* and include the need for sensory input, movement, exploration, curiosity, manipulation of objects, and body contact, the need to touch others.

Needs which have only a psychological basis are called *secondary needs*. Secondary needs include the need for security or the need to be free from fear, aggression, achievement, affiliation (the need for love, acceptance, and approval from others), and consistency.

## Primary Needs

**Needs for Survival of the Individual.** The motivation for many of a worker's behaviors can be traced to survival needs. For example, a worker may take a break from work because of fatigue, may stop work to eat because of hunger, or leave the work activity to get a drink of water because of thirst. Even engaging in work may be motivated by the hunger drive—to obtain money to buy food which can lead to the behavior of food intake. Frequently, the source of motivation for behavior is related to survival needs and the biological system. The hypothalamus in the brain is sensitive to the chemistry and temperature of the blood and produces the desire for food, liquids, or temperature change (Davis, Gallagher, & Ladove, 1967; Epstein, Fitzsimmons, & Simons, 1969). Some researchers believe that even one's hunger for a specific food may be activated by some chemical imbalance in the blood (Davis, 1939). Pain is the signal system that activates voluntary behaviors that allow the individual to escape or avoid whatever is threatening him or her. If a worker is in need of food, liquids, temperature change, or relief from pain, behaviors will be exhibited that attempt to maintain a physiological state of equilibrium while on the job.

Impulses from the reticular formation in the brain are the sources of different brain wave patterns related to different levels of arousal. Each of the senses—vision, hearing, smell, taste, touch—stimulates the reticular formation which then arouses the higher brain centers. Sometimes arousal level is very low, as in sleep, and sometimes it is extremely high, as when very excited. Different brain wave patterns differentiate the various levels of arousal.

Five different brain wave patterns differentiate the stages of sleep (Kleitman, 1963). (See Figure 9-3). The typical sleep pattern of a young adult involves five stages. An average of 10 to 15 minutes is spent in each stage, descending from Stage 1 to Stage 4, then ascending back to Stage 1 to enter REM sleep. Stage 1 with *REM* (rapid eye movement) is when dreaming most frequently occurs. About 90 minutes is required to complete a cycle. These cycles continue during the sleep period until about five have been completed. The first period of REM sleep is about 10 minutes. But these periods gradually become longer until they last maybe 30 to 45 minutes so that the average dream time is about 1½ to 2 hours per sleep period (See Figure 9-4.)

When one has been deprived of REM sleep and is then allowed to sleep undisturbed, the REM periods will be longer to make up for the

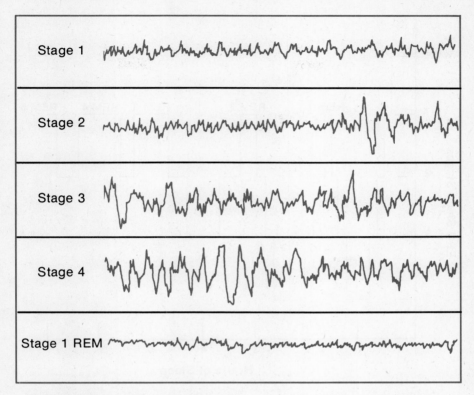

Figure 9-3   The brain wave
patterns typical of each of the five
stages of sleep.

deprivation; thus, there seems to be a need for a certain amount of
dreaming. One recently advanced theory (Hobson & McCarley, 1977)
proposes that involuntary mechanisms send impulses to stimulate the
brain when impulses are not being sent from sensory stimulation as they
are in the waking state. Dreams then are an attempt by the brain to make
a coherent interpretation out of essentially incoherent bursts of impulses
in the cortex of the brain during sleep. The cortex recalls memories that
can be associated with the impulses it is receiving. If no logical connections are found, illogical and remote associations are made or the gaps are
filled with recent memories. According to Sigmund Freud and later psy-
choanalysts, dreams are symbolic expressions of unconscious desires and
serve as sources of wish fulfillment to drain off tensions created during
the day. This view proposes that REM sleep is needed for a worker's
psychological well-being, unconsciously satisfying emotional needs.

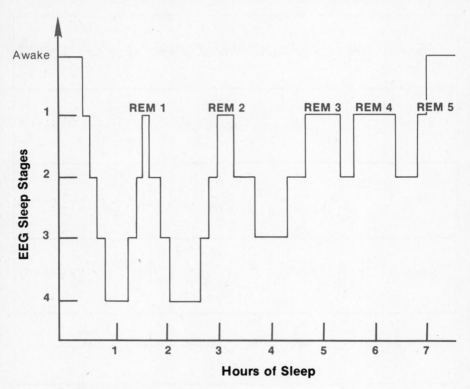

Figure 9-4    Typical sleep pattern for a young adult.

During the waking state and thus during job performance, the individual also progresses through cycles of varying levels of arousal indicated by varying brain wave patterns. These varying levels of arousal or alertness may be significant in the explanation of some work behaviors. For example, the level of alertness may be a factor in poor job performance resulting in accidents or in a lower level of production.

Although a physiological need or internal conditions may be the basis for some work-related behaviors, the environment or external condition may also activate a desire for food, liquids, or sleep. (See Figure 9-5.) In addition, learning may affect the way in which one responds to the desire whether the desire is internally or externally activated.

**Needs for Survival of the Species.** Drives related to survival of the species seem to be very powerful. In lower animals such as rats, cats, or dogs, hormones appear to account for sexual arousal and behavior. In primates and humans, however, experience or learning may override the influence of hormones as the cerebral cortex of the brain becomes more involved in the sex drive. A particular song, special perfume, candlelight,

Figure 9-5　The desire for food is more likely to be activated by external conditions in overweight people while the desire is more likely to be activated by internal conditions in normal or below normal weight people.

or soft music may become a stimulus for sexual arousal. A decrease in the involvement of purely biological factors and an increase in the environmental factors seems to occur the higher an animal is on the evolutionary scale. Sexual behavior depends on a combination of hormones, involuntary mechanisms—particularly the hypothalamus reactions—and external stimuli which are learned. External or learned stimuli play a greater role in the sexual arousal of humans since humans are highest on the evolutionary scale and have a more advanced development of the cortex of the brain which allows a greater ability to learn. The sex drive seems to differ from the other drives in several ways: (1) It is not essential for individual survival. (2) Its arousal is not dependent on deprivation. (3) It can be aroused by almost any conceivable stimulus. (4) Arousal of the drive is sought as actively as the reduction of the drive once it is aroused. (5) It motivates an unusually wide variety of behaviors and psychological processes (Ruch & Zimbardo, 1971).

Studies with rats show that the maternal drive is more powerful in determining behavior than hunger, thirst, or sex (Warden, 1931). Maternal behavior of lower animals appears to depend primarily on hormones and the stimulus conditions (Rosenblatt, 1969). As with the sex drive, experience and learning may override the influence of hormones in primates and humans. Experiments with monkeys indicate that maternal behavior requires learning and experience (Harlow & Harlow, 1966). In higher animals and humans, the maternal drive seems to consist of a complex set of motives and emotions.

A recent biological theory of motivation called sociobiology suggests that behavior is preprogrammed for one and only one function—to ensure the survival of the DNA molecules that make up one's genetic identity. All living organisms, including humans, are proposed to be designed to behave in such a way as to protect and propagate the genes. It is not the survival of the individual organism or the species that motivates behavior; it is the survival of the genetic material in the cells.

**Stimulus Needs.** The stimulus needs (activity, curiosity, exploration, manipulation, and body contact) apparently have a biological basis and are innately programmed. Usually, external stimuli rather than internal conditions arouse the behavior that seeks to satisfy stimulus needs. The need to move about and to be active seems to provide external stimuli to insure sensory stimulation. Experiments with sensory deprivation indicate that the need for sensory stimulation is so strong that in its absence visual sensations like dots and geometric forms and eventually hallucinations begin to occur (Heron, 1957).

The need to manipulate and to have body contact seems to be related to the need to know something at the tactile level and the need to be soothed. The desire to manipulate is associated with a specific object and involves handling with the fingers or toes. The desire for contact is associated with more general touching of objects and touching of other people. Studies with baby monkeys separated from their mothers at birth (Harlow, 1958) indicate that a biological basis exists for the needs of cuddling and closeness.

Curiosity and the desire to explore are activated by the new and unknown and are satisfied by knowledge. Exploration is more spatial; curiosity is more intellectual. These stimulus needs seem to provide the new and changing sensory input necessary for learning and for the development of intelligence necessary for survival.

### Secondary Needs

**Affiliation Motive.** During psychological development each person acquires or learns certain needs and may acquire them in different strengths. For example, an infant's biological needs are satisfied by people; then people become goal objects themselves. The child develops a need to be with people, to be accepted by some people, and to be loved by people. This need is referred to as the *affiliation motive*. The development of a need to be with other people is not completely understood, but research clearly suggests that the family, the first group with which one is associated, plays an important role. Children brought up to be dependent or who are raised with close family ties show stronger affiliation motives than those who are not. Also, firstborn and only children have stronger affiliation motives than those born later (Sarnoff & Zimbardo, 1961). Research on simple tasks has shown that people with a high need for affiliation perform better than people with a low need for affiliation. This is explained by the fact that people who have a high need for affiliation have a greater desire to please, to cooperate, and to be friendly (French, 1958).

**Need for Approval.** The need to be approved as a person and to have one's actions approved is an important motive in understanding much of social behavior. (See Figure 9-6.) For example, why do people tend to conform and do what others do or what they think others would do?

*"You really handled this job extremely well."*

Figure 9-6    Receiving praise
satisfies a need for approval.

People with a high need for approval tend to agree more with the judgment of others.

**Achievement Motive.** If the people in a child's life value and reward achievement, the child will develop a need to achieve in order to win approval. In the United States this need to achieve, referred to as the *achievement motive,* has been so strongly learned that the term motivation is often used to mean achievement. Two factors seem to be involved in achievement motivation: a need for success and a fear of failure. Different people have different combinations of these two factors. The probability of success or failure and the incentive value of success or failure are related to these two factors. For example, if a task is so difficult that a person is rarely able to accomplish it, then failure would have no negative incentive value since there would be no shame associated with failure. If the task is so easy that almost anyone can do it, then achieving success is not worth much and has little positive incentive.

Some research indicates a relationship between occupational choice and the need for achievement (McClelland, 1965). In a group of college graduates, 83 percent with high need for achievement went into occupations characterized by a high degree of risk, challenge, and decision making like sales, management, or business ownership. Seventy percent of those who did not choose an occupation like this had a low need for achievement. People high in need for achievement choose people who are professionally competent as working partners; people high in need for affiliation tend to choose friends as working partners. People high in need for affiliation will not be motivated to affiliate with people or groups who are extremely unpleasant and disliked; instead they will be motivated by a friendly request to cooperate and to help out for the common good, provided the request is from a person or group that has positive incentive value (French, 1958).

**Aggression.** Aggression refers to any behavior consciously or unconsciously intended to inflict physical or psychological harm. If children observe people in their lives using aggression as a means of achieving or gaining power over others, they may develop a need to be aggressive. Another view is that aggression is not a motive at all but simply a behavior that results from frustration produced by the nonfulfillment of other motives. Freud proposed that people are born with an aggressive drive and that aggression has a biological basis. According to this concept, aggression is constantly generating energy and, if it is not released in small aggressive acts, will build up greater tension and will be released in more extreme aggressive acts. Competitiveness in the world of work might be viewed as the release of innate aggression. Recent research studies, however, suggest that the release of energy through aggressive acts tends to increase aggressive behaviors rather than decrease them (Lazarus, 1974); therefore, the view that aggression is an innate characteristic is unpopular among the majority of psychologists today.

**Fear.** Fear can be attached to almost any stimulus. One learns a need to avoid or escape from whatever is causing the fear. One particular kind of fear that may be learned is fear of success. The motive to avoid success has been associated primarily with females, since our society has traditionally stereotyped women who achieve outside the home as being sexless, unfeminine, and cold; and assumed that a woman's need for affiliation was usually stronger than her need to achieve (see Figure 9-7). In a recent study (Hoffman, 1974), about 65 percent of the female subjects gave responses that indicated a fear of success, but 77 percent of the male subjects also expressed this fear. Evidently, fear of success is a general kind of fear for many people, both male and female.

**Need for Cognitive Consistency.** Humans seem to have a need for consistency or agreement in their attitudes, beliefs, and behaviors. The

Figure 9-7    Attitudes which keep women from pursuing their personal needs for achievement are changing, and more women are moving into management positions in the world of work.

tendency to change or reevaluate discrepancies in order to bring about agreement or balance is referred to as the need for *cognitive consistency*. If a person behaves in a manner inconsistent with what is believed to be appropriate behavior, disagrees with another person, or holds two conflicting attitudes, ideas, or opinions, the inconsistency usually makes the person so uncomfortable that he or she will do something to restore balance or agreement. The state of tension that is created in such a conflict is referred to as *cognitive dissonance* (Festinger, 1957). This dissonance motivates the person to engage in behavior that will reduce the conflict.

In order to reduce dissonance, a person may use a number of different strategies. Some people may seek out information to support a belief that differs from another person's belief. Since new information may be in conflict with information or beliefs previously held, some people may avoid seeking information to avoid further dissonance. If new information is encountered that is inconsistent with information or beliefs previously held, some people find a way to deny or reject the information. If a person's behavior is inconsistent with what he or she believes to be appropriate behavior, either the behavior may be changed or the attitude may be changed to bring about consistency. People with low self-images are more likely to retain their previously held beliefs, while very confident people are more likely to change their beliefs when faced with a conflict based on new information. Another way to reduce dissonance is to discredit the person who holds a conflicting attitude or belief. If one receives information about a person that conflicts with one's image of that person, either the information will be rejected or the image of the person will change. Any time a decision is made between two conflicting alternatives dissonance is present. Dissonance may be resolved after the decision is made by reevaluating the alternatives in a more biased manner in order to justify the decision.

Dissonance theory suggests that the harder one works for a goal, the more attractive or highly valued that goal will become for that person. Also, research has shown that people may perform acts that are not in accordance with their own values if the acts can be justified as submission to the demands of authority or if the reward is great enough to justify it. If the reward is not great enough to justify the act or the act is not performed as submission to authority, people are likely to either change their values or not perform the act (Festinger & Carlsmith, 1959).

**Need to Work.** Sometimes a behavior is a result of *intrinsic motivation* rather than *extrinsic motivation*. A behavior that in itself satisfies a need is a result of intrinsic motivation. When the consequence of a behavior satisfies a need, the behavior is a result of extrinsic motivation. For example, satisfaction may come from work rather than from the money obtained for the work. One may engage in gardening simply because of the pleasure derived from it. The need for work may stem from a need to demonstrate a mastery of the environment and a need to feel competent and self-determining. One may seek out activities and challenges to demonstrate mastery. Although there does seem to be a need to work, to be motivated by the work activity itself, employers usually rely on extrinsic motivation rather than intrinsic motivation. Only external reinforcers like money, prizes, and fringe benefits are thought of as conditions that motivate a workers's behavior. Research studies have shown (Deci, 1972; Lepper, Greene, & Nisbett, 1973) that sometimes imposing external rewards on an activity that is intrinsically motivated has the unexpected after-effect of lowering intrinsic motivation for the activity. For example, if one reads books just for the enjoyment of reading (intrinsic motivation) and then is paid money to read books, reading when the pay stops may become less frequent than it was prior to the application of extrinsic motivation. Managers should consider the role of intrinsic motivation in the behavior of workers and realize that employees may seek activities that allow them to demonstrate competence, self-determination, and mastery of the environment.

---

### BIORHYTHMS

Scientists are just beginning to consider body cycles, or *biorhythms*, as a possible source of motivation. One cycle that is known to be shared by individuals is the 24-hour circadian cycle of body activity. The 28-day menstrual cycle in females clearly can affect mood. Scientists now believe many kinds of body rhythms exist which begin at birth and rise and fall at different rates.

Three cycles—emotional, intellectual, and physical—have been charted, but the only scientific proof of their existence is statistical. The physical cycle is 23 days, the emotional cycle is 28 days, and the mental cycle is 33 days. Critical days occur when one of the cycles is at its lowest point. Double or triple critical days occur when two or three of the cycles are at the lowest point simultaneously. Critical days are not predetermined as dangerous; they only give an idea of the energy potential. Energy potential is highest when the three cycles are at the highest point simultaneously.

Industry is paying attention to biorhythms. Johns-Mansville Manufacturing Corporation, United Airlines, and Denver Yellow Cab are among those who have made use of biorhythms to reduce accidents and increase efficiency (Frazier, 1977). All the evidence on biorhythms is not in, but they do seem to be a small but significant part of the explanation of human behavior. More cycles and more human behaviors that depend on these cycles will probably be discovered.

## Assessment of Motivation

Since motivation is a theoretical concept and cannot be directly observed, behavior which is indicative of a motivational state is assessed. A variety of techniques have been developed for measuring the strength of a motive. Sometimes a person can analyze his or her own behavior and determine the need that is the source of motivation; however, very frequently the motive for a specific behavior is not consciously known to the person exhibiting the behavior.

### Unconscious Behavior

*Unconscious motivation* is not a particular kind of motivation; instead it refers to any need that one is acting to satisfy without knowledge or awareness of the need as a source of the behavior. Freud's view of unconscious motivation was probably the most extreme in that he viewed every act, regardless of how trivial, as derived from a host of unconscious motives. Most psychologists agree that unconscious motives exist, but not to the degree of Freud's view. They prefer to think in terms of degree of awareness. For example, one may be vaguely aware of the need to dominate others, the need for social approval, or the sex drive but not really aware of the extent to which this need is dominating behavior. Unconscious motivation explains many examples of consumer behavior. One may be unconsciously motivated to buy certain products and a particular brand of that product. Some unconscious motivation may be a defense reaction by which a person psychologically protects himself or herself from reality. Sometimes motivations are unconscious because one cannot pinpoint a complex motive that is derived from a combination of needs.

### Measurement Techniques

**Direct Observation.** In everyday life, observations are made in an unsystematic manner and inferences about motivation are made concerning one's self and especially others (see Figure 9-8). Psychologists, however, use systematic ways of assessing motivation. In order to conduct scientific studies, several techniques have been developed for measuring motivation. Since one function of motivation is the energizing of behavior, one can expect that increased motivation would lead to increased restlessness or activity or performance; therefore, the general activity level may be measured as an indication of motivation level. Once one has learned a response to satisfy a motive, the rate of responding may be used to measure the strength of motivation. A highly motivated individual will sometimes endure a great deal of hardship in order to reach a desired goal; therefore, the stronger the motivation, the more pain one will accept to satisfy that need. In most real-life situations, several motivations are operating at once and behavior is generally determined by the stronger motivation; therefore, the relative strength of competing motives can be assessed just by observing what behaviors are exhibited.

**Standardized Self-Report Inventories.** Psychologists may use standardized self-report inventories in which an individual gives information about his or her likes and dislikes and emotional reactions to certain situations. The self-report inventory is valuable in that it goes below the surface appearance of the behavior to tap the individual's own personal experience and feelings. Self-report inventories are convenient to give and score because interviews or groups of raters are not required, and they usually may be scored objectively. One disadvantage is that the person responding to the inventory often does not know and cannot always give an accurate report.

**Projective Tests.** Sometimes a person's motives are assessed in an indirect manner through use of *projective tests* whereby the person

Figure 9-8    Often inferences are made in an unsystematic manner concerning the motives for one's behavior—especially the behavior of others.

projects himself or herself into a stimulus situation. One of the most widely used tests of which motives are present in a person is the Thematic Apperception Test (TAT) originally developed at Harvard University by H. A. Murray and his associates. The Thematic Apperception Test is used to assess motivation as reflected in the content of stories created in response to certain standard pictures. Twenty cards containing pictures of one or more human figures with very few plot hints are shown to the subject. The subject is allowed enough time to make up a complete story for each picture. The story should include what has led up to the situation, what is happening, what the characters are doing, what their thoughts and feelings are, what is wanted and by whom, and what will happen or be done or what the outcome will be. Various scoring systems have been devised to assess the stories on their content, language, and themes—all of which are indicative of particular needs. For example, references to competition against a standard of excellence, unique accomplishment, achievement of a long-term goal, or strong effort or actions concerning the attainment of achievement-related goals would count toward achievement motivation. See the boxed material below and Figure 9-9 which illustrate the Thematic Apperception Test.

Other tests may be used to assess motivation, particularly unconscious motivation. Some of these other techniques are free associations (word associations or picture associations), open-ended sentences, the Rorschach inkblots test, or the depth interview.

People come to work with different needs, both physiological and learned, which predispose them to behave in particular ways. Also, the work situation provides cues which can arouse particular behavioral tendencies. These cues let the individual know what particular behaviors may lead to satisfaction of needs.

---

### AN ILLUSTRATION OF THE TAT

Look at the picture carefully and make up a brief story about it. In your story tell what is happening, who the individuals are, what has led up to this situation, what has happened in the past, what is being thought and what is wanted and by whom, and what will happen and be done in the future. Then analyze your story sentence by sentence and relate each sentence to an appropriate need—need for achievement, need for affiliation, need for power, etc. Some sentences probably cannot be classified. Total the number of sentences that relate to each motive and see if one occurs more frequently than the others. This is similar to how the Thematic Apperception Test is used to assess motivation.

Figure 9-9    The Thematic
Apperception Test  is one of the
most widely used means of
assessing a person's motives.

## SUMMARY

1.    Motivation, a hypothetical construct, is that which activates and
gives direction to behavior.

2. Different theories of motivation propose that different internal sources exist as causes of behaviors which are not reflexive.

3. Two basic assumptions exist about behavior: free will, the assumption that humans freely choose their own behavior, and determinism, the assumption that every behavior is the consequence of prior physical, psychological, or environmental events that are independent of the human will.

4. Philosophers have attributed behavior to conscious reasoning (rationalism), natural physical laws (mechanism), the desire for pleasure and the avoidance of pain (hedonism), an interaction of mind and body (dualism), lawfulness of stimuli and responses (empiricism), and instinct.

5. Drive theory attributes the source of motivation to biological distress brought about by deprivation.

6. Incentives are a pulling force and give direction to behavior. Motivation is seen as a combination of drives or pushing forces and incentives.

7. Need theory expanded drive theory to include psychological (social or learned) needs as well as physiological needs, both of which serve as sources of behavior to relieve physiological and psychological distress.

8. Arousal theory maintains that behavior is influenced by the need to maintain equilibrium and is a function of being arousable by a stimulus—being sensitive and reactive to a stimulus, rather than being a direct effect of deprivation.

9. Reinforcement theory proposes that behavior is a function of the learned association between the behavior and the environmental consequence of that behavior.

10. Expectancy theory sees behavior as a function of the expectancy of a particular consequence and the value that the person places on the expected consequence.

11. Homeostasis sets forth the idea that the source of motivation is an automatic adjustment of behavior to maintain equilibrium and includes either involuntary or voluntary mechanisms.

12. The hypothalamus and the reticular formation in the brain seem to be implicated in motivation. The hypothalamus is sensitive to the chemistry and temperature of the blood; impulses from the reticular formation are the sources of different brain wave patterns related to different levels of arousal.

13. Basic needs may be classified as primary or secondary.

14. Primary needs are those having a physiological basis which are necessary for survival—food, fluid, temperature, pain, sleep and dreaming, sex, care of the young, activity, curiosity, exploration, manipulation, and bodily contact.

15. Secondary needs are learned or acquired and have a psychological basis—affiliation, approval, achievement, aggression, security, and cognitive consistency.

16. A need for consistency results when conflict produces a state of tension referred to as cognitive dissonance.

17. Motivation may be intrinsic as when the satisfaction is in the behavior itself or extrinsic whereby the satisfaction is in the outcome of the behavior.

18. Motivation may be unconscious as well as conscious; one may act to satisfy a need without being aware of the need that is the source of the behavior.

19. Motivation must be assessed indirectly. Sometimes it is assessed by observing general activity levels, rates of responding, and endurance levels.

20. Self-report inventories are standardized objective techniques for indirectly assessing motivation.

21. Motivation may be assessed indirectly by techniques such as the Thematic Apperception Test.

## SUGGESTIONS FOR FURTHER READING

Atkinson, J. W., & Birch, D. *An introduction to motivation* (2nd ed.). New York: Van Nostrand Reinhold, 1978.

The authors focus on learned human motives, particularly the need for achievement.

Atkinson, J. W., & Feather, N. T. *A theory of achievement motivation.* Huntington, New York: Krieger, 1974.

This treatment of achievement motivation is comprehensive and well done.

Bolles, R. C. *Theory of motivation* (2nd ed.). New York: Harper & Row, 1975.

This excellent text deals with many motivational concepts, particularly as they are studied in research with animals. The focus is on biological drives and reinforcement theories.

Carlson, N. R. *Physiology of behavior.* Boston: Allyn and Bacon, 1977.

> Information on the biological bases of hunger, thirst, sex, and maternal behavior is contained in this text.

Deci, E. L. *Intrinsic motivation.* New York: Plenum, 1975.

> A well-written book that combines many different concepts of intrinsic motivation. The role of cognition in motivation is also included. Key studies regarding effects of rewards on intrinsic motivation are presented.

Madsen, K. B. *Modern theories of motivation.* New York: Wiley, 1974.

> Part II of this book contains a detailed presentation of twelve single theories of motivation plus a brief presentation of a few others. The order of presentation of the theories follows a historical sequence.

Seligman, M. E. P. *Helplessness: On depression, development, and death.* San Francisco: Freeman, 1975.

> The research on learned helplessness is summarized and then applied to human behavior in this study.

Weiner, B. *Human motivation.* New York: Holt, Rinehart and Winston, 1980.

> A good general overview of motivation is presented in this book.

# M̲otivation and Work

**A** **totally** unifying theory of motivation applicable to work behaviors that can account for variables within the individual, the job and the work environment, and the interactions among these variables does not exist. In the absence of one unifying theory, several theories of motivation specifically applicable to industrial and organizational settings will be reviewed in this chapter. The first two parts of the chapter are concerned with the use of theories of motivation and how those theories apply to human behavior in industrial and organizational environments. The last part of the chapter is related to the application of the concepts of motivation to specific problems and situations encountered in the world of work.

## Use of Theories

The functions served by work provide an opportunity for the application of motivation theory in work situations. The various specific theories of motivation help one understand a worker's behavior. If an employee is viewed as a resource or investment, the various specific theories of motivation are useful in realizing the maximum potential of the worker.

### Tools for Understanding

Several theories of motivation have been proposed which may be used as tools for understanding the everyday work performances of people. Some of the theories may be used as tools for looking at the needs people bring with them into organizations—needs that predispose them to behave in particular ways. Some may be used for seeing how these individual predispositions and situational characteristics come together to produce particular ways of behaving on the job. Some theories of motivation may serve as tools for increasing the probability that employees will perform effectively.

Different theories of motivation are not necessarily contradictory and may be complementary. Therefore, it is more important to decide which theory is most helpful in understanding a particular aspect of employee behavior rather than which theory is valid. Each theory presented has something to offer in the attempt to understand motivation. This means that more than one theory or parts of several theories may be validly used to explain, predict, and control on-the-job behavior.

### Functions Served by Work

Theories of motivation may be used as tools for understanding behaviors in industrial and organizational settings if one is aware of the functions served by work activities in this modern society. With an understanding of the functions of work, the motivation theories presented in this chapter may be more meaningful. First, work provides some form of reward in exchange for service; a worker has an expectation of the type and amount of reward to receive. Second, the workplace provides social interaction—an opportunity for developing friendships. (See Figure 10-1.) Third, a job serves as a source of status. Fourth, work is an important source of identity, self-esteem, and self-actualization. Work may provide a person with a sense of purpose or a sense of value to society and be a source of meaningfulness in his or her life. Or work may be humiliating, frustrating, or boring and be a source of anxiety.

Figure 10-1   The workplace provides an opportunity for social interaction and the development of friendships that satisfy affiliation needs.

## The Human Resources Approach

Most business firms operate according to the philosophy that an employee is an investment. The employee has some knowledge, skills, abilities, etc. (resources) that are an asset to the organization for certain conditions. Motivation may be a key factor in how much of the potential resource an organization realizes from an employee. The human resources approach to management attempts to account for the amount that has been invested in human resources in a business or industry and to determine how well these human resources are being used. For example, an accounting department may be using employees below their optimum level of skill or the employees may not be motivated to perform at their optimum level of performance. The human resources approach proposes that not making maximum use of human resources is just as undesirable for a business firm as not making maximum use of economic resources. This view is characterized by a strong social emphasis which portrays humans as being motivated by a complex set of interrelated factors such as money, the need for affiliation, the need for achievement, or the desire for meaningful work. Use of various theories of motivation may be useful to organizations in utilizing human resources to the maximum.

## Theories Applicable to Work

Since there are many different ways to view human motivation, different theorists and researchers have developed a variety of conceptual frameworks called theories of motivation to help a person, possibly a manager, understand on-the-job behavior of others. A knowledge of motivational theories provides one with the tools for analyzing motivational problems and for making practical application of the theories. Thus, a knowledge of motivational theories may enable a manager to predict the consequences of a course of action. Several of these theories of motivation will be briefly examined—specifically, the network of three basic motives, Maslow's hierarchy of needs, McGregor's Theory X and Theory Y, Herzberg's two-factor theory, and VIE (valence-instrumentality-expectancy) theory.

### Network of Three Basic Motives

A theory of motivation related to socially acquired needs has been proposed by several researchers (McClelland, 1961, 1962; Atkinson, 1964; Stringer, 1971). The theory consists of a network of three basic motives which identifies patterns of behavior—information necessary to the creation of the right kind of work climate for individuals. This network of motives includes the need for achievement, the need for affiliation, and the need for power.

The need for achievement (*nAch*) is the need for success as measured against some internalized standard of excellence. The need for affiliation (*nAff*) is the need for close interpersonal relationships and friendships with other people. The need for power (*nPow*) is the need for direct control or influence over others or the need for control over the means of influencing others. These three basic needs may exist in varying degrees in employees. Extremely high needs for both power and affiliation in an individual are somewhat incompatible; however, extremely high affiliation needs and achievement needs may be compatible. Also, extremely high achievement and power needs would be compatible, although the presence of one does not necessarily indicate the presence of the other.

People with a high need for achievement tend to seek and assume more personal responsibility, to take more risks, to set more challenging but realistic goals, to seek and use more feedback concerning the results of their actions, and to seek out more opportunities in business that will enhance their desire to achieve (McClelland, 1961). Although they are competitive, they tend to avoid intense clashes which may be a common occurrence for those with a need for power.

People with a high need for affiliation seek warm relationships and friendships, are not as concerned with getting ahead as are high achievers, and tend to enjoy jobs that have many interactions with other people. Many people find more satisfaction in being loved than in being powerful or in achieving. In fact, such a person may avoid power because often people in positions of power must make decisions that alienate others. People with a need for affiliation care very much what others think of them.

People with a high need for power seek and enjoy work where power, influence, or authority rests within the job. Individuals with a high need for power may strive intensely for promotions, play organizational politics, and try to win arguments and persuade others.

### Hierarchy of Needs

The American psychologist, Abraham H. Maslow, proposed a simple but very influential theory of motivation with the central theme that human needs are arranged in a hierarchy (Maslow, 1954, 1970). This theory places those needs with a physiological basis, or the primary needs, lowest in the hierarchy because they are the most basic. The secondary needs which have a psychological basis follow a specific order of rank. Maslow's proposed *hierarchy of needs* is shown in Figure 10-2. A

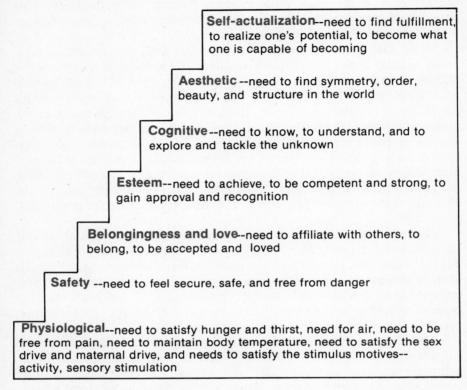

Figure 10-2    Maslow's
hierarchy of needs.

need higher in the hierarchy will become a motive of behavior if the
needs below it have been satisfied. Unsatisfied lower needs will dominate
over unsatisfied higher needs. For *self-actualization*, the need highest in
the hierarchy, to become a motive for behavior all the other needs below
it must be satisfied to some degree. Only unsatisfied needs are motivating; therefore, when one need is satisfied a higher need becomes a motive
for behavior.

The motivational life of a person may be described as a growth
process—a climbing toward self-actualization. Infants are dominated by
hunger and thirst, while young children add the need to feel safe and
secure and the need to be loved and accepted (affiliation and safety needs)
to the physiological needs of infancy. Older children may be driven by
achievement and esteem needs; but self-actualization needs do not arise
until one reaches adulthood. Since people are believed to progress
through this hierarchy in a developmental fashion, many never reach the
self-actualization stage of motivation. Maslow formulated a list of 15
characteristics of self-actualized persons which are presented in the box

on this page. Probably no one is ever completely self-actualized since there are varying degrees of self-actualization; self-actualization itself is a growth process. Self-actualized persons are especially capable of loving and being loved to the fullest extent.

---

CHARACTERISTICS OF SELF-ACTUALIZED PERSONS

a. Self-actualized persons perceive reality more effectively than most people do and have more comfortable relations with it. That is, they *live close to reality* and to nature, can judge others accurately, and can tolerate ambiguity or uncertainty more easily than most people can.

b. They can *accept themselves* and their various characteristics with little feeling of guilt or anxiety and, at the same time, can readily *accept others*.

c. They show a great deal of *spontaneity* in both thought and behavior, although they seldom show extreme unconventionality.

d. They are *problem-centered*, not ego-centered, often devoting themselves to broad social problems as a mission in life.

e. They have a *need for privacy* and solitude at times and are capable of looking at life from a detached, objective point of view.

f. They are relatively *independent of their culture and environment* but do not flaunt convention just for the sake of being different.

g. They are capable of *deep appreciation* of the basic experiences of life, even of things they have done or seen many times before.

h. Many of them have had *mystic experiences* such as having felt a deep sense of ecstasy, having felt limitless horizons opening to them or having felt very powerful and at the same time very helpless but ending with a conviction that something significant had happened.

i. They have a *deep social interest* and identify in a sympathetic way with people in general.

j. They are capable of very *deep, satisfying interpersonal relations,* usually with only a few rather than many individuals.

k. They are *democratic* in their attitudes toward others, showing respect for all people, regardless of race, creed, income level, etc.

l. They discriminate clearly between means and ends but often *enjoy the means toward their ends* ("getting there") more than impatient persons do.

m. They have a good *sense of humor*, tending to be philosophical and nonhostile in their jokes.

n. They are highly *creative*, each in their own individual way. They have "primary creativeness that comes out of the unconscious" and produces truly original, new discoveries. This shows itself in whatever field the self-actualized person has chosen.

o. They are *resistant to enculturation.* That is, although they fit into their culture, they are independent of it and do not blindly comply with all its demands. (Zimbardo, 1979, p. 488)

A person is constantly fluctuating from one need to the other due to temporary conditions and situations. A person is in some state of need all the time. Even though one's behavior may be generally motivated by achievement needs or self-actualization needs, a reverting to lower needs may occur at any time the lower needs become unsatisfied to a certain degree. For example, one may be motivated to accomplish a task (achieve), but finally become hungry enough to stop and eat. Just as unsatisfied needs can drive one down the hierarchy, satisfied needs open up higher needs.

The application of Maslow's theory to the motivation of people at work has important implications. Since managers attempt to influence human behavior, they need to consider what needs are relatively unsatisfied and, thus, can serve as motives. If an employee is not hungry or insecure, offering only rewards that are seen as food and security will not motivate the employee. If an employee has affiliation needs, rewards in the form of social relations might be a good source of motivation. If social needs are relatively satisfied, however, esteem needs tend to become dominant (See Figure 10-3). One's job plays an important role in determining one's self-esteem and the esteem received from others. Just being associated with a prestigious company may help satisfy esteem needs. Rewards for work in the form of fringe benefits such as a new car to drive or a private office may satisfy esteem needs. When all the lower needs are satisfied to a certain degree, the need for the individual to do what is personally satisfying, to realize his or her potentials, and to be self-fulfilled or self-actualized will be the basis for motivation.

Although Maslow's hierarchy of needs has proved to be a useful tool for management to use in considering the relationship of the job to motivation, questions have been raised concerning the fact that adequate scientific research is not available to substantiate it (Cofer & Appley, 1964). When the theory has been tested directly in industrial settings, the empirical results have not always provided clearly supportive evidence (Alderfer, 1969; Beer, 1968; Hall & Nougaim, 1968).

## Theory X and Theory Y

Maslow's theory of motivation has influenced the theories of others. Douglas McGregor (1960) drew heavily on Maslow's theory and proposed that management by direction and control fails to provide effective motivation of human effort toward organizational objectives. Management by direction and control fails because the two methods are useless for motivating people whose physiological and safety needs are reasonably satisfied and whose affiliation, self-esteem, and self-actualization needs are dominant. McGregor believed that a theory of managing people based on concepts of motivation and human nature as an integrative view was

Figure 10-3  Esteem needs may be satisfied when a manager polishes an employee's ego and causes him or her to feel more important.

needed. He proposed such a theory and labeled it *Theory Y*. He labeled the conventional management theory, based on external direction and control, *Theory X*. The assumptions in Theory X are as follows:

1. The average human being has an inherent dislike of work and will avoid it if possible.
2. Because of this human characteristic of dislike of work, most people must be coerced, controlled, directed, or threatened with punishment to get them to put forth adequate effort toward the achievement of organizational objectives.
3. The average human being prefers to be directed, wishes to avoid responsibility, has relatively little ambition, and wants security above all (McGregor, 1960, pp. 33-34).

The assumptions in McGregor's Theory Y, the integrative view, are listed below:

1. The expenditure of physical and mental effort in work is as natural as play or rest.
2. External control and the threat of punishment are not the only means for bringing about effort directed toward achieving organizational objectives. People will exercise self-direction and self-control in the service of objectives to which they are committed.
3. Commitment to objectives is a function of the rewards associated with the achievement of those objectives.
4. The average human being learns, under proper conditions, not only to accept but also to seek responsibility.
5. The capacity to exercise a relatively high degree of imagination, ingenuity, and creativity in the solution of organizational problems is widely, not narrowly, distributed in the population.
6. Under the conditions of modern industrial life, the intellectual potentialities of the average human being are only partially fulfilled (McGregor, 1960, pp. 47-48).

Some people seem to have developed qualities that fit the assumptions of Theory X and require direction and control based on imposed authority. They seem to prefer to be told what to do. But to assume that Theory X characteristics are innate or inherited and are applicable to all employees is not justifiable. Attempts to use Theory Y assumptions to manage employees who fit Theory X assumptions will probably fail. Likewise, management of those who fit the Theory Y assumptions with Theory X assumptions will probably result in a great deal of difficulty. McGregor proposes that everyone has the potential for the behaviors and attitudes described in Theory Y and is capable of being intrinsically motivated although some people may have developed qualities that fit Theory X because of environmental situations.

Theory X organizations try to increase the quantity and quality of work by offering extrinsic rewards such as increased pay, fringe benefits, or shorter work weeks. Theory Y organizations prefer to rely on intrinsic rewards for producing positive results in the quantity and quality of work performed.

Critics of McGregor's theory point out that the behavioral characteristics of both Theory X and Theory Y represent extreme examples of motivation and human nature in the general population. Perhaps in reality very few people consistently demonstrate the characteristics of either theory. To view the characteristics of people on a continuum from the extreme of Theory X to the extreme of Theory Y would be more realistic. McGregor's theory, like Maslow's, has been criticized because it is not consistently in accord with research. Some Theory X organizations do not seem to have problems; but for those that do application of Theory Y does not always solve the problems.

## A Two–Factor Theory

Frederick Herzberg, a well-known industrial psychologist, was also influenced by Maslow when he proposed a two-factor theory of motivation. Herzberg proposed that workers have two independent sets of needs that function differently (Herzberg, 1968). One set he called *hygiene* or *maintenance factors* which are part of the job content but are external to the job itself. A favorable work environment, financial rewards, fringe benefits, relations with peers and supervisors, and company policies are hygiene factors. Herzberg concluded that when a person believes these factors to be inadequate, dissatisfaction occurs. But when these factors are believed to be adequately present, they do not generate satisfaction or motivate to greater productivity. Positive feelings aroused by these factors, such as a word of praise from a supervisor or an increase in pay, are of very short duration. Hygiene factors are needs which must be satisfied merely to avoid worker dissatisfaction. However, these factors may attract a person to accept a job in an organization, help reduce turnover, prevent rebellion, or make it possible for a worker to be motivated.

Herzberg called the second set of job-related needs *motivation factors*. These factors occur at the time the work is performed and make the work rewarding in and of itself. The situation in which the work is performed is not a motivating factor. When present, motivating factors lead to job satisfaction and increased productivity; but their absence, according to Herzberg, rarely produces dissatisfaction. Examples of motivating factors are: achievement, recognition, advancement, responsibility, growth possibilities, and the work itself. Figure 10-4 is a diagram of the relationships in Herzberg's theory.

Some research supports the two-factor theory of motivation. Herzberg (1968) conducted 12 different studies assessing job-related events which lead to extreme dissatisfaction and to extreme satisfaction. The 1,844 events classified as motivation factors were found to be associated primarily with job satisfaction; the 1,753 events classified as hygiene factors were found to be associated primarily with job dissatisfaction.

Probably the most controversial part of Herzberg's two-factor theory is that "satisfaction" and "dissatisfaction" are viewed as two separate and distinct variables rather than as opposite ends of a continuum of a single variable. Some critics believe the theory is oversimplified since some studies of job attitudes have not found the existence of two independent factors corresponding to Herzberg's "motivators" and "hygienes" (Campbell, Dunnette, Lawler, & Weick, 1970). In addition, a high level of job satisfaction has not always been found to result in a high motivation to produce (Kahn, 1960; Smith, Kendall, & Hulin, 1969). Herzberg's theory has, however, received much attention and has been useful in the world of work in drawing attention to intrinsic motivation.

**Motivational Force**

← ─────────────────          ───────────────── →

| Force in a<br>Dissatisfied Direction | No Force | Force in a<br>Satisfied Direction |
|---|---|---|
| Hygiene factors absent | Hygiene factors present<br><br>Motivation factors absent | Motivation factors present |

Figure 10-4    Herzberg's two-factor theory.

## VIE Theory

In the 1930s, Kurt Lewin and E. C. Tolman developed a theory of motivation based on the expectation or anticipation of reward which involved the mental processes—information processing in the brain. Since information processing involves the cognitive processes such as perception, memory, thinking, and intelligence, this theory of motivation is called a cognitive theory. Several psychologists have built on this theory. Their research has developed a theory of work motivation (Atkinson, 1964; Campbell et al., 1970; Edwards, 1954; Peak, 1955; Porter & Lawler III, 1968; Rotter, 1955; Vroom, 1964) which has come to be known as valence-instrumentality-expectancy or *VIE theory*. The expectancy or anticipation of reward energizes behavior while the valence or perceived value of various outcomes gives direction to behavior. Outcomes may be first-level outcomes—a direct result of the behavior. For example, the direct outcome (first-level outcome) of meeting some set production quota may be to receive an award certificate. However, this outcome may lead to some other outcomes called second-level outcomes. For example, the worker may be chosen over another applicant for a job at a later date because of the award certificate received, or the worker may receive praise from friends and relatives who see the certificate.

VIE theory has several assumptions. (1) The work behavior of an individual is the result of a deliberate, conscious choice in order to attain a predetermined outcome (see Figure 10-5). (2) The individual worker has a belief that a certain behavior will lead to a particular outcome (expectancy). (3) The individual worker has a belief concerning the value of a

"*I chose to work on this job because I expect a paycheck at the end of each week with which I can purchase a camera that I want and need very much.*"

Figure 10-5    A worker makes a choice to work based on an expected reward, the value of that reward, and the instrumentality of that reward.

particular outcome (*valence*). (4) The belief concerning the value of a particular outcome (first level) is dependent on the ability of the outcome to achieve or secure other outcomes (second level) and the value or valence of these other outcomes (*instrumentality*). In other words, a relationship is perceived between achievement of the first- and second-level outcomes. (5) Both intrinsic and extrinsic rewards are recognized; however, neither is recognized as more desirable or more significant. (6) The individual worker has a perception of the ratio between effort and reward obtained from the effort as well as a perception of the relation of the ratio to another person's ratio between effort and reward obtained. A perception of inequity between a person's own ratio of effort to reward and another person's ratio may lead to a greater expenditure of effort in order to increase the reward. Or the inequity between ratios may result in a withdrawal from the work situation. If a worker perceives his or her reward as excessive he or she may continue to exert the same amount of effort for the reward or may decrease the amount of effort being exerted.

In VIE theory, one should note that it is perception that is important, not reality, and that outcomes gain their valence or value from their relationship to the needs of the individual. Valence or value of the outcome toward which work behavior is directed may be specified internally by the individual's own value system as well as by external specifications of others. For example, the outcome of working seven days a week to meet a production quota by a particular deadline might be very valuable economically, but one's internal value system may place a higher value on time spent with a family member or in religious activities. Additionally, one should keep in mind that a primary determiner of expectancy may be an employee's perception of personal skills, talents, or abilities to accomplish a particular outcome.

VIE theory encompasses many factors and is more complex than the previously mentioned theories since an individual is viewed as seeking a network of many interrelated outcomes rather than a single outcome. VIE theory does seem to offer one of the best understandings of motivation, and the theory is currently being given much attention by those concerned with behavior in organizations. For instance, many research studies have been launched during the past decade in an effort to obtain empirical support of the expectancy theory. Although expectancy models have not done very well in demonstrating relations among expectations, effort, and performance (Bass & Barrett, 1981), they have led to asking the right questions about what motivates a person to work. Questions that are being asked today are questions such as: What outcomes does an employee expect from work? How much are the expected outcomes valued? How important are the expected outcomes in comparison with other outcomes? To what extent will the expected outcomes interfere with obtaining other outcomes? To what extent are employees dependent on other outcomes to obtain the expected outcomes? To what extent can other people block obtaining the outcomes? How much effort will be required to obtain the expected outcomes? Are there shortcuts to obtaining the expected outcomes?

## Application of Motivation Concepts

Explaining why a person behaves in a particular way in order to predict and influence human behavior has practical applications for organizations in such areas as marketing, decreasing absenteeism and employee turnover, increasing job satisfaction, increasing production, and building morale. Psychologists are often consulted by organizations and asked to make studies of human factors involved in these areas.

### Marketing

The area of marketing is concerned with the buying and selling of products and services. Of course, the person producing and marketing products needs to know who will buy, how many will buy, how much will be bought, and where the buying will occur. Going beyond these questions and finding out why a product or service is bought is extremely important in marketing. Psychologists call the study of why people buy things *motivation research*. Motivation research tries to discover what drives, motives, needs, desires, emotions, attitudes, or preferences of consumers are involved in the choice of a product or service (see Figure 10-6). Motivation research tries to uncover the unconscious motives for the choice of a product or service.

After a motive has been uncovered for selecting a product or service, questionnaires and field interviews may be used to find how many people have this specific motivation. No new research techniques are used by psychologists doing motivation research, but the findings are valuable for improving marketing programs. Influences in buying, new markets, and direction for new advertising can be revealed through motivation research. Motivation research is increasing because it offers a better understanding of the unconscious motivation as well as the conscious motivation of consumers. It provides the marketer with more than statistics concerning the number or percentage of people who buy a product; it finds out why some people buy and others do not so that more effective appeals may be used in advertising.

Figure 10-6   Motivation research identifies motives, perhaps unknown to the consumer, for buying a product.

## *Job Satisfaction and Organizational Problems*

*Job satisfaction* has been related to a number of organizational problems. According to motivation theories, job satisfaction depends on whether one's personal needs, wants, desires, and expectations are fulfilled or satisfied by the job. Also, job satisfaction may depend on whether the job is compared favorably to some reference group.

Consistently, studies indicate that dissatisfied workers are absent more often from their jobs and have greater turnover than employees who are satisfied (Atchison & Lefferts, 1972; Herzberg, Mausner, Peterson, & Capwell, 1957). In general, it seems that people have a tendency to avoid situations that are not satisfying. If this line of reasoning is applied, workers who are dissatisfied can be expected to quit their jobs or to be absent more frequently than workers who are satisfied. Perhaps absenteeism, which is temporary withdrawal, may be the easiest and least painful way for an employee to express dissatisfaction, especially since many companies give employees full pay when they are absent due to illness (Bass & Barrett, 1972). Other actions such as tardiness, leaving early, and taking longer than authorized lunch or coffee breaks are ways of temporarily avoiding the job situation. Fulfillment of needs has been related to turnover in a study of the needs of a group of workers who had quit their jobs compared to a matched group who had not quit. No difference was found in the needs and their strengths between groups; however, a significant difference was found in the degree to which their needs had been fulfilled (Ross & Zander, 1957).

Research studies have found significant correlations between job satisfaction or dissatisfaction and physical symptoms such as fatigue, shortness of breath, headaches, and ill health (Burke, 1969/1970). The fact that a dissatisfied worker usually experiences more stress thus producing biochemical changes which lead to physical illness is a factor in accounting for these findings. Since one's job is part of one's life, significant correlations between job satisfaction and life satisfaction and mental health have been found (Barrett, 1972; Kornhauser, 1965). The strongest relationship between specific job attributes and mental health was for the attribute of opportunity to use abilities.

A series of investigations in the 1960s referred to as the Michigan Studies was carried out by the Survey Research Center at the University of Michigan. The purpose of these studies was to determine the relationships between productivity and supervisory practices. A successful leader or supervisor was defined in terms of productivity and employee satisfaction. The group of studies revealed two general concepts (Higgins, 1982). To be successful the supervisor or leader must be employee-oriented enough to maintain some degree of job satisfaction as well as production-oriented enough to get the job done. The leader must consider employees as human beings who may be intrinsically motivated and who have individual and personal needs. The leader must also stress production and technical aspects of the job and view employees as the means of achieving the goals of the organization. The leader must behave in both behaviors in varying degrees. The researchers concluded that there is no clearcut relationship between job satisfaction and increased productivity (Kahn, 1960).

## Motivational Strategies

*Job redesign* is a procedure employed by some organizations in an effort to fulfill employees' intrinsic needs by applying principles of motivation. Fulfillment of intrinsic needs should lead to greater job satisfaction according to Herzberg's theory that motivation factors lead to satisfaction while hygiene factors only avoid dissatisfaction. Job redesign includes elements of increased responsibility, autonomy, job rotation, and increased employee participation.

Much has been written about job redesign in two automobile plants in Sweden—Volvo and Saab-Scania. In a job redesign experiment in the upholstery department at Volvo which included job rotation, it was reported that jealousy and bickering among employees disappeared since jobs were no longer inequitable. Employees came to realize they had exaggerated the differences between jobs. Also, turnover that had been running 35 percent fell to 15 percent. The managing director of Volvo became convinced that a correlation existed between increased motivation, increased job satisfaction, and a decrease in the turnover of employees through the use of job redesign. A new Volvo plant architecturally planned to include job redesign concepts was justified by the expected decrease in turnover, improvement in quality of production, and reduction in absenteeism. The managing director of Volvo strongly believes a way must be found to create a workplace that meets the needs of the modern worker for the purpose of increasing satisfaction in daily work without adversely affecting productivity (Dowling, 1978).

Inspired by Herzberg's theory, American Telephone & Telegraph Co. (AT & T) has undertaken programs of job redesign directed toward making the work itself more rewarding, challenging, and meaningful to employees (Alderfer, 1976). For job redesign programs to be successful, theoretically, they must motivate growth needs.

Another innovation becoming more popular in an effort to meet workers' needs is *flexible scheduling* (see Figure 10-7) which allows workers to schedule their own 40 hours of work a week within the time the organization is in operation. This system has been shown to decrease tardiness and absenteeism and to increase productivity (Laird, Laird, Fruehling, & Swift, 1975). The four-day work week is another innovation allowing workers to schedule their working hours according to their own

*"Now that both our jobs allow for flexible scheduling, we can take more family trips, have one of us home with the children most of the time, and plan our schedules to attend our community service club meetings."*

Figure 10-7    Such innovations as flexible scheduling are a result of the recent trend for organizations to focus on the interrelationships between the world of work and the family, the community, and changing sex role definitions.

desires and needs in an effort to increase job satisfaction. Job satisfaction has been shown to be partly determined by the worker's perception of the degree to which the hours of work facilitate or interfere with valued off-the-job activities (Mott, Mann, McLoughlin, & Warwick, 1965).

Various *job enrichment* programs have been put into effect in an effort to increase job satisfaction. Job enrichment is the process of making jobs more challenging and interesting by increasing personal responsibility for one's work, by providing the opportunity for personal achievement and recognition, and by expanding opportunities for psychological growth and development. For example, the Monsanto plant in Florida eliminated dull and dirty jobs by automation and made workers their own managers. The reported results indicated waste dropped to zero and production was up by 50 percent (*Work in America*, 1972). Many firms are providing educational courses at the job site as well as implementing refund programs to pay for all or part of tuition costs for courses at schools outside the organization to meet the growth needs of workers.

Job enrichment is the introduction of elements for increasing job satisfaction—the introduction of motivation factors as proposed by Herzberg's two-factor theory, while job redesign introduces hygiene as well as motivation factors and has elements for avoiding dissatisfaction as well as increasing satisfaction. The terms are often incorrectly used interchangeably in industry.

Goal setting is considered to be related to job satisfaction and productivity (Myers, 1970). Expectancy theory suggests that whether one's expectancies are met is a factor in job satisfaction. Job satisfaction then depends on whether there is a discrepancy between what the environment offers, what is expected, and what is attained. Goal setting could possibly reduce such discrepancies. Goals may create a sense of meaningfulness by providing the employee with a greater sense of worthwhile contribution to the organization, may provide challenge, may shift greater responsibility to the employee while reducing supervisory control, and may provide reinforcement through some form of feedback.

Individual differences play an important role in goal setting. For example, research suggests that individuals with high need for achievement performed tasks better than individuals with low need for achievement (Steers, 1975, 1976). When assigned clear and specific goals, individuals with high need for achievement pursued goals no matter how much freedom they were given and tended to prefer more difficult goals than individuals with low need for achievement. Also, higher correlations between goal setting and job involvement were found for people with low need for affiliation than for those high in need for affiliation. Identifying and effectively dealing with individual differences may determine whether a job redesign program, flexible scheduling, job enrichment, or goal setting program will be a success or failure.

### Morale

*Morale* is often discussed in the context of motivation, but exactly what the term means is not always clear. Morale seems to be a word with many meanings such as degree of happiness, amount of conflict, extent of ego involvement, and attitudes. Guion (1961) has defined morale to include all these meanings: "Morale is the extent to which an individual's needs are satisfied and the extent to which the individual perceives that satisfaction as stemming from his total job situation" (p. 303). High morale then would be indicated by little conflict, a feeling of happiness, good personal adjustment, many favorable attitudes, and cohesiveness—a "we feeling" which comes from finding personal need satisfaction within a group. Correlations found between morale and overall satisfaction suggest that morale may be a function of general satisfaction (Motowidlo & Borman, 1978).

Another view proposed that high morale exists when the individual perceives a high probability of achieving both individual and group goals through a course of action and that whenever the individual perceives a considerable difference between group goals and personal goals, morale will suffer (Stagner, 1958). To raise morale within an organization, situations in which group and individual goals coincide to the greatest extent possible must be created. In military organizations, morale has traditionally been thought to be extremely important for group effectiveness and to be related to motivation.

### The Hawthorne Effect

Reports have been published of cases in which the satisfaction of needs resulted in the improvement of various aspects of an employee's life and the job situation. For example, the satisfaction of needs has been related to the improvement of satisfaction with life in general, the quantity and quality of work and morale, and to a reduction of absenteeism, turnover, jealousy and bickering, and wasted materials on the job. The reported results, however, are not always conclusive as to the role of the satisfaction of needs in these areas because of the phenomenon known as the *Hawthorne effect*. The Hawthorne effect refers to the effect on responses due to the attention given to the participants during the research.

Studies to test the effects of light intensity on productivity were conducted at the Hawthorne plant of the Western Electric Company. The studies began in 1924, gained recognition by 1927, and were published in 1930 (Pennock, 1930). Productivity increased when the light intensity was increased; and a decrease in the light intensity also increased productivity. The control group in the experiment had no change in the light intensity but also experienced an increase in productivity. Something other than the light intensity, the variable being manipulated, was causing the increase in productivity (Roethlisberger & Dickson, 1939). The attention and concern shown by management affected the temporary favorable results. Sometimes it is difficult to determine whether subjects participating in an experiment are responding to fulfillment of needs or to the knowledge that they are participating in an experiment. The Hawthorne studies emphasized the importance of correctly identifying the causes and effects of motivation. Desiring to please the researcher, reacting to special status, or noticing the introduction, removal, or reintroduction of treatment may, in some situations, affect responding.

The conclusion was drawn from the Hawthorne studies that employees are social in nature and group themselves informally to meet social needs. Thus, meeting social needs by providing a friendly, cooperative, and conflict-free workplace for employees became important to supervisors who were concerned with increased production. The interpretations of the Hawthorne studies down-graded the role of economic incentives on the grounds that workers were more interested in social relationships than money. The interpretations of the studies shaped the trend of job satisfaction research for the next two decades. This trend became known as the human relations movement—the view that stressed the central importance of the supervisor and work group in determining productivity and employee satisfaction. The workplace came to be viewed more as an informal social organization.

In summary, the conclusion may be drawn from the theories of motivation applicable in work situations and studies of motivation as related to marketing, job satisfaction, morale, and increased productivity that behavior on the job is both a function of what the person brings to the job situation and what the job situation brings to the person. Each worker brings different needs which predispose him or her to behave in particular ways. The work situation provides cues which can arouse particular behavioral tendencies. The cues can signal to the individual that particular behaviors may lead to particular outcomes that will or will not satisfy needs. An individual's needs and the satisfaction of those needs explains that individual's behavior whether on or off the job.

## *SUMMARY*

1. Various theories and parts of theories contribute to understanding motivation in the work situation, but no totally unifying theory of motivation applicable to work behaviors exists.

2. The human resources approach to motivation recognizes that the workplace provides rewards and social interactions and serves as a source of status and self-actualization.

3. The need for affiliation, need for achievement, and need for power are three basic socially acquired motives which identify patterns of individual behavior important in the creation of the right kind of work climate for individual employees.

4. Maslow's theory of a hierarchy of needs proposes a ranked order of priority for need satisfaction. Motivation is a general progression up the hierarchy; however, needs constantly fluctuate due to temporary conditions.

5. McGregor proposed an integrative view of managing people which assumes that any person is capable of being intrinsically motivated (Theory Y) versus the traditional view that assumes an inherent lack of ambition which requires external direction and control (Theory X).

6. Herzberg proposed that two factors exist in the work situation—hygiene factors which are external to the job itself and motivation factors which are related to what the worker does in performing the job. The satisfaction of hygiene factors only avoids dissatisfaction with the job, while satisfaction of the motivation factors produces job satisfaction and increased productivity.

7. VIE theory portrays behavior as being energized and directed by valence, instrumentality, and expectancy. In other words, behavior is energized and directed by the expected probability of the outcome, the believed value of the outcome, the ability of the outcome to achieve other outcomes and the value of the other outcomes.

8. Motivation research to discover why people buy a particular product or service has a practical application in marketing.

9. Job satisfaction resulting from satisfaction of needs seems to be a factor in organizational problems such as absenteeism, tardiness, and turnover and also in the physical health, life satisfaction, and mental health of employees.

10. Some strategies which have been employed in organizations to enhance job satisfaction are job redesign, flexible scheduling, job enrichment programs, and goal setting.

11. Employee morale seems to be related to satisfaction of needs within a group and the perceived probability of achieving the goals and meeting the needs of the individual and the group.

12. In the Hawthorne effect, attention to employees resulted in increased productivity. This shifted the importance of employee satisfaction and productivity to the role of the supervisor as well as the group under study and drew attention to the possibility of mislabeling cause and effect in research studies.

## SUGGESTIONS FOR FURTHER READING

Herzberg, F. *Work and the nature of man*. Cleveland: World Publishing Company, 1966.

Herzberg's ideas concerning motivation and work are presented in this book.

Herzberg, F. Motivation, morale, money. In T. J. Cottle & P. Whitten (Eds.), *Readings in personality and adjustment*. New York: Harper & Row, 1978.

This is an article about the research study from which the motivation-hygiene concepts arose. Misconceptions about money as a motivator and morale builder are discussed and job examples are given of how challenge can be put into a routine job.

Lawler, E. E., III. *Motivation in work organizations*. Monterey, Calif.: Brooks/Cole, 1973.

The application of motivational principles to the world of work is discussed in this book.

Maslow, A. H. *Motivation and personality* (2nd ed.). New York: Harper & Row, 1970.

This book is the most complete version of Maslow's general theory of motivation. It is a highly readable and systematic presentation of his own views.

McClelland, D. C. The two faces of power. *Journal of International Affairs*, 1970, *24* (1), 29-47.

This article explains the need for power.

McClelland, D. C. *Power: The inner experience*. New York: Irvington, 1975.

The power motive and its influence are discussed. The discussion includes the relationship of power to individual maturity, cultural ways, and war.

Packard, V. *The hidden persuaders*. New York: McKay, 1957.

An intriguing book which covers motivational research and unconscious motivation.

Steers, R. M., & Porter, L. W. (Eds.). *Motivation and work behavior* (2nd ed.). New York: McGraw-Hill, 1979.

This text uses journal articles to demonstrate the application of motivational principles to work in organizations. It also illustrates and gives contrasting viewpoints on how to motivate employees.

Vroom, V. H. *Work and motivation*. New York: Wiley, 1964.

This book reviews the factor analytic studies on measures of job satisfaction.

Winter, D. G. *The power motive*. New York: Free Press, 1973.

A detailed study of the need for power which includes an analysis of the famous lover, Don Juan, in terms of the power motive. It is a comprehensive look at the motive to seek and acquire power and mastery over others.

# Chapter 11
# Emotion and Stress

**P**eople experience feelings such as fear, anger, sadness, guilt, happiness, joy, pleasure, and love. If people were incapable of feeling, life would be rather colorless and monotonous. Individuals would be more like computers or robots—able to think and behave but without feeling.

Emotions are related to stress and how a person reacts to stressful events in life. Stress in the form of competition at work, deadlines to meet, or financial concerns makes emotional demands on a person. Emotional stress is unavoidable and, up to a point, may be beneficial; however, intense emotional stress over an extensive period of time may have adverse effects. Sometimes an emotion may be a very positive force, or an emotion may be a very negative force that overwhelms and destroys a person. This chapter will focus on human emotion and psychological stress which people may experience in their personal and work lives.

## Concept of Emotion

Emotion involves many different feelings and constantly fills an individual's life. Though commonly experienced, emotion is not easy to define. Psychologists do tend to agree that emotion is composed of physiological changes in the body and mental activity such as perception and appraisal. And emotion seems to vary according to intensity, degree of pleasantness or unpleasantness, and the desire to approach or avoid.

### Nature of Emotion

**Definition.** Emotion has been defined as a feeling that involves physiological changes and may be expressed through behavior (Morris, 1979). Some psychologists make no attempt to define the concept proposing that it is really too complex and subjective. Many psychologists, however, believe that emotion is a combination of three aspects—physiological changes, feelings, and expressive behavior. For example, fear may be associated with a pounding heart and increased blood pressure along with a subjective feeling of threat to one's well-being which may be expressed by withdrawing from the situation. Pleasure may be associated also with a pounding heart and increased blood pressure, but the subjective feeling enhances one's well-being and may be expressed by engaging in the activity. A person's behavior is motivated by feelings; she or he behaves in order to evade unpleasant emotional states such as fear or guilt and to obtain pleasant emotional states such as happiness, love, pleasure, or joy. A wide range of individual differences exists in emotional experiences—in physiological changes, in the depth of feeling, and in the behavioral expression of the feeling.

**Components.** Emotion consists of a physiological component and a cognitive component. Emotions differ according to the two components—the cognitive component is based on the appraisal of the external situation and the physiological component is based on the intensity of the bodily changes. Some of the physiological changes are controlled by the endocrine glands and the autonomic nervous system (see page 71) and are experienced as bodily sensations. The cerebral cortex and other parts of the brain are also involved in emotions, particularly the cognitive component. Whether one experiences fear, anger, love, or some other emotion depends on the cognitive component which involves the perception of the external stimuli, appraisal of what is perceived, thinking, imagination, and the recall of past experiences. The hypothalamus in the brain is involved in activating the endocrine system to serve as a pathway to and from the cerebral cortex. Particular points in the limbic system (see page 74) are associated with particular feelings of pleasure, rage, and sexual sensations, also. The physiological component determines the intensity of the emotion while the cognitive component determines the kind of emotion.

**Dimensions.** All emotions can be described in terms of three dimensions: approach-avoidance, intensity, and pleasantness-unpleasantness. Because of variations in these dimensions, people respond differently to the same external situations in the same environment (Mehrabian, 1976).

Some of the individual differences in emotion are the result of learning. For example, the roles of classical conditioning and modeling are discussed in Chapter 6. Because of classical conditioning, one individual may have an intense emotional reaction to something that produces no emotional response in another individual. Individuals also vary greatly in the more complex cognitive processes (intelligence, perception, thinking, and memory) which help determine emotional experience. Some differences seem to be inborn. Two inborn differences seem to be (1) the sensitivity of the autonomic nervous system and (2) the size and activity of the endocrine glands both of which play a role in the bodily changes associated with emotion.

Whether the emotion causes a person to run toward or away from an object, person, or event is the basis for classifying an emotion on the approach-avoidance continuum. Generally, the positive emotions like love and pleasure cause approach reactions, and the negative emotions like fear and anxiety lead to avoidance reactions. Anger, however, may lead to approach reactions, but in an attacking and aggressive manner. Whether a person moves away from something or someone because of fear, or whether a person moves toward something or someone because of anger depends on how one feels about herself or himself in relationship to the object, event, or person. If there is no hope of controlling the object, situation, or person, a person may want to avoid it. But if there is hope of controlling, a person may approach the object, situation, or person. Thus, the same situation may evoke fear—an avoidance reaction—in one person and anger—an approach reaction—in another person. For example, one employee might like the management of Department X and ask for a transfer to that department. Another employee may not like the management of Department X and request not to be transferred to that department for fear of being fired from the job. Another employee might not like the management of Department X but would ask for a transfer to that department with the hope of "battling it out" and getting the management changed.

The intensity of emotion is the dimension represented by the level of arousal—a person may be a little irritated, angry, or in a rage. Some psychologists suggest that all emotion is just the degree to which a person is stirred up, but all psychologists do not agree with this idea. Robert Plutchik (1962; 1970; 1980) formulated a theory that defines eight primary emotions derived from evolutionary processes in terms of eight basic functions which are essential to the survival of the human species. All other emotions are believed to be varying intensities of these primary emotions or mixtures of these primary emotions. Love, for example, is seen as a combination of joy and acceptance. Hostility or contempt is seen as a combination of anger and disgust.

Plutchik's eight primary emotions and the emotions formed by combinations of these eight emotions are shown in Figure 11-1 on page 258. Emotions across from each other in the wheel are opposites. Plutchik associates each primary emotion with a basic function necessary for species survival. For example, humans must reproduce, protect themselves from dangerous things, deprive themselves of some things, and have an awareness or an orientation of the environment—all of which are necessary for survival of the species. The basic functions necessary for species survival and the primary emotions with which they are associated along with examples of a higher and a lower intensity of each emotion are shown in Table 11-1.

Probably the most obvious dimension used in classifying emotion is pleasant-unpleasantness. A person's feeling may be described as a point on a continuum from extremely unpleasant to extremely pleasant. Sometimes an individual may have both pleasant and unpleasant feelings about an object, person, or event simultaneously. For example, an employee may experience such mixed emotions as joy over the raise received with a promotion and also fear of performing the tasks required with the promotion.

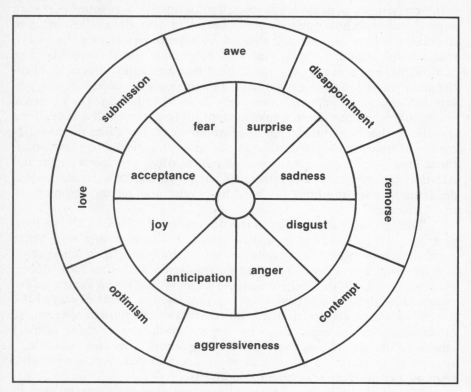

Figure 11-1 Plutchik's eight basic emotions and the emotions formed by combinations of adjacent pairs.

| TABLE 11-1 | Primary Emotions | | |
|---|---|---|---|
| **Function** | **Emotion** | **A Higher Intensity** | **A Lower Intensity** |
| Protection | Fear | Terror | Apprehension |
| Destruction | Anger | Rage | Annoyance |
| Reproduction | Joy | Ecstasy | Pleasure |
| Deprivation | Sadness | Grief | Pensiveness |
| Incorporation | Acceptance | Interest | Attention |
| Rejection | Disgust | Loathing | Boredom |
| Exploration | Anticipation | Watchfulness | Readiness |
| Orientation | Surprise | Amazement | Distraction |

## *Physiology of Emotion*

When people experience intense emotion, they are aware of some but not all of the changes in the body. *Psychophysiologists* who study bodily changes brought on by emotion indicate that the autonomic nervous system, which is part of the peripheral nervous system, produces the physiological changes that occur in emotion.

**Autonomic Nervous System.** The autonomic nervous system consists of nerve fibers leading from the brain and spinal cord to the smooth muscles of the internal organs of the body, certain glands, and blood vessels. As was noted in Chapter 4, the autonomic nervous system consists of two parts: the sympathetic nervous system which is activated by stressful conditions, such as the emotions of fear and anger, and the parasympathetic nervous system which is in control when a person is calm and relaxed. The two systems usually work in opposition to each other, but not always.

The hormones epinephrine (adrenaline) and norepinephrine (noradrenaline) are secreted when the adrenal glands are activated by nerve impulses in the sympathetic nervous system. Epinephrine helps mobilize sugar in the blood to make more energy available to the brain and muscles and causes the heart to beat faster. Norepinephrine constricts the peripheral blood vessels and raises the blood pressure. More norepinephrine is released in anger and more epinephrine is released in fear (Funkenstein, 1955). Consequently, there are some differences between bodily responses in fear and anger. Muscle tension is usually greater in anger; rate and depth of breathing are greater in fear; and the rise in blood pressure is usually higher in anger.

The *relaxation response* is almost the opposite of the bodily emergency reaction of the sympathetic nervous system activated when a person experiences fear, anger, and other strong emotions. The relaxation response consists of bodily responses which include decreased activity in both the sympathetic and somatic nervous systems. Practitioners of *yoga*, a form of meditation derived from an Eastern religion, can induce a state of inner tranquility in which heart rate and breathing rate are reduced and brain wave patterns are indicative of relaxation. *Transcendental meditation*, a simple technique introduced by Maharishi Maheah Yogi, produces relaxation, heightened awareness, and more efficient performance of both mental and manual skill tasks. Another method of relaxation, devised by Herbert Benson (1977) and his colleagues, requires no elaborate training or belief in a religious philosophy. The description of this method appears in the box on page 260.

The parasympathetic nervous system helps to conserve the energy stored in the body by decreasing the heart rate, reducing blood pressure, and directing blood to the digestive tract. The parasympathetic nervous system takes over and returns the body to its normal state as the emotion gradually disappears.

---

### A METHOD OF RELAXATION

1. Sit quietly in a comfortable position and close your eyes.
2. Deeply relax all your muscles, beginning at your feet and progressing up to your face. Keep them deeply relaxed.
3. Breathe through your nose. Become aware of your breathing. As you breathe out, say the word "one" silently to yourself. For example, breathe in . . . out, "one"; in . . . out, "one"; etc. Continue for 20 minutes. You may open your eyes to check the time but do not use an alarm. When you finish, sit quietly for several minutes with closed eyes and later with opened eyes.
4. Do not worry about whether you are successful in achieving a deep level of relaxation. Maintain a passive attitude and permit relaxation to occur at its own pace. Expect other thoughts. When these distracting thoughts occur, ignore them by thinking "Oh, well" and continue repeating "one." With practice, the relaxation response should come with little effort. Practice the technique once or twice daily, but not within two hours after any meal, since the digestive processes interfere with the changes in the autonomic nervous system that bring about relaxation (Benson, Kotch, Crassweller, & Greenwood, 1977, p. 442; Morgan, King, & Robinson, 1979, p. 254).

---

**Central Nervous System.** The brain, primarily the cortex, is involved in (1) perception and appraisal of situations that produce emotion; (2) control of the bodily responses in somatic and autonomic activity; and (3) direction of the behavior motivated by the emotion. As mentioned in Chapter 4, in the core of the brain is a complex group of structures, including the hypothalamus, known as the limbic system. Stimulation of certain points in the limbic system and hypothalamus has produced great change in emotional behavior. Humans have experienced great pleasure when the posterior hypothalamus was stimulated and experienced sexual sensations when the *septal region*, a structure in the core of the brain, was stimulated (Delgado, 1969).

## Communication of Emotion

Whenever people are together, they are constantly communicating how they feel and monitoring the feelings of others. Emotion is perceived from many sources and may be communicated verbally and nonverbally.

## Verbal Communication

Although people may be aware of their feelings and are willing to communicate the emotion verbally, they often find it hard to describe their own emotions. In some situations, people do not know what their emotions really are; consequently, they cannot verbally communicate their feelings. Sometimes the emotion is minimized or denied entirely to avoid hurting another person or to conform to how a person believes he or she is supposed to feel. Sometimes a person verbally states the opposite of the emotion really felt. For example, a secretary fails to show up for work one day, and the office manager has a busy day trying to manage without any help. When the secretary comes to work the next day, the office manager may say, "I hope you enjoyed your day yesterday" rather than saying, "I'm furious that you did not show up for work yesterday."

Sometimes an individual has difficulty determining another person's emotions based on verbal communication. Almost everyone at times, consciously or unconsciously, attempts to hide his or her emotions to protect his or her self-image or to conform to social expectations. Sometimes words are inadequate to describe emotions, and often the same word may be used in many different ways. The verbal communication of emotion is, therefore, usually considered to be inadequate.

## Nonverbal Communication

Since the bodily changes associated with emotions are not normally under the control of the individual, emotions are communicated through facial expressions, body postures and gestures, vocal intonations, and *proxemics* (physical distance and eye contact). These nonverbal communications are probably more reliable indications of emotion than verbal communications.

**Facial Expression.** Facial expression is an indicator of emotion that seems to be at least partially innate. Some psychologists believe that facial expressions are the key factor in emotional experience. These psychologists believe that every basic emotion is accompanied by a characteristic facial pattern that occurs automatically as a result of hereditary programming (Izard, 1977). The various patterns are believed to be the product of evolution. Charles Darwin noted that most animals, including humans, share a common pattern of facial expressions. For example, they all bare their teeth in rage. Children who are born blind and deaf exhibit the same facial expressions for emotions as do children born without these defects. For example, they smile for joy or raise their eyebrows for surprise. Further evidence for universal facial expressions for the basic emotions is provided by Paul Ekman and his associates (1975). They showed photographs of six facial expressions to college students in five countries and found that the students in all countries accurately identified most of the emotions. (See Figure 11-2.)

The pupils of the eyes enlarge involuntarily whenever one experiences pleasant emotions. People with large pupils are usually perceived as being more attractive, warmer, or happier while people with smaller pupils are usually perceived as being angrier, less friendly, or more selfish (Hess, 1975). A salesperson may unconsciously rely more on watching the eyes of prospective buyers to know what they really like than on what is verbally communicated.

In an experiment, people were shown groups of three photographs similar to the group in Figure 11-3 on page 263. Photograph *a* is a picture that has not been altered. Photograph *b* is composed of two right halves of the face shown in the original photograph with one half flipped over to form the left side. Photograph *c* consists of two left halves of the face shown in the photograph with one half flipped over to form the right side. The left-face combinations were found to give the clearest, strongest expression of the emotion (Sackeim, Gur, & Saucy, 1978). In Chapter 4, it

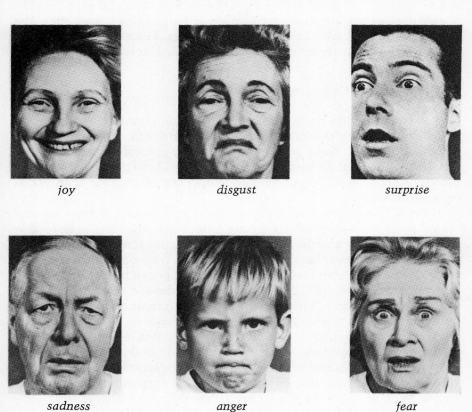

*joy*  *disgust*  *surprise*

*sadness*  *anger*  *fear*

Figure 11-2 Facial expressions of emotions.

was pointed out that the right and left hemispheres of the brain are not equal partners. The right half of the brain which controls the left side of the face and body seems to specialize in spatial relationships, form, music, and achieving the overall picture instead of details. Also, there is some evidence that the right half of the brain is dominant in controlling the muscles of the face. The left half of the brain which controls the right side of the face and body specializes in language, logic, and details. The left half of the brain is the analytical brain, and the right half is the feeling brain. This research suggests that a person should concentrate on the left side of the face and ignore the right side to perceive how another person really feels.

**Kinesics.** Body postures and gestures as well as facial expressions have been studied as nonverbal expressions of emotion. The study of body language has been made into a science called *kinesics* (Birdwhistell, 1952). When a person directly faces and leans toward another person, the emotion of interest and acceptance is indicated. The body of a person experiencing anxiety may be rather rigid and straightbacked. A person who is feeling relaxed will likely be loose rather than rigid in his or her movements. When people are consciously trying to keep an emotion from showing in their faces, they are less conscious about their bodies, legs, feet, and hands which may give cues also. For example, a poker player may be able to avoid communicating a facial expression that would indicate the joy and excitement of having a good hand, but the player may unconsciously lean forward in expectancy of collecting the chips. Gestures such as a handshake, a slap on the back, a touch, and an embrace communicate feelings. Clenching the fist usually indicates anger; covering the eyes, shame or embarrassment; and rubbing the hands together, anticipation or excitement.

|  |  |  |
|:--:|:--:|:--:|
| *a* | *b* | *c* |

Figure 11-3 Three facial expressions of an emotion. Most people perceive photograph *c* as a clearer and stronger expression of the emotion.

**Paralanguage.** Communication of emotion by voice intonations, not words, is called *paralanguage.* For example, the pitch and loudness of the voice, pauses, exclamations, stuttering, and voice inflections are para-language. Screams may be indicative of fear; sobs, sorrow; laughter, joy; and groans, pain or unhappiness. A tremoring voice may mean grief or great sorrow, and a loud, high-pitched voice usually means anger. Also, the pitch of the voice has been found to have a tendency to rise when the person is lying (Freedman, Sears, & Carlsmith, 1978).

**Proxemics.** Another way emotions are communicated nonverbally is by the physical distance kept from the person or by the eye contact that is maintained. *Proxemics* is the word used to describe this form of emotional communication. A standard distance seems to prevail that is appropriate for normal conversation. This standard distance varies from culture to culture. Whenever someone stands closer than this standard distance, it indicates an approach emotion—perhaps aggression or affection. Whenever someone stands farther away than the standard distance, it indicates an avoidance emotion—perhaps fear or disgust.

The eyes are prominent in facial features, and eye contact may be an indicator of an overall emotional state. A psychological distance seems to be maintained through eye contact. Looking into a person's eyes is like "going inside the person." A number of studies suggest that frequent eye contact with another person is a sign of an approach emotion, but eye contact may be interpreted as friendliness or hostility associated with anger. As in physical distance, a standard or normal amount of time seems to prevail for eye contact. Gazing for a longer than standard time may indicate unusual dislike or hostility or unusual attraction as in love or sexual attraction. Gazing for less than a standard amount of time may indicate a fear of psychological closeness, guilt, negative thoughts, the desire to withdraw from the other person, a general lack of interest as in depression, or a fear of people in general as in shyness. An individual is often aware of another person's feelings from cold stares or warm glances.

The more a person looks at another person, the more dominant, potent, or self-confident that person appears (Argyle, Lefebvre, & Cook, 1974). Eye contact then can communicate liking and self-confidence, but it can also communicate dominance, anger, and hostility. This sounds perplexing, but a person usually has no trouble distinguishing between a stare of love and a stare of hate.

Emotions that occur in work situations are often communicated through nonverbal behaviors. Being aware of this and developing the ability to perceive the emotions of others from these behaviors can be an invaluable asset in the world of work. In addition, people may improve their nonverbal communication by consciously attending to it, just as people may improve their verbal communication. Five suggestions for improving nonverbal forms of communication are: (1) Obtain feedback by asking others to comment upon gestures and facial expressions you use, or use videotape to study these yourself. (2) Learn to relax while communicating by using tension-reducing techniques. (3) Increase the impact of enthusiastic comments by using gestures. (4) Avoid overusing a particular gesture indiscriminately such as nodding approval to everything even though a statement is not necessarily liked, or patting everyone on the back even though the person is disliked. (5) Maintain the proper physical distance when conversing with a person—about one and a half feet if the purpose is strictly business (DuBrin, 1980).

### Measurement of Emotion

Although an individual's emotions are assessed constantly by the people with whom the individual has contact, the assessments are usually based on verbal and nonverbal behavioral cues and the situation in which the behavior occurs. This type of assessment is indirect and subjective. The measurement of physiological responses associated with emotion has been used by researchers and other interested individuals as an attempt to measure emotion more directly and objectively. The specific emotion experienced cannot be identified, but the level of emotional arousal can be measured.

In ancient cultures it was observed that emotional arousal was often associated with a dry mouth. People of these cultures determined if a person was guilty of something by giving the suspect a slice of bread and cheese; those who could not swallow it were declared guilty. A suspect might be asked to chew rice powder and spit it out; those who spit out dry powder were considered guilty (Rubin & McNeil, 1981).

Pupil enlargement has been used more recently as a measure of emotion (Hess & Polt, 1960); but pupil enlargement also seems to be indicative of mental activity and attention-arousing stimuli. Pupil responses are often used to measure the interest value of advertisements. Activation of the sympathetic division of the autonomic nervous system causes pupils to enlarge and inhibits the production of saliva along with other bodily changes.

The *polygraph*, commonly called a lie detector, is another modern attempt to measure several physiological responses associated with emotion. The polygraph records changes in heart rate, blood pressure, respiration, and the *galvanic skin response* (GSR), a measure of the resistance of the skin to the conduction of electricity. The theory of lie detection is that lying produces feelings of guilt and fear of being "found out" which would be exhibited in physiological responses measured by the polygraph. A polygraph test is sometimes used as part of a job application to measure emotional responses to questions that may be of interest to the prospective employer—perhaps questions about stealing or drug use (see Figure 11-4).

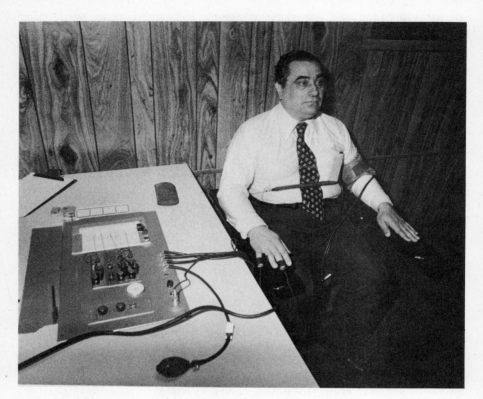

Figure 11-4 A polygraph test is
sometimes used as part of a job
application.

The *psychological stress evaluator,* a new kind of lie detector, has
been recently developed to measure changes in a person's voice that are
undetectable to the human ear. The activity of the sympathetic nervous
system suppresses the vibration of the muscles controlling the vocal
cords when a speaker is under stress. A device called a *voice stress
analyzer* is used to replay the recording of a person's voice four times
slower than the recorded speed and produce a voice printout in graphic
form. Voices may be recorded over the telephone, from radio or television, or from tape recordings as well as in person without the person's
knowledge. The person does not have to be hooked up to any equipment
as with the polygraph.

Psychologists have spent considerable time studying and measuring
the bodily processes that take place during emotional states. The polygraph and the voice stress analyzer give a fairly accurate indication of
nervousness, tension, anxiety, or stress; but these do not always indicate

lying. Although many theories propose that lying arouses emotional responses, this may not be true in some cases.

## Theories of Emotion

Various attempts have been made to explain emotion; however, most of the early theories do not account for all three aspects of emotion—the physiological changes, the feelings, and the expressive behavior. A comprehensive theory should explain all three aspects of emotion. In some theories, the physiological changes are thought to be the result of the psychological feeling expressed. In other theories, the physiological changes are thought to be the cause of the psychological feeling experienced. A theory is needed that explains the interaction of the three aspects of emotion. Some of the major theories of emotion are briefly reviewed on the following pages.

### James-Lange Theory

The psychologist, William James (1884), mentioned in Chapter 1, and the physiologist, Carl Lange (1885/1922), proposed that a stimulus may produce a physiological change, and the sensation of this change is the emotion or feeling experienced. Specifically, this theory proposes that individuals feel sorry because they cry; angry because they strike; afraid because they retreat or tremble; happy because they smile; or tickled because they laugh. Although most people think the reverse—that they cry because they are sorry, strike because they are angry, retreat because they are afraid, laugh because they are tickled, or smile because they are happy—the theory does have some limited value today. This theory suggests that by acting a certain way a person may come to feel that way. Perhaps, in some cases a person could overcome feelings of depression by engaging in pleasant activities or overcome fear by approaching the cause of that fear rather than running away. In research with depressed and nondepressed people, a significant relationship was found between mood and the number and type of pleasant activities a person becomes involved in (Rehm, 1978).

### Cannon-Bard Theory

In 1927, Walter Cannon objected to the James-Lange theory, partially on the basis that the physiological arousal of one feeling is not different from the physiological arousal of other feelings. Cannon, with Philip Bard (1928), proposed that a stimulus triggers bodily responses and psychological feelings simultaneously. According to this theory, the thalamus in the brain adds the emotional quality to incoming sensory impulses. The emotional quality, usually inhibited by the cortex, sometimes breaks through the inhibition when strong enough or when earlier associations arouse the cortex. The thalamus then releases a pattern of impulses. The pattern sends messages up to the cortex to mediate the physiological changes. Some situations do not result in emotion because the cortex inhibits the thalamus.

More recent research, however, has shown the Cannon-Bard theory to be inadequate to explain emotion. The thalamus is merely a relay station between the sense organs and the cortex, and emotion is not something that is added to sensory impulses as they pass through the thalamus. The key brain structures for emotion have been found to be those in the limbic system. The adrenal gland is now known to produce both adrenaline (epinephrine) and noradrenaline (norepinephrine), either of which raises blood pressure. Adrenaline, however, has an inhibitory effect and depresses muscular contractions while noradrenaline has an excitatory effect. The immediate spurt of energy brought forth from the emotion of fear may begin and end before the adrenaline or noradrenaline has had much effect on voluntary muscles.

### Cognitive Theory

Neither the James-Lange theory nor the Cannon-Bard theory considered that such mental activities as thinking, evaluating, appraising, or interpreting play a role in emotion. According to cognitive theory, emotion results from an interpretation of perceived bodily arousal. Previous experience and interpretations of the present situation directly affect the psychological feeling.

**Schachter's Theory.** Research conducted by Stanley Schachter and Jerome Singer (1962) has suggested that a stimulus produces an aroused state of the nervous system. This includes both the cerebral cortex in the central nervous system where appraisal (perception and interpretation) occurs and the autonomic nervous system where physiological changes are produced. Emotion is the result of both the appraisal of the stimulus and the aroused bodily condition. Appraisal and arousal are interrelated. If appraisals can be changed, bodily changes could be influenced; and if bodily changes can be changed, cognitive appraisals of a situation could be affected. For example, if a supervisor is angry because of a situation at home or a recent occurrence in a management meeting, a mistake made by a secretary may be appraised differently than when the supervisor is in a relaxed state. If the mistake is appraised as nonthreatening and only involves the cost of retyping a page, the supervisor will not be aroused to anger as intensely as he or she might be if the mistake is evaluated as possibly causing the company to lose a $100,000 contract or as threatening the supervisor's ego by causing the supervisor to appear stupid.

Schachter supported his theory by demonstrating in an experiment that people aroused physiologically with an injection of adrenaline (epinephrine) adopted the psychological feeling of their partners who had been instructed to be either euphoric and friendly or angry and resentful. When the individual was correctly informed as to the effects of the adrenaline and knew what to expect, he or she was not as euphoric or angry as those who had not been informed or were incorrectly informed (Schachter & Singer, 1962). Schachter believes that the situation a person is in when aroused gives clues as to the label for the specific psychological feeling. Whether the arousal is labeled as love, hate, fear, etc., depends on the situation and the person's appraisal.

**Arnold's Theory.** Magda Arnold (1960) emphasized appraisal—perception and interpretation—in her theory of emotion. Emotion is viewed as a tendency toward something that is appraised as good or away from something that is appraised as bad. Attraction and aversion are each accompanied by the pattern of physiological changes that prepares the body for action—approach or withdrawal. If a stimulus is appraised as neutral, these physiological changes are not elicited. Appraisal of a stimulus is believed to occur almost instantaneously and precedes emotion which includes bodily arousal. According to Arnold's theory, the feeling experienced and the physiological changes that lead to expressive behavior are both determined by the appraisal that occurs in the cerebral cortex. A business executive might see a person approaching and appraise the situation as good based on memories or imaginations of sales made; or the executive might appraise the situation as bad based on memories or imaginations of being robbed and mugged. In either case, the appraisal would produce a physiological response and the business executive would experience a psychological feeling that would produce a direct action—joy with approach and attempts to sell, anger with approach and attack action, or fear with withdrawal and attempts to escape.

The more recent theories of emotion indicate that emotion is more complex than was originally believed. Cognition—perception, memory, thinking, and intelligence—is now theorized to be related to emotion. Thus, the capacity to respond emotionally increases with age—the range of a person's emotions and the number of stimuli that produce them increases with cognitive development.

A summary of the major theories of emotion is provided in Figure 11-5. The James-Lange theory proposes that the body responds first to a stimulus, then the cognitive processes occur in the cortex based on the physiological responses. According to the Cannon-Bard theory, a stimulus activates cognitive processes and physiological responses simultaneously. In Schachter's theory, the cognitive and physiological responses occur simultaneously in response to a stimulus, but the responses from

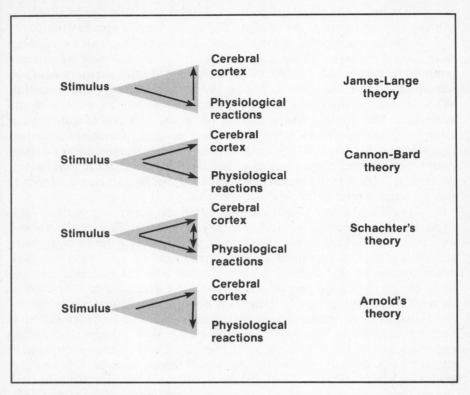

Figure 11-5 A diagrammatic summary of four theories of emotion.

the cerebral cortex also elicit physiological responses and the physiological responses in turn affect cognition. Arnold believes the cerebral cortex responds first to a stimulus, and then the cognitive appraisal elicits the physiological response.

## Stress

The autonomic nervous system was described in Chapter 4 as consisting of two systems—the parasympathetic system which functions to carry out the physiological processes for normal life and the sympathetic system which functions to change the physiological processes to handle unusual conditions which place stress on the body. The activation of the sympathetic nervous system is sometimes referred to as the "fight or flight" response. This response handles emergency needs of the body and is present in emotion. Any situation which makes a special demand on the body is referred to as *stress*. If the body is injured, damaged, or diseased, special demands are made for healing of the injury, overcoming the damage, or conquering the disease. Heavy physical work, injury on the job, loss of sleep, poor nutrition, or illness might be sources of physiological stress for a worker. The body has mechanisms for adapting to or coping with physiological stress. Of course, the stress may be so intense or prolonged that the mechanisms can no longer handle the stress.

Psychologists are more concerned with *psychological stress*—demands that are placed on the body by the cognitive or mental processes. The sympathetic nervous system is activated to produce bodily changes to adjust to psychological stress as well as to adapt to physiological stress.

### Sources of Psychological Stress

Interactions between a person and the person's environment produce stress. Small amounts of stress constantly appear and disappear. Large amounts of stress may arise when an individual faces a demanding situation and is unsure of his or her ability to cope with it. When an individual is unsure of whether he or she can take advantage of an opportunity that arises, large amounts of stress may arise. Thus, psychological stress may be produced from a variety of situations.

As previously noted in this chapter, any emotion or feeling produces stress whether the emotion is love, joy, anger, hate, or grief. *Anxiety* is a psychological state characterized by apprehension, tenseness, dread, and foreboding. The causes of anxiety are usually not as specific as the causes of fear. Anxiety produces stress whether the anxiety is recognized or not, or whether the cause is identified or not. Pressure, frustration, and conflict are also sources of psychological stress. Psychological stress is an ever-present feature of most job settings. From the assembly line worker, to the supervisor, to the project superintendent, employees experience psychological stress. Workers experience pressure to meet deadlines and quotas, frustration caused by events which interfere with reaching goals, and conflict in decision making.

**Emotional Stress and Anxiety.** An individual's perception and/or evaluation of a situation and of his or her ability to cope with or to take advantage of the situation is a key factor in stress. Evaluation consists of two stages. During *primary appraisal*, a person interprets a situation as either threatening or harmless. During *secondary appraisal*, a person evaluates the action called for and the resources available for the required action. New information or the development of new skills makes it possible for a person to reappraise a situation.

Anxiety develops when an individual's perception or evaluation of the situation, of the action called for, and of his or her resources to handle the action are not in balance. Anxiety is so uncomfortable that a person may attempt to reduce the anxiety either by reappraising the situation, by reappraising what action is necessary, or by doing something to obtain the resources for carrying out the necessary action. How much stress a person experiences then in a given situation may partially depend on the personal skills, information, and resources the person actually has available and on the person's self-confidence. Having the qualifications to perform a job and being confident of those qualifications are deterrents to anxiety in the work situation.

Most people cannot escape some anxiety on the job, which is good. Anxiety in the right amount is necessary for a person's top performance, but a great deal of anxiety interferes with rational planning and effective performance and may contribute to failure which in turn produces more anxiety and future failure. Different individuals reach peak job performance at different levels of anxiety. In other words, a particular level of stress may activate the sympathetic nervous systems of some people but not others and may disrupt the performance behavior of some people but not others. Also, different job tasks may be disrupted by different levels of stress or anxiety. For example, the performance of a routine task such as an assembly line worker repeatedly putting a rivet in a certain place on a car body would probably not be disrupted by a level of anxiety that would interfere with the performance of a mental task such as developing a computer program which would require high levels of concentration.

The psychoanalytic view of anxiety proposes that anxiety is the result of internal, unconscious conflict—evaluations and emotions of which a person is not aware. If the emotion conflicts with a person's conscious values or feelings of self-worth, anxiety develops; and the person may engage in particular behaviors to keep the emotion out of consciousness in order to lower the anxiety. These behaviors may become the source of even more anxiety; the original source of anxiety may be unconscious but is still present. For example, an interior decorator may keep feelings of incompetency submerged in his or her unconscious by criticizing other interior decorators. Anxious people experience all the bodily changes that occur when the sympathetic nervous system is aroused; however, they sometimes do not know what the source of arousal is. They may not be able to explain why they feel as they do, or what it is they fear will happen. They may assign various sources to their feelings that are not true sources of their anxiety.

Charles Spielberger (1966) distinguished between two types of anxiety. One type of anxiety, called *trait anxiety*, represents the general level of anxiety that is characteristically exhibited by an individual over time. This type is a relatively stable aspect of the personality. Some people seem to experience anxiety whether they are on the job, attending a party, going to school, or vacationing. They worry about many things and have a vague uneasiness about the outcome of events in general. The other type, *state anxiety*, refers to temporary situational anxiety. People who are generally free of anxiety may experience anxiety in a specific situation such as when taking a test, when making a speech before an audience, or when a robber is pointing a gun at them. The level of state anxiety is usually affected by the length and severity of the stressful event and by whether or not the stressful event was expected.

**Pressure.** When a demand for a particular performance is made on a person and the person feels that the demand must be met, pressure occurs which produces stress. People set standards of behavior for themselves based on their ideals. If they do not meet these ideals, they hold themselves in low esteem. Therefore, they are under a lot of *internal pressure* to perform in accordance with these ideals in order to maintain their self-esteem. Internal pressure can be good and can bring great pleasure to a person when the ideal performance is accomplished. However, if a person's ideals are too difficult to achieve, internal pressure may be a source of extreme stress.

Demands to meet a particular standard of behavior are also made on a person by other people who are significant in his or her personal and work lives. Pressure from this source is referred to as *external pressure.* The general manager of Company X may demand that a project bid be submitted by a particular time in order to be considered. Or the president of Company Y may demand that an average number of projects be completed each day in order for the manager to remain in the position of manager. A new procedure may be demanded by the supervisor, and the employee must learn the procedure or resign from the job. Family members and close friends also may place demands on a person which result in external pressure and the accompanying stress.

**Frustration.** When something or someone interferes with or prevents a person from reaching a goal that is important to him or her, the person experiences frustration which produces stress. The person must either give up the goal or overcome the barrier that is encountered in reaching the goal. Frustration is one of the main sources of stress on the job. Delays, lack of resources, losses, lack of ability (failure), and meaninglessness of the goal are five basic sources of frustration (Coleman & Hammen, 1974).

Some people can tolerate more frustration than others. A person with a low frustration tolerance may respond with anger and verbal or physical aggression to remove the barrier immediately. Or they may respond in counterproductive defensive behavior; they may minimize the importance of achieving a goal or deny the reality of the barrier. People with a high frustration tolerance are more likely to do something constructive to remove the source of their frustration. They may devise and initiate a systematic approach to remove the barrier, modify the goal to evade the barrier, or compensate by working to achieve some other goal.

**Conflict.** Probably the most common source of stress is conflict which arises when one is faced with incompatible motives (drives or needs), demands, opportunities, or goals. There is no complete solution to conflict. This type of stress involves decision making. Kurt Lewin (1935) described four types of conflict. These are *approach-approach, avoidance-avoidance, approach-avoidance,* and *double approach-avoidance.* Approach represents an attraction or positive feeling, and avoidance represents a withdrawal or negative feeling.

In approach-approach conflict, a person is simultaneously attracted to two opportunities, goals, or demands. Two equally attractive alternatives are present, but the person cannot have or do both. This type of conflict is illustrated by the fable about the donkey who stood between two delicious bales of hay yet starved to death because he could not make a decision as to which bale of hay to eat. In the world of work, humans may have to choose or decide between two equally attractive jobs, two equally attractive applicants to employ, two equally attractive meetings to attend, or two equally attractive contracts to accept. Unlike the donkey in the fable, humans usually can make a choice in these types of conflict without experiencing a great amount of stress. This is probably the least serious form of conflict.

Avoidance-avoidance conflict involves making a decision between two equally unattractive alternatives. The person must face one of the unpleasant situations. These conflicts are more stressful to resolve than the approach-approach conflicts, and the individual is more likely to vacillate back and forth longer. As the person approaches making a choice and moves closer to one of the unattractive situations, more stress is experienced, and there is a tendency to back up and move toward the other unattractive situation to reduce the stress. But as the individual moves closer to it, more stress is experienced again, and the individual backs up and moves toward the other situation. In these kinds of conflict, many people simply wait for something to happen that will make the decision for them, or they try to find a way to avoid making the decision, thus prolonging the stress. This type of stress might be illustrated when an employer has to either fire an employee or put up with the problem behavior of the employee. As the time to fire the employee approaches, the employer may change the decision and decide to put up with the behavior. As the behavior becomes unbearable, the decision to fire the employee may be made again, but as the time approaches the employer may back off again.

In approach-avoidance conflicts, a person has to decide whether to engage in a single activity, pursue a single goal, or take advantage of a single opportunity that has both desirable and undesirable characteristics or advantages and disadvantages. A shy person may have to decide whether to apply for a new job opening. Getting the job means an increase in salary which is desirable; but getting the job also means having an interview with the company president which is undesirable. When a person is further away from the goal, the tendency to approach is stronger, and the shy person may make an appointment for an interview. The desire to approach increases in strength as a person gets nearer the goal. But, the desire to avoid also gets stronger as a person gets nearer the goal. (See Figure 11-6.) Thus, the shy person may make preparations for the interview. But as time for the interview gets closer, the avoidance tendency strengthens faster than the approach tendency until the point is reached where avoidance is stronger. Then the appointment may be cancelled, or the shy person may turn around and walk away as the door to the interview office is approached. As the person walks away or cancels the appointment and gets further from the goal, the point may be reached at which the tendency to approach becomes stronger again. Then the individual may turn around and go back toward the office or make another appointment. This may happen repeatedly until the conflict is resolved by the individual being forced to make a decision, or the situation changes and the job is no longer available. This type of conflict may be faced often in work situations. Someone wants a pay raise but fears criticism. Someone wants to perform in front of an audience but fears being laughed at. Sometimes action must be taken to reduce the avoidance tendency by seeking new information, developing new skills, or obtaining professional help to overcome irrational fears.

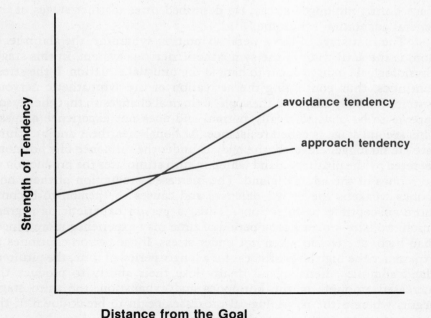

Figure 11-6 Approach-avoidance conflict.

When a person must make a choice between two goals and each goal has desirable as well as undesirable tendencies, the conflict is more complex and produces even more stress. Such conflict is referred to as double approach-avoidance conflict. A person experiencing this most stressful type of conflict is said to be in a *double bind*. For example, a supervisor may want an employee to work overtime. The spouse may want the employee to go to a party. If the employee chooses to work overtime, the decision has the advantage of pleasing the supervisor but the disadvantage of upsetting the spouse. If the employee chooses to attend the party, the decision has the advantage of pleasing the spouse but the disadvantage of upsetting the supervisor.

### General Adaptation Syndrome

Stress activates the sympathetic part of the autonomic nervous system which produces a set of physiological responses which prepare the body for action. These responses include rises in the blood sugar level, acceleration of the heartbeat and breathing, inhibition of the digestive processes, tensing of the muscles, shifting of blood away from the skin, increases in blood pressure, and the secretion of adrenaline. Hans Selye (1956), a medical researcher, coined the phrase *general adaptation syndrome* to represent the entire pattern of the sequence of events that takes place during prolonged stress. He described three distinct stages of the general adaptation syndrome.

The first stage of the general adaptation syndrome, the alarm reaction, is the activation of the sympathetic nervous system. In this stage, physiological changes occur to handle the unusual situation. If the stress continues, thus continuing the activation of the sympathetic nervous system, the body adapts to these physiological changes so that the person appears to be physiologically normal and does not experience arousal. This second stage is called resistance. Although heartbeat and breathing rate are no longer elevated, the body is under the influence of a hormone secreted by the pituitary gland which in turn stimulates the production of hormones of the adrenal gland. The increased production of these hormones weakens the body's defenses and causes the person to become more susceptible to infections. Thus, a person experiencing a great amount of stress over a long period of time may experience more illness than he or she would when not under stress. If the person continues to experience the high level of stress for a longer period of time, the pituitary gland and the adrenal gland finally lose their ability to produce the increased amounts of the hormones and exhaustion, the third stage, begins wherein the physiological processes begin to break down. If the stress continues, the eventual outcome will be death.

Thomas Holmes and Richard Rahe (1967) developed a scale to quantify the amount of stress a person experiences based on the impact of life experiences and the degree of adjustment involved in coping with the experience. (See Table 11-2 below.) A total of 150 to 199 units accumulated in any one year indicates mild stress; 200 to 299 units indicates moderate stress; and 300 units and above indicates major stress. Holmes (1978) found that individuals who experienced a greater amount of stress ran a higher risk of physical illness or accidental injury. It is difficult, however, to predict stress-related illness because of the differences in individual reactions to stress.

## TABLE 11-2 Scale of Life-Change Units

| Life Event | Value | Life Event | Value |
|---|---|---|---|
| Death of spouse | 100 | Trouble with in-laws | 29 |
| Divorce | 73 | Outstanding personal achievement | 28 |
| Marital separation | 65 | | |
| Jail term | 63 | Wife beginning or stopping work | 26 |
| Death of a close family member | 63 | Begin or end school | 26 |
| Personal injury or illness | 53 | Change in living conditions | 25 |
| Marriage | 50 | | |
| Fired at work | 47 | Revision of personal habits | 24 |
| Marital reconciliation | 45 | | |
| Retirement | 45 | Trouble with boss | 23 |
| Change in health of family member | 44 | Change in work hours or conditions | 20 |
| Pregnancy | 40 | Change in residence | 20 |
| Sex difficulties | 39 | Change in schools | 20 |
| Gain of new family member | 39 | Change in recreation | 19 |
| Business readjustment | 39 | Change in church activities | 19 |
| Change in financial state | 38 | | |
| Death of close friend | 37 | Change in social activities | 18 |
| Change to different line of work | 36 | Mortgage or loan less than $10,000 | 17 |
| Change in number of arguments with spouse | 35 | Change in sleeping habits | 16 |
| Mortgage over $10,000 | 31 | Change in number of family get-togethers | 15 |
| Foreclosure of mortgage or loan | 30 | Change in eating habits | 15 |
| | | Vacation | 13 |
| Change in responsibilities at work | 29 | Christmas | 12 |
| Son or daughter leaving home | 29 | Minor violations of the law | 11 |

## Psychosomatic Illness

Physical disorders that have a psychological origin—caused by psychological stress—are referred to as *psychosomatic disorders*. Psychosomatic illnesses are real disorders, not imagined ones, and require medical attention. Some cases of ulcers, migraine headaches, asthma, high blood pressure, and heart disease are related to psychological stress. People who consistently exhibit excessive aggressiveness, competitive drive, impatience, and time urgency suffer twice as many heart-related deaths as people who are consistently calm and relaxed (Friedman & Rosenman, 1974). Herbert Benson (1975) of Harvard University has shown that prolonged stress can lead to high blood pressure which can lead to diseases such as hardening of the arteries, strokes, and kidney malfunctions. Stress has also been shown to play a role in such diseases as arthritis, premenstrual syndrome, colitis, diabetes, and low blood sugar (Selye, 1976).

## Coping with Stress

Some employees are fortunate in that they have developed effective skills for coping with stress. Other employees have not developed effective skills for coping with stress, and job performance can be an aversive and threatening experience. Inability to cope with the stress associated with a job detracts from the enjoyment of the work activity, negatively affects performance, and promotes the development of psychosomatic disorders. In addition, the inability to cope with stress increases the likelihood of accidents and injury.

Effective coping involves learning to use socially acceptable methods that can (1) reduce the impact of stress, (2) alter the environment to reduce the amount of stress, and (3) change one's own behavior so that less stress will be experienced. Humans begin to learn and use strategies for coping with psychological stress at birth. The strategies that one learns to use account for how one characteristically behaves—one's personality. The word "adjustment" or "well-adjusted" is emphasized by most psychologists in defining normal personality. Mental health is related to a person's ability to adjust to the environment and to other people.

Some of the strategies one learns to use are unconscious processes called *defense mechanisms*. These strategies will be explained in the next chapter concerned with personality. The use of these strategies is called *defensive coping* because self-defense is a form of self-deception. When the individual cannot identify the source of the stress, or when the source of the stress is internal conflict that threatens the person's sense of identity or self-esteem, the defensive coping strategies may be used. Apathy, an extreme form of withdrawal, is another way of coping defensively.

Direct or active coping is action oriented—consciously taking action to alter the uncomfortable stress-provoking situation. The source of the stress must be consciously recognized before this can be done. Psychologists sometimes apply the term *assertive coping* to meaningful, constructive attempts to change situations that produce high levels of stress. Psychologists sometimes apply the term aggression to destructive attempts to alter the uncomfortable stress-provoking situation. If a truck driver's rig gets a flat tire and the truck driver gets busy changing the tire or finds a phone and calls a service station for help, he or she would be exhibiting assertive coping. If the truck driver hit the tire rim with a sledge hammer or attacked the codriver verbally for being incompetent, aggression would be exhibited. A secretary who experiences stress when taking shorthand dictation and transcribing it may cope assertively by attending night school and taking courses to improve these skills. In situations of genuine helplessness where nothing can be done about the source of stress, action can only be taken to try to control the effects. In some situations, the most effective action may be to withdraw or physically escape the stress.

Because stress can be damaging, some organizations utilize training programs developed by psychologists to teach coping skills to employees which enable them to gain greater control over stress and to keep emotional arousal within manageable limits. Such training programs may include training in voluntary muscle relaxation skills. Several recently devised methods for reducing levels of arousal are meditation, biofeedback, progressive relaxation, and diaphragmatic breathing. Some training programs for practicing coping skills may use mental rehearsal techniques whereby an employee imagines the introduction of stressful elements to the job situation. In some programs, actual stressful elements are introduced gradually to allow for realistic practicing of coping skills. Other programs attempt to alter one's thinking—to help a person become aware of self-defeating thoughts and to practice thinking thoughts that are incompatible with the self-defeating thoughts. For example, thinking "I cannot make 50 sales this week" is self-defeating, and thinking "I can make 50 sales this week" is incompatible with that self-defeating thought.

## SUMMARY

1. Emotion has been defined as a feeling that involves physiological changes and may be expressed through behavior.

2. Emotion consists of a physiological component controlled by the responses of the endocrine glands and the autonomic system which determines the intensity of the emotion and a cognitive component which determines the quality of the emotion based on appraisal.

3. Emotions may be described in terms of approach-avoidance, intensity, and pleasantness-unpleasantness; however, individuals may respond differently along these dimensions because of inborn differences and differences in what has been learned.

4. The dimension of approach-avoidance depends on whether the emotion is positive or negative and whether there is hope of controlling the situation eliciting the emotion.

5. According to Plutchik, the basic emotions are fear, anger, joy, sadness, acceptance, disgust, anticipation, and surprise; all other emotions are varying intensities and/or mixtures of these.

6. Sometimes a person may have both pleasant and unpleasant emotions about a specific object, person, or event that exist simultaneously.

7. The autonomic nervous system, composed of the parasympathetic and the sympathetic systems, is under the control of the central nervous system and produces the physiological changes associated with emotion.

8. The hormones epinephrine and norepinephrine are secreted during emotional arousal; but more norepinephrine is released in anger and more epinephrine is released in fear.

9. The relaxation response consists of decreased activity in both the sympathetic and somatic nervous systems. The relaxation response may be elicited by yoga, transcendental meditation, and muscle relaxation techniques.

10. The cortex and limbic system of the central nervous system are involved in appraisal, control of bodily responses, and the behavioral expression of emotion.

11. Emotions may be communicated both verbally and nonverbally.

12. Facial expressions, a type of nonverbal communication, seem to be innate for basic emotions, and research suggests that the left side of the face gives the clearest, strongest expression of a particular emotion. The enlargement of the pupils of the eyes is also a facial expression that communicates emotions.

13. Body postures and gestures, called kinesics, and paralanguage communicate emotion.

14. Emotion is also communicated by proxemics, the physical distance kept from a person and the eye contact that is maintained.

15. Both verbal and nonverbal communication of emotion may be improved by consciously attending to them.

16. Emotion is usually assessed indirectly and subjectively; however, physiological responses may be measured objectively.

17. Dryness of the mouth; pupil enlargement; the polygraph which records heart rate, blood pressure, respiration, and the galvanic skin response; and the voice stress analyzer which produces a voice printout in graphic form have been used to give an indication of emotional arousal.

18. The James-Lange theory of emotion suggests that stimuli produce physiological changes in the body. The sensation of these changes is emotion.

19. The Cannon-Bard theory of emotion proposes that stimuli produce physiological changes in the body and psychological changes simultaneously.

20. Schachter's cognitive theory of emotion proposes that emotion is the result of bodily changes and the simultaneous appraisal of the stimulus. However, appraisal and arousal are interrelated—a change in appraisal influences a change in arousal and a change in arousal influences appraisal.

21. Arnold's cognitive theory of emotion proposes that appraisal occurs first and elicits a pattern of physiological responses appropriate to the appraisal.

22. Stress is any situation which makes a special demand on the body whether the demand is of a physiological nature or a psychological nature.

23. Psychological stress is produced by mental activity, emotion, anxiety, pressure, frustration, and conflict.

24. The evaluation of a situation, of action called for, and of resources called for is a key factor in stress; anxiety develops when an imbalance exists between the parts of the evaluation.

25. Anxiety may be reduced by reappraisal or action; therefore, some anxiety increases performance, but too much anxiety may be disruptive to performance.

26. According to the psychoanalytic view, anxiety is the result of internal, unconscious conflict that produces bodily changes even though the anxiety may be denied or assigned to sources that are not responsible for the feeling.

27. Spielberger's research distinguished between trait anxiety, the general level of anxiety that is a typical aspect of an individual's personality, and state anxiety, a temporary situational anxiety.

28. Pressure to meet a particular standard of behavior may be in the form of internal pressure (a standard set by one's self) or external pressure (a standard set by others). While some pressure can be good, too much pressure may be a source of extreme stress.

29. Frustration which produces stress results when something or someone interferes with or prevents one from reaching an important goal. Individual differences exist in tolerance of frustration.

30. Conflict which produces stress exists when an individual must make a decision between incompatible motives, demands, opportunities, or goals.

31. Approach-approach conflicts are those where a choice must be made between two equally attractive alternatives.

32. Avoidance-avoidance conflicts are those where a choice must be made between two equally unattractive alternatives.

33. Approach-avoidance conflicts involve a decision as to whether to pursue a single activity or goal which has both desirable (approach) and undesirable (avoidance) characteristics. As the goal is approached, both approach and avoidance tendencies increase in strength, but the avoidance tendency increases faster than the approach tendency.

34. When a choice must be made between two alternatives and each one has desirable and undesirable characteristics, the conflict is more complex and produces more stress. This is referred to as a double bind.

35. The general adaptation syndrome refers to the sequence of physiological events that takes place during prolonged stress. Three stages—the alarm reaction, resistance, and exhaustion—comprise the syndrome.

36. Holmes and Rahe developed a scale to determine whether the impact of stress is mild, moderate, or major for an individual.

37. Psychosomatic illnesses are physical disorders such as some cases of ulcers, migraine headaches, asthma, high blood pressure, colitis, and heart disease—all of which may be caused by psychological stress.

38. Characteristic patterns of behavior are learned, beginning at birth, for coping with or adjusting to stress. Some people have learned more effective coping skills than others.

39. Defensive coping (unconscious behaviors), direct coping (conscious, assertive, or aggressive actions), withdrawal, or apathy may be strategies used to manage stress.

40. Some organizations utilize such training programs as muscle relaxation techniques (biofeedback, meditation, progressive relaxation, and diaphragmatic breathing) and mental rehearsal techniques to teach coping skills to employees.

## SUGGESTIONS FOR FURTHER READING

Alberti, R. E., & Emmons, M. L. *Your perfect right: A guide to assertive behavior.* San Luis Obispo, Calif.: Impact, 1974.

The authors of this book discuss how people can increase their sense of personal power by overcoming anxiety through assertive action.

Benson, H. *The relaxation response.* New York: Morrow, 1975.

The relaxation response and how to elicit it are explained in detail.

Cooper, C. L. *The stress check.* Englewood Cliffs, N. J.: Prentice-Hall, 1981.

This is an excellent review of the stress one experiences in life, especially in work situations.

Ekman, P., & Friesen, W. V. *Unmasking the face.* Englewood Cliffs, N. J.: Prentice-Hall, 1975.

A nontechnical book on identifying emotions and identifying when a person is trying to disguise an emotion. The authors are two of the leading researchers on facial expressions and emotions.

Fast, J. *Body language.* New York: Evans, 1970.

Detailed descriptions of gestures and body positions and the emotions they are communicating are included in this book.

Hall, E. T. *The hidden dimension.* Garden City, N. Y.: Doubleday, 1966.

How people use space in personal and business encounters is presented in this easy-to-read book.

Lazarus, R. S. *Patterns of adjustment* (3rd ed.). New York: McGraw-Hill, 1976.

A scholarly textbook on adjustment that touches on many topics related to coping with stress.

Martindale, D. Sweaty palms in the control tower. *Psychology Today,* February, 1977, 71-72, 75.

This article deals with the highly stressful work of the airflight controller and describes the physical and psychological effects that can be produced by stress.

Plutchik, R. *Emotion: A psychoevolutionary synthesis*. New York: Harper & Row, 1980.

A good general overview of emotion, particularly the innateness of emotion is presented here.

Schachter, S. *Emotion, obesity, and crime*. New York: Academic Press, 1971.

Research conducted by the author in the area of emotion, obesity, and crime is presented along with the reasons for supporting the cognitive theory of emotion.

Selye, H. *The stress of life*. New York: McGraw-Hill, 1976.

This book includes an excellent presentation of the functions of the endocrine glands and the nervous system in human adjustment to the constant changes encountered in life and work.

Strongman, K. T. *The psychology of emotion* (2nd ed.). New York: Wiley, 1978.

The physiology of emotion, the expression of emotion, the development of emotion, and the perception of emotion are topics attended to in this book in addition to a good review of the various theories of emotion.

# Part 5
## Individual and Social Processes

# P ersonality

Chapter **12**

I. **ASSESSMENT OF PERSONALITY**
  A. Interviews
  B. Direct Observations
  C. Objective Tests
  D. Projective Tests
  E. Personality Differences

II. **THEORIES OF PERSONALITY**
  A. Psychoanalytic Theory
  B. Learning Theory
  C. Humanistic Theory
  D. Type and Trait Theory
  E. Theory of Personality Adjustment

III. **ABNORMAL PERSONALITY**
  A. Views of Abnormality
  B. Neurotic Disorders
  C. Psychotic Disorders
  D. Other Disorders

IV. **PERSONALITY CHANGE**
  A. Therapy
  B. Management and Therapy

**SUMMARY**

**SUGGESTIONS FOR FURTHER READING**

The word *personality* may bring to mind statements such as the following: "He really has personality." "She has a good personality." "She has no personality." "He has a terrible personality." In all these statements, personality is used in the popular sense. Psychologists use the word personality to describe the characteristic way a person responds to other people, objects, or events in the environment—the persistent behavior patterns that are unique to an individual. Psychologists do not use the term to judge whether an individual's personality is good or bad or use the word to mean charming.

A study of personality is appropriate for those who are in or will be in a work situation. Most knowledgeable people in the world of work agree that most employees who lose their jobs are dismissed because of personality characteristics rather than lack of skill or ability in general. The personalities of the individuals under a manager's supervision influence the style of leadership that works best for that manager. For example, a permissive or democratic leadership style seems to work better for people who are highly motivated, above average in intelligence, and well trained; whereas people who have rigid, strict, or authoritarian personalities usually prefer a more direct or authoritarian leadership style. Personality also needs to be considered when attempting to motivate others. J. M. Higgins (1982) proposed that an individual's self-image—an important aspect of one's personality—and the maintenance, lowering, or enhancing of the self-image affects motivation and, in turn, performance. In other words, personality has an impact on motivation and performance. Personality also plays a role in communication. Attitudes developed through experience contribute to an individual's personality. Attitudes influence perception which gives meaning to sensation, and the meaning one gives to sensory inputs gives rise to a unique personality. No two people share exactly the same set of experiences; therefore, people cannot perceive things in exactly the same way.

The purpose of this chapter is to consider how personality is assessed, to explain how personality evolves, to differentiate between abnormal personalities and normal or well-adjusted personalities, and to identify approaches and therapeutic techniques that are used for changing maladjusted personality.

## Assessment of Personality

Informal personality assessment occurs all the time. Judgments are often made concerning the characteristics of an individual based on one's own private observation, one's own personal experience, or hearsay; but these judgments are apt to be biased. Reliable, unbiased measures of personality are frequently used by business organizations—especially when hiring personnel. Psychologists use four basic techniques in assessing personality: interviews, direct observations, objective tests, and projective tests.

## Interviews

An interview consists of a conversation wherein the interviewer directs questions to the person being interviewed in order to evaluate the person's personality. The interviewer also relies on nonverbal communications when making the evaluation. Although the success of this technique depends on the skill of the interviewer, most firms still rely heavily on the interview to assess personality and to select employees. (See Figure 12-1.) The validity of the interview technique is questionable because the interviewer may become too emotionally involved, because

Figure 12-1 Most firms still rely heavily on the interview to assess personality.

the interviewer's own personality may affect the evaluations, and because the interviewer may not be sensitive to unconscious cues such as changes in pitch of voice.

Interviews differ according to the method used to obtain information. The primary difference is the amount of structure imposed by the interviewer. In the nondirective interview, the interviewer asks broad, general questions in order to avoid determining the course of the interview and influencing remarks. The depth interview is somewhat more structured than the nondirective type, and the questions asked cover general areas. The patterned interview is highly structured and may consist of a set of detailed questions.

Interviewing has been the subject of much research. Some of the major findings listed by Chruden and Sherman (1980) are as follows: (1) Interviewers form an immediate, usually subconscious, first impression within the first five minutes of the interview on the basis of appearance and actions. Information is then sought throughout the remainder of the interview to substantiate this first impression. (2) The two most critical factors in an interviewer's decision are the appropriateness of the content of responses to the questions and the manner of speaking. (3) Structured interviews are more reliable than unstructured interviews. (4) The trait most validly evaluated is intelligence. (5) Unfavorable information influences the interviewer more than favorable information. These findings suggest that first impressions are indeed extremely important in interviewing for a job.

### Direct Observations

Psychologists often assess a person's behavior by observing his or her actions. If several observers report similar accounts of a person's behavior over a period of time, the assessment of a person's personality by observation can be quite reliable.

Objective observation consists of directly observing behaviors and recording the data. The first step in direct observation is to precisely define the behavior to be observed. Vague terms like "lazy" should be replaced with specific responses that can be measured such as "arrives late to work" or "completes fewer than five reports in a day." The next step is to observe the specified behavior and record the observation. The data collected over a period of time constitutes the assessment.

The data will probably be more reliable if it is collected without the person's knowledge. If two or more observers collect the data simultaneously, the assessment will be more reliable. Sometimes supervisory personnel are too quick to type a subordinate. Their observations may be based on too little data or may be biased by their own attitudes. If supervisors compare their perceptions of observed worker behaviors with others, a higher level of objectivity will be effected.

## Objective Tests

Objective tests, sometimes called personality inventories, have been created by psychologists to measure a variety of traits, interests, and dimensions of personality. Objective tests usually are paper-and-pencil tests and are in the form of questions about one's self. An individual may be asked to indicate on an answer sheet how various statements about behaviors, opinions, and feelings relate to him or her. Questions such as "Do you frequently have headaches?" or "Do you make friends easily?" are often included on these tests. Sometimes a choice must be made from a list of several activities. For example, the individual may be asked, "Which activity in this group would you choose if you had to be engaged in one?" Or the individual may be asked, "Which activity would you omit if you had to be engaged in all of the activities except one?" Sometimes individuals are asked to choose from a set of statements the one statement or those statements they feel best describe themselves.

Validity and ethics sometimes present problems in objective testing. Individuals may fake answers or have unrealistic self perceptions. The forced choice technique does reduce the possibility of falsifying one's answers on a test. Asking personal questions pertaining to an individual's habits, attitudes about sex, or likes and dislikes are sometimes considered an invasion of a person's privacy.

A few objective personality tests used to differentiate specific personality types are mentioned on page 293 of this chapter. The Minnesota Multiphasic Personality Inventory (MMPI) (Hathaway & McKinley, 1967) is the most widely used personality inventory. It is a true-false test which contains 550 statements about one's self and yields 13 different scores. Three of the scores are related to the validity of the responses. One of those three is related to the indecisiveness of the individual based on the number of responses in the "can't say" category; another of the three is related to attempts to falsify the outcome of the test by giving responses that would result in a more favorable appearance. The other one of the three is related to the carelessness of the individual in answering questions and is based on inconsistent answers. Ten other scores rate the person on traits used in psychiatric evaluations. The Minnesota Multiphasic Personality Inventory (MMPI) clinical scales are listed and described in the boxed material on page 291.

## Projective Tests

Projective tests use unstructured, vague, and ambiguous stimuli to obtain a response. The thoughts and perceptions that come to the person's mind are thought to reveal the conflicts, fears, fantasies, needs, and defenses that may be unknown to the person. It is believed that the person "projects" his or her personality into the stimulus situation and the response.

The Rorschach inkblot technique developed in 1921 by Hermann Rorschach consists of ten inkblots formed by dropping ink on a piece of paper and then folding the paper to create a symmetrical design. It is probably the best known and most widely used projective test. Figure 12-2 is an inkblot similar to those used in the test.

Another widely used projective test is the Thematic Apperception Test (TAT) developed by H. A. Murray and Christina Morgan in the 1930s. This test consists of 20 pictures of one or more people in various positions and/or settings. The person is asked to make up a story about each picture describing the events that led up to the pictured scene, what is happening in the scene, and the outcome of the situation. The TAT was described in Chapter 9 since it is often used to assess motivation.

Other projective techniques are sometimes used. These include a word association test wherein a person says the first word that comes to mind after a word is given by the psychologist administering the test. In other tests, the person may be asked to draw a picture instead of responding verbally or in writing.

---

### MMPI CLINICAL SCALES

1. Hypochondriasis (Hs). Extreme and persistent concerns about one's physical health.
2. Depression (D). Poor morale, pessimism, feelings of hopelessness and sorrow.
3. Hysteria (Hy). Physical ailments that have no organic basis and feelings of sadness and lack of satisfaction.
4. Psychopathic deviation (Pd). Difficulty in forming satisfactory personal relationships and inability to anticipate consequences of one's behavior.
5. Masculinity-femininity (Mf). Traditional masculine and feminine interest patterns.
6. Paranoia (Pa). Feelings of sensitivity, suspiciousness, persecution, and grandiosity.
7. Psychasthenia (Pt). Vague anxieties, insecurity, self-doubt, phobias, and obsessive-compulsive reactions.
8. Schizophrenia (Sc). Emotional isolation and poor reality contact, sometimes accompanied by hallucinations.
9. Hypomania (Ma). Hyperactivity, restlessness, distractibility, and unrealistic optimism.
10. Social introversion (Si). Shyness and feelings of uneasiness in and/or withdrawal from social situations. (Janda & Klenke-Hamel, 1982, p. 312).

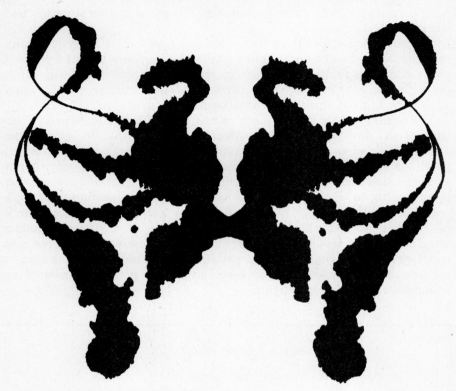

Figure 12-2 An inkblot similar
to those used in the Rorschach
technique to assess personality.

Projective tests are used primarily in clinical situations. This is
because a highly trained psychologist is required to accurately evaluate
the responses. Also, considerable time is usually needed to administer
projective tests.

## Personality Differences

By utilizing techniques for assessing personality, researchers are
able to differentiate basic personality types. For example, basic personality types have been found to exist for various occupational groups according to the manner in which they work (hurriedly or leisurely), their
degree of emotionality, and their need for sensory stimulation.

Studies concerned with the relationships between personality characteristics and occupational groups indicate that, overall, workers and
professionals in different occupational groups, as well as students pre-

paring for different occupations, have different personalities (Holland, 1980). Three sets of scales frequently used to determine basic interest areas are the Strong Vocational Interest Blank, the Kuder Preference Record, and the Vocational Preference Inventory.

The Strong Vocational Interest Blank, which measures 22 basic areas of interest, was developed by E. K. Strong, Jr., who learned that interests vary in people from occupation to occupation and that a person's interest pattern tends to remain stable, especially after age 21. The Kuder Preference Record distinguishes ten basic interest areas—outdoor, mechanical, computational, scientific, persuasive, artistic, literary, musical, social science, and clerical. The Strong Vocational Interest Blank and the Kuder Preference Record are widely used in vocational counseling to compare an individual's interests or personality with the interest and personality of individuals in the various occupational groups.

Holland (1972, 1973) proposes that occupations may be grouped according to six personality types. Table 12-1 lists and describes the personality types and lists a sampling of occupations associated with each personality type. The Vocational Preference Inventory was developed based on this theory. Research studies have shown that individuals tend to choose a career type that matches their personality type and that the closer the match the greater the job satisfaction and the longer the individual will stay with his or her work (Cole, Whitney, & Holland, 1971; Holland, 1962, 1968).

Cardiologists Meyer Friedman and Ray Rosenman have differentiated two major personality types called As and Bs. Workers who exhibit the typical personality pattern of always hurrying—striving to accomplish too much, too quickly, too frequently—are typed as As. Type A personalities are characteristically restless, ambitious, aggressive, and are often referred to as workaholics. In the world of work, this type is usually admired; however, they have been found to be prone to coronary heart disease. Type Bs, realizing their limitations, can relax and perform in a more leisurely manner (Friedman & Rosenman, 1974).

Individuals may be differentiated also according to how they attempt to control their environment (Rotter, 1966). *Internals* are those individuals who perceive themselves as being the center of control in their lives; *externals* perceive the center of control in their lives as being outside themselves. Internals are more likely to attempt to improve their environment and thus be more effective agents of change. They believe they can effect change. Internals are also more likely to see rewards as related to their own behavior and to be motivated to perform. They believe their skills can make a difference in the outcome of events. Externals, on the other hand, tend to believe that what they do will make no difference in the outcome. They are more likely to give up when they are hindered in meeting their goals and to see difficulties as threats. A

## TABLE 12-1 Holland's Personality Types and Corresponding Sample Occupations

| Personality Type | Description | Sample Occupations |
|---|---|---|
| Realistic | Likes work requiring physical strength; tends to avoid interpersonal and verbal types of work; prefers task problems that are concrete rather than abstract | Engineer, carpenter, architect, forester, machinist, printer, agriculturist |
| Intellectual | Prefers tasks involving the intellectual processes such as thinking and comprehension; tends to avoid work activities that require domination and persuasion of people or close interpersonal contact; tends to be more introverted than extroverted | Physician, home economist, paramedic, anthropologist, veterinarian, biologist, medical radiographer |
| Social | Exhibits skill in interpersonal relations and chooses work situations requiring interpersonal relationships; prefers work activities that help other people such as teaching or therapeutic service; tends to avoid high stress, intellectual problem-solving work activities. | Minister, teacher, psychologist, counselor, dental assistant, nurse, social worker |
| Artistic | Tends to dislike structure, to be more introverted than extroverted, and to exhibit a high degree of femininity; expresses feelings and may act on impulse | Actor or actress, musician, photographer, artist, journalist, cosmetologist |
| Enterprising | Desires power and status and likes work activities that involve manipulating and dominating others; tends to have good verbal skills | Attorney, salesperson, politician, manager, administrator, real estate agent, public relations worker, economist |
| Conventional | Prefers structure and order with rules and regulations governing the work activities; exhibits much self-control; identifies with power and status | Secretary, accountant, business teacher, clerk, data processing worker, financial advisor |

worker's reaction to the loss of a job, a supervisor's rating, or a promotion may be predicted based on whether the worker's basic personality type is internal or external.

Two major dimensions of personality, *emotionality* (prior to 1978 labeled neuroticism) and *extroversion-introversion*, have been identified by Eysenck (1947, 1951). The dimension of emotionality is related to emotional stability; changeability in mood; sensitivity to emotional stress, tenseness, anxiety; tendency to worry; concern about physical health; tendency to feel guilty; self-esteem; and feelings of fatigue. The dimension of extroversion-introversion is related to the individual's need to receive stimulation from the outside world. *Extroverts* tend to seek stimulation in the form of social activities and exciting, adventurous events as well as sensory stimulation in the form of loud noises and colors. *Introverts* are usually more withdrawn. Most individuals are probably *ambiverts*—a mixture of the two extremes—and vacillate from one extreme to the other in different situations. For example, a person in a supervisory position may be an introvert at a party, but an extrovert (aggressive and outgoing) while supervising a crew of construction workers.

Research has shown emotionality and extroversion-introversion to be important in a job environment. In general, an employee who has a lower dimension of emotionality makes a better worker at all levels. In order to perform at a higher level on the job, one must have good control over tension, anxiety, and emotional stress. DuBrin (1980) points out that the level of emotional arousal is related to job effectiveness. Job effectiveness increases when the optimum level of arousal is reached; however, optimum levels of arousal vary from person to person. One individual may need to be highly aroused in order to call on sales prospects while another individual may be able to do so at a lower level of arousal. A person who is generally in a high state of emotional arousal does not need much pressure from the environment in order to perform a task, and they may perform ineffectively if too much pressure is present from the environment. Understimulation is more apt to be a cause of job dissatisfaction and inadequate performance for extroverts than for introverts. Overstimulation is more likely to adversely affect job satisfaction and performance for introverts. Introverts are easier to condition. For example, introverts would be more likely than extroverts to improve on getting to work on time when given a reward for doing so (Hamner & Organ, 1978).

The development of techniques for assessing personality differences has contributed to the understanding of human behavior. Ways to measure dimensions of personality have made research studies possible which have provided new information, made predictions possible which have produced more satisfactory occupational choices, and made diagnosis of problems possible in some job situations.

# Theories of Personality

Many attempts have been made to describe how people establish a unique but fairly consistent pattern of behavior called personality. The personality theories can be grouped according to the approach used to explain how personality develops—psychoanalytic, learning, humanistic, or type and trait.

## Psychoanalytic Theory

**Freud's Theory.** Sigmund Freud (see Figure 12-3) focused on the unconscious in his theory of personality. He proposed that the personality is made up of three parts which continually interact with each other. The *id*, the unconscious part of the personality, operates to derive immediate pleasure. It is concerned only with immediate gratification of biological needs. The id's way of thinking, called *primary process thinking*, may generate mental images and wish-fulfillment fantasies (dreams), but it cannot actually obtain the things needed and desired. The *ego* is the conscious part of the personality that is in contact with reality. It is responsible for the voluntary processes, perceives the needs of the individual, evaluates the environment, adapts to social norms, plans ahead, and finds ways to actually obtain the things needed and desired. The conscious mental activity of the ego is called *secondary process thinking*. The *superego* consists of the internalized values and moral standards—the conscience. The id is the "wants" of the person; the superego is the "shoulds" of the person; and the ego is the "doing" of the functioning person. The id is the product of biological needs; the ego is the product of the intellectual processes; and the superego is the product of socialization.

Internal conflicts between the biological urges of the id and the internalized controls of the superego create anxiety or tension. The ego has to find ways to control the anxiety level. This is what was referred to earlier as coping strategies. The ego may use coping strategies that are conscious or unconscious. The unconscious coping strategies that a person uses are called defense mechanisms. Defense mechanisms distort, falsify, or deny reality, and everyone uses them to a certain extent. If they are overused, they may prevent a person from coping directly and taking action to resolve conflicts. Unresolved conflict creates more anxiety and necessitates more use of the defense mechanisms—a vicious cycle is put in motion and the distortions and denial of reality may reach serious proportions.

Major defense mechanisms are described in the boxed material on page 298. The ego finds or learns ways early in childhood to control the anxiety level. The ways tend to be repeated because their use is reinforced

Figure 12-3 Sigmund Freud.

whenever the anxiety is successfully reduced, and they come to constitute the person's personality—characteristic ways of responding to people, objects, or events in the environment.

According to Freud, pleasure is derived from the body's erogenous
zones—highly sensitive places on the body such as the mouth or genitals.
Different erogenous zones become the source of pleasure as one progresses through childhood—the *psychosexual stages* of development.
Whether the pleasure needs are satisfied at each stage of development has
major consequences for one's personality.

From birth to approximately the age of one or two, the mouth is the
principal erogenous zone. Gratification of the id comes though oral activities such as sucking or biting. If the id is not sufficiently satisfied as a
child, the adult may exhibit oral traits such as smoking, biting the nails,
chewing gum, overeating, or excessive talking.

## THE MOST COMMON DEFENSE MECHANISMS

1. Rationalization: a form of self-deception in which a socially acceptable justification is developed to avoid having to face a nonacceptable view of oneself. For example, an executive fails because of poor business decisions, but insists that the cause of failure was an unfavorable economy.
2. Flight into fantasy: inappropriate daydreaming. A management trainee who is frustrated by low status and unchallenging work daydreams about a future in the executive suite rather than creatively working to make such a future a reality.
3. Projection: unconsciously rejecting an unacceptable thought, desire, impulse, etc., by blaming it on someone else. The executive who has ceased to be promoted because of nonperformance projects failure onto superiors by believing that they block opportunities and favor other candidates.
4. Aggression: destructively attacking the real or imaginary source of frustration. This may be expressed verbally in slander and gossip or physically in such behaviors as sabotage or fighting.
5. Scapegoating: behaving aggressively toward someone who cannot fight back as a substitute for aggression toward the source of one's frustration. A foreman who is angry at his superior takes it out on subordinates or family.
6. Overcompensation: as a means of handling inadequacy in one area, exaggerated and inappropriate behavior is expressed in another. For example, an individual who feels ill at ease with people may talk too much or too loudly in a vain attempt to gain social acceptance. On a less extreme level, called compensation, students who flunk out of school make up for feelings of shame by intensively applying themselves in a substitute career. Various forms of substitution can be wholesome forms of defense, except when they involve giving up too soon on a worthwhile initial objective or lowering one's self-expectations when the going gets rough.
7. Repression: blotting out of consciousness certain ideas, memories, etc., that cause conflict and tend to lower self-esteem. This is exemplified by supervisors who selectively forget their own errors and blunders, refuse to accept constructive criticisms of superiors, and thus are unable to make the behavioral changes required for effective performance.
8. Reaction formation: a pendulum swing in the opposite direction from one's true desires or impulses as a means of maintaining self-control or self-respect. A highly ambitious manager whose career is stymied accepts defeat and becomes an extreme advocate of the stupidity of working hard and playing the upward mobility game.
9. Withdrawal: physically and/or psychologically pulling away from people and conflict. This is exemplified by the shy individual whose protection is to be excessively quiet or by the manager whose reaction to departmental conflict is to avoid becoming involved—to act as though the conflict were nonexistent (Williams, 1978, pp. 113-114).

From approximately the ages of one to three, the anus is the focus of sensation. Elimination of feces removes discomfort and tension and brings feelings of relief and pleasure. During the toilet-training period, the child learns to value holding back and to deliberately refuse to expel the feces. According to Freud, conflicts often arise during this power struggle between the child and the parent. If the conflicts are unresolved, the result will be a stingy, miserly, orderly, or obstinate adult personality.

Discovery of the sexual organs between the approximate ages of three to five brings both pleasure and anxiety. Probably the most controversial part of Freud's theory is his idea that the child unconsciously develops an attachment for the parent of the opposite sex, and then becomes jealous of the parent of the same sex which creates anxiety. Freud called this the *Oedipus complex* for a boy and the *Electra complex* for a girl. The conflict is resolved by identification with the parent of the same sex. If identification does not occur during this stage of development to resolve the conflict, the adult personality may be characterized by jealousy and problems with heterosexual relationships.

Freud placed little emphasis on the latency period which includes the time from about age six to puberty—a time when sexual impulses are dormant or repressed and no new conflicts occur. If all the other stages have been passed through successfully, the adolescent progresses toward heterosexual relationships and chooses a sexual partner. This genital stage with a renewed focus on sexuality continues through adulthood.

**Neo-Freudians.** Freud's basic theory was modified by *neo-Freudians*. Each one kept some or most of Freud's basic views but altered them to include social interactions rather than to emphasize the biological aspects and the erogenous zones. The modifications put less emphasis on the biological drives of the id and placed more emphasis on the ego. Erikson's theory of psychosocial stages of personality development is one of the best-known modifications of Freud's views. This theory of life stages was described in Chapter 5 on development.

### Learning Theory

Social learning theory contends that an individual's personality is learned. The principles of classical and operant conditioning presented in Chapter 6 are believed to account for the unique but characteristic ways a person responds to stimuli. Reinforcement is central to personality development, and social interactions are agents of reinforcement. The principles of classical and operant conditioning are extended to observational learning (also included in Chapter 6) which is sometimes called modeling or imitation.

## Humanistic Theory

**Rogers' Self Theory.** Carl Rogers, one of the most influential humanistic theorists, explains an individual's personality in terms of the *self-concept* and the *actualizing tendency* (Rogers, 1961). According to Rogers, humans are born with a tendency to seek experiences which protect and maintain the self and to grow psychologically as well as physiologically. This innate tendency is the motivation for personality development. People engage in and value activities that satisfy their need to grow and avoid those that hinder growth or are unpleasant. The self or ego, which is conscious, is the primary structure of personality. This is in contrast to the psychoanalytic concept of the unconscious id being a primary structure of personality.

As the infant experiences the world, the self is gradually separated from other things that exist in the environment, and the self-concept develops. How people come to perceive themselves depends on their social experiences. For example, if a child's parents are warm and accepting, frequently giving praise, the child comes to perceive himself or herself as competent and likeable and develops a positive self-concept. However, if a child's parents are cold, rejecting, and constantly criticizing, the child develops feelings of inadequacy that lead to a negative self-concept. Internalized attitudes, values, and standards serve as a gauge in the development of the self-concept. For example, if one has the attitude that any grade less than an "A" is unacceptable, and that person makes an "A – ", the person becomes defensive and anxious because his or her self-concept has been threatened. The person must either see the self as an unacceptable person, change the attitude, or perceive the experience in a distorted way through use of defense mechanisms.

Rogers believes that personality is related to the level of discrepancy between the person's perception of the self (self-concept), the person one would like to be (the ideal self), and the type of person one really is (the real self). The lower the level of disparity, the less anxious and ego defensive the person will be. The higher the level of disparity, the more anxiety the person will experience, the greater the likelihood that defense mechanisms will be overused, and the greater the likelihood that a low self-concept will be developed—all of which are characteristics of a maladaptive personality. The essentials then for the development of a healthy personality are a warm and accepting environment, an understanding of the real self, and realistic ideals.

**Maslow's Hierarchy of Needs Theory.** Abraham Maslow, another influential humanistic theorist, explained personality in terms of differing motivations which are arranged in a hierarchy. Maslow, like Rogers, proposes an actualizing tendency—a striving toward self-actualization. See Chapter 10 for a description of Maslow's theory.

## Type and Trait Theory

Early theories attempted to explain personality by grouping individuals by category or type. As mentioned earlier, Hippocrates explained a person's personality by typing the person according to which of the four humors dominated his or her body. William Sheldon (1940) classified people into three types based on the body build: *endomorphs*—those who have soft, wider bodies with a large proportion of the body weight in the abdomen; *mesomorphs*—those who have a firm bone structure and much accumulation of muscle; *ectomorphs*—those who have a thin body with small bones. (See Figure 12-4). Endomorphs are typically sociable, slow moving, jovial, and fond of food. Mesomorphs are characterized as being action oriented, risk taking, adventurous, aggressive, and loud. Ectomorphs are usually sensitive, quiet, restrained, self-conscious, and like privacy.

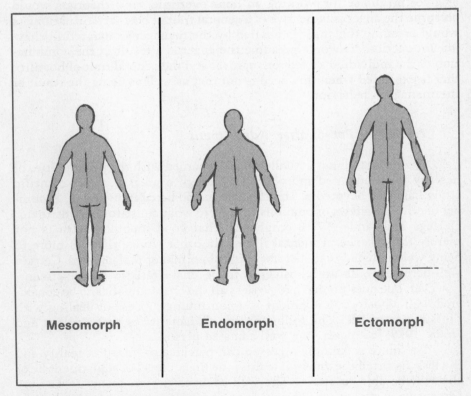

**Mesomorph**    **Endomorph**    **Ectomorph**

Figure 12-4 Sheldon's three basic body builds.

Many trait theories exist such as those previously mentioned in this chapter: Eysenck's typing of people according to extroversion-introversion and emotionality traits, typing of individuals as to whether they are externals or internals, and typing according to whether an individual is personality type A or B. Psychologists have identified many traits and developed techniques for identifying them. Two well-known theorists are Gordon Allport (1937) and Raymond B. Cattell (1946). They believe traits are relatively permanent and relatively consistent.

The trait view of personality has been challenged in recent years. Some psychologists, referred to as *situationists*, believe the environment plays a greater role in behavior than internal personality traits. They believe that behavior is not as consistent in different situations as trait theorists believe. Other psychologists, known as *interactionists*, believe the consistencies that are found are due to the interaction of the individual with the environment rather than to a general trait belonging to the individual. For example, if an employee becomes angry when the manager gives no praise for working an hour overtime, trait theorists would presume the anger is indicative of a general trait of hostility. Situationists would presume the anger is elicited by the manager's ungrateful behavior. Interactionists would presume the anger is a result of the combination of the individual's need for approval and the general trait of hostility that is exhibited when this need is not met as well as being the result of the manager's behavior.

## Theory of Personality Adjustment

Little research has actually been concerned with the personalities of healthy, well-adjusted individuals although a great deal of scientific study has been devoted to abnormal or maladjusted individuals. A number of different views or opinions exist as to what constitutes adjustment. Derlega and Janda (1978) emphasize that good mental health is not merely the absence of mental illness. In other words, there is more to being well adjusted than just not being abnormal or maladjusted. Certain well-defined skills are considered to be characteristic of adjustment; however, one does not have to possess all the characteristics to be considered well-adjusted. Adjustment is a continuing process of dealing with the stresses of life. The following are characteristics that Derlega and Janda (1978) feel describe a well-adjusted person.

The more accurately a person can perceive or interpret reality and the less distorted the views of reality, the higher level of adjustment he or she will be able to attain. The well-adjusted person seems to be very perceptive in evaluations of situations and in evaluations of other people. His or her personal motives do not unconsciously interfere as much with such evaluations as is true of maladjusted individuals. People who lack confidence and believe others dislike them, or who have a great deal of guilt regarding sexuality and view fairly innocent books, magazines, or movies as disgusting and shameful are allowing their personal motives to interfere with their evaluations of people and situations.

The more able one is to profit from past experience and plan for the future, the better adjusted one is likely to be. Well-adjusted individuals seem to be primarily concerned with the present; can achieve a better balance between the past, present, and future; and, thus, can realize a richer life. Although well-adjusted individuals remember, they do not brood over the past; and, although concerned with the future, they do not worry or become obsessed with it. They are able to find satisfaction in their present lives.

Additionally, well-adjusted individuals are committed to some form of work and have the ability to be productive. Also, adjustment includes the capacity to feel and to express a wide range of emotions. Well-adjusted people view themselves positively and are viewed positively by others. They are socially competent, feel comfortable in interacting with others, and are able to achieve intimacy in social relationships. They have the capacity to share their lives, feel close to others, and to form deep friendships and love relationships.

Personality adjustment seems to vary on a continuum from extremely maladjusted to extremely well adjusted. The degree of adjustment varies among individuals and may vary from time to time for an individual. One's work activity is related to adjustment. For example, well-adjusted individuals are more likely to choose occupations that provide challenge, and they are more likely to perform up to their real potential since they do not have a low self-concept. (See Figure 12-5.)

## Abnormal Personality

The literal meaning of "abnormal" is "away from normal," and abnormal behavior is considered to be behavior that deviates from normal behavior. But what is normal behavior? If the characteristics of the well-adjusted individuals are considered adaptive and normal, then maladaptive behaviors that create rather than solve problems or endanger one's life or the lives of others would be considered abnormal. If abnormal behavior is a deviation from normal behavior, what degree of deviation is classified as abnormal? The degree of deviation from normal most often is related to the amount of time spent engaging in a behavior. Normal behavior may be defined as customary or commonly occurring behaviors. Abnormal behavior then would be the unusual, uncommon, or rarely occurring behaviors. Normal behavior may be defined as realistic and accurate perceptions, and distorted perceptions of reality may be defined

Figure 12-5 Individuals tend to
work up to a level that fits their
self-concept.

as abnormal. Goleman (1982) lists norm violation, statistical rarity, personal discomfort, and deviation from an ideal as the criteria for defining abnormal behavior. Whether behavior is abnormal is sometimes difficult to differentiate.

Approximately one person in ten can expect to be treated during his or her lifetime for some form of abnormal behavior. This means that people suffering from abnormal behavior to such a degree as to interfere with performance and/or require treatment are often found in work environments. Since they have problems, they often are problems for supervisors and co-workers.

## Views of Abnormality

Some psychologists criticize the diagnosing of behaviors as abnormal on the basis that diagnostic procedures are too unreliable; the behavior may be diagnosed differently by different clinicians. Another objection to labeling behavior as abnormal is the long-lasting psychological effect the labeling may have on how a person is regarded by others and how a person regards himself or herself. Szasz (1974) is critical of such labeling because he feels the labeling is just a method for disposing of those who behave in a way disapproved by society—a form of punishment for nonconformity. An even more radical criticism is based on the view that the label of abnormal behavior is misleading because such behavior is really an act of heroism—daring to leave the extreme world of logic and explanation and move into one's own mind (Laing, 1967).

Several views or models of abnormal behavior exist currently. The *organic model* proposes that the basis for abnormal behavior is in the biochemical or physiological processes. Researchers have found physiological differences between those labeled as exhibiting normal and those exhibiting abnormal behavior. For example, some behavioral disorders are related to the deterioration of or destruction of brain tissue, and, as mentioned in Chapter 4, various concentrations of particular chemical substances in specific areas of the brain are associated with various behaviors. Also, the electrical stimulation of certain areas of the brain are associated with different behaviors. In Chapter 5, heredity was noted as being the basis for some abnormal behaviors due to abnormalities in the genes and chromosomes.

The *psychoanalytic model* was developed by Freud. He proposed that the condition causing a behavioral disorder could be psychological as well as physiological and that a disturbance in early childhood could cause it. For example, Freud believed that the severe mental disorder called schizophrenia was the result of a psychological disturbance in the first two years of a child's life. The most important aspect of this model is the theory that psychological problems are symptoms of underlying conflicts which are probably unconscious to the individual.

The *medical model* is based on both the organic and psychoanalytic models. It proposes that people who have psychological problems are sick and are no more responsible for their abnormal behavior than a person who exhibits abnormal body temperature from a physical illness such as measles or who hobbles from a broken leg. This model has greatly influenced clinical psychology and psychiatry as can be seen in the medical terminology used by psychologists and psychiatrists. For example, the "doctors" have "patients" with a mental "illness" treated with "therapy" in mental "hospitals" and when the patients respond they are "cured."

The *learning model* proposes that behavior is learned; therefore, abnormal behavior is explained as being the result of learning. Deviant behaviors are not believed to be symptoms of an underlying condition but instead have simply been conditioned by environmental experiences or learned by observation. This model, as does the psychoanalytic model, recognizes that biological factors may be an explanation for some abnormal behavior. In other words, learning is the major explanation for abnormal behavior, but learning may not be able to account for all abnormal behaviors. The learning model view holds that inappropriate behaviors may be decreased in frequency of occurrence and more appropriate behaviors may be learned by delivery of reinforcing consequences. An expanded version of the learning model view includes covert or unseen behaviors like thinking and emotions as well as the overt, observable behaviors. This expanded view emphasizes that behavior is determined by the cognitive processes such as thinking, memory, and perception and is referred to as the *cognitive-behavioral model*. The expanded learning model view proposes that abnormal behavior is a result of reinforcement of what the person thinks, feels, and does and the way a person thinks, feels, and behaves can be altered by changing the reinforcement.

The medical model view that people who have psychological problems are sick has led to the view that a mental disorder can be labeled or differentiated from other mental disorders by the symptoms exhibited. The *Diagnostic and Statistical Manual of Mental Disorders* or *DSM-III* (the third revision of the American Psychiatric Association's official classification) classifies mental disorders according to abnormal behavior patterns. The manual lists more than 230 types of disorders and gives a description which includes details such as essential features, occasional features, predisposing factors, frequency of occurrence in particular groups (age groups, ethnic groups, male and female groups, etc.), behavior patterns common to the family of the patient, and features which differentiate the disorder from similar ones (American Psychiatric Association, 1980). Only a few of the major types of disorders will be discussed in this chapter.

## Neurotic Disorders

In DSM-III, the term *neurosis* is no longer used as a general category of abnormal behavior. The behaviors that were previously listed in this category are now separated into more specific categories such as anxiety disorders and dissociative disorders. Most of these are currently listed in the category of anxiety disorders.

People with neurotic disorders are in contact with reality and maintain basic control over their thoughts and feelings. They deal ineffectively with the problems of living and thus experience much anxiety. Defense mechanisms are used excessively as coping strategies, and, since they merely repress the anxiety rather than remove the source of the anxiety, more and more anxiety is experienced. Such a great amount of the person's energy is used up in repressing the anxiety that new, more effective behaviors are not learned. Neurotic behaviors are extremely persistent because of the reinforcing consequence of relief from tension or anxiety provided by the defense mechanism and, also, because of the reinforcement received from significant people in a person's life in the form of sympathy, attention, and support. Neurotic behaviors are extremely difficult to change. Examples of neurotic behaviors are described in the following paragraphs. All people are neurotic in the sense that everyone uses defense mechanisms as coping strategies to some degree. A person would be labeled as neurotic only if the behavior is extreme, exhibited frequently, and interferes with normal functioning.

According to principles of classical conditioning, *phobias* are intense, irrational fears that are learned. However, according to psychoanalytic theory, they are symbolic expressions of some other anxiety. For example, an individual who has an extreme, unrealistic fear of riding in elevators may have had an experience sometime, perhaps in early childhood, in a small, closed place and conditioning occurred so that any similar stimulus now elicits fear or produces anxiety. Or the fear or anxiety may be displaced anger toward his or her parents. Displacing the anger with a fear of elevators is how the anger is kept repressed which prevents the person from acting directly on the anger.

In *obsessive-compulsive disorders*, the person repetitiously performs a behavior even though he or she may attempt to stop performing the behavior. Recurring or persistent covert thoughts are called obsessions, and recurring or persistent overt behaviors are called compulsions. The anxiety one has is repressed by cognitive means such as filling the mind with constant, trivial thoughts or by behavioral means such as staying busy so that anxiety-provoking thoughts or behaviors are avoided. This may be a learned coping strategy or, according to psychoanalytic theory, it may be a symbolic reaction. For example, a compulsion to wash one's hands may be related to guilt feelings about something.

*Anxiety states* occur when one is unable to repress anxiety. One may experience a feeling of anxiousness and tenseness that is free floating and generalized and is not associated with anything in particular. Such feelings may be intense enough to activate the sympathetic nervous system and cause the person to experience heart palpitations, choking sensations, etc. The source of the anxiety is kept repressed by attaching the anxiety to a less psychologically threatening condition such as a physical ailment.

In *dissociative disorders*, the part of the person's personality that is the source of the anxiety seems to be separated from the rest of the personality and repressed. Psychological amnesia, loss of memory for past events or personal identity, is one type of dissociative disorder. *Multiple personality* whereby a new identity arises to temporarily allow one to forget the old identity is another type. Rather than having only one identity, the person may be dominated by one or more alternative identities at various times as a coping strategy. The transition from one personality or identity to the other is a sudden reaction to stress. Another common dissociative disorder is called _depersonalization_. The person suddenly feels changed or different in a strange way. People may feel they are outside their bodies, that their actions are mechanical or that they are dreaming.

Sometimes an individual learns to displace anxiety by expressing it through physical symptoms known as _somatoform disorders_. The physical symptoms present are real but no organic cause of them can be found. The person is not conscious of the anxiety that is the source. Therefore, the person is not consciously trying to convince others that something is physically wrong and cannot bring the symptoms under voluntary control. There are four types of somatoform disorders.

In _somatization_ there is a pattern of vague, recurring physical complaints. The person usually has a long medical history that involves many physicians, a variety of physical disorders, unnecessary surgery, and the use of much medication. A similar neurotic disorder, _hypochondriasis_, involves a preoccupation with one's physical health. The person typically overreacts. For example, every small symptom is interpreted as a symptom of a serious disease, and the person rushes to the doctor. Or when people with this disorder read or hear about the symptoms of a particular illness, they may believe that they have those symptoms and will visit a physician. The meaning of normal aches and pains may be distorted, aches and pains may be imagined, and complaints of ill health are constant even though a physician can seldom find anything physically wrong with them.

When a person reduces anxiety by displacing the anxiety to a part of the body and then inactivating that part of the body, the response is called a _conversion disorder_. Blindness, deafness, and paralysis that have no physical cause are examples. Psychoanalytic theory suggests that the physical symptom is related to some traumatic past experience. After seeing someone murdered, a person might lose his or her sight; or a person might lose all feeling in one hand if that hand has been used in a way that brings about guilt and accompanying anxiety. This form of coping with anxiety is not as common today as in Freud's day. People are more knowledgeable of the physiological functioning of the body, and one of the preceding forms of coping is more likely to be used.

The _psychogenic pain disorder_ consists of feeling pain for which there is no physical basis in some part of the body. It is not faked; the pain is actually felt. Learning theorists propose that reinforcement may be motivating the pain. The individual may be receiving some benefit such as workmen's compensation, care and attention, or the privilege of evading some disliked task.

## Psychotic Disorders

Like neurosis, the term *psychosis* is no longer used as a general category in DSM-III, and the disorders formerly listed in this category are separated into more specific categories such as schizophrenia and affective disorders. The main distinction between neuroses and psychoses is that in psychoses the individual loses contact with reality. In psychosis, fantasy and actuality cannot be differentiated; thus, it is the most severe of the abnormal behaviors. Perception, thinking, and feeling seem to be guided more by internal stimuli than external stimuli. Typical symptoms of psychosis are *hallucinations*, the perception of things that are not really there; *delusions*, the belief of things that are not true; inappropriate affect, a feeling that does not match the situation; and withdrawal, the regard of self as alien to the external world. A person may have psychotic episodes which may vary in intensity and in length of time. No person is usually psychotic 24 hours of every day. Some theorists propose that the person uses the withdrawal from reality as a coping strategy.

Several types of schizophrenia are differentiated. *Undifferentiated* or *simple schizophrenia* includes several or all of the symptoms of psychosis mentioned in the preceding paragraph. The person may be incoherent and may exhibit bizarre or chaotic behavior at times along with hallucinations and delusions. *Catatonic schizophrenia* is primarily characterized by disturbed motor activity. The person becomes rigid and immobile and may remain motionless for hours or days. Catatonics may be mute and remain in whatever position they are placed. According to psychoanalytic theory, hostility and anxiety are handled through such immobility. In disorganized or *hebephrenic schizophrenia*, the behavior may be childish or immature. Inappropriate silliness and giggling, a refusal to wear clothes or use eating utensils, or the elimination of urine or feces at inappropriate times are typical symptoms. The coping strategy seems to be regression to an earlier stage of development. Symptoms of *paranoid schizophrenia* include suspiciousness and delusions along with hallucinations. Paranoid schizophrenics may appear normal in first interactions but their fear of persecution gradually takes control of them, and they become hostile and aggressive toward anyone who does not agree with their delusions. They may have *delusions of grandeur*—they are some great or grand person, *delusions of persecution*—others are attempting to do them harm or get something they have, or *delusions of reference*—everything others do is in reference to them. They seem to be using projection and denial as coping strategies. They deny their own hostility and desires and project them into the personalities of others. They are often extremely religious and use their religious beliefs to deny and keep repressed hostility and desires. The only symptom exhibited in *paranoia* is delusion. Other symptoms of schizophrenia are not exhibited. The delusions may be very specific and commonly involve one's spouse, a member of the family, a supervisor or employer, or perhaps a more remote enemy such as foreigners or a political group. Except for the specific delusion, a person with paranoia may function adequately.

In *affective disorders*, the person seems to fail to use a strategy to repress feelings of guilt and inadequacy and often even exaggerates them. The result is major *depression* characterized by listlessness, brooding, fatigue, feelings of worthlessness, slowing of the thought processes, and profound sadness and loneliness. The result may be a *bipolar disorder*, formerly called manic-depressive psychosis. The individual may suddenly change back and forth from depression to a wild, violent, or extremely elated mood. The manic behavior seems to be a defense against the depression and will continue until exhaustion occurs. Psychotic depressions are differentiated from normal depressions associated with some event in a person's life in that psychotic depression fails to disappear, gradually gets worse, or is not associated with any event in the person's life. Various explanations for affective disorders have been proposed. Some psychologists believe that biochemical factors or heredity play a role. Psychoanalytic theory proposes that the person has guilt and the depression is self-punishment, or that the person has anger toward someone or some situation but cannot express the anger and takes it out on himself or herself instead. Learning theory suggests that depression is a result of learned helplessness. When a person repeatedly experiences failure, or perceived failure, the punishment for failing inhibits future occurrence of that behavior. The person comes to believe he or she has no control over the successes and failures in life.

### Other Disorders

Other disorders include the excessive use of substances to cope with the problems of life. Some common substances used are alcohol, heroin, cocaine, or marijuana. Substance use is classified as a disorder in DSM-III under the following conditions: (1) When addiction occurs—the body chemistry changes and the drug becomes a biological need. (2) When dependence occurs—increasing amounts are required to achieve the same results, or physical or psychological symptoms appear when the substance is reduced or not taken. (3) When abuse occurs—using the substance when it interferes with one's health, interferes with one's ability to function adequately, or disturbs social relationships.

Psychosexual disorders are sexual behaviors that deviate from the cultural norms of the society. These behaviors may be grouped into three major classifications. In *psychosexual dysfunction*, the individual is unable to function effectively during sex—impotency or frigidity is experienced. Dysfunction occurs commonly in mild forms and under temporary conditions. It is considered to be a disorder only when it is typical and occurs in an extreme form. In *paraphilia,* objects or situations arouse the person sexually that normally do not arouse a person. These may become the preferred or exclusive method of sexual arousal thus interfering with the achievement of a loving sexual relationship. For example, sexual arousal may be associated with children, animals, aggression, or physical pain. In *gender identity disorders,* the individual is confused over his or her biological sex and prefers to behave in a manner typical of the opposite sex.

People with *personality disorders* formerly were referred to as sociopaths or psychopaths. They may fight, be sexually promiscuous, lie, cheat, steal, and show constant disregard for the rights of others. The "con artist" is one example. Often their behavior leads to imprisonment. They seem to have a weak superego.

## Personality Change

Clinical psychologists attempt to change personality or typical behavior that is abnormal or maladaptive. Often behavior change is sought to help one become better adjusted. *Therapy* is the term used for any attempt by a clinician to bring about desired personality or behavioral changes by applying particular psychological techniques (Korchin, 1976). Therapy has also been defined as "a corrective experience leading a person to behave in a socially appropriate, adequate, and adaptive way" (Bourne & Ekstrand, 1982, p. 442).

### Therapy

The approach used to influence or change behavior will depend on the theory of personality development and the theoretical model of abnormal behavior the therapist accepts.

The psychoanalytic approach attempts to bring repressed feelings and sources of anxiety into consciousness so the person can resolve conflicts and reevaluate. As the feelings are brought into consciousness, the psychologist helps the person interpret his or her feelings. The goal is to achieve insight into the cause of the symptoms and to reexperience the feelings associated with a memory. Freud developed several techniques to help a person overcome his or her resistance to insight and to experiencing feelings which are painful psychologically. The therapy may be called psychoanalysis.

Behavior modification is a technique used in *behavior therapy* to change behavior. Behavior therapists use conditioning techniques and tend to disregard the experiences that caused the behavior. The goal is to teach more satisfactory ways of behaving.

*Client-centered therapy* is based on Carl Rogers' theory of the development of the self-concept. According to this therapeutic theory, the goal of the therapist is to increase the person's sense of self-worth and help the person develop a more realistic self-concept thus giving the person the strength to face the repressed conflicts and feelings. This is accomplished by the therapist's ability to accurately understand the person's feelings and communicate this understanding, to truly like and accept the person, and to communicate this unconditional positive regard.

Two *cognitive therapies* are *rational therapy* and *reality therapy*. Cognitive therapy considers a person to be responsible for his or her own behavior. Rational therapy attempts to change a person's irrational beliefs which are considered to be the source of maladaptive behavior. The goal is to show the person that his or her interpretations of events are irrational and are the cause of their problems and to teach the person more rational interpretations. The primary goal of reality therapy is to help people develop responsible behavior by encouraging them to judge their own behavior, set goals, and make commitments; by accepting no excuses for failing to keep a commitment; and by inflicting no punishment or showing any rejection of the person.

Many different kinds of *group therapy* are used in a wide variety of settings. The basic assumption in group therapy is that the personality disorder is related to an inability to communicate, to relate to others, and to perceive accurately. The goal of group therapy is to provide feedback. A person may find out his or her problem is not unique, may find out how she or he affects others, may find needed encouragement to try out new behaviors, may find fulfillment through helping another person in the group, and may find a safe and accepting environment in which to try out new behaviors.

*Medical therapies* are based on the assumption that a physiological disorder is the source of the abnormal behavior. Medical therapies include brain surgery, shock therapy, and chemotherapy which involves the prescribing of vitamins, sedatives, minor tranquilizers, antidepressants, and antipsychotic drugs (major tranquilizers) which reduce delusions and hallucinations.

## Management and Therapy

J. C. Williams (1982, p. 93) comments that "since today only chronically ill psychotics and occasionally neurotics are hospitalized, managers must relate to large numbers of people who would be totally incapacitated except for their continued medication. . . . They are people with whom the supervisor has the most direct contact: the chronic absentee, the troublemaker, the low producer, and the person who has difficulty relating to others." Managers do become involved with people with maladaptive personalities and dealing with them as ordinary disciplinary problems may not be economically feasible. It is important then for managers to be able to recognize symptoms of maladjustment in order to consider the problem behavior in making decisions and to be able to make referrals to someone who can provide professional help.

Some large companies and a few labor unions are now utilizing the services of industrial psychologists who are trained to provide therapy to employees with maladaptive personalities and to provide consultation service to supervisors for dealing with employees with maladaptive personalities. "Industrial psychologists are just beginning to appraise the personality factors that bear directly on a person's fitness or nonfitness for work" (Janda & Klenke-Hamel, 1982, p. 540).

## SUMMARY

1. Personality is the characteristic or usual responses of a person to people, objects, or events in the environment—the persistent behavior patterns that are unique to an individual.

2. Four basic techniques are used to assess personality: interviews, direct observations, objective tests, and projective tests.

3. Nondirective, depth, and patterned interviews differ primarily in the amount of structure imposed by the interviewer.

4. Direct observation is more reliable when the behavior to be observed is precisely defined and two or more observers collect the data simultaneously.

5. The Minnesota Multiphasic Personality Inventory is one of the most widely used objective tests for personality assessment. Objective tests are usually paper-and-pencil tests in the form of questions to answer about one's self.

6. Projective tests use unstructured, vague, and ambiguous stimuli to obtain a response. The Rorschach inkblot technique and the Thematic Apperception Test are two widely used projective tests.

7. Workers in different occupational groups have different personalities. The Strong Vocational Interest Blank, the Kuder Preference Record, and the Vocational Preference Inventory are often used to determine a person's basic interest areas.

8. Workers may be categorized as to whether they have personality Type A or Type B, whether they are internals or externals, or extroverts or introverts.

9. The psychoanalytic approach to explaining personality focuses on the unconscious. Freud explained personality in terms of the interaction of the id, the ego, and the superego; the use of defense mechanisms to reduce tension or anxiety; and the psychosexual stages of development.

10. Reinforcement is central to the social learning theory approach which contends that an individual's personality is learned by reinforcement of both covert and overt behaviors and observations.

11. The humanistic approach to explaining personality is represented by Rogers' theory of the development of the self-concept and Maslow's self-actualization theory.

12. Sheldon's body type theory proposes that endomorphs, mesomorphs, and ectomorphs are characterized by typical personalities.

13. Situationists believe the environment plays a greater role in behavior than internal personality traits, and interactionists believe personality consistencies are due to the interaction of the individual with the environment; these two approaches challenge the trait view of personality which proposes that people possess a set of general traits that are relatively permanent and relatively consistent.

14. Theorists describe a well-adjusted personality as being more than the absence of maladjustment. A well-adjusted personality would include the ability to perceive reality accurately, the ability to profit from experience, a commitment to some form of work, the ability to form close or intimate social relationships, and the ability to express a wide range of emotions.

15. The criteria for defining abnormal behavior is norm violation, statistical rarity, personal discomfort, and deviation from an ideal.

16. Abnormal behavior is often difficult to differentiate, and some theorists are critical of labeling behavior as abnormal.

17. The organic model proposes that the basis for abnormal behavior is in the biochemical or physiological processes.

18. The psychoanalytic model proposes that abnormal behaviors are symptoms caused by underlying conflicts which are probably unconscious to the individual.

19. The medical model is a perspective based on both the organic and psychoanalytic models and treats abnormal behavior as an illness.

20. The learning model proposes that abnormal behaviors are learned, that they are not symptoms of an underlying condition, and that the person is not ill.

21. The cognitive-behavioral model proposes that the way one thinks and feels, as well as how one behaves, is learned by reinforcement, and that behavior is determined by the cognitive processes such as thinking, memory, and perception.

22. The DSM-III is the American Psychiatric Association's official classification of mental disorders according to abnormal behavioral patterns. The manual lists and describes more than 230 disorders.

23. People with neurotic disorders are in contact with reality and maintain basic control over their thoughts and feelings, use the defense mechanisms excessively, and are extremely difficult to change.

24. Phobias (irrational fears); obsessive-compulsive disorders (recurring and persistent thoughts or behaviors); anxiety states; and dissociative disorders such as amnesia (loss of memory for events), multiple personality (the transition from one identity to another), and depersonalization (out-of-body experiences) are examples of neurotic disorders.

25. The somatoform disorders labeled somatization (vague, recurring physical complaints), hypochondriasis (preoccupation with one's physical health), conversion disorder (inactivation of a part of the body), and psychogenic pain disorder (feeling pain for which there is no physical basis) are neuroses wherein the individual displaces anxiety by expressing it through physical symptoms.

26. People with psychotic disorders are out of contact with reality and have hallucinations, delusions, or inappropriate affect.

27. Four types of schizophrenia are differentiated: undifferentiated, which includes several or all the symptoms of psychosis; catatonic, which is characterized by disturbed motor activity; hebephrenic, which is characterized by immature behavior; and paranoid, which is characterized by delusions. Delusions of grandeur, persecution, or reference may be expressed.

28. Paranoia is characterized by a specific delusion which may be the only noticeable symptom.

29. Affective disorders consist of depression and bipolar disorder, formerly called manic-depressive psychosis.

30. Substance use disorders—addiction, dependence, and abuse; psychosexual disorders—psychosexual dysfunction, paraphilia, and gender identity disorders; and personality disorders, formerly called sociopathic or psychopathic, are other abnormal behaviors.

31. Therapy, the intentional application of psychological techniques to effect personality or behavioral changes, may take various forms of

approaches: psychoanalysis, behavior therapy, client-centered therapy, rational therapy, reality therapy, group therapy, or medical therapy.

32. Managers often supervise employees who have maladaptive personalities and need to be able to recognize symptoms of maladjustment in order to consider the problem in making decisions and to be able to make referrals to someone who can give them professional help.

## SUGGESTIONS FOR FURTHER READING

Becker, J. *Affective disorders*. Morristown, N. J.: General Learning Press, 1977.

A paperback book which presents information on depression and the various theories of its causes. Case histories illustrate important points.

Belkin, G. S. *Contemporary psychotherapies*. Chicago: Rand McNally, 1980.

Various methods of psychotherapies are discussed. Principles and procedures related to the various methods are identified in the discussion.

Bernheim, K. F., & Lewine, R. R. J. *Schizophrenia: Symptoms, causes, treatments*. New York: Norton, 1979.

A paperback book which gives a readable account of schizophrenia and includes descriptions, theories of causes, and clinical treatments.

Coleman, J., Butcher, J. N., & Carson, R. C. *Abnormal psychology and modern life* (6th ed.). Glenview, Ill.: Scott, Foresman, 1980.

A balanced presentation of abnormal behavior which emphasizes no particular approach or theory. This is one of the most widely used textbooks in the field of abnormal psychology.

Hall, C. S., & Lindzey, G. *Theories of personality* (3rd ed.). New York: Wiley, 1978.

A classic textbook that describes and evaluates the major theories of personality.

Orpen, C. The 'correct' use of personality tests: A view from industrial psychology. *Public Personnel Management*, May-June 1974, 3(3), 228-229.

A journal article that points out the special knowledge and understanding required to use personality tests and emphasizes using them for determining how performance on the test is related to job success.

Rachman, S. J., & Hodgson, R. J. *Obsessions and compulsions.* Englewood Cliffs, N. J.: Prentice-Hall, 1980.

A rather detailed review of what is known about obsessive-compulsive disorders and the treatment of such behaviors.

Schultz, D. *Growth psychology: Models of the healthy personality.* New York: Van Nostrand Reinhold, 1977.

A short paperback book that presents seven prominent theorists' views regarding the healthy personality.

Snyder, S. H. *Biological aspects of mental disorder.* New York: Oxford University Press, 1980.

A book that points out the relevance of the findings in the fields of biochemistry, genetics, and pharmacology to the study of behavior disorders.

Wilson, K. *Matching personal and job characteristics.* Washington, D. C.: U. S. Government Printing Office, 1978.

A guide that summarizes the personal characteristics and skills necessary for 282 occupations. It is useful in helping people make decisions about a career.

# Social Influences

# Social psychology is the area of psychology concerned

with how individual behavior is influenced by groups of people and how people behave within groups. Humans are social creatures who exist within a social environment and that environment influences their behavior. Much of a person's time on the job will be spent in a social environment with groups of people, and his or her behavior will be influenced by and representative of the group with whom he or she is involved. The group or social environment may consist of a circle of friends, a section of employees, a department of people, a larger group called a division, or the entire organization.

The study of attitudes and attitude change has been of primary interest to social psychologists because attitudes are assumed to be important determinants of behavior. A person's attitudes reflect social influences. The nature of attitudes, the development and measurement of attitudes, and the changing of attitudes and behaviors will be topics of discussion in this chapter. The study of attitudes includes the study of special aspects of attitudes—beliefs, opinions, values, prejudices, and discrimination. Since the attitudes of workers often influence their behavior and their effectiveness in a job situation, the study of social influences is highly relevant. Changing people's attitudes is an important means of behavior control in our society since one cannot force a person to buy a particular product, vote for a particular politician, like or dislike a particular person, or work for a particular goal.

## The Nature of Attitudes

Sometimes a person is said to have "a good attitude" or "a bad attitude" toward some person, object, idea, or situation. Sometimes a person is told to change or improve his or her attitude. Sometimes people wonder how a person came to have a particular attitude. In this section, attitudes will be defined, then theories explaining how attitudes develop will be discussed, and finally methods that have been devised to assess or measure a person's attitudes will be described.

### Components

An *attitude* is usually defined as a person's disposition to think, feel, and act either positively or negatively toward a person, idea, object, or situation. Attitudes are relatively long lasting and consist of a combination of intellectual, emotional, and behavioral aspects. (See Figure

13-1.) One aspect of attitude, a *belief*, may be true or false and does not involve feeling, emotion, likes or dislikes, but is accepted as fact. An *opinion* is similar to a belief; however, the evidence supporting an opinion is weaker than the evidence supporting a belief. For example, based on the age stated on an application form, an employer may have a belief that the job applicant is under 21 years of age. If the applicant is seen in the waiting area and there is no other information about the applicant's age, the employer may have an opinion that the applicant is under 21 years of age. *Prejudice* is a special aspect of attitude that involves prejudging without evidence such as judging an applicant to be irresponsible because the applicant's age is under 21. *Discrimination* is an action taken based on a prejudice. Discrimination would be demonstrated if the applicant is not hired for the job because of age even though he or she may be the best qualified applicant for the job. *Value* involves both thinking and feeling. The degree of worth of something and how positively or negatively one feels about something determines the value placed on that something—person, idea, object, or situation. For example, one employee may value a large, comfortable desk chair in the office more highly than other employees in the office if the chair prevents a backache for that employee or if it is a status symbol and that employee has a low self-esteem.

An attitude is characterized by three components: cognitive, affective, and conative. The cognitive component of an attitude is the belief or opinion held about a person, object, idea, or situation. The cognitive component consists of mental activities such as perception, memory, and thinking. Often the beliefs and opinions that accompany attitudes are not true or are only partially true. The affective component of an attitude is the feeling one has toward the person, object, idea, or situation. One may like, dislike, love, hate, fear, respect, and have positive or negative feelings in general toward something or someone. The conative component of an attitude is the action or response tendency. The response may be to approach or to avoid the person, object, or situation. The conative component consists of any directed effort toward action. For example, a person is said to have a favorable or positive attitude toward a new marketing concept if he or she believes the information that provides support for the concept (cognitive component), likes or has good feelings about the concept (affective component), and votes in favor of a proposal to incorporate the concept into the company's present marketing strategies (conative component).

### Formation

Attitudes are not inherited; they are acquired. How people acquire attitudes has been of interest to psychologists for many years. According

*"I'm not going to enjoy this new project because I know already I'm not going to like working with a female supervisor."*

Figure 13-1    Attitudes predispose a person to think, feel, and act in a particular way.

to learning theorists, a person's attitudes are acquired primarily through the process of learning and begin to be formed in infancy.

An individual's parents are a strong social influence on his or her attitudes. Parents serve as models for their children. Children identify with parents and act the way parents do by responding positively and negatively to the same things and situations. Parents reward and punish children for expressing certain attitudes. Likes, dislikes, and fears are often the result of associations formed in early childhood experiences. Most frequently these early attitudes remain with a person throughout his or her life. (See Figure 13-2).

As children grow older and begin school, peers and adults other than their parents begin to have a significant influence on the formation of attitudes and are thus a strong social influence on an individual's behavior. During adolescence, the influence of the peer group on attitude formation and therefore behavior is quite dramatic. The impact of peer influence on attitudes is also very strong among college students who are exposed to many and varied attitudes.

Figure 13-2    Attitudes are
often acquired in early childhood
through modeling, punishment, and
reward, and may remain with a
person throughout life.

Attitudes seem to be learned, just as anything is learned, through
conditioning, observation, and insight. Attitudes develop through classical conditioning—conditioning by association of two stimuli. For example, a salesperson may attempt to develop an attitude in his or her
customers by dressing attractively in the hope that the positive feeling

stimulated by his or her appearance will become associated with the product he or she is selling. If a positive attitude can be developed, the result will probably be the behavior of purchasing the product. Attitudes may be shaped through operant conditioning by following the expression of certain attitudes with reinforcing or punishing consequences. For example, a creative attitude may develop if a worker is praised and reinforced for exhibiting creativity in a job situation, but a creative attitude will probably not develop if the worker is criticized and punished for exhibiting creativity.

Television, newspapers, and other forms of mass media, as well as parents, family, peers, and other significant people such as teachers and famous people, have an impact on the formation of attitudes and are thus strong social influences on an individual's behavior. Information, lifestyles, social patterns, and values are presented to people through mass media. The fact that children become attracted to television at an early age suggests the strong influence of the mass media over attitude formation.

### Measurement

Numerous methods have been devised by psychologists to measure attitudes. The measurement of attitudes involves identifying the attitudes a person holds, determining the strength of each attitude, and determining whether the attitude is positive or negative. Frequently, employers have an interest in measuring an employee's or a potential employee's attitudes toward various things related to a job such as transfers, travel, promotions, shift work, or particular groups of people. Manufacturers may have an interest in measuring consumers' attitudes, and politicians often have an interest in measuring voters' attitudes.

A self-report method is the method most commonly used in measuring attitudes. This method involves asking the person to report how he or she feels about some person, object, idea, or situation. Usually a list of possible answers is provided that will indicate the strength and direction (positive or negative) of the attitude. This method is called an *attitude scale.*

The Thurstone attitude scale is attributed to the work of Thurstone and Chave (1929). Statements ranging from extremely favorable to extremely unfavorable about a person, object, idea, or situation are listed in jumbled order. The respondent must check those statements with which he or she agrees. Each statement was previously assigned a scale value which is used to determine an attitude score.

On the Guttman attitude scale (Guttman, 1950), respondents indicate the strongest statement they are willing to endorse in a series of successively more extreme statements. The statements are arranged along an attitude dimension so that anyone accepting a more extreme item would accept all of the preceding ones. The following is an example of an item of this type:

1. I would not mind living in the same city with a person of this particular ethnic group.
2. I would not mind living on the same street with a person of this particular ethnic group.
3. I would work beside a person of this particular ethnic group.
4. I would have a person of this particular ethnic group in my home to visit.
5. I would marry a person of this particular ethnic group.

A lot of time is required to construct Guttman scales and, consequently, this method is not widely used.

The Likert scale (Likert, 1932) is another type of attitude scale which consists of a series of statements to which the respondent indicates the extent of his or her agreement or disagreement on a five- or six-point scale as illustrated below:

The supervisor is fair in work-load assignments.

1 Strongly disagree
2 Disagree
3 Undecided
4 Agree
5 Strongly agree

An individual's score is determined by totaling the numeric values of his or her responses to the statements. This is the simplest attitude scale, and it has consistently been found to be more reliable and less time consuming to construct than the Thurstone or Guttman scales.

The semantic differential scale (Osgood, Suci, & Tannenbaum, 1957) presents a series of adjectives and their antonyms. The respondent rates a particular concept along a scale between the adjective and its antonym. For example, one might rate the concept of "supervisor" on adjective scales similar to the following examples:

Fair     1 2 3 4 5 6 7 Unfair

Pleasant 1 2 3 4 5 6 7 Unpleasant

Strong   1 2 3 4 5 6 7 Weak

Typically a concept is rated between many adjective pairs, perhaps 15 or 20, and the numeric values of the ratings are totaled to determine an attitude score.

Some psychologists believe that attitudes can be more accurately ascertained from actions or behaviors than from verbal statements. What a person says is not always consistent with what he or she does. For example, in one study landlords indicated they would rent apartments to interracial couples; yet when the couples appeared in person, many of the landlords would not even show the apartments to the couples (McGrew, 1967). A recent study (Zanna, Olson, & Fazio, 1980) suggests that the strength of the relationship between behavior and reported attitude varies from person to person according to the personality dimension of *self-monitoring*—the degree to which a person's behavior is guided by situational cues. The behavior of a person who is low in self-monitoring is guided more by his or her thoughts and feelings than by situational facts. For example, managers who have strong negative feelings toward a particular ethnic group and are low in self-monitoring are more likely to allow their negative feelings to influence the decision to avoid giving a promotion to a person of this particular ethnic group. The behavior of a person who is high in self-monitoring is guided more by the situation than by feelings. For example, managers who have strong negative feelings toward a particular ethnic group but are high in self-monitoring are more likely to be aware of their feelings and may make the promotion of a person of this particular ethnic group contingent on situational facts such as supervisor rating or production quotas. Low self-monitors are likely to show more consistency between reported attitudes and behavior, and high self-monitors are likely to show less consistency between reported attitudes and behavior. For example, managers who are low self-monitors are more likely to allow their attitudes to influence their behavior than managers who are high self-monitors.

## Changing Attitudes

Although attitudes are relatively enduring, they can and do change. Attempts to change attitudes generally focus on changing one of the components: cognitive, affective, or conative. Dissonance, fear, new information, and personality seem to be related to attitude change.

### Dissonance

Changing any one of the three components of attitude will create dissonance or inconsistency. This dissonance will be so uncomfortable the person will be motivated to eliminate it by establishing consistency. Consistency may be established by changing the other components also.

As was indicated in Chapter 9, individuals have a strong need for cognitive consistency which can be the motivation for attitude change and is the basic assumption of Leon Festinger's (1957) theory of cognitive dissonance. The need for cognitive consistency and thus the motivation for changing another component of the attitude occurs if one can change any one component of the attitude. Cognitive dissonance occurs when a person has two inconsistent beliefs, when a person's behavior is inconsistent with his or her beliefs or feelings, or when a person's beliefs and feelings are inconsistent. For example, the owner of a business firm would experience cognitive dissonance if he or she believes that all the employees of the firm are honest but also believes that money has been stolen from the cash register. Cognitive dissonance would also be experienced by a person who feels uncomfortable working with a person of a particular ethnic group but believes he or she should work with all people, or by a person who believes that people past 70 years of age are unproductive on the job but meets an employee past 70 years of age who is highly productive on the job.

Since people reduce dissonance by using a number of different strategies, attitudes may change in various ways or the dissonance may be resolved without attitude change. When a person's actions disagree with his or her beliefs or feelings, the behavior may be changed to fit the belief or feeling, or the belief or feeling may be changed to fit the behavior. When one encounters new information that is inconsistent with present beliefs and opinions, the new information may be regarded as unreliable; new facts may be sought to refute the new information; or the new information may be accepted and the belief or opinion changed to fit the new information. Sometimes a person may deny the inconsistency or discrepancy, minimize it, or rationalize it in such a way that the discrepancy is avoided. For example, the missing money from the cash register might be rationalized as an honest error in making change.

Some factors that seem to affect the degree of attitude change that occurs from dissonance are reinforcement, choice, and justification. When there is conflict between beliefs and feelings and one's behavior and the person receives reinforcement or a reward for the behavior, the belief or feeling is less likely to change because the behavior can be rationalized as being engaged in for the reward. If there is little or no reward, then the beliefs and feelings are more likely to change since the behavior cannot be rationalized as being engaged in for the reward. If a person freely chooses to behave in a manner that conflicts with beliefs and feelings, the beliefs and feelings are more likely to change than if he or she was forced to behave in such a manner. The behavior can be rationalized if it is believed to have been forced and the belief or feeling does not have to change to resolve the dissonance. Likewise, if a person has a very good reason for a behavior that is in conflict with his or her beliefs and feelings, the beliefs and feelings are less likely to change. If the behavior cannot be justified, the beliefs and feelings are more likely to change.

## Fear

Arousal of fear can be a useful technique for effecting attitude change. Slight to moderate fear arousal is effective in changing attitudes; however, if fear is aroused out of proportion to the actual situation and a person becomes too fearful, denial of the danger may be used as a defense mechanism, and fear arousal would not be very effective in changing attitudes. Results of experimental studies have produced conflicting results on the use of fear arousal as a means of attitude change. In an early study (Janis & Feshbach, 1953), three groups of high school students were exposed to messages which emphasized the importance of dental care and were designed to arouse varying degrees of fear. The group that had high fear arousal and was shown horrible pictures of rotten teeth and infected gums reported fewer changes in their dental care behaviors than a group that was exposed to a less threatening message which gave the information without such horrible pictures or the group that received information on dental care in a nonthreatening manner. More recent research, however, has shown that greater fear can be more effective in changing attitudes than low fear arousal (Dabbs & Leventhal, 1966). These conflicting findings were explained when an experiment on attitude change was conducted which coupled fear arousal with specific suggestions on how to change the behavior (Leventhal, 1970). A message which aroused greater fear generated more intentions to stop smoking but was not effective in actually reducing the number of cigarettes smoked unless specific suggestions on how to change the behavior were also given in the message. Giving specific suggestions on how to change without any fear arousal, however, was not effective in producing change.

## New Information

The introduction of new information is another method for changing attitudes. One's social environment constantly provides new information. Several factors determine how effective new information will be in changing attitudes; these are credibility, attractiveness, and power of the communicator. If the source of the information is perceived as being especially knowledgeable, objective, and trustworthy, the new information is more likely to be internalized. When the communicator of the new information is liked, is perceived as being similar to one's self, and is perceived as attractive, the information will probably be accepted in order to identify with the source or maintain a relationship with that person.

The more power a communicator of new information has to reward a person for accepting the new information or to punish a person for rejecting the new information, the more likely the person is to change his or her attitude. A person with a low self-image who is more ego defensive than a person with a high self-image will be less likely to accept the credibility, attractiveness, and power of the communicator and less likely to change an attitude based on new information.

The characteristics of the message may be a factor in attitude change. Printed material is usually more effective with people of higher socioeconomic status than with people of low socioeconomic status. Face-to-face communication is usually more effective than other forms of communication. A review of the literature on attitude changes (McGuire, 1969) indicates that a message is more likely to change attitudes if the following conditions exist: (1) The message begins with material that is agreeable rather than disagreeable to the person. (2) The intent to change attitude is not made obvious. (3) The conclusions to be drawn are made clear. (4) Both sides of the issue are presented. (5) The side of the issue which seeks to change the person's attitude is presented second. (6) The discrepancy between the position of the message and the person's view is only moderate rather than extreme. (7) The message is only moderately frightening rather than extremely frightening.

### Personality

The characteristics of a person also seem to be a factor in attitude change. An intelligent person is more likely to change his or her attitude than a person who is less intelligent. The more intelligent person is more likely to understand new information and is not as apt to hold on to a belief or opinion because of insecurity about his or her intelligence.

The general mood of a person is a factor in attitude change. When people are in a good mood, they are more likely to change their attitudes. Salespeople often entertain a prospective customer just prior to their attempts to sell their products or service.

A person who feels inadequate as a person and has low self-esteem is more likely to change his or her attitudes than someone with higher self-esteem. Obviously, if people do not think very highly of themselves, they will not put much value on their beliefs, feelings, and behaviors. If a person with low self-esteem finds his or her beliefs, feelings, and behaviors challenged, he or she may give them up without much hesitation.

Attitudes can be changed. Research indicates, however, that attitudes that have been formed early in life and to which the person is highly committed do not change much with time (Freedman, Sears, & Carlsmith, 1981). These attitudes are very resistant to change.

## Changing the Behavior

Sometimes social influence is used primarily to change the behavior of people without any concern for altering their attitudes. One may attempt to change the behavior of another in various ways—ranging from begging, pleading, and crying appeals to attempts to physically force the behavior. The methods most commonly used to change another's behavior without trying to change his or her attitudes are requesting, ordering or commanding, and showing that the behavior change is necessary to avoid violation of socially accepted standards.

### Conformity

The degree to which a person behaves in order to be in accordance with the norms or standards of society is called *conformity*. Most people acquire a strong disposition to conform during childhood. Conformity is reinforced with praise, approval, and acceptance. Nonconformity is punished by criticism, disapproval, and rejection.

Solomon Asch (1952) was the first to demonstrate experimentally that the technique of showing a person that behavior change is necessary to avoid violation of socially accepted standards is highly effective in modifying behavior. Subjects in his experiment were asked to decide which of three lines matched a given line in length. (See Figure 13-3.) Unknown to the subject, Asch placed seven other people in the experiment who had been previously told what response to make each time. On the first few trials the other seven people gave correct responses. Then they unanimously began giving incorrect responses. The subject was faced with responding according to his or her own perception and going against the group or going along with the group. The study indicated that about 75 percent of the subjects conformed at least once to the incorrect answer given by the group. Most people find it less anxiety arousing to contradict evidence received by their own senses than to publicly disagree with the judgments of many other people.

Many different experiments have been conducted since the Asch experiments which support Asch's findings and identify some of the factors influencing conformity. Two factors that are especially significant are the size of the influencing group and whether the individual has any social support—an ally. Early studies indicated that sex was a factor—females being more likely to conform than males. A later study (Sistrunk & McDavid, 1971) found males to be more conforming than females on "feminine" items with which the males were unfamiliar and females to be more conforming than males on "masculine" items with which the females were unfamiliar. No difference in the degree of conformity was

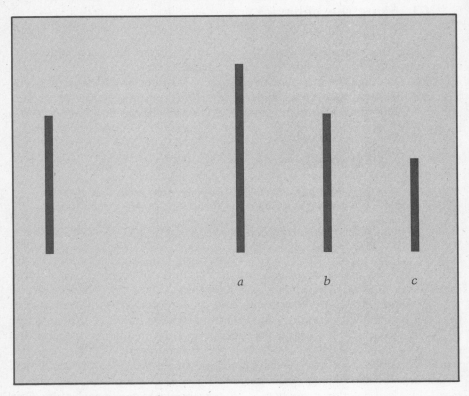

Figure 13-3    Sample item
used in the Asch experiment.
Subjects were asked to identify
which line—_a, b,_ or _c_—was the
same length as the given line.

found between males and females on neutral items that were equally familiar to both sexes.

## Compliance

Often people influence a person to change his or her behavior by requesting the person to behave in a particular way. Influencing others to comply with a direct request may involve causing the person to feel guilty if he or she does not comply, increasing one's attractiveness to the person, and asking the person to perform small or trivial behaviors before graduating to larger and more important requests or vice versa.

Getting a person to feel guilty is a commonly used technique for obtaining _compliance_ with a request. A person usually feels guilty when he or she does something that harms another person, especially if the harm was unintentional. The guilty person then tries to make amends by doing something good or helpful for the person harmed. People who can be convinced they have done harm to a person will be more likely to comply with the person's request than people who do not feel they have done harm to the person. Crying, playing the role of the martyr, or just looking sad and forlorn are effective techniques for convincing a person that harm has been done and, thus, for "getting your own way."

A person is more likely to comply with requests from those they like. Therefore, if a person can get others to like him or her, those people will be more likely to comply with that person's requests. Techniques for increasing one's own attractiveness to another person may include complimenting the other person, doing favors for the other person, and even bribing the other person. Another technique sometimes used is to agree with the views and opinions of the other person.

Once a person has complied with a small or trivial request, the chances are much greater that the person will comply with a larger request. Salespersons often ask customers to accept free gifts or some literature or ask for just one minute of their time. If the customer can be persuaded to agree to such a small request, the chances are much greater that the person can be persuaded to comply with a larger request. The reverse of this technique is also effective in obtaining compliance with a request. If a large response is asked for first, then reduced to the smaller response actually desired, the person is more likely to comply with the smaller response. For example, if a person is asked to donate eight hours of time, refuses and is asked for a donation of just one hour, the chances are greater that the person will comply with the second request than if he or she had just been asked initially for the one hour. This technique is often used in collective bargaining or in settlement of claims.

## Obedience

Obtaining the desired behavior of a person by simply ordering or commanding the person to behave in a particular manner is effective if the individual doing the ordering or commanding has enough power or authority to inflict punishment for failure to carry out the orders or commands. Otherwise, commands may not produce *obedience;* they will only produce anger and hate directed toward the person doing the commanding. If the person doing the ordering or commanding is a powerful authority figure, such as a company president, supervisor, military officer, parent or teacher, he or she may be able to successfully influence behavior by ordering or commanding.

Research studies have also indicated that a relatively powerless source of authority can obtain obedience to orders just from the appearance of authority. This is blind, unquestioned obedience to authority.

Stanley Milgram (1963) first tested this blind, unquestioned obedience to authority by having an experimenter order a subject to deliver electrical shocks of higher intensity each time another subject made an error. The second subject was actually an actor pretending to be receiving the shocks so that the real subject believed he or she was delivering shocks. If the subject found the task disturbing as the shocks became more intense and wanted to stop, the experimenter, using strong authoritative tones, ordered the subject to continue. The ordering became increasingly stronger each time the subject tried to stop. Total obedience to the final 450-volt shock was obtained from 65 percent of the subjects. This study and further experiments indicate that many people have a tendency to obey the commands of a person who gives the appearance of authority even when the commands do not make sense and are inhumane.

Whether a person obeys an order seems to be related to how much the person perceives himself or herself as responsible for the harm. If the person can rationalize that another person is the source of the harm, the person is more likely to obey the commands than if the person assumes responsibility for his or her own behavior. Another factor seems to be the degree to which the person given the commands has been exposed to disobedient models. If the person has been exposed to obedient models, he or she is more likely to obey. If the person has been exposed to disobedient models, he or she is more likely to disobey.

## Prejudice

Prejudice is an attitude toward a group of people which favorably or unfavorably predisposes a person's attitude toward the whole group. Discrimination is the behavior that expresses the prejudice. We usually think of a prejudice as being an unfavorable attitude; however, a person may be prejudiced in favor of a particular group. *Stereotyping*, or assigning identical characteristics to all members of a group, and holding on to the stereotype even when faced with conflicting information seem to be the two primary elements of prejudice.

### Sources

A number of theories have been proposed to explain the development of prejudice. Some historians suggest that prejudice may have its origin in years of conflict between groups. Often economic factors are important in generating conflict. A group may be stereotyped as inferior to justify exploitation of the group or the exploitation of the resources of the group. This may explain some prejudice, but it cannot explain all prejudice.

One group of theorists advanced the idea that people have an *ingroup* or reference group with which they identify and an *outgroup* which they do not consider their own. The outgroup has some characteristics which set it apart from the reference group or ingroup. A person comes to believe his or her ingroup is superior to the outgroup since it is the source of his or her satisfactions and its members are more similar to the person. The characteristics which set the outgroup apart from the ingroup come to be the source of the prejudice. This prejudice strengthens ingroup solidarity and cohesiveness. Prejudice seems to be more than just a means of developing group solidarity and cohesiveness, however.

Another popular theory explaining prejudice is that it is the result of displaced aggression. A group of people become a *scapegoat* for the frustrations of the prejudiced group. Scapegoat is the biblical term for a live goat over whose head all the sins of the children of Israel are confessed and who is sent into the wilderness symbolically bearing their sins. Psychologists use the term scapegoat to mean a person or group bearing the blame for others. One group displaces its anger, hostility, and frustration onto another group that is smaller, less powerful, and less threatening. Groups that are more likely to become scapegoats are those that are readily available, have previously been scapegoats, have no power to strike back, and are easily identified by their physical appearance (Allport, 1944).

Psychologists have not been able to explain all prejudices with a unified theory. Some psychologists believe the personality of the individual who is prejudiced may have much to do with explaining prejudice since research indicates that people who are prejudiced against one minority group also tend to be prejudiced against other minority groups and even imaginary groups that do not exist (Adorno, Frenkel-Brunswik, Levinson, & Sanford, 1950). Prejudice seems to be a personality trait that generalizes to many situations rather than being related to just one specific situation.

### Reducing Prejudice

Although prejudice can probably never be eliminated, psychologists have identified some methods of reducing prejudice. Experiments have shown that sometimes the prejudice is reduced by increased contact with the group against whom the prejudice is held. Sometimes, however, the prejudice may be increased with increased contact, if anger and competitiveness prevail. The nature and quality of the contact seems to be the determining factor. Although sometimes increased contact may help the person to see that his or her beliefs are not true and may change them, it is clear that just contact alone is usually not sufficient to reduce prejudice.

Five main conditions need to be present along with the contact before prejudice is reduced (Cook, 1978). First, the members of the two groups need to see each other in situations of equal status. Even when the contact is congenial and is not hostile, if the members of one group are of lower status, such as in lower status jobs or less educated, the contact will most likely continue the stereotypes.

Second, the members of the two groups need to become personally acquainted with each other. Often members of prejudiced groups may have frequent contact without really getting to know each other personally. If the contact does not bring about a knowledge of each other as individuals—knowing about each other's personal lives and innermost feelings—assumptions will probably continue to be made about the person on the basis of his or her group membership, and prejudice will not be reduced.

A third condition for reducing prejudice is for the contact to involve individuals who violate the stereotype. If the contact is with an individual who happens to have a stereotypical characteristic, the prejudice will not be reduced, only strengthened. For example, actually encountering men and women who are successful in nontraditional occupations is a condition for reducing the stereotyping of abilities of males and females. (See Figure 13-4.)

A fourth condition for reducing prejudice seems to be social support. Social support of the contact from family, friends, the law, custom, or just an atmosphere that favors equality, fair treatment, and the contact itself is needed to reduce the prejudice.

Cooperation seems to be a fifth condition for reducing prejudice. A situation wherein the prejudiced members of two groups must cooperate with one another to attain a common goal is a powerful factor. Mutual cooperation seems to produce a feeling of rapport or comradeship which can break through the prejudice. When cooperation is vital for survival, either physically, psychologically, or economically, it is difficult for a person to hold prejudices toward people with whom he or she is engaged in the struggle.

Prejudice resulting from scapegoating might be reduced by improving the emotional well-being of the prejudiced person and changing the person's coping strategy to a more satisfactory one. This might be accomplished through some form of psychotherapy. Since punishing child-rearing practices are considered by some psychologists to be the origin of scapegoating, changing child-rearing practices to less physically abusive techniques should reduce scapegoating which would in turn reduce some prejudices.

## Discrimination

Although prejudices may exist in the workplace, there are federal laws administered by the Equal Employment Opportunity Commission (EEOC) banning discrimination by an employer, manager, supervisor, or employee representing an employer. The most comprehensive law is

 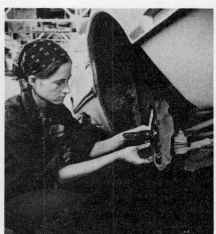

Figure 13-4   The success of males and females in nontraditional jobs aids in reducing stereotypes of abilities of males and females.

Title VII of the Civil Rights Act of 1964. Title VII prohibits discrimination in employment on the basis of race, color, religion, sex, or national origin. Discrimination against persons because of their being in the 40 to 70 age range is illegal under the Age Discrimination in Employment Act. The Equal Pay Act prohibits unequal wages for equal (or very similar) work because of sex. Discrimination against the physically handicapped is illegal under the Rehabilitation Act of 1973. However, this Act only applies to those companies holding at least $2500 worth of contracts with federal government agencies.

In addition to these laws, there are several Presidential Executive Orders requiring employers with government contracts to take affirmative action for minorities, women, handicapped persons, and Vietnam veterans. Failure to meet these requirements may result in the cancellation of contracts and denial of future business with the government.

Finally, many states have laws banning discrimination on the same bases as federal laws with agencies to enforce them. Most of these state laws prohibit physical handicap discrimination whether or not the employer does business with the federal government.

Discrimination in business is sometimes very subtle, disguised under "business reasons." However, sometimes only a visual investigation is necessary to reveal that there are no women or blacks or members of other ethnic groups in certain positions, or that women and members of certain ethnic groups are found in only certain positions, such as clerical or maintenance positions. A thorough investigation of personnel records will provide evidence that discrimination on the basis of sex, race, or national origin has occurred in hiring and possibly in promotions. Other forms of discrimination can be revealed through an investigation of a company's personnel records. Discrimination in business is an example of the effect of social influences on behavior.

Although social influences are a factor in discrimination which is one aspect of attitudes, other aspects of attitudes are also affected by social influences. Social influence is a primary source of a person's behavior. Therefore, an individual's behavior cannot always be explained without some understanding of this influence. An individual belongs to many different classifications of groups based on sex, age, educational level, occupation, special interests, etc. Each group with which a person is identified is a source of pressure to behave in a particular manner. A person's behavior is shaped to a large extent by social influences—the people in his or her environment.

## SUMMARY

1.  An individual's behavior is influenced by groups of people and how people behave within groups.

2.  Attitudes which are acquired in a social environment are assumed to be important determinants of behavior.

3.  An attitude is a person's predisposition to think, feel, and act either positively or negatively toward a person, idea, object, or situation.

4.  Beliefs, opinions, prejudices, discrimination, and values are aspects of attitudes.

5.  An attitude is characterized by three components—cognitive, affective, and conative.

6.  Attitudes may be acquired through learning by identification with parents, peers, and other significant people and by classical and operant conditioning. Learning of attitudes begins in infancy.

7.  Mass media is an important influence in the formation of attitudes.

8.  The attitudes a person holds, along with the strength and direction (positive or negative) of the attitudes, may be assessed through the use of attitude scales and the observation of behavior.

9.  Some attitude scales that have been developed to measure attitudes are the Thurstone scale, the Guttman scale, the Likert scale, and the semantic differential scale.

10. Although attitudes are relatively enduring, attitudes may change when dissonance, inconsistencies existing between the components of an attitude, is created.

11. Some sources of dissonance may be conflict between behavior and beliefs and feelings or new information that conflicts with beliefs.

12. Arousal of fear has been found to be an effective technique for changing attitudes.

13. Whether new information results in a change of attitude depends on the credibility, attractiveness, and power of the communicator and whether the message is printed or presented face-to-face, and meets certain conditions.

14. Some personality characteristics that seem to be factors in attitude change are intelligence, general mood, and self-esteem.

15. An individual's behavior may be changed without changing his or her attitude by requesting, ordering or commanding, and showing that the behavior change is necessary to avoid violation of socially accepted standards.

16. Conformity to socially accepted standards is learned during childhood, and most people find it anxiety arousing to disagree with socially accepted standards.

17. A person is more likely to comply with a request if he or she can be made to feel guilty. Crying, playing the role of a martyr, or looking sad and forlorn are often effective techniques for obtaining compliance with a request.

18. A person is more likely to comply with a request if he or she likes the person making the request. Thus, giving compliments and doing favors are often effective techniques for obtaining compliance with a request.

19. Making a small, trivial request first and getting compliance increases the likelihood of compliance with a larger request. Making a large request first and getting rejection increases the likelihood of compliance with a smaller request.

20. Obedience to an order or command may be obtained if the person doing the commanding has the power to inflict punishment for failure to obey or is an authority figure.

21. Milgram's study and further experiments indicate that many people have a tendency to obey the commands of a person who merely gives the appearance of being an authority figure—blind, unquestioned obedience to authority—particularly if they do not perceive themselves as responsible and have not been exposed to many disobedient models.

22. Prejudice is an attitude toward a group of people which predisposes

a person favorably or unfavorably toward the whole group. Discrimination is the behavior that expresses the prejudice while stereotyping is the assigning of identical characteristics to all members of a group.

23. Some theorists believe prejudice has its source in conflict between groups; some believe ingroups are the source; some believe scapegoating is the source; and some believe personality is the source.

24. Sometimes prejudice can be reduced through contact, particularly if the following conditions prevail: equal status, personal acquaintance, violation of stereotypes, social support, and cooperation.

25. A person may be prejudiced, but the law prohibits discrimination in employment situations. Sometimes discrimination in business is very subtle, disguised under "business reasons."

## SUGGESTIONS FOR FURTHER READING

Allport, G. W. *The nature of prejudice.* Reading, Mass.: Addison-Wesley, 1954.

This book is considered to be a classic and provides thorough coverage of the topic of prejudice.

Aronson, E. *The social animal* (3rd ed.). San Francisco: Freeman, 1980.

Several topics in the field of social psychology are presented in this introductory book.

Berscheid, E., & Walster, E. H. *Interpersonal attraction* (2nd ed.). Reading, Mass.: Addison-Wesley, 1978.

A short but comprehensive and readable summary of attraction.

Freedman, J. L., Carlsmith, J. M., & Sears, D. O. *Social psychology* (4th ed.). Englewood Cliffs, N. J.: Prentice-Hall, 1981.

A social psychology textbook that is easy to read.

Insko, C. *Theories of attitude change.* New York: Appleton-Century-Crofts, 1967.

A review of the research on each of the major theories of attitude change is presented in this book along with a description and evaluation of each of the theories.

Milgram, S. *Obedience to authority: An experimental view.* New York: Harper & Row, 1974.

A detailed description is given of the well-known series of experiments that demonstrated that most people are influenced by individuals perceived to be authority figures.

# **G**roup Dynamics — Chapter 14

## I. GROUPS
   A. Formation
   B. Group Influence on Individual Behavior
   C. Group Performance

## II. COMMUNICATION
   A. Patterns of Group Communication
   B. Transactional Analysis

## III. LEADERSHIP
   A. Approaches to the Study of Leadership
   B. Leadership Effectiveness
   C. Informal Group Leadership

## SUMMARY

## SUGGESTIONS FOR FURTHER READING

**F**or most people, the majority of the time spent working on a job is spent interacting with other people. Social psychologists refer to a collection of individuals who interact with each other, share some common identity, and share some common goals or desires as a *group*. A number of people merely standing or sitting near each other would not be called a group. A group may be composed of as few as two people or any number up to a huge crowd.

In the preceding chapter, the social influences on individual behavior through the formation and change of attitudes, the formation and change of prejudice, and the change of behavior by use of obedience to commands, conformity to norms, and compliance with requests were discussed. The influence of organized groups of people on individual behavior is perhaps even greater than some of those informal social influences. Thus, group dynamics will be examined in this chapter. The primary focus will be on the formation of groups, behavior changes of individuals as a result of being in a group, group performance, and communication within groups. A look at leadership in groups will conclude the chapter.

## Groups

Most groups come into existence to serve one of two basic purposes. Some groups form to serve people's social needs, and some groups form to accomplish a task. Other groups serve both a social function and a task-oriented function. Task-oriented groups form to accomplish some goal. The task may be anything—perhaps to widen a road, operate an effective mailing system, or build a profitable business. Social groups form to provide enjoyment. (See Figure 14-1.) In this section, group formation, including explanations for the formation, conditions for membership, and the structure of the group, will be discussed. Individuals may behave differently in a group than when alone. Group behavior and factors affecting group performance as a whole will be examined.

### Formation

Groups form, people are members of groups, and groups have structure. The reasons for formation, conditions for membership, and structure from the standpoint of developmental sequence, position, and norms will be considered.

Figure 14-1    Most groups come into existence to serve one of two basic purposes. A task-oriented group may form to accomplish a task. A socially oriented group may form to provide enjoyment.

**Reasons for Formation.** Groups may form for any number of reasons. Most often a group is formed to achieve a goal that can only be accomplished by or more easily accomplished by the interaction of two or more people. It would be impossible for a single individual to simultaneously perform all the tasks that are necessary for a space flight, for example. A house could be built more easily by a group combining their knowledge and skills in such areas as carpentry, electricity, plumbing, and roofing than by a single individual who would have to master all these skills in order to build the house alone.

Another explanation for the formation of groups is the social comparison theory (Festinger, 1954). The social comparison theory proposes that people are attracted to groups that contain individuals similar to themselves because such groups supply information or feedback that enables people to compare or evaluate their own opinions, attitudes, and abilities.

A reason for the formation of some groups is to provide support to individuals who are experiencing or anticipating stress. This reason for the formation of some groups is supported by experimental studies which demonstrated that a greater percentage of people chose to wait with others rather than alone when anticipating a very painful electric shock. The experiments also demonstrated that a greater percentage of people chose to wait with people who were also going to experience the shocks rather than with people who were not anticipating experiencing the shocks (Schachter, 1959).

Groups may form to satisfy people's needs such as emotional needs, esteem needs, status needs, or recreational needs. People have so many different needs such as reduction of tension, companionship, reduction of boredom, or need for reassurance that all of them cannot be listed. Sometimes groups form to satisfy members' needs to seek or share information or to share the same interests or concerns. People seem to have a basic need to belong to or affiliate with other people and thus form groups.

**Conditions for Membership.** More than likely, a person will belong to many groups. Why people join groups or belong to groups is of interest to social psychologists. An individual may be a member of a group under two conditions. Sometimes one has no choice about being a member of a group—a person may be ascribed to a group. For example, a worker might be a member of the Building II group merely because he or she works in that building. Or a worker might be a member of the group of female employees of a business firm as a result of being a female. Or an employee may be ascribed to the electrical department because of the nature of the work he or she performs. A person is born into some groups such as a family, a race, or a nationality.

Sometimes a worker is a member of a group because he or she chooses to join the group; membership is acquired or achieved voluntarily. For example, a worker may choose to join the group attending the annual company picnic, or the group subscribing to Plan A insurance, or the group taking the air traffic controller course.

The social exchange theory proposes that people join a group because being a member of the group is a means to an end. Being a member of the group yields rewards that are greater than the costs of not being a member of the group (Thibaut & Kelley, 1959). Furthermore, whether a person remains in a group or joins another depends on the rewards received in that group compared to the previous group.

**Structure.** When groups form there is some organizational structure—formal or informal. An understanding of the structure of groups is necessary to understanding the effect of groups on individual behavior.

The process of group formation has been described as a four-phase sequence (Rosenfeld, 1976). In the first phase, called the *orientation phase*, the members of the group are getting acquainted. Early in this phase there may be a general feeling of discomfort accompanied by some anxieties and uncertainties. Through interaction, the members confirm or change expectations of the activities of the group and the rewards rendered by membership in the group. Also, through interaction the members learn what behaviors are tolerated and expected by other members of the group and assess the goals and emotional atmosphere of the group. If a member continues through this phase, the general feelings of discomfort, anxiety, and uncertainty subside and a feeling of belonging is experienced.

During the second phase of group formation, called the *conflict phase*, members' individual personalities and needs begin to clash. Members may begin to experience anger, hostility, and aggression toward each other, particularly the leader.

Members may have to give up some of their own individual wants, desires, and needs for the benefit of the group as a whole. This compromising and reaching of agreements characterizes the *balance phase*. By the end of this phase, positions and roles are established, harmony exists in interpersonal relations, and members are working competently and enthusiastically to accomplish common goals.

Sometimes groups disband which is called the *parting phase*. Groups may fluctuate back and forth between the conflict phase and the balance phase and continue to exist; however, a group may dissolve when the balance stage cannot be reached following a conflict stage. Sometimes a group's existence is limited by time or situation. For example, a group may be formed to campaign for a political candidate and then disbands following the election. Or a grievance committee may be formed to function for one year and may disband and be replaced by a new group at the end of one year.

The structure of a group is often studied by assessing the positions, roles, and status of the individual members. "*Position* refers to a specific slot occupied by an individual in a group, and *role* refers to the behavior displayed by an individual in a certain position. . . . *Status* refers to an evaluation of the contribution of particular roles to the welfare of the group" (Harari & Kaplan, 1982, p. 212).

In some groups, particularly in work situations, positions and roles may be clearly defined. But in groups where positions, roles, and status are not clearly defined, they emerge as members of the group interact and come to behave in a systematic way. Sometimes the position itself may be defined but the role or behavior to be exhibited by the person in that position is not clearly defined. When role confusion exists, the individuals concerned often experience anxiety and stress. Since people are members of many groups, an individual has multiple roles.

A person may compete for a position because that role is valued higher than another role. The position of president is higher in status than vice president and the role of a committee chairperson is higher than that of a committee member. Being a member of the middle social class is higher in status than being a member of the lower social class.

Members of a group demand that other members conform to the rules and standards of the group. In groups, "standards with which members are expected to comply and against which the behavior of members is evaluated" (Williams, 1982, p. 134) are called norms. A group may be viewed in terms of norms, since group behavior depends on the norms probably more than any other aspect. Members of a group have a tendency to think and behave similarly. If they do not have similar attitudes and feelings, the group enters a conflict phase. Through continued interaction, the members' attitudes and behaviors become more similar and the group enters a balance phase. The attitudes and behaviors agreed upon by the members of a group compose the norms of the group. The boxed material on page 345 illustrates the effect of norms on individual behavior.

## Group Influence on Individual Behavior

People often behave differently in the presence of a group than they behave when alone. Being in the presence of a group affects individual behavior in a number of different ways. Some of the ways individual behavior is affected by the presence of a group are described in this section.

**Social Facilitation.** The presence of a group increases individual performance—a phenomenon called *social facilitation*. Under conditions of increased motivation, people who generally perform effectively perform even better. The presence of others engaged in a similar activity has been found to increase the motivational level and the anxiety level of the individual (Zajonc, 1965). This increased arousal results in faster working and greater productivity for most people than when they are less motivated or less aroused. However, if a person should happen to be so highly motivated or aroused that his or her optimum level of performance has already been reached, then increased motivation or arousal will interfere with performance. Also, those individuals who perform poorly may experience so much anxiety about performing in the presence of others that their level of performance may decrease.

**Shift Toward Polarization.** An individual may shift to a more extreme position when making a decision in the presence of a group than when making a decision alone. In other words, an individual is usually more willing to make riskier decisions as a member of a group than when alone—the *risky-shift phenomenon*. Or an individual is willing to make an even more conservative decision when in a group than when alone— the *stingy-shift phenomenon*. This tendency of people to shift to a more extreme position when making decisions in the presence of a group is called the *shift toward polarization* (Lamm & Myers, 1978).

Mere presence of a group does not seem to be the only condition required for the shift to occur. Research on this shift toward polarization indicates that two additional conditions must be present: group discussion and the expression of different initial opinions. A consistent finding in research is that group decisions made following discussion and the expression of different initial opinions will usually be more extreme in

## GROUP NORMS

Williams (1982) provided the following examples to illustrate how norms express the collective values of members of a group and provide guidelines that ensure the successful achievement of the goals of the group.

1. Group A consists of fifteen no-mobility employees who work in a chemical plant. They rotate over three shifts and are primarily involved in loading ships with pelletized fertilizer. The following norms are of central importance to this group:

   (a) One employee shall not exert so much effort that other employees appear to be unproductive by comparison.
   (b) When an employee is unable to perform well, because of a hangover or fatigue, others will cover for that individual, however, abuse of the off-day privilege will not be tolerated.
   (c) Employees will not discuss with management anything derogatory about another group member.
   (d) Employees will not express favorable attitudes toward management and the company in general.

The norms of Group A stand in stark contrast to those of this group:

2. Group B consists of eleven young women in a secretarial pool of the same organization. Each looks forward to promotion into a position as executive secretary. The promotion decision is usually made on the combined basis of seniority, competence, and ability to relate to a given executive. Group B reflects a need for nondestructive internal competition. The following are among its most obvious norms:

   (a) Dress and hair must always be smart and fashionable in order to maintain the image that "the pool" is the place for an executive to select an attractive, efficient secretary (rather than hire an outsider through the personnel department).
   (b) Taking the initiative with executives in order to be selected is taboo—especially if such initiative involves flirting.
   (c) It is never permissible to make remarks or stimulate rumors that may interfere with a peer's promotion, even though the remarks or rumors are true.
   (d) Poor productivity and poor quality work from anyone capable of high performance is unacceptable, since it reflects negatively on the group.
   (e) An employee does not recommend friends or acquaintances to fill vacancies unless they fit the model required to maintain the favorable image the group enjoys. (p. 134)

the same direction as the average preferences of the individual group members prior to discussion (Wrightsman, 1977). (See Figure 14-2.) When most members of a group are leaning toward taking a risk, the group takes

Figure 14-2    If each member
of a committee holds a mildly
liberal view, the committee
decision will most likely be very
liberal. If each member of the
committee holds a mildly
conservative view, the committee
decision will most likely be very
conservative.

an even riskier position than the average degree of risk that the individual
members are willing to take. When most members of a group are leaning
toward being conservative, the group takes an even more conservative
position than the average conservativeness of the individual members.
Once an individual participates in a group decision that is more extreme
than his or her initial position, that individual retains a more extreme
position than his or her initial position.

Several explanations for the shift toward polarization have been
offered. One explanation is that increased familiarity with the issues
occurs during discussion. The strength of the information that emerges in

the discussion is the source of the shift. Maybe those group members who support extreme views simply provide more information favoring their views. This explanation has not received much research support and, therefore, is not a widely accepted theory.

Another explanation is that members of a group who dare to have more extreme views initially also tend to be more dominant and exert more influence over other group members than those who are less daring and, thus, less dominant (Marquis, 1962). Research findings have not consistently supported this explanation either.

A third explanation is that there is a *diffusion of responsibility* in a group. No one individual is responsible for the decision. When a single individual decides on a course of action that ends in failure, that individual alone bears the total responsibility for the failure. If, however, a course of action decided on by a group ends in failure, the responsibility for the failure is shared among all the members of the group.

The shift toward polarization has also been explained in terms of social value (Brown, 1965). Because our culture values daring behavior, most people want to be at least as daring as the average person and usually perceive themselves as being daring. When they realize through group discussion that their positions are not as daring as they had perceived them to be, they are willing to shift to a position that will fit their perceived self-image. In other words, when the group norm is learned through discussion, group members conform to the new perception of the norm. This theory seems to have the most research support.

**Deindividuation.** When a person feels submerged in a group, that person does not feel that he or she is responding as an individual. That person loses his or her distinctive personality and adopts a perceived group personality. The individual sets his or her own personality aside. This phenomenon is referred to as *deindividuation* and is most often explained by the diffusion of responsibility theory and identification. A group identification rather than an individual identification exists. As a member of the group, the person may have a feeling of anonymity as an individual. A deindividuated person loses his or her inhibitions. The person is more likely to express emotions—behave affectionately, show joy or sorrow, behave aggressively, or release feelings of anger and hostility (Zimbardo, 1970). People have a tendency to act differently in a group setting than when they are alone. (See Figure 14-3.) Mob behavior can partly be explained by the deindividuation phenomenon. The larger the group, the more the members become deindividuated.

**Bystander Apathy.** One might make the assumption that if a group of people is present, help would be more likely in a time of need. Often, however, a person in need of help is ignored by bystanders or passersby. Research suggests that the presence of a group actually inhibits rather than facilitates helping (Latané & Darley, 1970). Several factors such as

Figure 14-3    Mob behavior
can partly be explained by the
deindividuation phenomenon.

diffusion of responsibility, modeling, deindividuation, and fear seem to account for this phenomenon referred to as bystander apathy.

One explanation for bystander apathy is the diffusion of responsibility that exists in a group. Individual members of a group of bystanders may not feel a personal responsibility to help. Additionally, the presence of others who are not helping sets the norm for the behavior of members of the bystander group, and usually members of a group conform to the norm. Third, deindividuation decreases the likelihood that members of the group will feel guilty about not helping. Members of a group lose their inhibitions for behaving in a manner unacceptable to themselves when deindividuated. A fourth explanation for bystander apathy is fear of embarrassment. Fear of embarrassment seems to increase with the number of people present who could observe any attempts at assistance and any blunders that are made. It appears that the presence of a group affects helping behavior—there is a relationship between the number of people who are present when a call for help is made and the likelihood that assistance will be offered.

### Group Performance

The efficiency of a group compared with the efficiency of a person working alone has been studied by psychologists. The findings are relevant to a study of behavior in work situations. Logically, one would reason that a group would be more efficient and thus more productive than a single individual. "Two heads are better than one" is an axiom often quoted and is often the basis for forming committees. However, in many situations, a group effort may be less efficient and, therefore, less productive than a person working alone.

**Factors Affecting Group Efficiency.** Several factors seem to determine how productive a group is—the nature of the task, the size of the group, the composition of the group, the acceptance of goals, cohesiveness, the nature of the communication network, the nature of the environment, and the style of leadership.

The size of the group has been shown to affect group performance, but people sometimes have different ideas about what is the ideal size. Studies of group size and performance have led to some conclusions. The larger the group is, the greater the possibility for interpersonal conflict. Smaller groups have been shown to be more creative, to express more ideas, to have a higher level of morale, and to need less supervision (Harari & Kaplan, 1982). In *parallel coaction tasks* where each member of the group is involved in a completely separate function and works independently but parallel, the larger the size of the group the more work that gets done.

Larger groups may accomplish more than smaller groups when group interaction and cooperation are required. People seem to work less when there are many to do the work, and they are not aware that individual effort is decreased with increase in group size. But even though increasing the size of the group may produce a gain in production when interaction and cooperation are required, a point will finally be reached where no further gain is made by increasing the size of the group. For example, one person might require four hours to complete a task (four hours of work time), but two people cooperating as a group might be able to complete the task in one hour (two hours of work time), producing as much in half the time. Three people cooperating on the task as a group might be able to complete the task in 40 minutes (two hours of work time), but there would be no gain in production. The task might be completed in 30 minutes by increasing the size of the group to ten (five hours of work time), but one more hour of work time would be used than for one person working alone and thus there would be a decrease in production. The *principle of least group size* states that the optimum group size for the performance of tasks requiring group interaction is the minimum number of individuals required to make available to the group all the requirements for performance of the task.

The composition of the group also affects performance. Groups that are composed of individuals who are compatible in terms of needs, beliefs, age, sex, seniority, marital status or other characteristics show higher morale and productivity than groups composed of individuals who are not compatible. A high degree of satisfaction and productivity is often displayed in groups composed of friends. Sometimes, however, in groups composed of friends, socializing may interfere with performance. Of course, the abilities of the members of the group as well as the sexes of the members affect the performance of the group. In a research study comparing the performance of all-male groups, all-female groups, and mixed-sex groups, mixed-sex groups performed better than same sex groups when incompatibility on variables other than sex were controlled by random sampling (Hoffman & Maier, 1961).

The climate in which a group functions, often determined by the style of the group's leadership, affects the productivity of the group. One study supporting this theory compared the effects of climate on productivity by using three groups of 10-year-old boys as subjects. Each group was supervised by an adult leader. In the *autocratic* climate, the adult leader was dictatorial, gave personal criticism, and did not actively participate with the group except when giving instructions. In the *democratic* climate, the leader acted more like a member of the group than an authority figure, held group discussions to aid in decision making, allowed members some freedoms such as choosing a working partner, gave praise, and gave criticism objectively. In the *laissez-faire* climate, the leader just did not function. Complete freedom was given, and the members were neither praised nor criticized. The leadership styles were rotated from one group of boys to another group every six weeks for a specified period of time. Productivity was highest with autocratic groups, but only when the leader was present. Members of such groups tended to be destructive and hostile or meek and submissive. The democratic groups maintained steady production, even when the leader was not present, and members tended to be friendly and content. In the laissez-faire climate, production was lowest and there was little satisfaction and a lot of horseplay (Lippit, 1940).

Leadership style may be classified by whether the leader is task-oriented or social/emotional-oriented (Bales, 1970). Task-oriented leadership creates a work climate that is all business, and the concern is only for getting the job done quickly and efficiently. Social/emotional leaders are concerned with getting the job done, but their primary concern is to maintain a climate of friendliness among members of the group and to foster good feelings. On a short-term basis, the task-oriented atmosphere is usually more productive; but on a long-term basis, the social/emotional atmosphere is usually more productive.

**Groupthink.** One of the advantages of a group decision is that the expertise necessitated by a decision that requires specialized information is more likely to be available in a group. Likewise, the biases, prejudices, and unconscious motives of some individuals may be counteracted by the insights of others in a group. Psychologist Irving Janis (1972) made a study of disastrous group decisions and argues that group decision making may be inefficient. *Groupthink* is the term Janis used to describe the type of thinking that occurs when people make decisions as a cohesive group based on a compulsion in order to maintain unanimity and each other's approval to the extent that critical, realistic thinking does not occur. In a cohesive group, members concede to the needs of the group rather than satisfy individual needs; the satisfaction of individual needs puts the group in a conflict stage. Group cohesiveness was found to be the major factor in groupthink (Janis, 1972). The more cohesive a group, the greater the members' tendency to rationalize or intellectualize its decisions will be; this results in the illusion that the group is invulnerable and thus should not be influenced by outsiders. Also, the more cohesive the group, the more pressure may be applied on dissenting members to conform. Individual members of such groups are not likely to take positions in decision making that would threaten the unity of the group. This may lead to inferior and often disastrous decisions.

A number of suggestions have been made for preventing groupthink (Janis & Mann, 1977). (1) Group leaders should encourage and reinforce the expression of doubts, fears, objections, or criticisms as an accepted part of a member's role in the group. (2) Group leaders should refrain from stating their own opinions first. The leader might divide the group into several small subgroups to reach tentative decisions, then have a discussion on the differences in ideas and decisions reached in the small groups. (3) Qualified outsiders' opinions should be brought into the group. The outsiders might meet with the group, or members of the group may be encouraged to seek opinions from outsiders they know and whose judgments they value. (4) At least one member of a group should be assigned the role of devil's advocate to challenge the majority's decision. (5) After a decision has been made, the group should hold a "second chance" meeting to reevaluate and voice any afterthoughts or misgivings and to reaffirm the decision.

## Communication

Communication is an important aspect of social interaction. The positions people hold in groups, the roles they play, and the power they have to influence groups depends considerably on their ability to communicate. How people communicate in groups will be examined in this section. Achieving effective communication in groups is not easy. Large business organization groups usually have flowcharts that clearly specify how and with whom members of the group are to communicate. In small and informal groups, role relationships usually determine the communication patterns. Individuals, usually leaders, speak for groups, and individual members within a group communicate with each other. Therefore, communication in groups can probably be better understood and improved through an understanding of *transactional analysis,* a system for analyzing the transactions or basic units of communication in individual-to-individual relationships.

## Patterns of Group Communication

Patterns of communication are an important factor in determining the efficiency with which a group operates and the morale of the group members. The patterns also provide an index of the distribution of power and status in groups. Communication patterns in groups may be directional in nature, may conform to a basic structure, and may consist of informal communication links.

**Directional Patterns.** In organized groups, messages may flow downward, upward, or horizontally. Downward communication involves conveying messages from higher levels to lower levels. For example, a group leader may convey a message from the division leader to his or her subordinates. The performance evaluation of a construction crew supervisor administered by the building contractor would be an example of a downward communication. Upward communication is the sending of messages from a lower level to a higher level. Examples of upward communication are: reporting the malfunctioning of a machine to the supervisor, or a supervisor reporting employee misconduct to the company's president. Horizontal communications consist of the exchange of information among employees at the same level. Some people may be better at communicating in one direction than another. For example, a person may communicate well with his or her supervisor (upward), especially if motivated to advance to a higher job level. The same person may not communicate as well with his or her peers (horizontal) or with lower-level employees (downward).

Some communication problems that may interfere with these *directional patterns* of communication are fear of reprisal in giving upward communications to supervisors and the fact that, in downward communication, employees often take directions from their supervisors as an indication of displeasure with their work. Sometimes the unavailability of the supervisor hinders upward communication. The grouping of employees into different departments, buildings, shifts, etc., particularly hinders horizontal communication (Sharma, 1979).

**Basic Communication Structures.** One of four basic communication structures seems to exist in any group regardless of whether the group is small or large, formal or informal. Generally, the more a basic structure allows a person to communicate with other people in the group, the greater the satisfaction that person will experience in the group (Leavitt, 1951). Also, the person at the center of the basic communication structure is named more frequently by the members of the group as the leader. Structures that are more centralized seem to be more effective when the operations are simple enough that the one person at the center can handle the directing. When the operations are very involved and complex and demand too much of the one person at the center, less centralized structures seem to be more effective.

The four basic structures of communication in groups are the *wheel*, the *Y*, the *circle*, and the *chain*. (See Figure 14-4.) The wheel is the most tightly centralized of the structures. In this pattern, all communication is channeled through one person. Communication flows from the

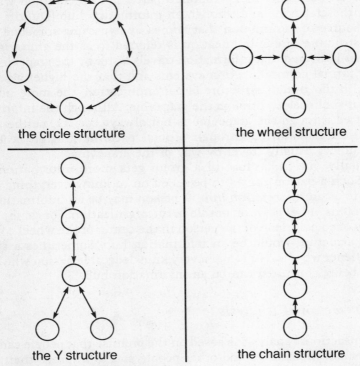

the circle structure

the wheel structure

the Y structure

the chain structure

Figure 14-4    Basic structures of communication (Leavitt, 1951).

hub of the wheel down the spokes and back up the spokes to the hub. The wheel is the most typical structure and usually the most efficient structure for small groups.

Communication in the Y structure starts with one person and branches out like an inverted Y. The branches of the Y may branch out to form other inverted Y structures. The Y is the most typical structure of large groups, and it is usually the most efficient. Although less centralized than the wheel, it is still tightly centralized.

The chain structure is less effective than other structures because a person only communicates with the people next to him or her, and the people on either end of the chain communicate with only one other person. In the circle structure, however, all members of the group tend to be equal, and communication circulates through the group. Although not the most efficient for problem solving, the circle pattern is especially effective in discussion groups. The circle is the least centralized of the basic structures. No person controls communication more than another person.

**Informal Communication Links.** Messages get transmitted to members of a group in many informal ways that are not designated on a flowchart or according to a structured pattern. Two common ways are through the grapevine and through an information hub (DuBrin, 1981).

A source of information that comes by bypassing someone in the official structure of communication is referred to as the *grapevine*. Research has indicated that information travels faster by the grapevine than through formal communication systems and that the higher a person's position in the group's structure of communication, the more information he or she receives through the grapevine. Although the information transmitted through the grapevine is not always correct, neither is the information transmitted through official patterns (Sutton & Porter, 1968). Rumors usually travel by way of the grapevine.

Usually one individual in a group gets more information than others. Such a person comes to be relied on to know everything and is referred to as an *information hub*. A person may be an information hub because of his or her position or role in the organization. For example, the secretary or social friend of the person in the center of the wheel communication structure would be an information hub. Sometimes a sympathetic listener who hears a lot, or a very knowledgeable person who learns a lot by being consulted can be an information hub.

## Transactional Analysis

Transactional analysis is based on the premise that people can learn to understand themselves and other people and to improve their interpersonal relations. The concept was originated by Eric Berne (1961) for use as a psychotherapy technique to help people improve their lives. It is also a theory of communication that provides the supervisor, the subordinate, the customer, the salesperson, the employer, and the employee with the tools for improving the way they communicate with people—either on or off the job. A knowledge of transactional analysis and its characteristic terms will help a person understand why he or she says certain things and why other people say the things they do.

**Strokes and Stamps.** Transactional analysis is based on the reinforcement principle of motivation—the fact that people need to be recognized and to maintain a positive self-image, good self-concept, and high self-esteem. Any communication that recognizes one's existence such as "Good morning, Pat" is called a *stroke.* Different types of strokes may be given. For example, a positive stroke causes a person to feel good about himself or herself, and a negative stroke causes a person to feel badly about the self. *Discounts* are strokes that are less positive than they should be or strokes not delivered. For example, a worker may be ignored when he or she arrives on the job site or when he or she completes a task. Or a person may not be given full credit for something when full credit is due. Mixed strokes have both positive and negative aspects such as "That's an excellent rate of responding (positive stroke) for a person as slow as you are (negative stroke)."

Feelings are called *stamps.* Stamps are obtained from strokes and build up over a period of time. In other words, people collect stamps. Good feelings are gold stamps and bad feelings are brown stamps. There are different kinds of stamps for different specific feelings such as red stamps for anger and yellow stamps for cowardice. Everybody collects stamps; but since it seems that most people have a tendency to give more negative strokes than positive strokes, more brown stamps are collected. People also seek out situations to increase their stamp collections if they are trying to collect a particular kind of stamp. The stamps a person collects are "cashed in" whenever enough have been collected and the person is ready to do so. Giving compliments, rewards, favors, or promotions and working overtime are some ways employees cash in gold stamps. Tardies, absences, thefts, accidents, or quitting a job are some ways employees may cash in brown stamps. In order to improve human relations on the job or anywhere else, a person must stop collecting brown stamps (or any negative stamps such as red or yellow stamps) and also not give any to those who are trying to get brown stamps. The way to prevent the "cashing in" of brown stamps is to not have any to cash in.

A person who works and communicates with others on a job especially needs to become aware of the kinds of strokes co-workers try to get and give. People have a tendency to trade stamps. If one gives negative strokes and thus brown stamps, that person will most likely receive negative strokes in return. If one gives positive strokes and thus gold stamps, that person will most likely receive positive strokes in return. If one discounts (does not stroke), negative strokes will be received in return, because people usually prefer a stroke of some kind to nothing at all. If a person does not receive a stroke in return for a positive stroke, they will try to get one in return for a negative stroke. The implication is that strokes must be given for any performance if human relations are to be improved. If positive strokes are not given for good performance, the good performance will cease and poor performance will replace it. People seeking negative strokes will give negative strokes and play psychological games to get them. Another condition for improving human relations in work situations is that one must not play games or return negative strokes for negative strokes. Poor performance must be stroked in the right way for it to cease such as through the use of extinction or through the use of reinforcement to shape more satisfactory performance.

**Life Scripts.** A person's general attitudes about life begin to be formed in infancy and are important in determining the behavior or personality of that person during his or her lifetime. According to the theory of transactional analysis, each person or group, such as a family or work organization, has a *life script* which consists of the attitudes (the affective element of the attitude) concerning things such as success, work, sex, love, education, or religion. Life scripts, unconscious lifetime plans, are like the script for a play. They are written before they are acted out. Life scripts are differentiated into three general categories: (1) The winner who communicates openly, honestly, easily, and gets along well with other people; (2) the loser who plays games, does not communicate openly, honestly, and easily, and does not get along well with other people; and (3) the nonwinner who sometimes communicates openly, is sincere, and gets along well with others but very often does not. Approximately 80 percent of the population have been estimated to be nonwinners, 15 percent winners, and 5 percent losers who are seldom seen in business firms. It is estimated that approximately 25 pecent of a person's life script is determined between the ages of 6 and 20 (Higgins, 1982). Relationships are sought with other individuals as in marriage, groups, and even work organizations to obtain strokes to play out life scripts.

**Life Positions.** Self-esteem is how one feels about one's self and, of course, a person also has an attitude or feelings about people in general. Transactional analysis proposes that there are four *life positions* that one may hold and act out: (1) I'm not OK—You're OK (the position of the very young child and often the position of subordinates); (2) I'm OK—You're not OK (the position of prejudiced individuals); (3) I'm not OK—You're not OK (usually the position of losers and individuals who are a menace to society); (4) I'm OK—You're OK (the position of well-adjusted individuals and usually the position of winners). Most people have a position that tends to prevail throughout their later childhood and adult life and, as with life scripts, a life position is the basis for many interactions with people which result in strokes that support the life position. Life positions may shift under certain environmental conditions just as life scripts might be rewritten sometimes.

**Ego States.** An individual's personality is viewed in transactional analysis as consisting of three parts—the *Parent*, the *Adult*, and the *Child*—called *ego states* (see Figure 14-5). The Parent ego state consists of values, opinions, dos and don'ts, shoulds and should nots, and stored memories of statements and actions of parents and authority figures. The Parent ego state is the criticizer and/or nurturer. The Parent ego state has a place in a worker's personality, but if it becomes too dominant in interactions with others, problems in human relations may arise.

The Adult ego state consists of the knowledge, logical reasoning, rational thinking, and information processing of the individual. The Adult is the manager of the Parent and Child states. The Adult state is the decision maker, the builder of self-esteem, and the problem solver. The Adult may dominate in well-adjusted individuals, but not to the extent that the Parent and the Child states are excluded.

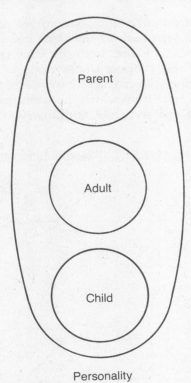

Personality

Figure 14-5    Ego states of the
personality according to transactional
analysis theory.

The Child ego state is made up of the feelings about everything the person has experienced and the person's current feelings. Feelings, of course, trigger behaviors. The source of openness, manipulation, spontaneity, sensuality, affection, creativity, happiness, rebellion, and hostility is in the Child ego state. The Child is the manipulator, the adaptor to demands of authority and power by use of coping mechanisms learned to survive childhood, and the expresser of the healthy, natural, spontaneous emotions. When an individual communicates with another person, he or she speaks or acts from one of the ego states. Understanding which ego state expressions are coming from and are directed toward will help a person to communicate more effectively and respond more appropriately to others.

**Transactions.** Analyzing the structure of social interaction is basic to using transactional analysis to improve communication. A social interaction that consists of a statement or stimulus directed toward a person and that person's response is a *transaction*. Three basic types of transactions may occur: complementary, crossed, and ulterior (see Figure 14-6).

In *complementary transactions*, sometimes called parallel transactions, the response is sent back to the same ego state from which the stimulus was received and is sent from the same ego state to which the stimulus was sent. These types of transactions do not produce conflict and may go on indefinitely. In *crossed transactions*, the response does not come back to the ego state from which the stimulus was sent nor does it come back from the ego state the stimulus was directed toward. In

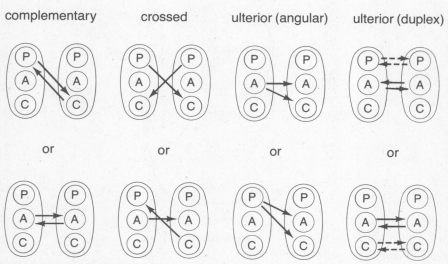

Figure 14-6   Basic transactions between two people.

crossed transactions, disagreement is present and either conversation on the topic ends or Child-to-Child negative complementary transactions occur. A crossed transaction may be used to stop psychological games. For example, an emloyee may ask a supervisor for an evaluation of a task just completed making the request from the Adult ego state and directing it to the Parent ego state unconsciously trying to hook the supervisor into giving a criticising response (a negative stroke). If the supervisor does not respond back from the Parent ego state with a "you should have" (a complementary transaction), but instead responds from the Adult ego state with an objective evaluation and praise for all the aspects of the task that are well done (a crossed transaction), the employee lost at the game and eventually the asking for an evaluation of tasks just completed may cease.

Hidden meanings characterize complementary messages referred to as *ulterior transactions*. In *duplex ulterior transactions*, the words have unspoken meanings that are understood by both the sender and receiver. The hidden meanings may be conveyed through body language. In the *angular ulterior transaction*, the message sent can be interpreted by the receiver as being directed toward either of two different ego states. Consequently, complementary transaction is more likely to occur than when directed to only one ego state because whichever one the sender responds back from, the response will be complementary. For example, a male employee may say to a female employee, "That new outfit you're wearing today is really sharp!" The remark could be directed to the Adult ego state, and the female employee could respond from the Adult ego state accepting the remark as a compliment. Or the remark could be directed to the Child ego state to obtain a feeling response with sexual connotations or anger to receive a negative stroke.

**Time Structuring.** Everybody has 24 hours of time every day which must be spent doing something. People spend their time either in activities that are physical or mental or in social interactions. Time may be spent in social interaction in five ways. (1) Intimacy is time spent with another person communicating openly, expressing genuine feelings, and developing a growing relationship in an atmosphere that is free of games. (2) Games are time spent communicating with another person in a deceitful way (as in ulterior transactions) in order to obtain strokes. (3) Pastimes are times spent in transactions that have no particular meaning and literally pass the time. (4) Rituals are time spent in stylized exchanges that require no thought to be performed. They are programmed by tradition and custom. (5) Withdrawal is time spent in any process or activity to avoid communicating with others. Withdrawal might include daydreaming, sleeping excessively, or watching television excessively.

**Psychological Games.** A game consists of a set or series of ulterior transactions that occurs repeatedly, has a predetermined end, and well-defined psychological strokes. A game may be either of two types. In one type, a person manages to get another person to give him or her a negative stroke. In the second type, a person tricks others into letting him or her give them negative strokes. A con is a part of all games but will not succeed unless it can hook into a weakness. All games are not completely undesirable, but all are time consuming and wasteful, involve deceitful communication, and lower someone's self-esteem. Games cause poor communication and hide real feelings. To improve communication, games should not be played. An effective technique to help a person stop playing games is for the person to become aware of the games he or she becomes involved in and then prevent the initiator of the game from giving or receiving a negative stroke. Workers will benefit from becoming aware of the games they and those they work with play.

## Leadership

Progress does not come from traits and abilities but from the organization that humans impose on themselves by creating groups. The creation and maintenance of organization depends "more on the quality of leadership than any other single event" (London, 1978, p. 573). A leader has been defined in many ways but is generally defined as the "group member who has the most influence on the other group members" (Seidenberg & Snadowsky, 1976, p. 426). The concern in this section will be with approaches to studying leadership, leadership effectiveness, and informal group leadership.

### Approaches to the Study of Leadership

Three approaches to the study of leadership have emerged: the *trait approach* which is concerned with the traits or characteristics of the leader; the *style approach* which focuses on methods and techniques used; and the *situational approach* which looks at the influence of environmental factors. Do traits, styles, situations, or a combination of these produce leaders? (See Figure 14-7.)

**The Trait Approach.** The trait approach to studying leadership was popular at one time, but this approach has practically vanished because it did not explain much about why relationships between some traits and leadership occurred. For example, research studies have shown leaders, compared to others, to be taller, more attractive in physical appearance, more domineering, more confident, more extroverted, more intelligent, and better adjusted psychologically (Gibb, 1969). The primary problem with this approach has been that individual traits do not predict who will become a leader, and a specific trait may not be found in leaders of all groups and situations. Intelligence, dominance, verbal fluency, and adjustment are traits found in leaders that are common to more groups and

Figure 14-7  Do traits, styles, situations, or a combination of these produce leaders?

situations than other traits. Many people associate *charisma* with leadership, but the term is too elusive to define objectively enough for research.

Charisma seems to refer to some magnetic quality that has the mysterious ability to draw people to a person and to allow that person to control them.

**The Style Approach.** The basic styles that have been identified as being used by leaders are autocratic, democratic, and laissez-faire. Autocratic leaders centralize the power in themselves, make the decisions for the group, and do not allow the members of the group to participate in the decision-making process. With this type of leadership, members of the group become increasingly dependent on the leader, and the leader becomes indispensable to the group.

Democratic leaders share their power with other members of the group and allow decisions to be made by the consensus of the group. Although the democratic leader has as much power as an autocratic leader, the power is used differently—to obtain input from the group members. Democratic leaders function in the interest of the group rather than in their own best interests. Laissez-faire leaders, on the other hand, have power over the group but do not exercise it. They are passive and allow the members of the group to make their own decisions.

Since the laissez-faire style cannot be considered as true leadership, leadership styles fall on a continuum somewhere between extremely autocratic and extremely democratic. The positions along the leadership continuum are as follows: (1) the leader decides then announces decisions to the group; (2) the leader decides then persuades the group to accept and support his or her decisions; (3) the leader presents ideas to and encourages questions from the group regarding a decision; (4) the leader presents tentative ideas subject to change by the group; (5) the leader presents alternatives from which the group makes a decision; (6) the leader establishes boundaries within which the group selects alternatives and makes a decision; (7) the group establishes the boundaries and the group decides (Napier & Gershenfeld, 1973).

**The Situational Approach.** The basic assumption in the situational approach to studying leadership is that special skills and competence appropriate to the goals of the group identify the leader. In other words, the particular task and particular situation determine the leader—a person emerges as a leader by happening to be in the right place at the right time. According to this theory, a person may be a leader in one group or at one time and a follower in another group or at another time. One situation that seems to be a factor related to the emergence of a leader is how much control the person has on the flow of communication—the more centralized the person's position in the communication structure, the more likely the person will become a leader.

## Leadership Effectiveness

Several theories related to the effectiveness of those in leadership positions have been proposed. The style of leadership, the banking of idiosyncrasy credits, and contingencies have been theorized to play a role in the effectiveness of a leader.

**Leadership Style.** An autocratic style of leadership has a tendency to foster negative feelings in members of the group. These negative feelings may be expressed openly in rebellious behaviors such as overt hostility and the destruction of property, may be repressed through the use of defense mechanisms, or may be expressed in indirect ways such as dropping out of the group. The democratic style of leadership has a tendency to lead to greater satisfaction, motivation, and cohesiveness among members of the group than other styles of leadership which, in turn, leads to greater achievement. In some situations, however, such as when a quick decision is needed, the democratic style may be less efficient. The result of laissez-faire leadership is often chaos as various members attempt to lead in various directions. Groups under an autocratic style of leadership compared to groups under a democratic style of leadership have been found to make fewer errors, require less communication, and require less time to complete a job which facilitates production.

The effectiveness of a leader has also been found to be related to the role played by the leader (Bales, 1970). The task-oriented leader is concerned with efficiency and moving the group toward a goal, while the socially oriented leader is interested in reducing tension and building morale. If a leader plays both of these roles, he or she will be more effective than if only one of the roles is played.

**Idiosyncrasy Credit.** One theory of leadership effectiveness suggests that effectiveness is related to the *idiosyncrasy credit* the leader builds up (Hollander, 1958). Idiosyncrasy credit is the label for the followers' perceptions of the leader—the sum total of positive impressions. Positive impressions accrue to the leader through helping the group accomplish its goals and by conforming to the expectations or norms of the group. The leader loses credits by deviating from the norms of the group or by failing to accomplish the goals of the group. The more idiosyncrasy credit the leader builds up the more effective he or she can be. This is because surplus credits allow the leader to deviate from the group norm and to fail to accomplish a goal without reducing the followers' perceptions of the leader to the extent of rejection. The theory explains why some leaders can engage in idiosyncratic behavior and still be perceived as effective leaders by the members of the group.

**The Contingency Theory.** Fred Fiedler (1967) proposed a contingency theory of leadership effectiveness. This theory views effective leadership as contingent on situational favorability—the degree to which the followers accept the way the leader uses power. Situational favorability is determined by (1) the degree of liking between the leader and followers (the more positive the personal feelings, the more favorable the situation); (2) the degree to which the task is structured (the higher the structure, the more favorable the situation); and (3) the leader's power (the stronger the power, the more favorable the situation).

In this theory, a relationship is considered to exist between the degree of esteem held for the least preferred co-worker referred to as an LPC score and leadership style. An LPC score is determined by rating the person liked least among all the people ever worked with according to a list of bipolar adjectives. An individual is then typed as a low-LPC leader or a high-LPC leader. Fiedler concluded from his studies that the higher the LPC score, the more the leadership style tends to be permissive, relaxed, nondirective, and concerned with group needs. The lower the LPC score, the more the leadership style tends to be autocratic and task oriented. Low-LPC leaders are more effective in either highly favorable or highly unfavorable situations; however, high-LPC leaders are more effective in moderately favorable situations. Although the assumption is usually made that years of experience as a leader are related to leadership effectiveness, this condition was not found by Fiedler to be a factor.

The specification of conditions under which leaders will be most effective is the primary strength of the contingency theory. Based on this theory and the research support for it, the conclusion has been drawn that no leader is effective in all situations.

## Informal Group Leadership

Although formal groups have a recognized leader, no one is usually assigned to a leadership position in informal groups. Members of informal groups may not even be aware of leader-follower relationships. Most groups, however, have one person who plays an influential role in the activities of the group. Even in small groups of friends, one person in the group often acts as the leader. A leader may emerge in small groups spontaneously as immediate needs arise and, when the immediate need vanishes, the person's position as leader may vanish with it.

In work situations, informal group leaders often emerge. Williams (1982) points out some major roles played by informal group leaders: the representative to management, the technical expert, the information source, the enforcer, the tension reducer, and the crisis manager. A worker who has good communication skills and a great deal of self-confidence and courage may emerge to represent a group to management. A worker who has highly specialized knowledge or skill may come to be respected as the authority on matters of his or her expertise. One worker may have privileged information needed by the group and may be looked to for direction. Sometimes a co-worker in a group needs to be chastised and a behavior change effected. A member of the group may voluntarily come forth and use persuasion or muscle and thus come to be elevated in respect by the group. Sometimes a person's skill in reducing conflict in the group results in that person coming to be recognized as a key person. This person who emerges as a leader in the group may be the comic, philosopher, or human relations expert. A member of an informal work group may emerge as a leader in some specific crisis situation such as when the group is threatened by some outside source.

In social interaction, groups form, communication occurs in the groups, and leaders of groups emerge. Understanding group dynamics is important to understanding human behavior.

## SUMMARY

1. A group is a collection of individuals who interact with each other and share something in common. Most groups that come into existence serve a task-oriented and/or a socially oriented function.

2. Some explanations for the formation of groups are that groups form to achieve a goal, to allow self-evaluations of the members, for emotional support, and to satisfy an unlimited number of needs such as the reduction of tension and boredom and the need for companionship.

3. Membership in some groups is ascribed—the members have no choice. However, membership in other groups is acquired or achieved voluntarily.

4. The four-phase sequence of group formation is the orientation phase, the conflict phase, the balance phase, and the parting phase.

5. The structure of a group may be described by the positions, roles, and status of the members and by the norms of the group.

6. Being in the presence of a group has been found to cause an individual to increase performance (social facilitation), to shift to a more extreme position in decision making (the risky-shift and stingy-shift phenomena), to lose his or her distinctive personality (deindividuation), and to be less willing to help in a time of need (bystander apathy).

7. The fact that responsibility is shared among all the members in a group (diffusion of responsibility) is frequently given as an explanation for individual behavior change in the presence of a group.

8. Group performance has been found to be related to such factors as size, composition, climate, and groupthink. Whether production is increased by increasing the size of the group depends on whether the task is a parallel coaction task or an interaction task. In interaction tasks, a point may be reached beyond which no further gain is experienced by increasing the size of the group.

9. Groups composed of members who are compatible or similar in some ways tend to show higher morale and productivity than other groups.

10. An autocratic and task-oriented climate in a group is usually more productive on a short-term basis than other climates; however, on a long-term basis, a democratic and social/emotional atmosphere is usually more productive.

11. Groupthink is the term for ineffective decision making in very cohesive groups and is thought to occur because of the compulsion to maintain unanimity and each other's approval.

12. Groupthink may be prevented if the group leader recognizes it and encourages such things as internal disagreements, outside opinions, and reevaluations.

13. Patterns of communication in a group provide an index of the distribution of power and status in the group.

14. Communications in a formal group follow directional patterns. Communications flow upward to higher levels, downward to lower levels, and horizontally to peers.

15. The basic communication structures that may exist in a group, in the order of degree of centralization, are the wheel (the most centralized), the Y, the chain, and the circle.

16. When operations are not too involved and complicated for one person to handle, the more centralized structures seem to be more effective than other structures. In very involved and complex operations and in discussion groups, the less centralized structures seem to be more effective than other structures.

17. The grapevine and information hubs may transmit messages by bypassing someone in the official pattern and thus travel faster.

18. Transactional analysis is a theory of communication explaining social interaction between two individuals in a group. The application of the theory can result in improved human relations.

19. Unique, catchy terms describe the principles of transactional analysis. For example, a stroke represents any communication that gives a person recognition, and stamps are the feelings one gets from strokes.

20. According to transactional analysis, stamps are collected, cashed in, and traded; therefore, to improve human relations, more positive stamps must be given and collected than negative stamps. Stamp collecting is the basis for much communication between individuals.

21. According to transactional analysis, a person acts out the life script of a winner, a loser, or a nonwinner based on unconscious attitudes

formed early in life. Life scripts explain many communications between individuals.

22. According to transactional analysis, how a person feels about himself or herself and about other people in general determines a person's life position which may be any one of four positions: I'm not OK—You're OK; I'm OK—You're not OK; I'm not OK—You're not OK; I'm OK—You're OK. Life positions explain many communications between individuals.

23. According to transactional analysis, an individual's personality consists of three ego states—the Parent, the Child, and the Adult. Transactions (communications between two people) may be sent from any one of the ego states to any one of the ego states of the other person.

24. In complementary transactions, there is no conflict because the response is sent to the same ego state from which the stimulus was received, and the response is sent from the same ego state which received the stimulus.

25. Crossed transactions produce conflict and occur when the response does not come back to the ego state that the stimulus was sent from, nor does it come back from the ego state the stimulus was directed toward.

26. Duplex ulterior transactions are complementary transactions with hidden meanings that are understood by both the sender and receiver.

27. One of the ways people structure their time is in social interaction which may be of several types: intimacy, games, pastimes, rituals, or withdrawal which is avoidance of social interaction.

28. Psychological games are a set or series of ulterior transactions that a person uses repeatedly and that have a predetermined end and well-defined psychological payoffs (strokes).

29. A game cons a person into giving the initiator a negative stroke or into letting the initiator give the person a negative stroke.

30. A leader is the member of a group who has the most influence over the other members of the group.

31. The three different approaches that have emerged to study leadership are the trait approach, the style approach, and the situational approach.

32. Three leadership styles have been identified: autocratic, democratic, and laissez-faire.

33. An autocratic style of leadership has a tendency to foster negative feelings in members of the group; while the democratic style tends to lead to satisfaction, motivation, and cohesiveness. The laissez-faire style often leads to chaos.

34. One theory proposes that a leader can be more effective if he or she builds up more idiosyncrasy credit.

35. The contingency theory of leadership effectiveness views effective leadership as contingent on the degree of situational favorability, task structure, power, and leadership style which is determined by a score derived from rating the least preferred co-worker (LPC).

36. Unrecognized leaders emerge in informal groups in such roles as the representative to management, the technical expert, the information source, the enforcer, the tension reducer, or the crisis manager.

## SUGGESTIONS FOR FURTHER READING

Berne, E. *Games people play*. New York: Grove Press, 1967.

Many psychological games that people play are described and illustrated in this book.

Berne, E. *What do you say after you say hello?* New York: Grove Press, 1972.

Although principles of transactional analysis are reviewed, this book deals primarily with the life script part of transactional analysis, discussing the process of script analysis in detail.

Fiedler, F., & Chemers, M. *Leadership and effective management*. Glenview, Ill.: Scott, Foresman, 1974.

This book provides a good background for further study of leadership and management by presenting a comprehensive review of the research on this topic.

Harris, T. *I'm OK, you're OK*. New York: Harper & Row, 1969.

This is an easy-to-read presentation of the theory of transactional analysis.

James, M., & Jongeward, D. *Born to win: Transactional analysis with gestalt experiments*. Reading, Mass.: Addison-Wesley, 1971.

Numerous examples are given in this book on transactional analysis. Experiments and exercises are included to help the reader understand and apply the principles of transactional analysis.

Jongeward, D. *Everybody wins: Transactional analysis applied to organizations.* Reading, Mass.: Addison-Wesley, 1973.

This book shows how the principles of transactional analysis can be applied in the world of work and how transactional analysis can be used as a training tool in industry.

Latané, B., & Darley, J. *The unresponsive bystander: Why doesn't he help?* New York: Appleton-Century-Crofts, 1970.

The experiments that were conducted on bystander behavior are described in this book. Several factors that influence whether a person will help another person are identified.

Shaw, M. E. *Group dynamics: The psychology of small group behavior.* New York: McGraw-Hill, 1971.

The reader is provided with a comprehensive review of what is known about groups. Issues and problems in the study of groups are identified.

Steiner, I. D. *Group process and productivity.* New York: Academic Press, 1972.

Task-group effectiveness is the theme of this book. Various types of group tasks are categorized, and the role of task demands in determining effects of size, reinforcement, and dissimilarity of members on production is discussed.

Stogdill, R. M. *Handbook of leadership.* New York: Free Press, 1974.

A handbook that is a very complete account of what is known about leadership. Over 3,000 books and articles have been surveyed and abstracted yielding 150 pages of bibliography.

Taylor, D. A. (Ed.). *Small groups.* Chicago: Markham, 1971.

This collection of selected readings provides the reader with a sampling of important research studies on small groups.

# GLOSSARY

## A

**Ability.** A current capability to learn that is based on both aptitude and experience.

**Accommodation.** An adaptation process whereby the rules or structures are changed in order to acquire new information that does not fit existing structures or rules.

**Achievement.** The knowledge and skills that a person has acquired through experience or learning.

**Achievement motive.** The need to accomplish something important or valuable, or to meet high standards.

**Activity theory.** The theory that activity is the essence of life and that aging people should maintain activities and work responsibilities for as long as possible.

**Actualizing tendency.** The innate tendency of humans to seek experiences which protect and maintain the self and which allow them to grow psychologically.

**Adaptation.** The innate ability of an organism to adjust to the environment such as when the cells in sense organs become less sensitive when exposed to a constant level of stimulation.

**Adrenal glands.** Endocrine glands located near the kidneys that release adrenaline (epinephrine) and noradrenaline (norepinephrine) as well as other hormones into the bloodstream during stress, resulting in a number of important changes in the body, all of which prepare it for action.

**Adult.** In transactional analysis, the ego state that consists of the knowledge, logical reasoning, rational thinking, and information processing of the individual.

**Affective disorders.** Maladaptive behaviors characterized by inappropriate emotional responses whereby the person seems to fail to use a strategy to repress feelings of guilt and inadequacy and often even exaggerates them.

**Afferent neuron.** A cell in the nervous system, sometimes referred to as a sensory neuron, that receives input directly from cells in the sense organs.

**Affiliation motive.** A learned need to be with people, to be accepted by some people, and to be loved by people.

**Ageism.** Discrimination, prejudice, or stereotyping on the basis of age.

**Alternate response technique.** The technique of engaging in responses which interfere with or replace the response to be controlled or eliminated when one is using a behavior modification program to achieve self-selected behavioral outcomes.

**Ambiverts.** Individuals whose personality type is a mixture of the extrovert and introvert and who vacillate from one to the other in different situations.

**Amnesia.** The partial or total loss of memory for past experiences which is often psychological in nature—an extreme form of repression.

**Amplitude.** The height or magnitude of the sound wave which is the primary determiner of the loudness of the sound.

**Angular ulterior transaction.** A message with a hidden meaning that can be interpreted by the receiver as being directed toward either of two different transactional analysis ego states.

**Anxiety.** A psychological state characterized by apprehension, tenseness, dread, and foreboding with causes that are usually not as specific as the causes of fear.

**Anxiety states.** A generalized feeling of anxiousness and tenseness that may be intense enough to cause the person to experience heart palpitations, choking sensations, etc.

**Approach-approach conflict.** Conflict resulting from a situation in which a person is simultaneously attracted to two opportunities, goals, or demands that are equally attractive.

**Approach-avoidance conflict.** Conflict resulting from a situation in which a person has to decide whether to engage in a single activity, pursue a single goal, or take advantage of a single opportunity that has both desirable and undesirable characteristics or advantages and disadvantages.

**Aptitude.** An innate or natural capacity for performing or learning to perform some task.

**Arousal theory.** The view that behavior is a function of being aroused or more sensitive to or more reactive to a specific stimulus.

**Assertive coping.** Meaningful and constructive attempts to change situations that produce high levels of stress.

**Assimilation.** An adaptation process whereby existing rules or structures are applied to new situations.

**Association value.** The degree to which a particular word can bring to mind other words that are related to it.

**Attitude.** A person's disposition to think, feel, and act either positively or negatively toward a person, idea, object, or situation.

**Attitude scale.** A self-report method in which a person reports his or her feelings about some person, object, idea, or situation to provide an indication of the strength and direction of his or her attitudes.

**Autocratic.** A type of leadership in which leaders centralize the power in themselves, make the decisions for the group, and do not allow the members of the group to participate in the decision-making process.

**Autonomic nervous system.** The division of the peripheral nervous system that serves the internal body organs and glands, thus regulating their activities.

**Avoidance-avoidance conflict.** Conflict resulting from a situation in which a person must make a decision between two equally unattractive alternatives or unpleasant situations.

**Axon.** A long, slender, tubelike fiber ranging in length from one to two inches to three feet extending away from the main body of a neuron.

**Belief.** One aspect of an attitude which does not involve feeling, emotion, likes or dislikes and may be true or false but is accepted as fact.

**Biofeedback.** Feedback in the form of an individual's physiological processes such as heart rate, blood pressure, galvanic skin response, or temperature which may be monitored and which provides a consequence stimulus enabling an individual to learn to control internal behaviors.

**Biorhythms.** Biological cycles such as emotional, intellectual, and physical cycles that are believed by some scientists to begin at birth and rise and fall at different rates and that seem to be a small but significant part of the explanation of human behavior.

**Bipolar disorder.** An affective disorder, formerly called manic-depressive psychosis, characterized by an individual who may suddenly change back and forth from depression to a wild, violent, or extremely elated mood.

**Blind spot.** The place on the retina where the optic nerve enters the retina that has neither rods nor cones and is, thus, insensitive to light rays.

**Bystander apathy.** Failure on the part of passersby to intervene when help is needed due to the presence of a group which inhibits rather than facilitates helping behavior.

# B

**Balance phase.** The third phase of a four-phase sequence in the process of group formation which involves members giving up some of their own individual wants, desires, and needs for the benefit of the group as a whole and is characterized by compromise and agreement.

**Behavior.** Any activity or movement of an organism in response to a specific stimulus or set of stimuli whether or not the activity is mental, physical, internal, or external.

**Behaviorism.** A view that defines psychology as the study of behavior focusing on the relationship between stimuli and responses and emphasizing objectivity and the empirical approach.

**Behavior modification.** The application of learning theory or the use of learning technologies to the modification of individual or group behaviors.

**Behavior therapy.** A method of psychotherapy that involves the application of learning principles in an attempt to modify behavior.

# C

**Case study method.** A method of studying behavior by conducting an intensive investigation of a single case which results in a large amount of information.

**Catatonic schizophrenia.** A type of schizophrenia primarily characterized by disturbed motor activity; such an individual becomes rigid and immobile and generally unresponsive.

**Central nervous system.** The division of the nervous system that consists of the brain and spinal cord.

**Cerebellum.** A lobed structure consisting of two hemispheres which is attached to the brain stem in the hindbrain and is involved in the control of motor behavior, especially balance and coordination.

**Cerebral cortex.** The mass of cell bodies and unmyelinated axons that covers the two hemispheres of the brain that form an umbrella over the structures in the center of the brain.

**Chain.** A basic structure of group communication in which a person only communicates with the person immediately above or below him or her in the chain of command.

**Charisma.** An elusive term which refers to some magnetic quality that has the mysterious ability to draw people to a person and to allow that person to control them.

**Child.** In transactional analysis, the ego state that consists of the feelings about the person's past experiences and the person's current feelings and is the source of openness, manipulation, spontaneity, sensuality, affection, creativity, happiness, rebellion, and hostility.

**Chromosomes.** A complex structure in the cell nucleus composed of thousands of genes which are the carriers of heredity threaded together like a string of beads.

**Circle.** A basic structure of group communication in which there is no chain of command and communication circulates through the group; all members of the group tend to be equal and no person controls communication more than another person.

**Classical conditioning.** A form of learning based on associations formed when a new event is paired with another event that brings forth a particular behavior, and the new event comes to signal the other event and brings forth the same behavior.

**Client-centered therapy.** A method of psychotherapy developed by Carl Rogers that involves helping the patient develop a more realistic self-concept and increase his or her sense of self-worth.

**Clinical psychology.** An area of psychology concerned with helping individuals achieve psychological well-being and with diagnosing and treating psychological disturbances.

**Cognitive-behavioral model.** An expanded version of the learning model of behavior which emphasizes that behavior is determined by the cognitive processes such as thinking, memory, and perception.

**Cognitive consistency.** Agreement or balance among one's attitudes, beliefs, feelings, and behaviors.

**Cognitive dissonance.** The state of tension that is created when there is inconsistency among an individual's attitudes, beliefs, feelings, and behaviors.

**Cognitive psychology.** One of the newer approaches to the study of human behavior which is based on the view that the mind is an information processing center and which emphasizes the role of memory and the thought processes in explaining behavior.

**Cognitive styles.** Ways individuals characteristically perceive events and draw inferences from them.

**Cognitive therapies.** Therapies based on the belief that the way a person perceives and structures his or her world determines his or her feelings and behavior and that a person is responsible for his or her own behavior.

**Common fate.** A principle of perceptual organization that perceives objects that move together as a single whole.

**Common sense assumptions.** Ideas one holds to be true without any proof that they are true.

**Complementary transaction.** In transactional analysis, a response sent back to the same ego state from which the stimulus was received; sometimes called a parallel transaction.

**Compliance.** The act of submitting to a direct request to behave in a particular way.

**Concrete operational stage.** The third stage in Piaget's theory of intellectual development, the period from about seven to eleven years of age for most children, during which the child develops the capacity to reason and solve problems in a logical manner.

**Conditioned (secondary) reinforcers.** Reinforcers that gain their effectiveness from their association with other reinforcers and are thus those which satisfy a learned need.

**Conditioned response.** A response that is learned; that is, a response that is brought forth by a conditioned or learned stimulus.

**Conditioned stimulus.** A previously neutral stimulus that, through learning or association with an unconditioned stimulus or another conditioned stimulus, comes to bring forth a response similar to the one brought forth by the stimulus with which it is associated.

**Cones.** Cells located on the back layer of the retina of the eye that respond to differences in wavelength and are involved in color vision.

**Conflict phase.** The second phase of group formation during which members' individual personalities and needs begin to clash.

**Conformity.** The degree to which a person behaves in order to be in accordance with the norms or standards of society.

**Conservation.** In Piaget's theory of intellectual development, the ability to recognize that the quantity (mass, volume, length, number, etc.) of a substance does not change, despite a change in appearance, if nothing is added or subtracted.

**Constancy principles.** Interpretative rules for judging occurrences that involve stabilizing processes that provide a standard, dependable way of interpreting events rather than following the movements.

**Consumer psychology.** The branch of psychology which studies the dynamics underlying decisions and behaviors regarding the acquisition, use, and disposition of products, services, times, and ideas.

**Continuity.** A principle of perceptual organization that groups together continuous contours.

**Continuous reinforcement.** A schedule of reinforcement in which a reinforcer follows the response every time it occurs.

**Control group.** In an experiment contrasting two groups, the group that does not receive the experimental treatment.

**Convergent thinking.** The type of thinking one uses to retrieve answers or solutions previously stored in long-term memory.

**Conversion disorder.** Maladaptive behavior whereby a person reduces anxiety by displacing the anxiety to a part of his or her body and then inactivating that part of the body.

**Cornea.** The transparent covering through which light rays first enter the eye.

**Corpus callosum.** The mass of nerve fibers that connects the two cerebral hemispheres of the brain.

**Correlated reinforcement.** Reinforcement in which the quantity of reinforcement varies in proportion to the quantity or intensity of the response.

**Correlation coefficient.** A numerical representation of the relationship that exists between two variables.

**Correlational method.** A scientific method of studying behavior that involves an investigation of the relationships between measurable events.

**Counseling psychologist.** A psychologist who may or may not have a doctoral degree and who works primarily with people who have less serious problems—perhaps problems associated with educational and vocational choices or individual and family adjustment problems.

**Critical periods.** A particular time in the developmental process during which an environmental condition will have a greater effect on behavior than at other times.

**Crossed transaction.** In transactional analysis, a transaction in which the response does not come back to the ego state from which the stimulus was sent nor does it come back from the ego state the stimulus was directed toward.

**Cross-validated.** The condition whereby the initial findings of a relationship between a performance measure and a variable believed to affect performance have been found in a repeated study with another sample.

**Crystallized intelligence.** The component of intelligence theorized by Cattell to reflect what one has learned through experience and which is believed to be able to increase for many years even after the end of formal schooling.

# D

**Data.** The observations in numerical form, often called scores, that represent a characteristic or a phenomenon.

**Defense mechanisms.** Strategies of self-deception that one unconsciously learns to use in order to avoid or prevent one from recognizing anxiety or something unpleasant or threatening to the ego.

**Defensive coping.** The use of strategies to cope with stress that one is not aware that he or she is using since they involve unconscious processes called defense mechanisms.

**Deindividuation.** The phenomenon in which an individual sets his or her own personality aside, becomes submerged in a group, and has a group identification rather than an individual identification.

**Delusions.** Beliefs that are not true and are characteristic of some psychological disturbances.

**Delusions of grandeur.** False beliefs or delusions one may have that he or she is some great or grand other person.

**Delusions of persecution.** False beliefs one may have that others are attempting to harm, persecute, or take something from them.

**Delusions of reference.** False beliefs one may have that things others do is in reference to them. For example, if a person sees a group of people talking, he or she believes they are talking about him or her.

**Democratic.** A type of leadership in which the leader shares his or her power with other members of the group and allows decisions to be made by the consensus of the group.

**Demonology.** One of the earliest explanations of behavior—the belief that spirits possess a person's body and direct a person's behavior.

**Dendrites.** The short, delicate, branchlike extensions that protrude from the main cell body of a neuron to receive messages or impulses from neighboring cells.

**Deoxyribonucleic acid (DNA).** A complex molecule in the nucleus of every cell in the body which carries chemically coded instructions that determine physical appearance, body functioning, and growth—the genetic code.

**Dependent variable.** The variable that is measured in an experimental study in order to observe the effect of the manipulation of the independent variable.

**Depersonalization.** A dissociative disorder characterized by individuals who suddenly feel changed or different in a strange way such as feeling they are outside their bodies, that their actions are mechanical, or that they are dreaming.

**Depolarization.** The state a neuron is in when the balance of electrical charges between the interior and the exterior of the cell is altered and the cell's interior is positive with respect to the exterior.

**Depressant.** Any drug that reduces nervous system activity.

**Depression.** An affective disorder characterized by listlessness, brooding, fatigue, feelings of worthlessness, slowing of the thought processes, and profound sadness and loneliness.

**Descriptive statistics.** The part of statistics that is concerned with describing the data collected and presenting the data in a convenient, usable, and understandable form.

**Determinism.** The assumption that every event, act, or decision is the consequence of prior physical, psychological, or environmental events that are independent of the human will.

**Developmental psychology.** The specialized area of psychology concerned with the growth and development of a person from the beginning of life until death and the behavior and behavioral changes characteristic of each period of development.

**Diagnostic and Statistical Manual of Mental Disorders (DSM-III).** The third revision of a manual published by the American Psychiatric Association which classifies mental disorders according to abnormal behavioral patterns.

**Dichromats.** Those individuals who have one type of cone missing, either the red-green cones or the blue-yellow cones, and do not perceive color normally.

**Differential reinforcement.** A situation in which two or more similar but physically different responses are made and one is reinforced while the others are extinguished.

**Diffusion of responsibility.** The phenomenon that, in a group, no one individual is responsible for the actions of the group.

**Directional patterns.** Upward, downward, or horizontal patterns of communication in organized groups.

**Discounts.** In transactional analysis, strokes that are less positive than they should be or strokes not delivered.

**Discrimination.** In social psychology, an action taken based on a prejudice.

**Disengagement theory.** The theory that assumes, as people grow older, withdrawal from society is natural and has psychological benefits.

**Disequilibration.** Piaget's term for dissatisfaction as a result of conflict, inconsistencies, and unresolved problems.

**Dissociative disorders.** Behavioral disorders used for coping with stress and anxiety in which the part of the person's personality that is the source of the anxiety seems to be separated from the rest of the personality in some way and repressed.

**Distributed practice.** A method of learning that involves practicing or repeating what is to be learned in short periods of time with rest periods intervening.

**Divergent thinking.** The type of thinking in which one uses his or her imagination to bring forth new, unusual, or unheard-of answers or solutions.

**Dominant.** In genetics, a gene in a pair which predominates over the other gene in the pair to influence the development of a particular characteristic.

**Double approach-avoidance conflict.** Conflict resulting from a situation in which a person is faced with a choice between two goals each of which has desirable as well as undesirable tendencies.

**Double bind.** The position a person is in when experiencing a double approach-avoidance conflict—two contradictory messages creating a dilemma from which one cannot escape since the advantages of one message are destroyed by the disadvantages of the other message.

**Down's syndrome.** A form of mental retardation produced by the presence of an extra chromosome.

**Drive.** The term referring to the force that arises from physiological conditions which signify some biological distress and, thus, compels behavior.

**Dualism.** The philosophy that human behavior is controlled by complex interactions of both the mind and the body, either of which may initiate behavior, which is based on the assumption that God is the source of behavior, having created humans in such a way that the mind guides behavior to satisfy bodily needs.

**Duplex ulterior transaction.** In transactional analysis, a complementary transaction with hidden meanings that are understood by both the sender and receiver.

# E

**Eclectic.** An approach used in applied psychology whereby the psychologist selects from the many theories and approaches available and uses what seems to fit the situation rather than relying on one approach only.

**Ectomorphs.** One of the three body types identified by Sheldon; typically thin and small boned.

**Educational psychology.** The specialized area of psychology concerned with increasing the efficiency of learning in schools; the study of behavior in educational settings.

**Efferent neuron.** A cell in the nervous system, sometimes referred to as a motor neuron, that carries messages out from the brain and spinal cord to muscle cells that control outward external movement as well as to the smooth muscles that control glands and internal organs.

**Ego.** Freud's term for the conscious part of the personality that is in contact with reality, is responsible for the voluntary processes, perceives the needs of the individual, evaluates the environment, adapts to social norms, plans ahead, and finds ways to actually obtain things needed and desired.

**Ego states.** In transactional analysis, the three parts of the personality—the Parent, the Adult, and the Child.

**Electra complex.** Freud's term for the conflict experienced by a young female child who has an erotic attachment to her father and hostile feelings toward her mother which is resolved by identification with her mother.

**Electrons.** Negative charges of electricity that are parts of all atoms.

**Emotionality.** One of the two major dimensions of personality identified by Eysenck—the dimension related to emotional stability; changeability in mood; sensitivity to emotional stress, tenseness, anxiety; tendency to feel guilty; self-esteem; and feelings of fatigue.

**Empirical approach.** The pursuit of knowledge through observation and experimentation—a method which deals with information that is available to the senses and can be validated and confirmed by other individuals.

**Empiricism.** The philosophy that behavior is determined, not chosen, and that relationships exist between stimuli and responses.

**Encoding.** According to the cognitive approach to explaining memory, the process of entering information into a system for immediate or later use; the transformation of a sensory input into a form that can be processed by the memory system.

**Endocrine glands.** The ductless glands of the body that empty secretions called hormones directly into the bloodstream, bringing about a widespread and immediate effect on behavior.

**Endomorphs.** One of the three body types identified by Sheldon; typically soft and wide, with a large proportion of the body weight in the abdomen.

**Engineering psychology.** A subdivision of the specialized area of psychology called industrial/organizational psychology which specializes in the discovery and application of information about the relationship between human behavior and machines, tools, jobs, and work environments.

**Engram.** A general term for a persistent structural change in the brain caused by stimulation of living neural tissue; the biological representation of memory in the brain.

**Environmental psychology.** A relatively new subdivision of the specialized area of psychology called industrial/organizational psychology which is concerned with the relationships between psychological processes and physical environments, both natural and human designed, such as the effects on human behavior of environmental conditions such as noise, air, and water pollution; physical space, and toxic agents.

**Equilibrium.** The sense of balance or an awareness of body position which makes it possible to maintain an upright posture.

**Existential psychology.** A loosely organized view of psychology that is more philosophical and less scientific than other views; stresses that human existence is in the here and now and that the goal of therapy is not to eliminate anxiety but to give it meaning; and focuses on feelings, attitudes, values, and one's immediate experience.

**Experimental group.** In an experiment contrasting two groups, the group that is subjected to a change in an independent variable.

**Experimental method.** A scientific method of investigation that seeks to define cause and effect relationships through the manipulation of certain variables.

**Experimental psychology.** An area of psychology in which rigorous research methods are used to experimentally investigate basic psychological processes in the study of behavior, usually in laboratory settings.

**External pressure.** Demands to meet a particular standard of behavior that are made on a person by other people who are significant in his or her life.

**Externals.** Individuals who perceive the center of control in their lives as being outside themselves.

**Extinction.** The weakening and eventual disappearance of a response when a learner no longer associates a conditioned stimulus with an unconditioned stimulus or a consequence stimulus with a response.

**Extrinsic motivation.** Motivation for behavior which may be satisfied with external reinforcers such as money, food, prizes, benefits, etc.

**Extrinsic reinforcers.** Tangible things that can be used as reinforcers.

**Extroversion-introversion.** One of the two major dimensions of personality identified by Eysenck—the dimension related to the person's need to receive stimulation from the outside world.

**Extroverts.** Individuals who tend to seek stimulation in the form of social activities and exciting, adventurous events as well as sensory stimulation in the form of loud noises and colors.

## F

**Feature analysis.** A theory of perception which explains perception as an active, hypothesis-testing process in which the person seems to abstract features of the signal or neural impulse and compares them with patterns stored in long-term memory.

**Figure-ground relationship.** One of the processes involved in perceptual organization—the principle that geometrical patterns are always organized as a figure against a background and appear to have a contour and boundary.

**Fixed interval schedule.** An intermittent schedule of reinforcement in which a reinforcer follows the response only after a set period of time.

**Fixed ratio schedule.** An intermittent schedule of reinforcement in which a reinforcer follows the response only after a set number of responses has occurred since the last reinforcer was given.

**Flexible scheduling.** A procedure which allows workers to schedule their own 40 hours of work a week within the time the organization is in operation.

**Fluid intelligence.** The component of intelligence theorized by Cattell to reflect a general perceptual capacity that is more dependent on the physiological functioning of one's brain and is determined by an individual's genetic endowment.

**Formal operational stage.** The fourth and last stage in Piaget's theory of intellectual development which occurs on the average between the ages of 11 and 15 and is characterized by abstract thinking.

**Fovea.** An area on the retina of the eye where the cones are most concentrated and is thus the area where vision is sharpest when the image is projected on the retina.

**Free recall.** A method of measuring memory in which an individual is given a list of items, such as Ebbinghaus' nonsense syllables, to recall at a later time in any order.

**Free will.** The assumption that humans freely choose their own behavior and have control of their own destinies.

**Frequency.** The number of cycles of the sound wave that arrive per second.

**Frequency distribution.** An arrangement of a set of data which consists of grouping together all scores which fall into a particular category.

**Frequency polygon.** A line graph in which the frequency associated with a score or a group of scores is plotted as a point.

**Functionalism.** The view of James that psychologists should study the functioning of the mind since the mind consists of the abilities to make decisions and to adapt to an environmental situation.

## G

**Galvanic skin response.** Changes in the resistance of the skin to the conduction of electricity.

**Gender identity disorders.** A personality disorder characterized by an individual who is confused over his or her biological sex and prefers to behave in a manner typical of the opposite sex.

**General adaptation syndrome.** A phrase coined by Hans Selye to represent reactions of the body to specific stimuli causing emotional stress.

**Generalized conditioned reinforcers.** Reinforcers such as money which are associated with many different reinforcers and, therefore, extinction from overuse does not usually occur.

**Genes.** Carriers of heredity that are composed of DNA molecules and are located on the chromosomes.

**Genetic engineering.** The modification of an individual's hereditary makeup through the manipulation of his or her genetic materials.

**Gestalt psychology.** The view that human behavior should be studied as an organized whole rather than as separate individual parts with emphasis on form, patterns, or wholes in perception.

**Grapevine.** A source of information that comes by bypassing someone in the official structure of communication for a group.

**Group.** A collection of individuals who interact with each other, share some common identity, and share some common goals or desires.

**Group therapy.** A form of therapy based on the assumption that personality disorders are related to an inability to communicate, to relate to others, and to perceive accurately which occurs with a group of people so that other members of the group can provide feedback.

**Groupthink.** The term coined by Janis to describe the type of thinking that occurs when people make decisions as a cohesive group based on a compulsion to maintain unanimity and each other's approval to the extent that critical, realistic thinking does not occur.

# H

**Hallucinations.** An inappropriate sensory experience; the perception of things that are not really there.

**Hallucinogens.** Drugs that usually produce changes in a person's ability to receive and interpret sensory information resulting in distorted perceptions and hallucinations.

**Halo effect.** A distorted perception of others in which a favorable impression of an individual is created by one characteristic which spreads to other characteristics so that virtually everything the individual does is judged in a favorable light.

**Hawthorne effect.** The phenomenon that the attention given to the participants during an experimental research project may have an effect on the responses of the participants.

**Hebephrenic schizophrenia.** A form of schizophrenia characterized by childish or immature behavior such as inappropriate silliness and giggling, a refusal to wear clothes or use eating utensils, or the elimination of urine or feces at inappropriate times.

**Hedonism.** The ancient philosophical idea that behavior is determined by the desire to avoid pain and the desire to seek pleasure.

**Hierarchy of needs.** Maslow's classification of motives responsible for behavior placed in a hierarchical order ascending from the physiological needs that must be satisfied first to the need for self-actualization—the highest motive for human behavior.

**Histogram.** A type of bar graph in which the frequencies of the scores or groups of scores are represented in terms of the lengths of the bars.

**Holistic approach.** An approach to the study of human behavior which deals with the whole individual as an organized system interacting within the context of the entire environment—the home environment, the work environment, the social environment, the religious environment, etc., each influencing the other.

**Homeostasis.** A central idea in biological psychology which sets forth the idea that the source of motivation is an automatic adjustment of behavior to maintain physiological equilibrium.

**Hormones.** Chemicals secreted by the endocrine glands directly into the bloodstream which have an effect on behavior.

**Humanistic psychology.** One of the newer approaches to the study of human behavior which emphasizes feelings and subjective experience, such as self-esteem and self-actualization, and psychological needs, such as the need for love, achievement, or creativity.

**Hygiene (maintenance) factors.** Factors which are part of the job content but are external to the job itself that Herzberg proposed must be satisfied to avoid worker dissatisfaction, but they do not generate satisfaction or motivate greater productivity.

**Hypochondriasis.** A neurotic disorder in which a person is constantly preoccupied with his or her health even though a physician can seldom find anything physically wrong.

**Hypothalamus.** A structure in the forebrain that functions as a thermostat for the body and plays an important role in motivation and emotion in order to maintain the needed balance for survival.

**Hypothesis.** A belief, hunch, tentative statement, or explanation that has not been proven or disproven.

**Hypothetical construct.** A mechanism which is inferred and assumed to exist but is invisible and impossible to measure directly.

# I

**Id.** Freud's term for the unconscious part of the personality which is concerned only with immediate gratification and employs primary process thinking such as wish-fulfillment fantasies or dreams.

**Identification.** Unconscious modeling of others' behavior such as their ways of coping with stress or sex roles and the unconscious internalizing of others' values, attitudes, and feelings.

**Idiosyncrasy credit.** The sum total of positive impressions in the followers' perceptions of the leaders.

**Illumination stage.** The third stage in creativity in problem solving which consists of sudden and unexpected insight into the problem resulting in the conception of an idea that seems to be a solution.

**Imagery rating.** The degree to which a word can bring to mind a concrete picture.

**Incentive.** A pulling force produced by external stimuli that is a source of motivation for behavior based on learning. For example, table laden with food is an incentive to eat.

**Incubation stage.** The second stage in creativity in problem solving which consists of the absorption and assimilation of the acquired information through unconscious mental activity.

**Independent variable.** The variable in an experimental study that is manipulated by the experimenter while all other variables are held constant.

**Industrial/organizational psychology.** An area of applied psychology that specializes in applying psychological principles in work-related situations and in conducting research to expand knowledge of psychological principles that are applicable in business or industry.

**Inferential statistics.** The part of statistics which is concerned with drawing conclusions and making inferences about populations based on samples taken from a population.

**Information hub.** An individual in a group who gets more information than others in the group perhaps because of his or her position or role in the organization or social position.

**Ingroup.** The reference group with which a person identifies.

**Instrumentality.** In VIE theory, the belief one has that a behavior will achieve or secure second level outcomes (outcomes that are a direct result of the behavior) and the value of these outcomes.

**Intelligence quotient.** The ratio of the mental age to the chronological age, multiplied by 100.

**Interactionists.** Psychologists who believe that the consistencies found in an individual's personality are due to the interaction of the individual with the environment rather than to a general trait belonging to the individual.

**Interference theory.** A theory of forgetting which proposes that the information gets mixed with other information and becomes harder to remember. The interference may be from previous or subsequent learning.

**Intermittent reinforcement.** The condition in which a reinforcer follows the response or behavior only some of the time rather than every time it occurs.

**Internal pressure.** Pressure on an individual to meet a particular standard of behavior that is self-imposed and is based on the need to meet ideals in order to maintain self-esteem.

**Internals.** Individuals who perceive themselves as being the center of control in their lives.

**Interneurons.** Neurons, sometimes referred to as association neurons, that carry messages from other neurons in the brain and spinal cord.

**Interval schedules.** Intermittent schedules of reinforcement in which a reinforcer follows the response only after a specific period of time has elapsed.

**Intrinsic motivation.** Motivation for behavior which is satisfied by the behavior itself rather than by the consequence of the behavior.

**Intrinsic reinforcers.** Internal feelings of satisfaction that one gets from performing a particular behavior such as feelings of competence, achievement, or self-actualization.

**Introspection.** The method used by the structuralists to investigate the contents of the mind by asking a person to describe his or her feelings or conscious awareness of the stimulus presented.

**Introverts.** Individuals who characteristically tend to withdraw into themselves and do not need to receive stimulation from the outside world as much as those classified as extroverts.

**Ions.** Particles formed when a neutral atom or group of atoms loses or gains one or more electrons.

# J

**Job analysis.** In personnel psychology, the act of describing the work to be done, the skills needed, and the training required for a particular job.

**Job description.** In personnel psychology, a description of the standard performance expected for a particular job.

**Job enrichment.** The process of making jobs more challenging and interesting by increasing personal responsibility for one's work, by providing the opportunity for personal achievement and recognition, and by expanding opportunities for psychological growth and development.

**Job evaluation.** In personnel psychology, the assessment of the relative value of a job to the organization.

**Job redesign.** A procedure employed by some organizations in an effort to fulfill employees' intrinsic needs by applying principles of motivation.

**Job satisfaction.** Overall positive feelings one has in job performance that results from the fulfillment of personal needs, wants, desires, and expectations and the favorable comparison of the job to some reference group.

# K

**Kinesics.** The science of body language—the study of body postures and gestures.

**Kinesthetic sense.** The sense that enables one to be aware of the movements and positions of different body parts.

# L

**Laissez-faire.** A style of leadership which cannot be considered as true leadership since the leader does not function and gives complete freedom to members of the group, neither praising nor criticizing.

**Leader.** The group member who has the most influence on the other group members.

**Learning model.** A view of abnormal behavior based on learning theory which proposes that deviant behaviors have simply been conditioned by environmental experiences or learned by observation.

**Learning sets.** Specific approaches that have been learned and that may be used in solving new but similar problems.

**Lens.** A transparent structure of the eye that focuses light rays entering through the pupil to form an image on the retina.

**Life position.** The transactional analysis term for a position that tends to prevail throughout a person's later childhood and adult life concerning one's self-esteem and attitudes or feelings about people in general.

**Life script.** In transactional analysis, unconscious lifetime plans which are based on attitudes concerning such things as success, work, sex, love, education, or religion and will be acted out like the script of a play.

**Limbic system.** An interconnection of several structures in the center core of the brain, including parts of the thalamus and hypothalamus, which seems to be related to motivation and emotion and includes the pleasure centers of the brain.

**Logical error.** A type of distorted perception of others in which one has a tendency to see different traits as belonging together when they logically do not.

**Logos.** A word which comes from a Greek word meaning knowledge, study of, or wisdom.

**Long-term memory.** In the structural view of memory, the third level or the storage system that holds information relatively permanently.

# M

**Massed practice.** A method of learning that involves practicing what is to be learned from start to finish in one long, unbroken time interval.

**Maturation.** The control that the genes exert over the unfolding of biological events from conception to death.

**Mean.** The familiar arithmetic average obtained by totaling all the items of data and dividing by the number of items of data.

**Measure of central tendency.** A representative point or score for a set of data which tends to be near the middle of the score range.

**Mechanism.** René Descartes' view that the physical aspect of humans obeys mechanistic laws and is explainable by them.

**Median.** A measure of central tendency based on the rank distribution—the point or score below which half (50 percent) of the items of data fall when they are arranged in rank order.

**Medical model.** A view of abnormal behavior based on the organic and psychoanalytic explanations for behavior which proposes that people who have psychological problems are sick and have a mental illness with descriptive symptoms that need to be treated and cured.

**Medical therapies.** Therapies for the treatment of psychological disorders based on the assumption that a physiological disorder is the source of the abnormal behavior.

**Medulla.** The structure in the lowest part of the brain adjoining the spinal cord which controls reflex behaviors such as breathing and heart rate and helps maintain our upright posture.

**Mesomorphs.** One of the three body types identified by Sheldon; typically muscular and well developed.

**Mode.** A measure of central tendency which is the score in a set of data that occurs most frequently.

**Modeling.** Bandura's term for learning something by watching or observing another person.

**Monochromats.** Those individuals who have two types of cones missing, both the red-green cones and the blue-yellow cones, and do not perceive color.

**Morale.** A word sometimes used to mean degree of happiness but, more specifically, the degree to which one's needs are satisfied, and the degree to which the satisfaction is perceived as stemming from the total job situation.

**Motivation factors.** Factors of a job that occur at the time the work is performed and make the work rewarding in and of itself which Herzberg proposed leads to job satisfaction and increased productivity, but their absence rarely produces dissatisfaction.

**Motivation research.** The study of why people buy things which tries to discover the unconscious motives, attitudes, and preferences involved in the choice of a product or service.

**Multiple personality.** A dissociative disorder whereby a new identity arises to temporarily repress the old identity.

**Myelin sheath.** Fatty nodules which cover the axons of some neurons serving as a sheath to insulate the fiber of the axon and speed up the transmission of the message.

# N

**nAch.** The term for need for achievement which is the need for success as measured against some internalized standard of excellence.

**nAff.** The term for need for affiliation which is the need for close interpersonal relationships and friendships with other people.

**Naturalistic or field method.** A scientific method of collecting evidence to test hypotheses which involves careful observation and recording of behavior in a natural setting with as little interference by the investigator as possible.

**Needs.** A term which refers to the learned or psychological needs of an individual as well as the physiological drives of the body.

**Negative reinforcement.** A consequence of a behavior that increases the frequency of occurrence of the behavior by either removing an aversive stimulus, providing escape from it, or preventing it from occurring.

**Neo-Freudians.** A term which literally means new Freuds and refers to those psychologists who kept some or most of Freud's basic views but altered them to include social interactions and to deemphasize the biological aspects and the erogenous zones.

**Nerve.** A bundle of axons from many neurons much like a telephone cable that consists of many wires.

**Neurons.** The specialized cells of the nervous system.

**Neurosis.** A general term referring to behavioral disorders in which the person is in contact with reality and maintains basic control over thoughts and feelings, but deals ineffectively with the problems of living and anxiety by using defense mechanisms. The term is no longer used as a general category of abnormal behavior in the DSM-III.

**Neutral stimulus.** A person, place, event, or object that does not bring forth a specific response from a person.

**Nonsense syllable.** A vowel between two consonants that does not form a meaningful word such as BAX, JUP, HEB, or LOM.

**Norms.** The average or standard performance of a specific group under specific conditions which provides the comparison for determining if an individual's performance is average, above average, or below average or for determining the percentile rank of the performance. Also, in social psychology, the standards with which members of a group are expected to comply and against which the behavior of members is evaluated

**nPow.** The term for need for power which is the need for direct control or influence over others or the need for control over the means of influencing others.

**Null hypothesis.** A statistical hypothesis that no differences exist among groups other than chance differences. If the null hypothesis is rejected, the researcher accepts that the difference is great enough or significant enough that it is unlikely to be a chance difference and the experimental condition is the source of the difference.

# O

**Obedience.** The act of carrying out an order or command authorized by another person.

**Observation-of-others technique.** A technique used in self-control in which others who have achieved the same goal are observed and their behavior modeled.

**Obsessive-compulsive disorders.** Behavioral disorders in which the person repetitiously performs a behavior even though he or she may attempt to stop performing the behavior. Obsessions are persistent thoughts, and compulsions are persistent overt actions.

**Oedipus complex.** Freud's term for the conflict experienced by a young male child who has an erotic attachment to his mother and hostile feelings toward his father which is resolved by identification with the father.

**Operant conditioning.** A type of learning which involves the learning of a relationship between a response and the environmental consequence and which results in the increase or the decrease in the frequency of the response.

**Opinion.** A type of belief that an individual may hold even though no factual evidence is available to support the belief.

**Optic nerve.** Either of the two nerves which connect the retinas of the eyes to the brain and through which the neural impulse is carried to the brain.

**Organic model.** A view of abnormal behavior which proposes that the basis for the abnormality is in the biochemical or physiological processes.

**Organizational behavior.** An area of psychology that is primarily concerned with understanding, predicting, and influencing human behavior in organizations and attempts to understand individuals in organizations in order to meet individual needs and achieve organizational objectives.

**Orientation phase.** The first phase of group formation during which the members of the group are getting acquainted and confirming or changing expectations of the activities of the group and the rewards rendered by membership in the group.

**Outgroup.** A reference group with which a person does not identify and which has some characteristics that set it apart from the reference group with which one identifies.

**Ovaries.** The female sex glands that release hormones such as estrogen and produce egg cells.

**Overlearning.** A learning procedure which refers to the continuation of practice or repetition of what is being learned beyond the point when the material has been learned.

**Ovum.** The egg cell produced by the ovaries of the female.

# P

**Pancreas.** A gland located near the stomach that secretes two hormones, insulin and glucagon, that work against each other to control the level of sugar in the blood.

**Paralanguage.** A form of nonverbal communication by voice intonations such as pitch and loudness of the voice, pauses, exclamations, stuttering, and voice inflections.

**Parallel coaction tasks.** Tasks in which members of the group work separately and independently but parallel.

**Paranoia.** A behavioral disorder characterized by a very specific delusion that commonly involves one's spouse, a member of the family, a supervisor or employer, or perhaps a more remote enemy such as a political group.

**Paranoid schizophrenia.** A form of schizophrenia characterized by suspiciousness and delusions along with hallucinations.

**Paraphilia.** A psychosexual disorder in which objects or situations arouse the person sexually that normally do not arouse a person such as children, animals, aggression, or physical pain.

**Parasympathetic system.** The subsystem of the autonomic nervous system which is activated in the normal maintenance of life support functions.

**Parathyroids.** The endocrine glands embedded in the thyroid which release a hormone which controls the calcium and phosphate levels in the blood.

**Parent.** In transactional analysis, the ego state that consists of values, opinions, dos and don'ts, shoulds and should nots, and stored memories of statements and actions of parents and authority figures—the criticizer and/or nurturer.

**Parting phase.** The fourth phase of a group which involves the disbanding or dissolving of the group either from failure to reach a balance phase following a conflict phase or because of a limited existence due to time or situation.

**Patterning.** Processes in perception called perceptual organization which permit rapid interpretations of sensory input by putting together large amounts of information quickly and integrating the elements into meaningful wholes.

**Perception.** The process of assembling sensations into a meaningful and usable mental representation of the world—one's immediate experience of the world.

**Perceptual learning.** A type of cognitive learning which increases one's ability to extract information from the environment as a result of practice or experience with environmental stimulation.

**Perceptual organization.** The processes of perception which are the bases for patterning or putting together large amounts of information quickly and integrating the elements into meaningful wholes.

**Perceptual sets.** Perceptual expectancies which prepare a person to perceive or misperceive in a particular way as a result of prior experiences, suggestions, and motivations.

**Perinatal.** The period of time in the development of an individual during which birth occurs.

**Peripheral nervous system.** The division of the nervous system which consists of all the nerves carrying messages to and from the brain and spinal cord and which go out to all parts of the body.

**Person perception.** An individual's perception of other people.

**Personality.** The sum total of the characteristic ways a person responds to other people, objects, or events in the environment—the persistent behavior patterns that are unique to an individual.

**Personality disorders.** Behavioral disorders in which the person shows constant disregard for the rights of others by fighting, lying, cheating, or sexual promiscuity; formerly referred to as sociopaths or psychopaths.

**Personnel psychology.** The study of individual differences in performance of employees and of methods to assess such differences; the application of principles of psychology to management and employee training, supervision of personnel, communication, and employee counseling.

**Phobias.** Intense, irrational fears.

**Physical restraint technique.** A technique sometimes used to control behavior whereby physical restrictions are used in order to achieve a particular end such as not having any cigarettes in the house to avoid smoking.

**Physiological psychology.** An area of psychology in which behavior is studied as a function of physical changes in the body, especially in the brain, the nervous system, and the biochemistry of the body.

**Pitch.** The qualitative dimension, highness or lowness, of hearing that is determined by the frequency of the sound waves that are the stimulus.

**Pituitary gland.** An endocrine gland located in the brain which produces many hormones that control the timing and amount of growth of the body and control the other endocrine glands.

**Polarization.** The state of a neuron when the electrical charges of the cell's interior and exterior are stable; the state of a neuron when it is at rest, neither receiving nor transmitting a message.

**Polygenic.** Characteristics of a person, such as intelligence, temperament, or personality, that are influenced by a variety of genes operating in a complex interaction.

**Polygraph.** A device, commonly called a lie detector, which measures or records changes in the physiological responses associated with emotion—heart rate, blood pressure, respiration, and galvanic skin response.

**Pons.** The mass of nerve fibers that connects the higher and lower levels of the brain and the two hemispheres of the cerebellum.

**Population.** The total set of all possible cases from which a sample is selected.

**Position.** In social psychology, the specific slot occupied by an individual in a group.

**Positive reinforcement.** A consequence of a behavior that increases the frequency of the occurrence of the behavior since it pleases, rewards, or satisfies the person.

**Postnatal.** The period of time in the development of an individual from birth until death.

**Prejudices.** The special aspects of attitude that involve prejudging an individual without evidence; attitudes toward a group of people which favorably or unfavorably predisposes a person's attitude toward the whole group.

**Premack principle.** The principle demonstrated by Premack that a behavior which occurs often can be used as a reinforcer of a behavior which occurs less frequently.

**Prenatal.** The period of time in the development of an individual from conception until birth.

**Preoperational stage.** The second stage in Piaget's theory of intellectual development; the period from approximately two to seven years of age during which the child becomes increasingly able to represent objects and events symbolically but is unable to reverse the thought processes, is still egocentric, and tends to focus attention on a single aspect of a visual stimulus, ignoring other relevant attributes.

**Primary appraisal.** The first stage of evaluation of a perceived stimulus in which a person interprets the stimulus as either threatening or harmless.

**Primary needs.** Needs which have a biological basis and are necessary for survival.

**Primary process thinking.** According to Freud, the id's way of thinking to obtain immediate gratification which may include the generation of mental images, dreaming, and wish-fulfillment fantasies.

**Primary reinforcers.** Reinforcers that are effective in increasing a behavior by satisfying a biological need and thus may lose their effectiveness due to overuse but, subsequently, may regain their effectiveness after a period of deprivation.

**Principle of least group size.** The principle that the optimum group size for the performance of tasks requiring group interaction is the minimum number of individuals required to make available to the group all the requirements for performance of the task.

**Proactive inhibition.** The interfering effect of previous learning upon the recall of recently learned information.

**Programmed instruction.** A teaching technique based on the operant conditioning principle of shaping whereby an individual is presented with small segments of information that moves the individual closer and closer to the final object of the course of study.

**Projective tests.** Personality tests that use unstructured, vague, and ambiguous stimuli to obtain a response that is thought to reveal the conflicts, fears, fantasies, needs, and defenses that may be unknown to the person.

**Proxemics.** Nonverbal communication exhibited by the physical distance kept from others or by the eye contact that is maintained.

**Proximity.** A principle involved in perceptual organization whereby parts seem separate or grouped together depending on how close together they are.

**Psyche.** A word which comes from a Greek word meaning mind, life, spirit, or soul.

**Psychiatrists.** Medical doctors who have followed their medical school training with three to five years of specialized schooling in psychological disorders.

**Psychoanalysis.** Therapy based on the psychoanalytic approach to behavior which attempts to bring repressed feelings and sources of anxiety into the patient's consciousness so that he or she can resolve inner conflicts and reevaluate.

**Psychoanalyst.** A psychologist or psychiatrist whose approach to treatment is based on psychoanalytical theory.

**Psychoanalytic model.** A view of abnormal behavior developed by Freud that proposes that psychological problems are symptoms of underlying conflicts which are probably unconscious to the individual and could have occurred in early childhood.

**Psychogenic pain disorder.** One of four types of somatoform disorders which consists of feeling pain in some part of the body for which there is no physical basis.

**Psychological stress.** Demands that are placed on the body by the cognitive or mental processes such as anxiety, pressure, frustration, and conflict.

**Psychological stress evaluator.** A device that is a new kind of lie detector developed to measure changes in a person's voice that are undetectable to the human ear but occur as the activity of the sympathetic nervous system suppresses the vibration of the muscles controlling the vocal cords when a speaker is under stress.

**Psychology.** The scientific study of behavior and mental processes and the application of knowledge gained through that study.

**Psychophysiologists.** Specialists who study bodily changes brought on by emotion.

**Psychosexual dysfunction.** A psychosexual disorder, such as impotency or frigidity, in which the individual experiences an inability to function effectively during sex.

**Psychosexual stages.** The stages of development proposed by Freud, each of which is characterized by an interest in or gratification of a highly sensitive place on the body such as the mouth or the genitals. The stages in sequence are the oral stage, anal stage, phallic stage, latency stage, and genital stage.

**Psychosis.** A general term referring to behavioral disorders in which the individual loses contact with reality and exhibits symptoms such as hallucinations, delusions, and inappropriate affect.

**Psychosomatic disorders.** Physical disorders, such as some cases of ulcers, migraine headaches, asthma, high blood pressure, and heart disease, that have a psychological origin and are caused by psychological stress.

**Punishment.** An aversive consequence that is either physiologically or psychologically unpleasant to the person that follows the occurrence of a response and decreases the occurrence of that response.

**Pupil.** The small hole in the front of the lens through which light rays enter the eye.

**Pygmalion effect.** The tendency of an individual to act, perhaps unconsciously, in such a manner as to ensure the expected perception.

### R

**Randomization.** The process of randomly selecting a sample of subjects in such a way that each member of the population has an equal chance of being selected.

**Range.** The amount of variation between the highest and the lowest items of data.

**Rank distribution.** The arranging of the items of data or scores in a hierarchical order from highest to lowest.

**Ratio schedules.** Intermittent schedules of reinforcement in which a reinforcer follows a response only after a certain number of responses have been emitted.

**Rational therapy.** A cognitive type of therapy which is based on the assumption that a person's irrational beliefs are the source of maladaptive behavior and which attempts to show the person that his or her beliefs are irrational and attempts to teach more rational beliefs.

**Rationalism.** The philosophical idea that attributes one's behavior to thinking—conscious intentions and reasonings.

**Reality therapy.** A cognitive type of therapy which is based on the assumption that a person is responsible for his or her own behavior and which has the primary goal of helping people develop responsible behavior by encouraging them to judge their own behavior, set goals, and make commitments; by accepting no excuses for failing to keep a commitment; and by not inflicting punishment or showing rejection of the person.

**Recessive.** The term used for a gene that, when paired with a dominant gene, does not produce an effect; a gene that defers to a dominant gene.

**Recognition.** The term which applies to the method of measuring retention or memory by determining the percentage of material learned that can be recognized.

**Reconstruction theory.** A theory that proposes that memory of events may be distorted since it is a reconstruction of an event.

**Refractory period.** The period of time required for a neuron to return to the polarized state after it depolarizes.

**Relaxation response.** Bodily responses, almost the opposite of the bodily emergency reaction, which involve decreased activity in both the sympathetic and somatic nervous systems and lead to a state of inner tranquility.

**Relearning method.** A method of measuring memory or retention based on percentage of savings computed by determining the difference between the original amount of time or number of trials it took to achieve perfect recall and the relearning amount of time or number of trials to achieve perfect recall after some time lapse period and then dividing by the original amount of time or number of trials it took to achieve perfect recall.

**Reliability.** The degree to which a test produces consistent or stable measures for an individual on different occasions.

**REM.** Rapid eye movements characteristic of sleep during which dreaming occurs.

**Repression.** The unconscious blocking out of memories which may be unpleasant, emotionally disturbing, or in conflict with one's belief system—the psychoanalytic explanation for forgetting.

**Response.** Any behavior—body movement, glandular secretion, or mental activity—that is a result of stimulation.

**Response-cost.** A type of punishment in which the punishing consequence is the removal of some pleasant stimulus situation.

**Response discrimination.** The process that occurs when two or more similar but physically different responses are emitted in a particular situation, and one response is reinforced and maintained while the other responses are extinguished.

**Response generalization.** The emission of a response to a stimulus or in a particular situation that is similar but slightly different than the response originally learned.

**Reticular formation.** A structure in the brain extending through the hindbrain and into the center core of the brain that is important in regulating levels of awareness and that serves as an arousal system to activate large areas of the higher parts of the brain.

**Retina.** The area at the back of the eyeball which contains the receptor cells that are activated by light rays.

**Retrieval.** The process of locating information in memory storage and bringing it into consciousness.

**Retrieval cue.** Any stimulus that helps retrieve a memory.

**Retroactive inhibition.** Interference with remembering previously learned material that is related to subsequent learning.

**Reverberating circuit.** A circuit in the brain formed as sensory information travels from one cell to the next until a full round is made and a structural change occurs so that the circuit may be repeated when cued into.

**Ribonucleic acid (RNA).** A molecule produced in a nerve cell that controls the production of protein molecules and is theorized to be the chemical mediator in memory.

**Risky-shift phenomenon.** The fact that an individual is usually more willing to make riskier decisions as a member of a group than when alone.

**Rods.** Receptor cells on the retina of the eye that are sensitive to brightness or differences in light intensity and are involved in night vision.

**Role.** The behavior displayed by an individual in a certain position or the expected behavior of an individual in a certain position.

**Rule modeling.** Learning to govern one's behavior by the same rules models have been observed to follow.

# S

**Scapegoat.** A person or group bearing the blame for others as in displaced aggression.

**Scattergram.** A visual representation of the correlation of two variables which is a two-dimensional plot of points—each point representing the paired measurements of the two variables.

**Secondary appraisal.** A process related to the perception of a stimulus whereby a person evaluates the action called for and the resources available for the required action.

**Secondary needs.** Needs that an individual has which have only a learned or psychological basis such as need for achievement.

**Secondary process thinking.** In Freud's theory of personality, the ego's way of thinking—the conscious mental activity of the ego.

**Self-actualization.** In Maslow's theory of motivation, the need highest in the hierarchy which is the tendency of an individual to realize his or her maximum potential.

**Self-concept.** A person's perception of the self which is a composite of all the beliefs, feelings, and attitudes one has concerning the self.

**Self-instruction technique.** A technique used in a behavior modification program whereby an individual makes specific comments or suggestions in order to achieve self-selected behavioral outcomes.

**Self-monitoring.** A personality dimension reflecting the degree to which a person's behavior is guided by situational cues. A person with a high self-monitoring score is guided more by the situation than by feelings and thoughts.

**Self-monitoring technique.** A technique used in a behavior modification program to achieve self-selected behavioral outcomes whereby the individual becomes aware of the extent to which he or she engages in a behavior by keeping records.

**Sensorimotor stage.** The first stage in Piaget's theory of intellectual development, the period from birth to approximately two years of age, during which the child learns relationships between sensations and motor responses—the stage that occurs prior to the development of language.

**Sensory memory.** In the structural view of memory, the first level or storage system where information is stored in the sensory register.

**Septal region.** A structure in the core of the brain that when electrically stimulated seems to produce sexual sensations in a person.

**Serial recall.** A method of measuring memory in which an individual is given a list of items (Ebbinghaus used nonsense syllables) to recall in the order learned at a later time.

**Set.** A habit or predisposition to respond in a certain way because of experiences.

**Sex-linked characteristics.** Characteristics of an individual that are determined by the pair of chromosomes containing the genes that determine sex, the X and Y chromosomes.

**Shaping.** Creating a new behavior by reinforcing closer and closer approximations of the desired or target behavior.

**Shift toward polarization.** The tendency of people to shift to a more extreme position when making decisions in the presence of a group.

**Short-term memory.** In the structural view of memory, the second level or storage system where memory is held in the present consciousness.

**Significant difference.** A difference between experimental groups in some measurable characteristic that is great enough that it is unlikely that the difference is due to chance factors.

**Similarity.** One of the processes involved in perceptual organization—the principle that parts seem separate or grouped together depending on how much alike they are.

**Situational approach.** An approach to the study of leadership which looks at the influence, of environmental factors.

**Situationists.** Psychologists who have challenged the trait view of personality and believe that the environment plays a greater role in behavior than internal personality traits.

**Social facilitation.** The phenomenon that the presence of a group increases individual performance.

**Social learning theory.** A larger, more general approach to learning which expands on operant conditioning and focuses on modeling whereby a person learns to do something by watching someone else do it.

**Social psychology.** The specialized area of psychology which deals with the behavior of people in groups and is concerned with how other people influence an individual's behavior.

**Sociobiology.** A recent biological theory of motivation which suggests that behavior is preprogrammed for one and only one function—to ensure the survival of the DNA molecules that make up one's genetic identity.

**Somatic nervous system.** A division of the peripheral nervous system which consists of the spinal nerves and the cranial nerves such as the auditory nerve and the optic nerve.

**Somatization.** A type of somatoform disorder which consists of a pattern of vague, recurring physical complaints, the use of much medication, and the involvement of many physicians.

**Somatoform disorders.** Psychological disorders involving the displacement of anxiety by expressing it through physical symptoms.

**Sperm.** The male gamete or reproductive cell which contains 23 chromosomes.

**Spontaneous recovery.** The reappearance, after a lapse of time following extinction, of a conditioned response.

**Stamps.** In transactional analysis, feelings that are obtained from strokes.

**Standard deviation.** The square root of the variance in a frequency distribution.

**Standardization.** The process of obtaining a distribution of scores for a test from a large sample of people to provide the comparison for determining if an individual's score is average, above average, or below average or for determining the percentile rank of the score.

**Standardized test.** A test that has norms available from a large representative sample of people to provide the comparison for determining if an individual's score is average, above average, or below average or for determining the percentile rank of the score.

**Standard normal curve.** A theoretical, bell-shaped, symmetrical curve (frequency polygon) which represents the distribution of scores for any population.

**State anxiety.** The term used to refer to anxiety that is experienced temporarily in a specific situation.

**Statistics.** A body of scientific methods consisting of mathematical ways of handling data and deciding whether a difference in behavior is attributable to independent variables rather than to chance factors. Also, a collection of numerical facts which have been collected through observation or from other numerical data such as averages, tables, and graphs.

**Status.** An evaluation of the contribution of particular roles to the welfare of the group.

**Stereotyping.** The assigning of identical characteristics to all members of a group, and the maintaining of the stereotype even when faced with conflicting information.

**Stimulant.** Any drug that increases activity in the nervous system.

**Stimulus.** A stimulus is any physical event either internal, such as a pain or thought, or external, such as something heard, seen, felt, or smelled.

**Stimulus control technique.** A technique used in behavior modification programs to achieve self-selected behavioral outcomes in which the environment is designed so that certain cues increase the likelihood that specific behaviors are performed such as selecting a place to relax where there are few cues associated with work.

**Stimulus discrimination.** Learning to differentiate between similar stimuli; recognizing differences between similar stimuli.

**Stimulus generalization.** In conditioning, the principle that when a new stimulus comes to be associated with a stimulus that already elicits a particular response, any stimulus similar to that new stimulus may also elicit the response, even if direct conditioning has not occurred.

**Stimulus motives.** Needs that cause an individual to seek out environmental stimulation which promotes learning such as the need for sensory input, movement, exploration, curiosity, manipulation of objects, and body contact.

**Stingy-shift phenomenon.** The fact that an individual is willing to make a more conservative decision when in a group than when alone.

**Storage.** In the process view of memory, the process of holding information in a system or the process of permanently storing information in a system.

**Stress.** Any situation, physical or psychological, which makes a special demand on the body.

**Stroke.** In transactional analysis, any communication that recognizes one's existence whether the communication is verbal or nonverbal.

**Structuralism.** A view held by early psychologists, Wilhelm Wundt and his followers, that the structure of the mind could be discovered by analyzing conscious sensory experience and reducing it to its basic elements.

**Style approach.** An approach to the study of leadership which looks at the type or style of leadership—autocratic, democratic, or laissez-faire.

**Subjects.** The participants—those whose behavior is observed—in a scientific study.

**Superego.** Freud's term for the part of the personality that consists of an individual's internalized values and moral standards—the conscience.

**Superstitious behavior.** A relationship between a response and reinforcement which occurs when reinforcement follows the response by chance and there is no schedule of reinforcement.

**Survey method.** A scientific method of studying behavior in which questions are usually prepared to which answers are obtained through direct interviews, by mail, or by telephone usually to investigate attitudes, feelings, traits, opinions, or behaviors of large groups of people.

**Sympathetic system.** The subsystem of the autonomic nervous system which is activated in emergency situations, in emotional experience, and in times of stress whether the stress is physical or psychological in nature.

**Synapse.** The small space that separates the terminal branch of one neuron from the dendrites of the next neuron.

## T

**Terminal branches.** Small fibers that extend from the end of an axon of a neuron, each of which has a knob on the end from which chemical substances are released.

**Testes.** The male sex glands that release hormones, primarily androgens.

**Thalamus.** A structure in the forebrain that functions as a relay station for messages coming in from the sense organs and directs the messages to particular areas of the brain.

**Theory.** An integrated set of interrelated hypotheses that satisfactorily explains a specific phenomenon.

**Theory X.** McGregor's label for the theory of managing people based on external direction and control.

**Theory Y.** McGregor's label for the theory of managing people based on concepts of motivation and human nature as an integrative view that everyone is capable of being intrinsically motivated.

**Therapy.** The term used for any attempt by a clinician to bring about desired personality or behavioral changes by applying particular psychological techniques.

**Threshold.** The minimum level of energy that is required for transduction to occur.

**Thyroid gland.** An endocrine gland located in the neck that secretes a hormone that regulates the rate at which energy is produced and used by the body.

**Timbre.** The quality or texture of the sound which is determined by a complex pattern of overtones produced by accompanying sound waves that are different multiples of the basic frequency.

**Time-out.** A type of punishment in which the punishing consequence is the delay for some period of time of some pleasant stimulus situation.

**Trace decay theory.** An explanation of forgetting which proposes that the strength of the memory is weakened with the passing of time, making the memory itself harder to retrieve.

**Trait anxiety.** The term that is used to refer to the general level of anxiety that is characteristically exhibited by an individual over time.

**Trait approach.** An approach to the study of leadership which is concerned with the traits or characteristics of the leader.

**Transaction.** In transactional analysis, a social interaction that consists of a statement or stimulus directed toward a person and that person's response.

**Transactional analysis.** A system for analyzing the transactions or basic units of communication in individual-to-individual relationships.

**Transcendental meditation.** A simple technique introduced by Maharishi Maheah Yogi which produces relaxation, heightened awareness, and more efficient performance of both mental and manual skill tasks.

**Transduction.** A process whereby energy received from the environment is translated at the sense organ level and relayed to the peripheral nervous system.

**Trichromats.** Those individuals who have all three kinds of cones and have normal vision.

# U

**Ulterior transaction.** In transactional analysis, a transaction or social interaction of the complementary type that has an unspoken or hidden meaning.

**Unconditioned response.** A response brought forth by an unconditioned (unlearned) stimulus; a reflex response.

**Unconditioned stimulus.** A stimulus that always brings forth a specific response, even the first time it is presented.

**Unconscious motivation.** Any motivation for behavior (motive, drive, or need) one is acting to satisfy without knowledge or awareness of the need as a source of the behavior.

**Undifferentiated or simple schizophrenia.** The type of schizophrenia which is characterized by several or all of the symptoms of psychosis—hallucinations, delusions, and inappropriate affect and perhaps withdrawal.

# V

**Valence.** The value an individual places on a particular outcome.

**Validity.** The extent to which a test measures what it is designed to measure.

**Value.** The worth of something determined by how positively or negatively one feels about that something.

**Variable.** Any characteristic, attribute, or event that may vary in amount when measured or may be present or absent.

**Variable interval schedule.** An intermittent schedule of reinforcement in which a response is reinforced after a variable time period.

**Variable ratio schedule.** An intermittent schedule of reinforcement in which a response is reinforced after a variable number of responses have been emitted.

**Variance.** A measure of variability which reflects the dispersion of the scores composing a set of data that is calculated by determining how much each score deviates from the mean of all the scores, squaring each deviation, then finding the average of the squared deviations.

**VIE theory.** A theory of work motivation based on expectation of reward, perceived value of direct outcomes, and instrumentality—indirect or second level outcomes and their value.

**Visual cliff.** An apparatus with a glass surface where a simulated drop-off appears used to test depth perception in infants.

**Voice stress analyzer.** A device used to replay the recording of a person's voice four times slower than the recorded speed that produces voice printout in graphic form.

# W

**Wheel.** A basic structure of group communication whereby all communication is channeled through one person, the hub of the wheel.

# X, Y, and Z

**Y.** One of the four basic structures of group communication in which communication starts with one person and branches out like an inverted Y, the branches of which may branch out to form other inverted Y structures. Usually, it is the most typical and most efficient communication structure of large groups.

**Yoga.** A form of meditation derived from an Eastern religion which can induce a state of inner tranquility in which heart rate and breathing rate are reduced and brain wave patterns are indicative of relaxation.

# REFERENCE LIST

Adorno, T. W., Frenkel-Brunswik, E., Levinson, D. J., & Sanford, R. N. *The authoritarian personality.* New York: Harper & Row, 1950.

Alderfer, C. P. An empirical test of a new theory of human needs. *Organizational Behavior and Human Performance,* 1969, *4,* 142-175.

_____. Change processes in organizations. In M. D. Dunnette (Ed.), *Handbook of industrial and organizational psychology.* Chicago: Rand McNally, 1976.

Allport, G. W. *Personality: A psychological interpretation.* New York: Holt and Co., 1937.

_____. *ABC's of scapegoating.* New York: Anti-Defamation League of B'nai B'rith, 1944.

American Dental Assistants Association, Personal communication, April 11, 1977, from the Executive Director, 211 East Chicago Ave., Chicago, Illinois 60611. In Fernald, L. D., & Fernald, P. S. *Introduction to psychology* (4th ed.). Boston: Houghton Mifflin, 1978.

American Psychiatric Association. *Diagnostic and statistical manual of mental disorders* (3rd ed.). Washington, D. C.: American Psychiatric Association, 1980.

Amoore, J. E., Johnston, J. W., Jr., & Rubin, M. The stereochemical theory of odor. *Scientific American,* 1964, *210*(2), 42-49.

Argyle, M., Lefebvre, L., & Cook, M. The meaning of five patterns of gaze. *European Journal of Social Psychology,* 1974, *4,* 125-136.

Arnold, M. B. *Emotion and personality* (2 vols.) New York: Columbia University Press, 1960.

Asch, S. E. *Social psychology.* New York: Prentice-Hall, 1952.

Atchison, T. J., & Lefferts, E. A. The prediction of turnover using Herzberg's job satisfaction technique. *Personnel Psychology,* 1972, *25,* 53-64.

Atkinson, J. W. *An introduction to motivation.* Princeton, N. J.: Van Nostrand, 1964.

Atkinson, R. C., & Shiffrin, R. M. Human memory: A proposed system and its control processes. In K. W. Spence & J. T. Spence (Eds.), *The psychology of learning and motivation: Advances in research and theory* (Vol. 2). New York: Academic Press, 1968.

_____. The control of short-term memory. *Scientific American,* 1971, *225*(2), 82-90.

Ausubel, D. P., & Youssef, M. The effect of spaced repetition on meaningful retention. *Journal of General Psychology,* 1965, *73,* 147-150.

Axelrod, J. Neurotransmitters. *Scientific American,* 1974, *230*(6), 58-71.

Baddeley, A. D., & Hitch, G. Working memory. In H. G. Bower (Ed.), *The psychology of learning and motivation* (Vol. 8). New York: Academic Press, 1974.

Bales, R. F. *Personality and interpersonal behavior.* New York: Holt, Rinehart and Winston, 1970.

Ball, W., & Tronick, E. Infant responses to impending collision: Optical and real. *Science,* 1971, *171,* 818-820.

Bandura, A. Influence of models' reinforcement contingencies on the acquisition of imitative responses. *Journal of Personality and Social Psychology,* 1965, *1,* 589-595.

_____. *Social learning theory.* Englewood Cliffs, N. J.: Prentice-Hall, 1977.

Bard, P. A. A diencephalic mechanism for the expression of rage with special reference to the sympathetic nervous system. *American Journal of Physiology,* 1928, *84,* 490-515.

Barrett, G. V. Research models of the future for industrial and organizational psychology. *Personnel Psychology*, 1972, *25*, 1-17.

Barrow, G. M., & Smith, P. A. *Aging, ageism, and society*. St. Paul, Minn.: West, 1979.

Bass, B. M., & Barrett, G. V. *Man, work and organizations*. Boston: Allyn and Bacon, 1972.

——————————————————. *People, work and organizations* (2nd ed.). Boston: Allyn and Bacon, 1981.

Beer, M. Needs and need satisfaction among clerical workers in complex and routine jobs. *Personnel Psychology*, 1968, *21*, 209-222.

Benson, H. *The relaxation response*. New York: Morrow, 1975.

——————————, Kotch, J. B., Crassweller, K. D., & Greenwood, M. M. Historical and clinical considerations of the relaxation response. *American Scientist*, 1977, *65*, 441-445.

Berne, E. L. *Transactional analysis in psychotherapy*. New York: Grove Press, 1961.

Birdwhistell, R. L. *Introduction to kinesics*. Louisville, Ky.: University of Louisville Press, 1952.

Boneau, C. A., & Cuca, J. M. An overview of psychology's human resources. *American Psychologist*, 1974, *29*, 821-839.

Bourne, L. E., Jr., & Ekstrand, B. R. *Psychology: Its principles and meanings* (4th ed.). New York: Holt, Rinehart and Winston, 1982.

Broadbent, D. E. Effects of noise on behavior. In C. M. Harris (Ed.), *Handbook of noise control*. New York: McGraw-Hill, 1957.

Brown, R. W. *Social psychology*. New York: Free Press, 1965.

Burke, R. J. Occupational and life strains, satisfaction and mental health. *Journal of Business Administration*, 1969/70, *1*(2), 35-41.

Buss, A. H., & Plomin, R. *A temperament theory of personality development*. New York: Wiley, 1975.

Campbell, J. P., Dunnette, M. D., Lawler, E. E., III, & Weick, K. E., Jr. *Managerial behavior, performance, and effectiveness*. New York: McGraw-Hill, 1970.

Cannon, W. B. The James-Lange theory of emotions: A critical examination and an alternative theory. *The American Journal of Psychology*, 1927, *39*, 106-124.

Cartwright, R. D. *A primer on sleep and dreaming*. Reading, Mass.: Addison-Wesley, 1978.

Cattell, R. B. *Description and measurement of personality*. New York: World, 1946.

——————————. *Abilities: Their structure, growth, and action*. Boston: Houghton Mifflin, 1971.

Chruden, H. J., & Sherman, A. W., Jr. *Personnel management* (6th ed.). Cincinnati: South-Western, 1980.

Cofer, C. N., & Appley, M. H. *Motivation: Theory and research*. New York: Wiley, 1964.

Cole, N. S., Whitney, D. R., & Holland, J. L. A spatial configuration of occupations. *Journal of Vocational Behavior*, 1971, *1*, 1-9.

Coleman, J. C., & Hammen, C. L. *Contemporary psychology and effective behavior*. Glenview, Ill.: Scott, Foresman, 1974.

Combs, A. W., & Snygg, D. *Individual behavior*. New York: Harper, 1959.

Cook, S. W. Interpersonal and attitudinal outcomes in cooperating interracial groups. *Journal of Research and Development in Education*, 1978, *12*, 97-113.

Coombs, J. A. *A nationwide study of women in United States dental schools*, Doctoral dissertation. Cambridge, Mass.: Harvard University, 1975.

Coppen, A. Indoleamines and affective disorders. *Journal of Psychiatric Research*, 1972, *9*, 163-171.

Cotman, C. W., & McGaugh, J. L. *Behavioral neuroscience.* New York: Academic Press, 1980.

Craik, F. I. M., & Lockhart, R. S. Levels of processing: A framework for memory research. *Journal of Verbal Learning and Verbal Behavior,* 1972, *11,* 671-684.

Crockenberg, S. B. Creativity tests: A boon or boondoggle for education? *Review of Educational Research,* 1972, *42,* 27-45.

Dabbs, J. M., Jr., & Leventhal, H. Effects of varying the recommendations in a fear-arousing communication. *Journal of Personality and Social Psychology,* 1966, *4,* 525-531.

Darwin, C. *On the origin of the species by means of natural selection.* London: Murray, 1859.

————————. *The expression of the emotions in man and animals.* London: Murray, 1872.

Davis, C. M. Results of self-selection of diets by young children. *Canadian Medical Association Journal,* 1939, *41,* 257-261.

Davis, J. D., Gallagher, R. L., & Ladove, R. Food intake controlled by a blood factor. *Science,* 1967, *156,* 1247-1248.

Deci, E. L. Intrinsic motivation, extrinsic reinforcement, and inequity. *Journal of Personality and Social Psychology,* 1972, *22,* 113-120.

Deese, J. *The psychology of learning.* New York: McGraw-Hill, 1958.

Delgado, J. M. R. *Physical control of the mind.* New York: Harper & Row, 1969.

Derlega, V. J., & Janda, L. H. *Personal adjustment.* Morristown, N. J.: Silver Burdett, 1978.

DiVesta, F. J., & Thompson, G. G. *Educational psychology: Instruction and behavioral change.* New York: Appleton-Century-Crofts, 1970.

Dowling, W. F. Job redesign on the assembly line: Farewell to blue-collar blues. In D. R. Hampton, C. E. Summer, & R. A. Webber, *Organizational behavior and the practice of management* (3rd ed.). Glenview, Ill.: Scott, Foresman, 1978.

DuBrin, A. *Effective business psychology.* Reston, Va.: Reston, 1980.

————————. *Human relations: A job oriented approach* (2nd ed.). Reston, Va.: Reston, 1981.

Duffy, E. *Activation and behavior.* New York: Wiley, 1962.

Dunnette, M. D. Toward fusion. In M. D. Dunnette (Ed.), *Handbook of industrial and organizational psychology.* Chicago: Rand McNally, 1976.

———————————— (Ed.). *Handbook of industrial and organizational psychology.* Chicago: Rand McNally, 1976.

Ebbinghaus, H. *Über das Gedächtnis* (On Memory). Leipzig: Duncker & Humblot, 1885.

Edwards, W. The theory of decision making. *Psychological Bulletin,* 1954, *51,* 380-417.

Ekman, P. The universal smile: Face muscles talk every language. *Psychology Today,* September 1975, pp. 35-36.

Elardo, R., Bradley, R., & Caldwell, B. M. The relation of infants' home environments to mental test performance from six to thirty-six months: A longitudinal analysis. *Child Development,* 1975, *46,* 71-76.

————————————————————————————. A longitudinal study of the relation of infants' home environments to language development at age three. *Child Development,* 1977, *48,* 595-603.

Elias, M. F., Elias, P. K., & Elias, J. W. *Basic processes in adult developmental psychology.* St. Louis: Mosby, 1977.

Engel, M. Children who work. *Archives of General Psychiatry,* 1967, *17,* 291-297.

Epstein, A. N., Fitzsimons, J. T., & Simons, B. Drinking caused by the intracranial injection of angiotensin into the rat. *Journal of Physiology* (London), 1969, *200,* 98P-100P.

Erikson, E. H. *Childhood and society* (2nd ed.). New York: Norton, 1963.

Eysenck, H. J. *Dimensions of personality.* London: Kegan Paul, 1947.

_____. The organization of personality. *Journal of Personality*, 1951, *20*, 101-117.

Fantz, R. L. The origin of form perception. *Scientific American*, 1961, *204*(5), 66-72.

Ferguson, L. W. The development of industrial psychology. In B. Von Haller Gilmer (Ed.), *Industrial psychology.* New York: McGraw-Hill, 1961.

Fernald, L. D., & Fernald, P. S. *Introduction to psychology* (4th ed.). Boston: Houghton Mifflin, 1978.

Ferster, C. B., & Skinner, B. F. *Schedules of reinforcement.* New York: Appleton-Century-Crofts, 1957.

Festinger, L. A theory of social comparison processes. *Human Relations*, 1954, *7*, 117-140.

_____. *A theory of cognitive dissonance.* Evanston, Ill.: Row, Peterson, 1957.

_____. *A theory of cognitive dissonance.* Palo Alto, Calif.: Stanford University Press, 1957.

_____, & Carlsmith, J. M. Cognitive consequences of forced compliance. *Journal of Abnormal and Social Psychology*, 1959, *58*, 203-210.

Fiedler, F. E. *A theory of leadership effectiveness.* New York: McGraw-Hill, 1967.

Finkelman, J. M., & Glass, D. C. Reappraisal of the relationship between noise and human performance by means of a subsidiary task measure. *Journal of Applied Psychology*, 1970, *54*, 211-213.

Frazier, D. Industry finding value in charting biorhythms. *The Houston Post*, July 25, 1977, p. 14A.

Freedman, J. L. *Introductory psychology.* Reading, Mass.: Addison-Wesley, 1978.

_____, Sears, D. O., & Carlsmith, J. M. *Social psychology* (3rd ed.). Englewood Cliffs, N. J.: Prentice-Hall, 1978.

_____. *Social psychology* (4th ed.). Englewood Cliffs, N. J.: Prentice-Hall, 1981.

French, E. G. Effects of the interaction of motivation and feedback on task performance. In J. W. Atkinson (Ed.), *Motives in fantasy, action and society.* New York: Van Nostrand, 1958.

Freud, S. *The standard edition of the complete psychological works.* J. Strachey (Ed.). London: Hogarth Press, 1953.

Friedman, M., & Rosenman, R. H. *Type A behavior and your heart.* New York: Knopf, 1974.

Funkenstein, D. H. The physiology of fear and anger. *Scientific American*, 1955, *192*(5), 74-80.

Ghiselli, E. E. *The validity of occupational aptitude tests.* New York: Wiley, 1966.

Gibb, C. A. Leadership. In G. Lindzey & E. Aronson (Eds.), *Handbook of social psychology* (2nd ed.). Reading, Mass.: Addison-Wesley, 1969.

Gibson, E. *Principles of perceptual learning and development.* New York: Appleton-Century-Crofts, 1969.

Ginzberg, E. Toward a theory of occupational choice. *Occupations*, 1952, *30*, 491-494.

_____. The development of a developmental theory of occupational choice. In W. H. VanHoose and J. J. Pietrofesa (Eds.), *Counseling and guidance in the twentieth century.* Boston: Houghton Mifflin, 1970.

Glass, D. C., & Singer, J. E. *Urban stress: Experiments on noise and social stressors.* New York: Academic Press, 1972.

Goleman, D., Engen, T., & Davids, A. *Introductory psychology* (2nd ed.). New York: Random House, 1982.

Guilford, J. P. Factorial angles to psychology. *Psychological Review*, 1961, *68*, 1-20.

_____. *The nature of human intelligence*. New York: McGraw-Hill, 1967.

_____, & Hoepfner, R. *The analysis of intelligence*. New York: McGraw-Hill, 1971.

Guion, R. M. Some definitions of morale. In E. A. Fleishman (Ed.), *Studies in personnel and industrial psychology*. Homewood, Ill.: Dorsey, 1961.

Guttman, L. The problem of attitude and opinion measurement. In S. A. Stouffer, et al. (Eds.), *Measurement and prediction*. Princeton, N. J.: Princeton University Press, 1950.

Haire, M. Projective techniques in market research. *Journal of Marketing*, 1950, *14*, 649-656.

Hall, D. T., & Nougaim, K. E. An examination of Maslow's need hierarchy in an organizational setting. *Organizational Behavior and Human Performance*, 1968, *3*, 12-35.

Hamner, W. C., & Organ, D. W. *Organizational behavior: An applied psychological approach*. Dallas: Business Publications, 1978.

Hampton, D. R., Summer, C. E., & Webber, R. A. *Organizational behavior and the practice of management* (3rd ed.). Glenview Ill.: Scott, Foresman, 1978.

Harari, H., & Kaplan, R. M. *Social psychology: Basic and applied*. Monterey, Calif.: Brooks/Cole, 1982.

Harlow, H. F. The nature of love. *American Psychologist*, 1958, *13*, 673-685.

Harlow, M. K., & Harlow, H. F. Affection in primates. *Discovery*, 1966, *27*, 11-17.

Hathaway, S. R., & McKinley, J. C. *The Minnesota Multiphasic Personality Inventory* (Rev. ed.). New York: Psychological Corporation, 1967.

Hebb, D. O. *The organization of behavior*. New York: Wiley, 1949.

Held, R., & Freedman, S. J. Plasticity in human sensorimotor control. *Science*, 1963, *142*, 455-462.

Helms, D. B., & Turner, J. S. *Exploring child behavior*. Philadelphia: Saunders, 1976.

Hepner, H. W. *Psychology applied to life and work*. Englewood Cliffs, N. J.: Prentice-Hall, 1973.

Heron, W. The pathology of boredom. *Scientific American*, 1957, *196*(1), 52-56.

Herzberg, F. One more time: How do you motivate employees? *Harvard Business Review*, January-February 1968, *46*(1), 53-62.

_____, Mausner, B., Peterson, R., & Capwell, D. F. *Job attitudes: Research and opinion*. Pittsburgh: Psychological Service of Pittsburgh, 1957.

Hess, E. H. The role of pupil size in communication. *Scientific American*, 1975, *233*(5), 110-119.

_____, & Polt, J. M. Pupil size as related to interest value of visual stimuli. *Science*, 1960, *132*, 349-350.

Higgins, J. M. *Human relations: Concepts and skills*. New York: Random House, 1982.

Hilgard, E. R., Atkinson, R. L., & Atkinson, R. C. *Introduction to psychology* (7th ed.). New York: Harcourt Brace Jovanovich, 1979.

Hilts, P. J. *Behavior modification*. New York: Harper's Magazine Press, 1974.

Hintzman, D. S. Theoretical implications of the spacing effect. In R. L. Solso (Ed.), *Theories in cognitive psychology: The Loyola Symposium*. Hillsdale, N. J.: Erlbaum, 1974.

Hobson, J. A., & McCarley, R. W. The brain as a dream state generator: An activation-synthesis hypothesis of the dream process. *American Journal of Psychiatry*, 1977, *134*, 1335-1348.

Hoffman, L. R., & Maier, N. R. F. Quality and acceptance of problem solutions by members of homogeneous and heterogeneous groups. *Journal of Abnormal and Social Psychology,* 1961, *62,* 401-407.

Hoffman, L. W. Fear of success in males and females. *Journal of Consulting and Clinical Psychology,* 1974, *42,* 353-358.

Holland, J. L. Some explorations of a theory of vocational choice: I. One- and two-year longitudinal studies. *Psychological Monographs,* 1962, 76(26, Whole No. 545).

_____. Explorations of a theory of vocational choice: VI. A longitudinal study using a sample of typical college students. *Journal of Applied Psychology Monograph,* 1968, *52*(1, Pt. 2).

_____. The present status of a theory of vocational choice. In J. M. Whiteley & A. Resnikoff (Eds.), *Perspectives on vocational development.* Falls Church, Va.: American Personnel and Guidance Association, 1972.

_____. *Making vocational choices: A theory of careers.* Englewood Cliffs, N. J.: Prentice-Hall, 1973.

Holland, M. K. *Introductory psychology.* Lexington, Mass.: D. C. Heath, 1981.

Hollander, E. P. Conformity, status, and idiosyncrasy credit. *Psychological Review,* 1958, *65,* 117-127.

Holmes, T. H. Life situations, emotions, and disease. *Psychosomatics,* 1978, *19,* 747-754.

_____, & Rahe, R. H. The social readjustment rating scale. *Journal of Psychosomatic Research,* 1967, *11,* 213-218.

Holzman, P. S., & Gardner, R. W. Leveling, sharpening, and memory organization. *Journal of Abnormal and Social Psychology,* 1960, *61,* 176-180.

Hurvich, L. M., & Jameson, D. Opponent processes as a model of neural organization. *American Psychologist,* 1974, *29,* 88-102.

Hyden, H. Biochemical aspects of learning and memory. In K. Pribram (Ed.), *On the biology of learning.* New York: Harcourt Brace Jovanovich, 1969.

Iversen, L. L. The chemistry of the brain. *Scientific American,* 1979, *241*(3), 134-149.

Izard, C. E. *Human emotions.* New York: Plenum, 1977.

Jacobs, P. A., Brunton, M., Melville, M. M., Brittain, R. P., & McClemont, W. F. Aggressive behaviour, mental sub-normality, and the *XYY* male. *Nature,* 1965, *208,* 1351-1352.

Jacoby, J. Toward a definition of consumer psychology: One psychologist's view. *Proceedings of the 77th Annual Convention of the American Psychological Association,* 1969, Part 2, pp. 987-988.

_____. Consumer and industrial psychology: Prospects for theory corroboration and mutual contributions. In M. D. Dunnette (Ed.), *Handbook of industrial and organizational psychology.* Chicago: Rand McNally, 1976.

James, W. What is an emotion? *Mind,* 1884, *9,* 188-205.

Janda, L. H., & Klenke-Hamel, K. E. *Psychology: Its study and uses.* New York: St. Martin's Press, 1982.

Janis, I. L. *Victims of groupthink: A psychological study of foreign-policy decisions and fiascoes.* Boston: Houghton Mifflin, 1972.

_____, & Feshbach, S. Effects of fear-arousing communications. *Journal of Abnormal and Social Psychology,* 1953, *48,* 78-92.

_____, & Mann, L. *Decision making.* New York: Free Press, 1977.

Jencks, C., Smith, M., Acland, H., Bane, M. J., Cohen, D., Gintis, H., Heyns, B., & Michelson, S. *Inequality: A reassessment of the effect of family and schooling in America.* New York: Basic Books, 1972.

Kagan, J. Personality development. In I. Janis (Ed.), *Personality dynamics.* New York: Harcourt Brace Jovanovich, 1969.

Kahn, R. L. Productivity and job satisfaction. *Personnel Psychology*, 1960, *13*, 275-287.

Kass, L. R. The new biology: What price relieving man's estate? *Science*, 1971, *174*, 779-788.

Kazdin, A. E. *Behavior modification in applied settings*. Homewood, Ill.: Dorsey Press, 1975.

Kimble, D. P. *Psychology as a biological science*. Santa Monica, Calif.: Goodyear, 1977.

Klatzky, R. L. *Human memory: Structures and processes*. San Francisco: Freeman, 1975.

Kleitman, N. Patterns of dreaming. *Scientific American*, 1960, *203*(5), 82-88.

_____. *Sleep and wakefulness* (2nd ed.). Chicago: University of Chicago Press, 1963.

Kohler, I. Experiments with goggles. *Scientific American*, 1962, *206*(5), 62-72.

Korchin, S. J. *Modern clinical psychology*. New York: Basic Books, 1976.

Kornhauser, A. *Mental health of the industrial worker*. New York: Wiley, 1965.

Kübler-Ross, E. *On death and dying*. New York: Macmillan, 1969.

Laing, R. D. *The politics of experience*. New York: Pantheon, 1967.

Laird, D. A., Laird, E. C., Fruehling, R. T., & Swift, W. P. *Psychology: Human relations and motivation* (5th ed.). New York: McGraw-Hill, 1975.

Lamm, H., & Myers, D. G. Group-induced polarization of attitudes and behavior. In L. Berkowitz (Ed.), *Advances in experimental social psychology* (Vol. 11). New York: Academic Press, 1978.

Lange, C. G. *[The emotions]* (English translation). Baltimore: Williams & Wilkins, 1922. (Originally published, 1885).

Latané, B., & Darley, J. M. *The unresponsive bystander: Why doesn't he help?* New York: Appleton-Century-Crofts, 1970.

Lazarus, R. S. *The riddle of man*. Englewood Cliffs, N. J.: Prentice-Hall, 1974.

Leavitt, H. J. Some effects of certain communication patterns on group performance. *Journal of Abnormal and Social Psychology*, 1951, *46*, 38-50.

Lekberg, C. The tyranny of qwerty. *Saturday Review*, September 30, 1972, pp. 37-40.

Lepper, M. R., Greene, D., & Nisbett, R. E. Undermining children's intrinsic interest with extrinsic reward: A test of the 'overjustification' hypothesis. *Journal of Personality and Social Psychology*, 1973, *28*, 129-137.

Leventhal, H. Findings and theory in the study of fear communications. In L. Berkowitz (Ed.), *Advances in experimental social psychology* (Vol. 5). New York: Academic, 1970.

Levinson, D. J. *The seasons of a man's life*. New York: Knopf, 1978.

Lewin, K. *[A dynamic theory of personality]* (D. K. Adams & K. E. Zener, trans.). New York: McGraw-Hill, 1935.

Liebeskind, J. C., & Paul, L. A. Psychological and physiological mechanisms of pain. *Annual Review of Psychology*, 1977, *28*, 41-60.

Likert, R. A technique for the measurement of attitudes. *Archives of Psychology*, 1932, *1*(1, whole No. 140), 5-55.

Lippit, R. O. An experimental study on the effect of democratic and authoritarian group atmospheres. *University of Iowa Studies in Child Welfare*, 1940, *16*(3), 43-195.

Livant, W. P. Grammar in the story reproductions of levelers and sharpeners. *Bulletin of the Menninger Clinic*, 1962, *26*, 283-287.

London, P. *Beginning psychology* (Rev. ed.). Homewood, Ill.: Dorsey Press, 1978.

Marquis, D. G. Individual responsibility and group decisions involving risk. *Industrial Management Review*, 1962, *3*, 8-23.

Martindale, C. Creativity, consciousness and cortical arousal. *Journal of Altered States of Consciousness*, 1978, *3*, 69-87.

Maslow, A. H. *Motivation and personality*. New York: Harper & Row, 1954.

——————————. *Motivation and personality* (2nd ed.). New York: Harper & Row, 1970.

McClelland, D. C. *The achieving society*. Princeton, N. J.: Van Nostrand, 1961.

——————————. Business drive and national achievement. *Harvard Business Review*, July-August 1962, *40*(4), 99-112.

——————————. Achievement and entrepreneurship. *Journal of Personality and Social Psychology*, 1965, *1*, 389-392.

McConnell, J. V. *Understanding human behavior* (2nd ed.). New York: Holt, Rinehart and Winston, 1974.

McGeoch, J. A., & Irion, A. L. *The psychology of human learning*. New York: Longmans Green, 1952.

McGregor, D. M. *The human side of enterprise*. New York: McGraw-Hill, 1960.

McGrew, J. M. How 'open' are multiple-dwelling units? *The Journal of Social Psychology*, 1967, *72*, 223-226.

McGuire, W. J. The nature of attitudes and attitude change. In G. Lindzey & E. Aronson (Eds.), *The handbook of social psychology* (2nd ed., Vol. 3). Reading, Mass.: Addison-Wesley, 1969.

Mehrabian, A. *Public places and private spaces: The psychology of work, play, and living environments*. New York: Basic Books, 1976.

Melzack, R., & Wall, P. D. Pain mechanisms: A new theory. *Science*, 1965, *150*, 971-979.

Milgram, S. Behavioral study of obedience. *Journal of Abnormal and Social Psychology*, 1963, *67*, 371-378.

Miller, G. On turning psychology over to the unwashed. APA paper, 1969. In D. Coon, *Introduction to psychology: Exploration and applications*. Los Angeles: West, 1977.

Miller, L. K. *Principles of everyday behavior analysis*. Monterey, Calif.: Brooks/Cole, 1975.

Miller, N. E., & DiCara, L. Instrumental learning of heart rate changes in curarized rats: Shaping and specificity to discriminative stimulus. *Journal of Comparative and Physiological Psychology*, 1967, *63*, 12-19.

Morgan, C. T., King, R. A. & Robinson, N. M. *Introduction to psychology* (6th ed.). New York: McGraw-Hill, 1979.

Morgan, R. *Introduction to psychology: Self-instructional, unit I*. Palo Alto, Calif.: Westinghouse Learning Press, 1970.

Morris, C. G. *Psychology: An introduction*. Englewood Cliffs, N. J.: Prentice-Hall, 1979.

Motowidlo, S. J., & Borman, W. C. Relationships between military morale, motivation, satisfaction, and unit effectiveness. *Journal of Applied Psychology*, 1978, *63*, 47-52.

Mott, P. E., Mann, F. C., McLoughlin, Q., & Warwick, D. P. *Shift work*. Ann Arbor, Mich.: University of Michigan, 1965.

Myers, M. S. *Every employee a manager*. New York: McGraw-Hill, 1970.

Nadler, D. A., & Lawler, E. E., III. Motivation—a diagnostic approach. In J. R. Hackman, E. E. Lawler, III, & L. W. Porter (Eds.), *Perspectives on behavior in organizations*. New York: McGraw-Hill, 1977.

Napier, R., & Gershenfeld, M. *Groups: Theory and experience*. Boston: Houghton Mifflin, 1973.

Olton, D. S. Spatial memory. *Scientific American*, 1977, *236*(6), 82-98.

Osgood, C. E., Suci, G. J., & Tannenbaum, P. H. *The measurement of meaning*. Urbana: University of Illinois Press, 1957.

Paivio, A. Language and knowledge of the world. *Educational Researcher*, 1974, 3(9), 5-12.

Pavlov, I. P. *[Conditioned reflexes]* (G. V. Anrep, trans.). London: Oxford University Press, 1927.

Peak, H. Attitude and motivation. In M. R. Jones (Ed.), *Nebraska Symposium on Motivation* (Vol. 3). Lincoln: University of Nebraska Press, 1955.

Pennock, G. A. Industrial research at Hawthorne. *Personnel Journal*, 1930, 8, 296-313.

Phillips, J. D. Report on discussion 66. *Adult Education Journal*, 1948, 7, 181-182.

Piaget, J. *[The origins of intelligence in children]* (M. Cook, trans.). New York: International Universities Press, 1953.

Plutchik, R. *The emotions: Facts, theories, and a new model.* New York: Random House, 1962.

——————————. Emotions, evolution, and adaptive processes. In M. B. Arnold (Ed.), *Feelings and emotions: The Loyola symposium.* New York: Academic Press, 1970.

——————————. *Emotion: A psychoevolutionary synthesis.* New York: Harper & Row, 1980.

Porter, L. W., & Lawler, E. E., III. *Managerial attitudes and performance.* Homewood, Ill.: Dorsey-Irwin, 1968.

Premack, D. Reinforcement theory. In D. Levine (Ed.), *Nebraska Symposium on Motivation* (Vol. 13). Lincoln: University of Nebraska Press, 1965.

Pylyshyn, Z. W. What the mind's eye tells the mind's brain: A critique of mental imagery. *Psychological Bulletin*, 1973, 80, 1-24.

Rathus, S. A. *Psychology.* New York: Holt, Rinehart and Winston, 1981.

Rehm, L. P. Mood, pleasant events, and unpleasant events. *Journal of Consulting and Clinical Psychology*, 1978, 46, 854-859.

Robinson, F. P. *Effective behavior.* New York: Harper & Row, 1941.

Roethlisberger, F. J., & Dickson, W. J. *Management and the worker.* Cambridge, Mass.: Harvard University Press, 1939.

Rogers, C. R. *On becoming a person: A therapist's view of psychotherapy.* Boston: Houghton Mifflin, 1961.

Rosenblatt, J. S. The development of maternal responsiveness in the rat. *American Journal of Orthopsychiatry*, 1969, 39, 36-56.

Rosenfeld, L. *Now that we're all here: Relations in small groups.* Columbus, Ohio: Merrill, 1976.

Ross, I. C., & Zander, A. Need satisfactions and employee turnover. *Personnel Psychology*, 1957, 10, 327-338.

Rotter, J. B. The role of the psychological situation in determining the direction of human behavior. In M. R. Jones (Ed.), *Nebraska Symposium on Motivation* (Vol. 3). Lincoln: University of Nebraska Press, 1955.

——————————. Generalized expectancies for internal versus external control of reinforcement. *Psychological Monographs*, 1966, 80(1, Whole No. 609).

Rubin, Z., & McNeil, E. B. *The psychology of being human.* New York: Harper & Row, 1981.

Ruch, F. L., & Zimbardo, P. G. *Psychology and life* (8th ed.). Glenview, Ill.: Scott, Foresman, 1971.

Rush, H. M. F., & Wikstrom, W. S. The reception of behavioral science in industry. *The Conference Board Record*, 1969, 6(9), 45-54.

Sackeim, H. A., Gur, R. C., & Saucy, M. C. Emotions are expressed more intensely on the left side of the face. *Science*, 1978, 202, 434-436.

Salapatek, P. Pattern perception in early infancy. In L. B. Cohen & P. Salapatek (Eds.). *Infant perception: From sensation to cognition* (Vol. 1). New York: Academic Press, 1975.

Sarnoff, I., & Zimbardo, P. G. Anxiety, fear, and social affiliation. *Journal of Abnormal and Social Psychology,* 1961, *62,* 356-363.

Scarr, S., & Weinberg, R. IQ test performance of black children adopted by white families. *American Psychologist,* 1976, *31,* 726-739.

Schachter, S. *The psychology of affiliation.* Standford, Calif.: Stanford Univeristy Press, 1959.

_____, & Singer, J. E. Cognitive, social, and physiological determinants, of emotional state. *Psychological Review,* 1962, *69,* 379-399.

Schwartz, G. E. Biofeedback, self-regulation, and the patterning of physiological processes. *American Scientist,* 1975, *63,* 314-324.

Segall, M. H., Campbell, D. T. & Herskovits, M. J. *The influence of culture on visual perception.* Indianapolis: Bobbs-Merrill, 1966.

Seidenberg, B., & Snadowsky, A. *Social psychology: An introduction.* New York: The Free Press, 1976.

Selye, H. *The stress of life.* New York: McGraw-Hill, 1956.

_____. *The stress of life* (Rev. ed.). New York: McGraw-Hill, 1976.

Senden, M. V. *[Space and sight]* (P. Heath, trans.). New York: Free Press, 1960.

Shapiro, D. H., Jr., & Zifferblatt, S. M. Zen meditation and behavioral self-control: Similarities, differences, and clinical applications. *American Psychologist,* 1976, *31,* 519-532.

Sharma, J. Organizational communications: A linking process. *The Personnel Administrator,* 1979, *24*(7), 35-39; 43.

Sheldon, W. H. *The varieties of human physique: An introduction to constitutional psychology.* New York: Harper & Row, 1940.

Shepard, R. N., & Metzler, J. Mental rotation of three-dimensional objects. *Science,* 1971, *171,* 701-703.

Sistrunk, F., & McDavid, J. W. Sex variable in conforming behavior. *Journal of Personality and Social Psychology,* 1971, *17,* 200-207.

Skeels, H. M. Adult status of children with contrasting early life experience: A follow-up study. *Monographs of the Society for Research in Child Development,* 1966, *31*(3), 1-65.

Skinner, B. F. 'Superstition' in the pigeon. *Journal of Experimental Psychology,* 1948, *38,* 168-172.

_____. *Science and human behavior.* New York: Macmillan, 1953.

_____. Pigeons in a pelican. *American Psychologist,* 1960, *15,* 28-37.

Smith, P. C., Kendall, L. M., & Hulin, C. L. *The measurement of satisfaction in work and retirement.* Chicago: Rand McNally, 1969.

Snyder, S. H. Opiate receptors and internal opiates. *Scientific American,* 1977, *236*(3), 44-56.

Spearman, C. 'General intelligence' objectively determined and measured. *The American Journal of Psychology,* 1904, *15,* 201-293.

Spielberger, C. D. The effects of anxiety on complex learning and academic achievement. In C. D. Spielberger (Ed.), *Anxiety and behavior.* New York: Academic Press, 1966.

Stagner, R. Industrial morale: 2. Motivational aspects of industrial morale. *Personnel Psychology,* 1958, *11,* 64-70.

Steers, R. M. Task-goal attributes, *n* achievement and supervisory performance. *Organizational Behavior and Human Performance,* 1975, *13,* 392-403.

_____. Factors affecting job attitudes in a goal setting environment. *Academy of Management Journal,* 1976, *19,* 6-16.

Sternberg, R. J. The nature of mental abilities. *American Psychologist,* 1979, *34,* 214-230.

Sternberg, S. High-speed scanning in human memory. *Science,* 1966, *153,* 652-654.

_____. Memory-scanning: Mental processes revealed by reaction-time experiments. *American Scientist*, 1969, *57*, 421-457.

Stevens, C. F. The neuron. *Scientific American*, 1979, *241*(3), 55-65.

Stringer, R. A., Jr. Achievement motivation and management control. In G. W. Dalton & P. R. Lawrence (Eds.), *Motivation and control in organizations.* Homewood, Ill.: Irwin-Dorsey, 1971.

Super, D. E. *The psychology of careers: An introduction to vocational development.* New York: Harper & Row, 1957.

Sutton, H., & Porter, L. W. A study of the grapevine in a governmental organization. *Personnel Psychology*, 1968, *21*, 223-230.

Szasz, T. S. Our despotic laws destroy the right to self-control. *Psychology Today,* December 1974, pp. 20-29; 127.

Thibaut, J. W., & Kelley, H. H. *The social psychology of groups.* New York: Wiley, 1959.

Thornton, G. C. Image of industrial psychology among personnel administrators. *Journal of Applied Psychology*, 1969, *53*, 436-438.

Thurstone, L. L. Primary mental abilities. *Psychometric Monographs*, 1938, *1*, 1-121.

_____, & Chave, E. J. *The measurement of attitude.* Chicago: University of Chicago Press, 1929.

Tobias, S. Anxiety research in educational psychology. *Journal of Educational Psychology*, 1979, *71*, 573-582.

Tolman, E. C. The nature of instinct. *Psychological Bulletin*, 1923, *20*, 200-218.

_____. *Purposive behavior in animals and men.* New York: Appleton-Century-Crofts, 1932.

Travers, R. M. *Essentials of learning* (3rd ed.). New York: Macmillan, 1972.

Troll, L. E. *Early and middle adulthood: The best is yet to be—maybe.* Monterey, Calif.: Brooks/Cole, 1975.

Vandenberg, S. G. Hereditary factors in normal personality traits. In J. Wortis (Ed.), *Recent advances in biological psychiatry* (Vol. 9). New York: Plenum, 1967.

VanRijn, P. *Instructor's manual to accompany psychology: Its principles and meanings.* Hillsdale, Ill.: The Dryden Press, 1973.

Vroom, V. H. *Work and motivation.* New York: Wiley, 1964.

Warden, C. J. *Animal motivation: Experimental studies on the albino rat.* New York: Columbia University Press, 1931.

Watson, D. *Psychology: What it is/how to use it.* San Francisco: Canfield Press, 1978.

Watson, J. B., & Rayner, R. Conditioned emotional reactions. *Journal of Experimental Psychology*, 1920, *3*, 1-14.

Wechsler, D. Intelligence defined and undefined: A relativistic appraisal. *American Psychologist*, 1975, *30*, 135-139.

Wertheimer, M. Psychomotor coordination of auditory and visual space at birth. *Science*, 1961, *134*, 1692.

Williams, J. C. *Human behavior in organizations.* Cincinnati: South-Western, 1978.

Williams, J. C. *Human behavior in organizations* (2nd ed.). Cincinnati: South-Western, 1982.

Wilson, E. O. *Sociobiology: The new synthesis.* Cambridge, Mass.: Harvard University Press, 1975.

*Work in America.* Report of a special task force to the Secretary of Health, Education and Welfare. Cambridge, Mass.: MIT Press, 1973.

Wrightsman, L. S. *Social psychology in the seventies* (2nd ed.). Monterey, Calif.: Brooks/Cole, 1977.

Zaidel, E. Auditory vocabulary of the right hemisphere following brain bisection or hemidecortication. _Cortex,_ 1976, _12,_ 191-211.

Zajonc, R. B. Social facilitation. _Science,_ 1965, _149,_ 269-274.

Zanna, M. P., Olson, J. M., & Fazio, R. H. Attitude-behavior consistency: An individual difference perspective. _Journal of Personality and Social Psychology,_ 1980, _38,_ 432-440.

Zimbardo, P. G. The human choice: Individuation, reason, and order versus deindividuation, impulse, and chaos. In W. J. Arnold & D. Levine (Eds.), _Nebraska Symposium on Motivation_ (Vol. 17). Lincoln: University of Nebraska Press, 1969.

Zimbardo, P. G. _Psychology and life_ (10th ed.). Glenview, Ill.: Scott, Foresman, 1979.

Zuckerman, M., Kolin, E. A., Price, L., & Zoob, I. Development of a sensation-seeking scale. _Journal of Consulting Psychology,_ 1964, _28,_ 477-482.

# ACKNOWLEDGMENTS

Page

1 Reproduced with permission by A.T. & T. Co. (left).

6 Sybil Shelton—Peter Arnold, Inc.

56 © Joel Gordon 1980.

59 NASA.

63 The Southland Corporation (left); Greg Booth for Associates Corporation of North America (center); CIBA-GEIGY Corporation (right).

85 Photo—Merck & Co., Inc.

107 Dennis Hallinan/FPG.

109 Ginger Chih—Peter Arnold, Inc.

113 Photo courtesy of Kimberly-Clark Corporation (left); McDonald's Corporation (center); Jefferson-Pilot Corporation (right).

122 Sybil Shelton—Peter Arnold, Inc.

133 Searle.

161 Sybil Shelton—Peter Arnold, Inc.

163 American Family Mutual Insurance.

174 © Joel Gordon 1978.

178 Photo by William Vandivert, courtesy of Scientific American.

Page

189 From "Factorial Angles to Psychology" by J. P. Guilford, Psychological Review, 1961, 68, 1-20. Copyright 1961 by the American Psychological Association. Adapted by permission of the author.

203 American Electric Power System (left); The Cincinnati Reds (center).

205 Renaud Thomas/FPG

215 From "Patterns of Dreaming" by N. Kleitman, Scientific American, November 1960, 203 (5), 84-85. Copyright by Dr. William Dement. Reprinted by permission.

216 Cartwright, A PRIMER ON SLEEP AND DREAMING, © 1978. Addison-Wesley, Reading, MA. Figure 1.6. Reprinted with permission.

219 Eastman Kodak Company.

225 Federal-Mogul Corporation.

258 Fig. 11.5 (p. 164) in EMOTION: A PSYCHOEVOLUTIONARY SYNTHESIS by Robert Plutchik. Copyright © 1980 by Robert Plutchik. Reprinted by permission of

*Page*

Harper & Row, Publishers, Inc.

262 Photos by Edward Gallob.

266 © Len Speier 1982.

270 Charles G. Morris, PSYCHOLOGY: An Introduction, 3rd ed., © 1979, p. 397. Reprinted by permission of Prentice-Hall, Inc., Englewood Cliffs, N.J.

277 Reprinted with permission from *Journal of Psychosomatic Research*, 11(2), pp. 213-218, T. H. Holmes and R. H. Rahe, "The Social Readjustment Rating Scale,"

*Page*

1967, Pergamon Press, Ltd.

291 From PSYCHOLOGY: ITS STUDY AND USES by Louis Janda and Karin Klenke-Hamel. Copyright © 1982 by St. Martin's Press, Inc., and reprinted by permission of the publisher.

297 The Bettmann Archive.

322 Mary Ellen Mark/Archive.

335 Delta Air Lines, Inc. (left); © Susan Lapides 1981/Design Conceptions (right).

348 Roger Malloch-Magnum.

361 The Bettmann Archive.

# NAME INDEX

## A

Acland, 196
Adams, 169
Adorno, 333
Alberti, 283
Alderfer, 238, 247
Allport, 302, 333, 338
Altman, 61
Amoore, 82
Anastasi, 200
Anderson, B. F., 40
Anderson, J. R., 170
Appley, 238
Argyle, 264
Aristotle, 8
Arnold, 269, 270, 281
Aronson, 338
Ary, 40
Asch, 329, 330
Atchison, 246
Atkinson, J. W., 229, 234, 242
Atkinson, R. C., 17, 151
Ausubel, 160
Axelrod, 69

## B

Bacon, 9
Baddeley, 152
Bales, 350, 363
Ball, 178
Bandura, 132
Bane, 196
Bard, 254, 267-268, 269, 281
Barrett, 62, 86, 244, 246
Barron, 200
Barrow, 108
Bass, 62, 86, 244, 246
Becker, 316
Beer, 238
Belkin, 316
Benson, 90, 259, 260, 278, 283
Berne, 354, 368
Bernheim, 316
Berscheid, 338
Binet, 191, 199
Birch, 229
Birdwhistell, 263
Block, 200
Bolles, 229
Boneau, 48

Borman, 249
Bourne, 311
Bradley, 99
Brittain, 96
Broadbent, 57
Brody, E. B., 200
Brody, N., 200
Brown, 347
Brunton, 96
Burke, 246
Buros, 200
Buss, 94
Butcher, H. J., 200
Butcher, J. N., 316

## C

Caldwell, 99
Calvin, 144
Campbell, D., 201
Campbell, D. T., 179
Campbell, J. P., 241, 242
Cannon, 254, 267-268, 269, 281
Cantell, 191
Caplan, 111
Capwell, 246
Carlsmith, 222, 264, 328, 338
Carlson, 230
Carson, 316
Carterette, 201
Cattell, 188, 302
Chaplin, 17
Chave, 323
Chemers, 368
Chruden, 289
Claiborne, 145
Cofer, 238
Cohen, 196
Cole, 293
Coleman, 273, 316
Combs, 176, 194
Cook, M., 264
Cook, S. W., 333
Coombs, 196
Cooper, 283
Coppen, 75
Cotman, 75
Craik, 153
Crassweller, 260
Crockenberg, 185
Cronbach, 201
Cuca, 48

## M

## N

## O

## P

# SUBJECT INDEX

## A

ability, 175

ability tests: examples of, 191-193; reliability, 193-194; shortcomings, 194; standardization, 194; validity, 194

abnormal personality, 303-311; views of, 305-306

abnormal personality, views of: cognitive-behavioral model, 306; learning model, 305-306; medical model, 305; organic model, 305; psychoanalytic model, 305

absenteeism, 86

Abstracts, Psychological, 38

accommodation, 99

achievement, 173

achievement imagery, in children's stories, 23

achievement motive, 220

actions, reflex, 8

activity theory, 108

actualizing tendency, 300

adaptation, 76

adolescence, 104-106

adrenal glands, 84

Adult, 357-358

adulthood, 106

affective disorders, 310

afferent neuron, 66-67

affiliation motive, 219

Age Discrimination in Employment Act, 335

ageism, 108

alternate response, 139

ambiverts, 295

amnesia, 155

amplitude, 79

angular ulterior transaction, 359

anvil, 80

anxiety states, 307

approach-approach conflicts, 274

approach-avoidance, 256-257

approach-avoidance conflict, 274-275; double, 274, 276

aptitude, 175

aptitude tests, 191-193

arousal theory, 210

assertive coping, 279

assimilation, 99

association value, 160

attitude: change, 325-328; components of, 319-320; defined, 319; formation, 320-323; measurement, 323-325; scale, 323

## B

autonomic nervous system, 71-72, 259

avoidance-avoidance conflict, 274

axon, 65

axonal transmission, 68-69

## B

balance phase, 343

behavior: defined, 4; organizational, 58-59

behaviorism, 10-11

behavior modification, 136-139; defined, 136; self-control, 138-139; steps in, 137

behavior therapy, 311

belief, 320

biofeedback, 131-132

biological-physiological approach, to psychology, 15

biological processes, 63-112; cycles of, 87; effect on worker, 84-87

biological rhythms, 87

bipolar disorder, 310

blind spot: defined, 77; locating, 78

bystander apathy, 347

## C

Cannon-Bard theory, 267-268

case study method, 22

catatonic schizophrenia, 309

central nervous system, 72-75, 260

cerebellum, 72

cerebral cortex, 73-74

chain, 353-354

Child, 357-358

chromosomes: defined, 94; sex, 95

circle, 353-354

Civil Rights Act of 1964, 335

classical conditioning: basic principles of, 119-120; defined, 115-120; discovery of, 115-117; emotional reactions, 117-118

client-centered therapy, 312

clinical psychology, 46

cochlea, 80

cognitive development, stages of: concrete operational stage, 101; formal operational stage, 101; preoperational stage, 100-101; sensorimotor stage, 99-100

cognitive dissonance, 222

cognitive processes, 113-202; intelligence, 172-200; learning, 114-144; remembering and thinking, 148-169

413

## U

## V

## T